Terrorists and Social Democrats

Russian Research Center Studies, 82

Terrorists and Social Democrats

The Russian Revolutionary Movement Under
Alexander III

Norman M. Naimark

Harvard University Press
Cambridge, Massachusetts
and London, England
1983

Copyright © 1983 by the President
and Fellows of Harvard College

Printed in the United States of America
10 9 8 7 6 5 4 3 2 1

This book is printed on acid-free paper, and its binding materials have
been chosen for strength and durability.

Library of Congress Cataloging in Publication Data

Naimark, Norman M.
    Terrorists and social democrats.

    (Russian Research Center studies ; 82)
    Bibliography; p.
    Includes index.
    1. Rossiiskaia sotsial-demokraticheskaia rabochaia
partiia — History.   2. Soviet Union — History — Alexander
III, 1881–1894.   3. Radicalism — Soviet Union — History.
4. Terrorism — Soviet Union — History.   I. Title.
II. Series.
JN6598.S6N24   1983   322.4′2′0947   82-23303
ISBN 0–674–87464–1

For Lila and Sarah

Acknowledgments

Most of the research for this book was carried out in Leningrad and Moscow with the support of the International Research and Exchanges Corporation (IREX) and the Fulbright-Hays Program. I owe a great debt of gratitude to the staffs of the archives and libraries in those cities, particularly the Central State Archives (TsGIA SSSR) in Leningrad. In addition, thanks are due the librarians and archivists of the Hoover Institution, the International Institute of Social History, and Widener Library. At the final stages of the research, and for the writing of this book, I was fortunate to have received financial support from the Alexander von Humboldt Stiftung, the Deutsche Forschungsgemeinschaft, Harvard University's Russian Research Center, and the Boston University Graduate School. The writing particularly has benefited from the quiet office and congenial atmosphere at the Russian Research Center. My special thanks to the Center's Director, Adam B. Ulam, and Administrative Assistant, Mary Towle, for their help and encouragement. I also wish to express my gratitude to the Osteuropa Institute of the Free University of Berlin and its Director, Hans-Joachim Torke, for providing a friendly home for this work during the year 1977–78.

More than most authors, I am beholden to my colleagues in the field. Joan Axelrod, Harley Balzer, Terence Emmons, Daniel Field, William Fuller, Abbott Gleason, Manfred Hildermeier, Ronald Suny, Nina Tumarkin, and Reginald Zelnik read parts or all of the manuscript and offered valuable criticisms. I am especially indebted to those hearty friends – John Ackerman, Gregory Freeze, and David Powell – who read and commented on more than one version of the manuscript. I also thank *The Russian Review* for permission to publish in somewhat altered form my spring 1978 article, "The Workers' Section and the Challenge of the 'Young.'"

Contents

Terrorists and Social Democrats

For convenience, soft signs have been dropped in first names, in Russian terms commonly used in English, and in the names of cities, towns, and provinces. Where an individual is known by two names, the assumed name is noted in parentheses. Names of Poles and of all but the main towns and cities in the Kingdom of Poland are rendered in Polish, though without the Polish diacritical marks; Russian spelling is used for the names of Russianized Poles, of Jews, Georgians, and other nationalities in the empire. The American system of transliteration has been used and Russian spelling has been modernized; only place names retain their late nineteenth-century spelling.

The terms "narodovolets" and "narodovol'ka" (singular, masculine and feminine) and "narodovol'tsy" (plural) are used to indicate members or adherents of the party Narodnaia Volia. For the sake of simplicity, "narodovol'tsy" will also be used instead of the Russian adjective form "narodovol'cheskii": thus "narodovol'tsy ideas" or "narodovol'tsy propaganda." All dates are in the old style unless otherwise indicated.

Introduction

This book seeks to recover a missing act in the nineteenth-century Russian revolutionary drama — from the 1 March 1881 assassination of Alexander II to the aftermath of the great famine of 1891–92 — and to do so in the context of the period itself, rather than from the perspective of 1917 and after. Since the lifting of the Stalinist ban on the study of early revolutionary history, Soviet historians have tread ever so carefully on the uncharted territory of the 1880s, eagerly discussing and fastidiously documenting the officially acceptable "heroic period" of Narodnaia Volia (People's Will), 1878–81, yet all but ignoring the more sensitive issue of the origins of the anathemized Socialist-Revolutionary party, which overlap with the fate of Narodnaia Volia after 1881. Social democracy was on the ascendancy in the 1880s, so the Soviet wisdom goes; Plekhanov was already at work in Switzerland, and therefore the *narodovol'tsy* (adherents of Narodnaia Volia and its offshoots) obstructed revolutionary progress. Several Soviet works explore in detail the history of domestic social-democratic groups in the 1880s, but they, like the works on Narodnaia Volia in the heroic period, never talk about the two movements in the same breath and avoid the major issues of their interrelationship.

It is more surprising that Western historians of the revolutionary movement have also ignored the 1880s, for their work is free of the formal ideological strictures that hamper their Soviet colleagues. Still, Franco Venturi ends the history of Narodnaia Volia and concludes his classic *Roots of Revolution* with the 1 March 1881 assassination. Following his example, other Western historians assume the instant demise of Narodnaia Volia after March 1 and discount the movement altogether under Alexander III, instead characterizing the 1880s as a period of "small deeds" or as a decade whose most important develop- ment was the establishment, in emigration, of the intellectual founda- tions of Russian Marxism. The rare excursions into the period are usually prompted by an effort to find the seeds of Bolshevism rather than by an attempt to assess the importance and diversity of the revolutionary movement as a whole. And generally, Western historians of Russian social democracy or the Socialist-Revolutionary party, when concerned at all with the movement inside the country, begin their studies with the famine of 1891–92, which sparked a renewed interest in revolutionary questions on the part of the Russian intelligentsia, among them the young Lenin.

Clearly, the victory of the Bolsheviks influences this and any other book on the revolutionary movement, if only because the choice of subjects is in part determined by the memoirs that the Soviets decided to publish in the 1920s and early 1930s. Fortunately, however, the ar- chives of the imperial government, which are now available to Western historians, can provide a valuable corrective to the selective memories of the movement's participants and the teleological inten- tions of the movement's historians. I rely most heavily on the archives of the Ministry of Justice's Second Criminal Department (TsGIA SSSR, fond 1405), which contain approximately two thousand cases against radical groups from the period 1881–1894. A critical reading of the radicals' depositions and letters, the prosecutors' correspon- dence with the police, the indictments, the appeals, and the police re- ports contained in each *delo* (case) produces a reasonably accurate picture of radical activities and ideologies. The material evidence in the cases was also collected by the Ministry of Justice (TsGIA SSSR, fond 1410), while the archives of the Ministry of Internal Affairs's Department of Police (TsGAOR, fond 102–DP) contain depositions, letters, and secret police reports that are not always duplicated in the prosecutors' cases. Finally, a year-by-year gendarme survey of the main political cases (*Obzor vazhneishikh doznanii* . . .) was printed by the government for internal use, providing an invaluable overview of the revolutionary movement.

Even if historians have not taken the approximately five thousand narodovol'tsy and social democrats of this period seriously, the tsarist government certainly did. Its job was to suppress the revolutionary movement and punish its participants, and in doing so tsarist officials have left us with remarkably detailed and judicious accounts of their victims' thoughts and activities. The archives also make it clear that the government's struggle against the revolutionaries influenced not only radical politics but the politics of the tsarist government itself. By their actions, each party, government and underground, altered the tactics, even the ideas, of its adversary.

In a sense, this is a guide book to revolutionary Russia in the 1880s. It was not possible to discuss all of the period's radical circles, a number of which could themselves be subjects of monographs, but the attempt has been made to treat the most important. Before beginning our tour of revolutionary Russia, however, several ground rules must be established. First, the groups and circles will be identified by their original names rather than by the names given them by Soviet historians. Neither in the political nor in the historiographical sense did the cult of personality perish with Stalin. For Soviet historians every party and every revolutionary group must have a recognized (and acceptable) leader, and groups and circles are usually named after the chosen leader. This habit of mind is followed by Western historians, in part because of its convenience — the names of the individual groups are sometimes long and cumbersome. But in most cases the Soviets have chosen the leaders for various political reasons, obscuring one of the most significant characteristics of all these groups: they had no clearly acknowledged leaders and formed and operated much more spontaneously than the Soviets care to admit. Therefore the "Blagoevtsy" (after the Bulgarian Communist leader Dimitr Blagoev) will be called the Party of Social Democrats, the "Ul'ianov conspiracy" (after Lenin's older brother) will be called the Terrorist Fraction of Narodnaia Volia, and the "Brusnevtsy" (after the supporter of the Bolsheviks, Mikhail Brusnev) will be called the Workers' Union.

Second, it is important to draw a clear distinction between the intellectual history of the period 1881–1894 and the contemporaneous history of the revolutionary movement. The day-to-day, year-to-year activities of Russian radicals developed out of practical experience in the movement itself. Prominent thinkers — Plekhanov, Mikhailovskii, Lavrov, or Tikhomirov — played a secondary role in shaping the activists' ideas or determining their actions. These figures were even less important as leaders of the revolutionary movement, at least in the period 1881–1894. In the underground, Russian radicals faced severe government repression, even as they attempted to comprehend firsthand the emerging social forces unleashed by rapid industrialization. It was a period that confronted them with fresh opportunities and new obstacles, and their response was shaped by strong revolutionary traditions that at once hindered and sustained them. Old labels no longer fit, and new initiatives resulted in constantly shifting alliances. As they attempted to come to terms with the complex and rapidly changing Russia of Alexander III, the radicals accomplished much and left a considerable legacy: they revised the tenets of Narodnaia Volia, established the foundations of Russian social democracy (independent of Plekhanov's influence), and formed the groups that evolved into the Socialist-Revolutionary party.

To make sense of the history and historiography of the movement, it is necessary to understand this basic division between the intellectuals and the underground activists without overemphasizing it. In the West, we have solid biographies of Martov, Aksel'rod, Lavrov, Zasulich, Mikhailovskii, Plekhanov, and Struve; we have numerous accounts of the young Lenin; and we have monographs on the debates between the "Legal Marxists" and "Legal Populists." And, to be sure, in the realm of pure theory Plekhanov did help to define the contours of revolutionary activity for social democrats, as did Tikhomirov for narodovol'tsy and Mikhailovskii for populists. But the underground radicals adapted these definitions to their own purposes, combined them in ways unacceptable to the theorists, and gave new meaning to them by their actions. Thus it is from the perspective of the underground that one can most usefully describe the major ideological divisions in the movement.

Despite great confusion during the period 1881–1894 in the use of the terms "narodovol'tsy," "social democrats," and "populists" and the significant blurring of distinctions among the circles they identified, it is possible to sketch the general characteristics of each group. The narodovol'tsy, the most numerous and influential of the groups in this period, associated themselves in diverse ways with the still glorious name of Narodnaia Volia. Essentially, they believed in terrorism of one sort or another and in the use of state power to introduce socialist institutions at some stage of the revolution. Power might be seized simultaneously with the socialist revolution or prior to it. The forcible seizure of power might even be obviated by the introduction of a parliament, which then could be used by the workers' party to introduce socialist institutions. In comparison with the remaining populists or the more numerous social democrats, the narodovol'tsy emphasized political rather than social goals in the short run: they were ready to use any methods that would succeed in bringing about the desired change, be it liberalization of government institutions, the introduction of an assembly of the people, or the eventual social revolution. They were also less patient than the social democrats or the populists; they sought to force change by their direct participation in underground politics.

It is important to note that the narodovol'tsy were no more and no less the direct heirs of the populists of the 1870s than were the social democrats. When the populist party Land and Liberty split in 1879, the two successor groups, Narodnaia Volia and Black Repartition, took with them an equal measure of populist thought. Initially, Black Repartition represented the mainstream of populist traditions, but in emigration, Plekhanov led the group in the direction of social democracy. Narodnaia Volia also evolved, but into urban circles of political street-fighters who seemed very different from the peasant propagandists of the 1870s. Strictly speaking, most narodovol'tsy of the 1880s no longer considered themselves populists at all. Although they still believed in a unique path for Russia's development, they understood that capitalism had made significant inroads into the countryside, that the peasant commune was severely threatened, and that the notion of a flourishing peasant socialism was a myth appropriate to an earlier "unscientific" age. Though they saw no valid reason to leave the peasants out of the revolutionary process, they recognized that urban workers were the most important popular force for revolution. It was clear to the narodovol'tsy that, ultimately, a social revolution could not take place without political changes; therefore, in complete contradiction to populist norms, they engaged in political struggle.

The variety of social democrats in this period was equally profuse. More directly than either the narodovol'tsy or the populists, the social democrats expressed their devotion to the Russian working class without unanimously rejecting the socialist possibilities of the peasantry. Most looked to the German social democrats as a model and tried to prepare Russian workers for a future role in parliamentary institutions. The narodovol'tsy argued that their theoretical platforms were as "scientific" and "objective" as those of the social democrats, but the latter were no doubt more "deterministic" than the "voluntaristic" narodovol'tsy. In fact, most social democrats accepted terrorism as a legitimate means of struggle by *other* parties, but like the populists they avoided direct participation in the political struggle. Some insisted, as did Plekhanov, that a bourgeois revolution would have to precede a socialist one and that the social revolution must await the full development of capitalism. But for the most part social democrats defined themselves in opposition to the narodovol'tsy's active politics. They were exclusively propagandists rather than street-fighters; they were organizers of workers' groups rather than of terrorist conspiracies; they were willing to wait and hope for a role in the future democratic society; and they rejected the notion of a forcible seizure of state power — a notion still found in some narodovol'tsy groups.

The social democrats, like the narodovol'tsy, generally followed Marx's analysis of the development of capitalism and of capitalism's pernicious removal of the means of production from labor's control.

Most social democrats in Russia were not doctrinaire Marxists, however. They did not believe in the inevitability of a revolution caused by escalating conflicts between the proletariat and the bourgeoisie. Their political model was the German Social-Democratic party, which in the 1880s managed to exert considerable influence on German politics despite Bismarck's antisocialist laws. Like the Germans, the Russian social democrats sought not to overthrow the government but to enhance labor's role within it. In this approach they were influenced more by the writings of Lassalle than by those of Marx and Engels, or for that matter of Plekhanov. One of the many anomalies of the Russian underground in the 1880s was that Russian radicals considered those self-designated Marxists "more Marxist than Marx himself." After all, Marx and Engels had supported the narodovol'tsy, advocated terrorism, and lent credence to the doctrine that Russian development followed a separate path, whereas Russian Marxists emphasized the inevitability of capitalism's development and the science of social progress, while they shunned terrorism and disparaged the political struggle. Sometimes, like many populists, they withdrew from the underground altogether and turned to pure economic studies. When they engaged in illegal activities, they usually formed circles devoted to discussing or disseminating the censored works of Marx.

Complicating the spectrum of ideological opinion even more was the emergence at the end of the 1880s of a small contingent of Russian revolutionary social democrats who considered themselves the sole true advocates of Marx's economic and political theories. Bolstered by the formation of the Second International in 1889, the lifting of Bismarck's antisocialist legislation, and the adoption by the German Social Democrats of the Erfurt Program (1891), the Russian revolutionary Marxists, Plekhanov included, began to exert a more decisive influence on social-democrat circles in the country. Their problem was not so much how to interpret Marxist politics in the Russian situation, but how to bring the more abstract ideas of the "dictatorship of the proletariat" and the class struggle to domestic social democrats and workers absorbed by educational and day-to-day organizational issues.

The populists, difficult to define even in their classical phase of the 1870s, were dispersed and their ideas became comparatively insignificant by the 1880s. After 1881 some joined narodovol'tsy circles, whereas others became part of the domestic social-democratic movement, a development which paralleled that of their comrades in emigration—Plekhanov, Zasulich, and Aksel'rod. In fact, the remaining populists and social democrats of the early 1880s held much in common: an aversion to terrorism, a devotion to raising the people's consciousness to a level that would allow them to make the revolution themselves, and a patient, evolutionary view of the tasks at hand. Nevertheless, the populists continued to emphasize the unique path of Russian development in contrast to the social democrats, who saw themselves as part of a European movement and were confident of the coming Westernization of Russia.

A few populists continued the work of the *derevenshchiki* (village propagandists) of the 1870s and taught school or engaged in various kinds of work related to the *zemstvos* (district and provincial organizations of local self-government). But most returned to the cities, where they either attempted to conduct peaceful educational work among urban laborers or became advocates of Legal Populism, which asserted that capitalism could not succeed in Russia and that political activities were irrelevant to the eventual flowering of communal self-government. At the end of the 1880s and the beginning of the 1890s, however, a majority of the populists moved closer to the narodovol'tsy, shedding their utopian dreams by adopting the experiences of the political struggle and thus becoming much more involved in the revolutionary movement as a whole.

These three movements—better represented as three emphases within the same movement—interacted, shifted, and combined in kaleidoscopic fashion, constantly altering the picture of revolutionary thought and activity between 1881 and 1894. The picture was unquestionably dominated by the narodovol'tsy, though room was soon made for the social democrats and later the neopopulists. But in the underground this was not a time of sharply defined struggles between narodovol'tsy and social democrats, terrorists and labor socialists, Marxists and populists. Rather, the end of the period witnessed a new consensus among revolutionary groups that the time had come to create a democratic, parliamentary Russia that would reflect the needs and interests of the entire population.

Background to Radicalism

1

On 1 March 1881, Tsar Alexander II was making his way along St. Petersburg's Catherine Canal to take afternoon coffee at the palace of the Grand Princess, Ekaterina Mikhailovna. The tsar's small convoy had not quite reached the Theater Bridge when, at 1:45, a bomb was tossed at his carriage, damaging the vehicle and injuring several passersby. Unhurt, Alexander alighted from his carriage and proceeded to the spot where the bomb-thrower was being held by two marines when suddenly a second bomb was hurled; it exploded at his feet, causing a deafening roar and shattering glass in the neighboring buildings. Fatally injured, the tsar murmured "Help me, help me," and then, while being carried to the Winter Palace, spoke again, "I'm cold, I'm cold." At 3:35 in the afternoon, surrounded by the imperial family, Alexander II died.[1]

Members of Narodnaia Volia had tried so often to assassinate Alexander II and suffered so many arrests as a result of their failures that the actual killing sent a shudder of relief through the remaining ranks of the party. The nightmare of autocracy was over, they believed. The combined social and political revolution, which they had advocated but had begun to doubt, could start now that the dragon was slain. The people would rise to seize their freedom and establish their own forms of socialism. The more astute narodovol'tsy, less prone to the illusions of their populist past, argued that at the very least there would be genuine liberal reforms, which would begin the process of revolution.

Lev Tikhomirov, the chief publicist of Narodnaia Volia, quickly understood not only that the people were more inclined to mourn the death of the tsar than to rebel because of it, but also that the very liberals who had generally cheered the terrorists were shaken by the reality of regicide and would not dare to take part in the conflict between the government and the revolutionaries. Hoping to salvage some gains from the assassination, Tikhomirov on March 10 sent a remarkably judicious letter to Alexander III, which promised an end to terrorist activities if the government granted amnesty to the radicals and instituted a broad range of reforms guaranteeing democratic institutions and civil rights. Tikhomirov also explained to the new tsar (and Russian society) the causes of terrorism: "Revolutionaries are created by circumstances: the general discontent of the people, the desire of Russia to bring it toward a new social system. It is impossible to exterminate all the people or to do away with discontent by enforcing repression; indeed, this will only make it grow. And it is this that makes new elements rise from the people in ever increasing numbers to take the place of those who have been killed; and it is this that gives life to ever more energetic and violent passions."[2] Although Tikhomirov's letter was an attempt to compensate for the weaknesses of Narodnaia Volia in the spring of 1881, his analysis of the dynamics of terrorism proved correct. Terrorist conspiracies became a normal part of Russian radical life from 1881 until the first years of the Soviet regime.

Lambs to Tigers

At the end of the 1870s, Russian social revolutionaries — the populists (narodniki) as they were later called — turned from propaganda to terrorism as the primary means to accomplish their revolutionary goals. The story of how the lambs became tigers, to paraphrase Kviatkovskii's trial speech, is one of the best known chapters in all of Russian history.[3] The lambs were mostly students and ex-students who had dropped their studies in Zurich, left their homes in Kiev, or joined workers' artels (communal workshops) in Petersburg, to "go to the people" during that "mad summer" of 1874, to bear the message of socialism and freedom to the Russian peasantry.

They were pilgrims as well as preachers, called by Petr Lavrov to know the people and teach them, exhorted by Mikhail Bakunin to rouse the people to revolution. They were "repentant nobles," who donned the boots and blouses of the peasant folk and trudged around the countryside to repay their debt to the people. Some of the more successful populists used their own estates as centers for rural agitation; others carefully concealed their ultimate revolutionary aims in the villages and were able to attract a loyal peasant following; and yet a third group concentrated its efforts among city workers. The program of the populists consisted of a number of hazy and idealistic pronouncements. They believed in the village commune, or *mir*, convinced it was the fundamental guarantee of justice and freedom in Russia and a natural form of socialist organization among the peasantry. For the mir treated all its members equally — unlike the government and the upper classes which conspired to deprive the peasants of their land and their liberty. The commune was also an antidote for the sickness of capitalism, which had destroyed the laboring man in the West and was threatening the integrity of communal self-administration in Russia. Were the masses to declare themselves free, to think and feel free, their might would be felt throughout the land; government oppression would disappear, replaced by a federation of communes based on free association whose reverberations would be felt all over Europe. So preached the populists from their rural pulpits.

Initially the form of government was a matter of indifference to them, and in this sense they have been described as apolitical. It was the social and economic system that mattered, far more than the government. Only a social revolution, the affirmation of communal self-administration on a countrywide basis, could solve the problems of Russia. A political revolution, the seizure of power by an elite, as advocated by some Russian radicals like Petr Tkachev, was anathema to most populists, as was reform from above. The Russian government, however, was indeed political, and it did not look upon the populists with indifference. The police and local authorities intervened, arresting them and sending them back to their homes. Hundreds were placed in pre-trial detention, others put under police surveillance. To make matters worse, the populists' reception among the people often disappointed their expectations. Sometimes the peasants rejected them altogether, refusing to listen to them or to attend their schools. Even when they were favorably received, the populists faced poor food, inadequate shelter, and harsh working conditions. Exhausted by their long journeys around rural Russia, the sobered young idealists returned to the cities.

Rather than abandon their ideals in the face of government opposition, prison hardships, and the difficult conditions met in the countryside, the populists formed an underground party called Land and Liberty (1876–1879). It would direct their efforts and, through its Disorganizing Section, keep the government at a distance while the party better coordinated its propaganda in the countryside and in the cities. The general socialist-federalist ideas of the populists had not changed — land would be transferred to the peasants, factories to the workers; the Russian Empire would be broken up according to local wishes. The communes would administer their own affairs and would join in a free association with other communes on a regional and national level. What had changed was the populists' attitude toward the government. In Kiev and Odessa at first, and soon in most urban populist circles, they showed a determination to resist arrest and internment, to free imprisoned comrades, and to frighten off the police with threats of violence. Prison terms humiliated and embittered the high-minded propagandists, and their mood turned increasingly truculent.

The "Zasulich affair" in the beginning of 1878 was one of the events that crystallized the turn to violence in the populist movement. During a visit to a prison that held the defendants in the "Trial of the 193," St. Petersburg municipal governor F. F. Trepov ordered the flogging of a prisoner, Emel'ianov (Bogoliubov), who refused to remove his hat in the governor's presence. The flogging set off a series of disturbances among Emel'ianov's indignant fellow prisoners, and, on 24 January 1878, a day after the conclusion of the trial, Vera Zasulich shot and wounded Trepov in retaliation for Emel'ianov's beating. Hailed by *obshchestvo* (educated society) as a martyr for justice and acquitted by a liberal court in April 1878, Zasulich, against her will, became a model among radicals for the terrorist—noble, innocent, brave, and devoted to the cause, a Joan of Arc facing the overwhelming evil of government oppression. Between her assault, which was an act of pure retribution, and the 1 March 1881 assassination of Alexander II, the motives of the terrorists became increasingly political, that is, the radicals were driven by the desire to spark an overthrow of the government in a social and political revolution. Following the Trepov shooting, Chief of the Gendarmes General N. V. Mezentsev was killed (August 1878), as was Kharkov Governor General Prince D. N. Kropotkin (February 1879). In April 1879 A. K. Solov'ev attempted to kill Alexander II; it was the first of six unsuccessful terrorist attacks on the tsar, which included the mining of his train (November 1879) and the setting of an enormous explosion in the Winter Palace (February 1880).

The move toward terrorism affected the structure of the populist organization Land and Liberty, as well as the self-image of its members. Centralized and conspiratorial party cells, arranged hierarchically with clear chains of command, developed in response to the government's understandable determination to employ every means to capture the assassins and deter others from attempting acts of revolutionary violence. The struggle between the government and the revolutionary movement grew so intense that at the Land and Liberty congresses in Lipetsk and Voronezh during the summer of

1879, the terrorist-inclined majority moved to concentrate all efforts on the task of killing the tsar. The Disorganizing Section was replaced by an Executive Committee, whose job it was to direct the operations of the social-revolutionary party. Yet even in the Executive Committee there were significant differences of opinion on how terrorism should be applied and to what end. Lev Tikhomirov, the group's most talented publicist, believed that terrorism would ignite the social revolution, whereas Nikolai Morozov was more interested in the private duel between the government and the freedom fighters of the Executive Committee. Others, such as Mariia Oshanina, were Jacobins who saw terrorism as a means to weaken the autocracy in preparation for seizing power in the name of the people. Andrei Zheliabov, on the other hand, hoped the terrorist campaign would force the government to grant a constitution. In all four views action took precedence over theory, politics over economics, violence over passivity. The common goal was to force the autocracy to its knees; when this happened the social revolution would take care of itself.

In protest against the majority view, Georgii Plekhanov walked out of the Voronezh Congress and established his own Black Repartition group (*Chernyi Peredel*) along with Vera Zasulich, Lev Deich, Pavel Aksel'rod, and Iakov Stefanovich, most of whom had been abroad during the series of assassinations. The Executive Committee then formed its own party, Narodnaia Volia, and the split in Land and Liberty was complete. For Plekhanov and Black Repartition (so called because of its dedication to the communal repartition of land), terrorism was of conceivable use only in concert with the social revolution; nothing could be gained by altering political institutions. A constitution was an unlikely result of terrorism, Plekhanov argued, and even if one were granted it could not help the people: "political revolutions can *never* and in *no place* assure the people of economic and political freedom."[4] Regicide itself would only impede agitation in the villages and factories, postponing rather than initiating the social revolution.

In January 1880, with the police on their heels and the vast majority of populists in sympathy with Narodnaia Volia, Plekhanov and the leaders of Black Repartition left Russia for the West. Rejecting the growing cult of violence, they responded instead to "the voice of the people, demanding agrarian revolution, [which] is like the voice of god."[5] Of course the narodovol'tsy also assumed that the Lord was on their side: "our holy and inseparable principles are the welfare of the people and the will of the people." For the narodovol'tsy, the agrarian revolution advocated by Plekhanov was not possible as long as the tsar's government, like that of Genghis Khan, oppressed the people and denied their will to freedom. The people desperately needed help, and this the party would provide by "carrying out the political revolution with the goal of handing over power to the people." The narodovol'tsy prided themselves on a realistic assessment of the political situation, which, in 1880, meant their belief that a constituent assembly was the most likely means for transferring power to the people. The party would start the insurrection, seize power from the government, hand it over to the assembly, and then concentrate on pushing its own program of communal self-administration, giving the land to the peasants and the factories to the workers.

The split in revolutionary populism was therefore not about goals, which remained consistent with those of 1874, but about means: political struggle, advocacy of a constitutent assembly, and the use of terrorism. Especially the terrorist aspect of Narodnaia Volia's program differentiated the party from the revolutionary populism of the early 1870s: "Terrorist activity consists of destroying the most dangerous personages in the government, of defending the party against spies, of punishing [the perpetrators] of the most noted cases of oppression and arbitrariness on the part of the government, administration, and so on . . . The goal is to break the spell of government omnipotence, to provide uninterrupted evidence of the possibility of struggle against the government, in such a manner as to raise the revolutionary spirit of the people and the faith in the success of the cause, and, finally, to form suitable forces ready for battle."[6] The most "dangerous personage" of all was Alexander II; his assassination had the best chance of destroying the government, of sparking the social revolution; and all the forces and energies of the narodovol'tsy were subordinated to this end. The needs of the *derevenshchiki* were ignored and the *Workers' Newspaper* (*Rabochaia gazeta*), intended to spread propaganda among urban laborers, was shut down. Each of the failed attempts on the life of the tsar depleted the organization's personnel and funds, forcing the remaining terrorists further underground. The seventh and successful attack was in many ways the last chance for the terrorists. Their organization was bereft of resources and manpower, and their hopes for a spontaneous revolution had faded.

Rather than seizing the opportunity to rebel, educated society and the people mourned the death of the tsar. The government, after an initial period of hesitation, responded to the assassination with an unambiguous determination to reaffirm autocracy as the only law of the land. Terrorists, terrorist sympathizers, even the causes of terrorism would be rooted out of Russia and any means would be employed to reestablish the tranquillity of autocratic rule. During the spring and summer of 1881, the government arrested and later tried and hanged the main participants in the March 1 assassination. The Petersburg and Moscow organizations of Narodnaia Volia were completely destroyed. Tikhomirov went into hiding and in mid-1882 fled to ·Paris, where he reestablished an impoverished and politically weakened imitation of the original Executive Committee.

The Government and the Revolutionaries

Conservative contemporaries praised the reign of Alexander III (1881–1894) for its stability and good sense. The tsar appeared to be the epitome of the true autocrat (*samoderzhets*). His imposing size and dignified carriage were noted by both foreign visitors and court nobles. In contrast to his father, Alexander II, the new tsar impressed the outside world with personal austerity and devotion to family life. The scandals and sumptuous court fetes that had characterized the last decade of Alexander II's rule were shunned by his heir, the "Russian Victorian," who refused to receive divorced women at court and reprimanded Russian society for its lack of morals and its inadequate sense of duty.

For the thirteen years of his reign Alexander III kept Russia at peace. Despite clarion calls in the right-wing press for an expanded Russian role in European affairs, and despite his own nationalistic bent, Alexander for the most part was content to let Bismarck orchestrate the European peace. Even the hated "nihilists," who plagued the last years of Alexander II's reign with plots, assassinations, and spectactular courtroom appearances, seemed to have disappeared. True, the police continued to report on new conspiracies, but in contrast to the 1870s political trials were rare, closed to the public, and barely mentioned in the carefully censored press. The Ministries of Justice and Internal Affairs had streamlined the system of administrative exile; opponents of the autocracy were silently removed from public view and consciousness. To be sure, the students chafed under the retrogressive 1884 University Statutes; there were noisy demonstrations and expulsions. Periodic strikes also disturbed the empire's calm, but even the huge Morozov strike of 1885 was effectively contained by government countermeasures. If only the reign of Alexander III had lasted another thirteen years, Witte wrote in his memoirs, Imperial Russia might have resolved its problems and avoided the revolutionary strife of the new century.[7]

But Witte's perception was no doubt colored by his own extraordinary influence under Alexander III and his barely concealed disdain for the rule of Nicholas II (1894–1917). More astute observers of Russia in the 1880s — Polovtsov, Peretts, Valuev, and Bezobrazov, among others — understood that Russia was calm only on the surface.

More than twenty years had passed since the promulgation of the 1861 peasant emancipation. New economic and social forces had already propelled Russia into an age of industrialization and social transformation. The new Minister of Finance, I. A. Vyshnegradskii (1887–1892), undertook measures that would insure the expansion of factories and commerce, further exacerbating the tensions between the unreformed political structure of Russia and the dynamic influence of industrialization.

Though Alexander III may have looked back to the autocracy of Nicholas I (1825–1855) as the model for his rule, Nicholas would not have recognized the industrial landscape of St. Petersburg and Moscow, even of Kharkov, Kiev, Rostov-on-Don, Ekaterinoslav, or dozens of other Russian cities and towns. The juridical, military, educational, church, and governmental reforms associated with the elimination of serfdom in 1861 could not simply be reversed or ignored by decree, for they had been in part necessary responses to irreversible changes in the society and economy of Imperial Russia. Moreover, the process of reform had changed the mentality of government civil servants; it was now central to the world view of thousands of minor bureaucrats. At the same time, the government itself had become so complex and so unwieldy that it no longer responded automatically to the whims of the autocrat. Even Alexander III's advisers, the notorious "four horsemen of the Apocalypse" — Prince V. P. Meshcherskii, Minister of Internal Affairs Count Dmitrii Tolstoi, Procurator of the Holy Synod K. P. Pobedonostsev, and editor of *Moskovskie vedomosti* (Moscow News) Mikhail Katkov — could not agree on a common strategy to stem the onrush of modernity, or even to channel it into forms compatible in the 1880s with a reactionary conception of the autocracy. Especially Pobedonostsev, who attempted to direct the course of government actions through countless memoranda, reports, letters, and personal lobbying, was frustrated in his attempt to control bureaucratic factionalism, which hampered the government's ability to formulate, much less to carry out, a coherent program. Thus, despite efforts at counterreform, few concrete reversals of earlier tsarist policies occurred. Industrialization continued, the old estate (*soslovie*) structure became more complicated, and new social problems further undermined the political structure of the empire.

The fundamental instability of Russian society in the 1880s was only magnified by the government's erratic and ultimately unsuccessful attempts to destroy the revolutionary movement. After the assassination of his father, Alexander III immediately withdrew from St. Petersburg to Gatchina where, surrounded by soldiers, servants,

and boyhood friends, the new tsar anxiously awaited the terrorists'
next move. It came on March 10 when the Executive Committee sent
Tikhomirov's conciliatory open letter promising the cessation of
terrorist activities if Alexander would undertake sweeping reforms.
On the recommendation of Pobedonostsev, the tsar then appointed
the war hero N. M. Baranov to the post of municipal governor of St.
Petersburg. Baranov declared a state of siege and surrounded the city
and its islands with regular army troops and corps of volunteers,
directing the police and gendarme organizations to tear up whole city
blocks in search of what the governor termed "the league of nihilists,
scoundrels, and idiots."[8]

Success in tracking down the major perpetrators of the regicide
swelled Baranov's ambition, and in the late spring and early summer
of 1881 he pressured the government to give him complete control of
all police forces throughout the country. Baranov's efforts found support among a group of noblemen who were close to the tsar and constituted the core of the Holy Brotherhood (*Sviashchennaia Druzhina*).
Even after Baranov fell from favor (he was removed from office in
August 1881), the brotherhood continued to press his cause, demanding the transfer of police functions to Gatchina and the revival of the
Third Section dealing with political subversives. In part defeated in its
efforts by the implacable hostility of Pobedonostsev,[9] the brotherhood
formed itself into an unofficial secret police force which, until it was
disbanded in 1883, served as a private guard to the tsar, and, in an
attempt to stop terrorism, conducted covert negotiations with Narodnaia Volia and financed nonterrorist socialist publications.

In May 1881 Count N. P. Ignat'ev was named to the post of
Minister of Internal Affairs, replacing M. T. Loris-Melikov. One of
the crucial issues facing his administration was how to organize the
struggle against the revolutionaries. Confronted with growing
anarchy in government police practices on the one hand and the
dangerous emergence of nongovernmental or semiofficial antirevolutionary activity on the other, Ignat'ev supervised the drafting of
a series of measures that provided the government, particularly the
Ministry of Internal Affairs, with special powers to track down and
prosecute political criminals.[10] On 14 August 1881, the tsar authorized
for three years the provisional "Regulations on measures for the protection of state security and public tranquillity".[11] Provisional in name
only, Ignat'ev's Regulations were in fact renewed every three years
and formed the legal basis for tsarist suppression of the revolutionary
movement until February 1917. Expanding the already well-
established practice of sentencing revolutionary sympathizers or
peripheral activists through administrative exile and police

surveillance, the Regulations also strengthened the autonomy of police organs within designated administrative regions. This measure in turn made possible the creation of separate secret police organizations in St. Petersburg and Moscow.

Ignat'ev's tenure as Minister of Internal Affairs lasted only until May 1882, when he was replaced by the more trusted and experienced Count Dmitrii Tolstoi. Tolstoi was one of Russia's best-known conservatives, an intelligent and well-informed bureaucrat, and his appointment was greeted by his supporter Katkov as "in itself a manifesto and program" of counterreform.[12] Much was expected from the chief of the largest and most powerful ministry of a government whose ministries, more than any other institutions, determined policies and actions. It took only a few years for even the most conservative commentators to realize this was not the Tolstoi of old, however. He lacked resolve and energy and espoused no particular program or set of policies. Tolstoi became obsessed by fear of nihilists. He lived in "his damp little house," wrote Polovtsov, "surrounded by guards as if he himself were a state criminal."[13] He carried a loaded pistol at all times and in 1884 had a special retaining wall built around his summer house. E. M. Feoktistov noted that Tolstoi no longer took his customary walks. If he went out, it was in a carriage with a police officer sitting in the coach box. Special agents guarded the train station at Gatchina, protected him on the way to the palace, and remained on constant duty at his country home. Not satisfied even with this much security, Tolstoi stopped receiving petitioners and gave Deputy Minister P. V. Orzhevskii an increased allowance for his own personal protection.[14]

For Tolstoi, assassination had assumed the force of a tragic inevitability. He gave credence to the most unlikely plots, one of which involved a group of Kiev revolutionaries putting his guards to sleep with drugged cigarettes and then assassinating him.[15] Convinced that the revolutionaries would attack the tsar or himself at the coronation in May 1883, Tolstoi approved special measures to guard the ruler's movements and the processions. Gatchina was guarded like a prison. Militiamen and soldiers stood all along the railway from Petersburg to Moscow, the site of the coronation. The old capital itself was inundated with soldiers and with some six thousand special troops recruited from the Voluntary Guard, an auxiliary of the Holy Brotherhood. The guards, the soldiers, the secret routes, the undisclosed timetable, the spies on the street—all made, in Valuev's words, a "sad picture . . . The Union of Tsar and People! Our worshipped autocracy!"[16] When the coronation passed without incident Tolstoi became even more convinced an assassination was at hand and ordered that police surveillance of radicals "be strengthened to the ultimate." Still, Tolstoi added, "there is nothing that can be done to guard oneself from a person who might jump from the bushes."[17]

Tolstoi's obsessive fears were especially damaging to the reign of Alexander III because as Minister of Internal Affairs he was officially responsible for Russia's already badly disorganized police system. The failure of the Third Section to control terrorism in the last years of Alexander II had led to extensive restructuring of the police under his successor. The Department of Police was created in 1880 and placed under the Minister of Internal Affairs, while the Third Section was abolished. In theory the new department controlled secret police activity both at home and abroad, but it was too undermanned (it had only 125 staff members in 1881) to manage even the situation in the capitals.[18] Consequently the 1881 Regulations provided separate secret police establishments for St. Petersburg and Moscow and placed the local gendarme administrations, responsible for police activities in the provinces, directly under the regional governors or governors-general. Theoretically, each of these regional organizations reported directly to the Minister of Internal Affairs, but the channels of reporting and the hierarchy of police responsibility were so ill-defined that each regional unit acted as an autonomous satrapy.

Instead of restoring some coordination to the police services, Tolstoi only jumbled matters more. Fearing an assassin's bullet, he refused to assume any police functions whatever. Despite Pobedonostsev's attempts to calm Tolstoi's fears, he accepted the ministership only on the assurance that a deputy minister would be appointed to supervise the Department of Police, the gendarmes, and the empire's secret police operations. ("Let the responsibility for the police reside with him, and let them shoot at him, not at me."[19]) The Deputy Minister, P. V. Orzhevskii, was empowered to ensure the accountability of the St. Petersburg police authorities, themselves under the direction of the new chief of police.

When Orzhevskii was appointed to the post of deputy minister in charge of police affairs, P. A. Gresser was made St. Petersburg Chief of Police. Gresser immediately moved to expand the scope of his authority, setting up an office of city affairs and prompting Tolstoi to abolish the municipal governorship (1 November 1882). When it subsequently became clear that a police chief with a governor's responsibilities but without a governor's title could not effectively run both city government and police affairs, the old system was restored and the governorship brought back for Gresser (3 June 1883), this time under the direct supervision of Deputy Minister Orzhevskii.

The organization and reorganization of hierarchical authority between the St. Petersburg city police and the central government was partly the result of an inherent conflict of interest between the capital's police and the ministry's infant and understaffed Department of Police. In addition, there was a personality clash between Gresser and Orzhevskii, which greatly exacerbated this conflict. Feoktistov wrote that they were "like the Montagues and the Capulets."[20] They kept information from one another; their secret police establishments spied on one another; and Gresser seldom observed his official responsibility to report to his immediate superior, the deputy minister. Gresser in fact constantly subverted Orzhevskii's appeals to Tolstoi by reporting directly to the tsar, reinforcing the monarch's earlier wishes to resurrect the Third Section.[21]

It was in this complex of personal rivalries, institutional confusion, and semiofficial police action that G. D. Sudeikin began his successful rise to the top of Russia's secret police apparatus. Having begun his career as an officer in the Kiev gendarme administration in the early 1870s, Sudeikin first attracted attention with his successful actions against Odessa narodovol'tsy in 1879–80. St Petersburg's Governor Baranov was so impressed with Sudeikin's arrest record that he brought him to the capital in the spring of 1881 to replace the secret police functionary V. V. Fursov.[22] After Baranov was removed and Gresser began to devote himself to a personal vendetta against Orzhevskii, Sudeikin in effect controlled all official antirevolutionary activity in the capital.

Sudeikin's investigative methods diverged sharply from those of Baranov and were greatly appreciated by an administration that treasured calm. Instead of treating the city as a stage for open warfare, Sudeikin went underground and infiltrated the narodovol'tsy movement with provocateurs. More important, Sudeikin saw the secret police as his personal power base and sought to use it to promote his career, reasoning that the man who could control Russian terrorism would stand closest to the tsar.

That the secret police could in fact serve as just such a source of power is in part attributable to the confusing police system. Neither the Petersburg governor nor the city's chief of police had any jurisdiction over the secret police. And instead of making Sudeikin responsible to the Department of Police, Tolstoi and Orzhevskii created a new office of inspector of the secret police, investing it with control of all secret police activity throughout the empire.[23] As Valuev put it, Orzhevskii had simply "handed over all secret police power in the country to Sudeikin."[24] At the same time, rivalries within the Ministry of Internal Affairs were so intense that there was no effective personal brake on Sudeikin's initiatives. Tolstoi wanted no part of police jurisdiction. V. K. Plehve, director of the Department of Police

and a skilled and intelligent bureaucrat, claimed that Tolstoi's ineffec-
tual policies "made it impossible to fight nihilism," and he constantly
threatened to resign for that reason.[25] Orzhevskii remained heavily involved in his bureaucratic war with Gresser. Therefore, it should be
no surprise that when Tolstoi finally learned the full extent of
Sudeikin's alleged plans to organize the assassinations of high government officials to promote his advancement, he noted that "all of his
activities were unknown to us."[26]

On the orders of the Executive Committee, the narodovol'tsy
brutally murdered Sudeikin on 18 December 1883. The news "greatly
upset" Tolstoi; he was certain that Sudeikin's assassins would never be
caught and that his own murder was imminent.[27] In a letter to
Pobedonostsev Tolstoi revealed the depth of these fears: "Poor
Sudeikin does not go from my head, no matter what I do — he is before
me . . . this event has totally capsized me; pray God that it does not
have an effect on my health." In closing, Tolstoi returned to the theme
that he was the next target of "these scoundrels," and that "it would be
a good idea to think now of a person who could replace me."[28] By
1885–86 Tolstoi's nerves were so bad and his health so poor that he
spent half the year away from Petersburg. When he finally died in
early 1889, Polovtsov wrote, "one cannot but consider . . . [his death]
a very fortunate event."[29]

The fear, helplessness, and paranoia so evident in Tolstoi during
this period were only an extreme version of the conviction pervading
Russian government circles that nihilists were everywhere and
terrorism unavoidable. "You can never catch them," lamented
Pobedonostsev, "you can never cure all madness." Even Valuev wrote
that he could not escape the thought that Russian statesmen were
"fated and doomed." The tsar forbade officers on parade before him to
carry any weapons and even carried a gun himself, once seriously
wounding an adjutant who had surprised him from behind. Becoming
increasingly exasperated by the number of soldiers and secret police
who followed his every step, Alexander ordered that they be used
only on appropriate occasions and also noted that "we all know they
do no good anyway."[30]

Every train wreck or murder of a government official, every
accidental explosion or robbery, was initially assumed to be the work
of the omnipotent nihilists.[31] When former Minister of Internal Affairs
L. S. Makov committed suicide in February 1883, Pobedonostsev
blamed it on an ex-governess who had been associated with the
nihilists. Even when government officials knew that the events were
not caused by the radicals, their penchant for secrecy encouraged the
public to interpret these events as the work of the terrorists. When the

tsar became sick in December 1883, Pobedonostsev urged Tolstoi to break with normal procedures and publish lengthy descriptions of the illness in the hope of allaying the widely held view that he had been shot. After the October 1888 wreck of the tsar's train, A. F. Koni begged Pobedonostsev to put the negligent railway officials on trial. He felt this was the only way to squelch widespread rumors that this near disaster was also the result of a terrorist plot.[32]

The nihilist phobia of imperial officials also permeated discussions about administrative reorganization and counterreform during the 1880s. When Count Ignat'ev sought to convoke an assembly of the land (*zemskii sobor*) in 1881, Pobedonostsev objected that this was an "invitation to revolution," and Mikhail Katkov reminded his readers that the notorious revolutionaries Nechaev and Zheliabov also wanted to establish such assemblies.[33] The necessity to find and destroy the sources of revolution was of especially high priority for the officials who considered reform measures for the press, the judiciary, and the educational establishment. Newspapers and journals were leading Russian youth to join the radicals, Pobedonostsev wrote; the libraries and the reading rooms were spreading their literature; and the liberal press served "as a haunt for inveterate nihilists."[34] Plehve insisted that the schools were responsible for turning out nihilists, and even Polovtsov wrote that the universities were "overcrowded with student bombers." Polovtsov also blamed the courts for not understanding "the complete absurdity" of trying terrorists in an open courtroom.[35] After studying the university statutes of 1884, Senator V. P. Bezobrazov concluded that the government was interested in little else other than punishing students for their collective guilt for perpetrating nihilism: "And here our rulers think only of destroying rather than repairing and improving the edifice of the state."[36]

In the discussion of the land captain (*zemskii nachal'nik*) project of 1889 and the zemstvo regulations of 1890, both of which owed much to Tolstoi's initial sponsorship, the main idea, noted Polovtsov, was to take "the ground away from the anarchists of various types."[37] The Great Reforms of the 1860s were seen as the seedbed of liberalism, and liberalism, in Katkov's words, was merely "nihilism in its legal form."[38] Thus government leaders conceived their attempt to reverse the old reforms as one aspect of the sacred struggle against the revolutionary movement. The substantial opposition in government and society to the counterreforms was attacked for sedition and radical leanings by the conservatives, with Alexander III and Tolstoi in the lead. Tolstoi, for instance, called the State Council, which served as a brake on autocratic counterreform, "an assembly of revolutionaries — striving to put limitations on the autocracy."[39] And Katkov continually accused reformist bureaucrats and the liberal St. Petersburg press of maintaining contacts with exiled Russian revolutionaries.[40] Especially in the case of Pobedonostsev, antipathy for the so-called nihilists reached absurd lengths. An 1891 proposal to build a railway to Kazan occasioned Pobedonostsev's retort: "There, now they are building a railroad to Kazan, but why? Kazan was off the beaten path, one could not get to it easily except during summer, but now, with a railroad, the nihilists will swamp it and, just as things were getting better, get the people to take leave of their senses."[41]

As historians of the reign of Alexander III have demonstrated, the counterreforms were neither unilaterally successful nor undertaken without considerable opposition. Often, the reactionary measures only continued the procedures of the last decade of the preceding reign. The leading Soviet historian of this period, P. A. Zaionchkovskii, suggests that it was precisely the absence of a revolutionary movement inside Russia in the 1880s that made possible the full program of counterreform; in other words, the revolutionary movement of the 1870s had kept reaction in check.[42] But the predisposition of tsarist officials to see nihilist conspiracies in every social disturbance, natural accident, or instance of administrative liberalism grew more pronounced in the 1880s, despite the fact that the revolutionary movement was badly dispersed. In his diaries, D. A. Miliutin claimed that the problem with the leaders of Imperial Russia was that instead of searching out the basic causes of the revolutionary movement, "they thought only about protective police measures."[43] The real problem, however, was that they not only searched everywhere for these causes, but, indeed, claimed to find them everywhere: in court decisions, in student meetings, and even in the country tavern which, wrote Pobedonostsev, "was the primary bearer of nihilist theories among the people."[44]

The officials also claimed that certain elements of the empire's population, the Poles and even more so the Jews, had become dangerous breeding grounds of radicalism. "Do you want to know what constitutes the soil for this organization of nihilists?" asked Count Ignat'ev: "It is the Poles and the Jews."[45] "Nihilism is a disease," Tolstoi explained to the English correspondent John Baddeley, "it is the moral cancer of our time. You can no more stamp it out or abolish it than the Hebrew leprosy."[46] At the end of 1888, the nihilist phobia of the leading figures of Alexander III's reign coalesced with their "Judaophobia"[47] to produce the abhorrent Department of Police order that doubled the maximum term of all politicals administratively exiled to Siberia (from five to ten years) and confined all Jewish exiles to the northern portion of Iakutsk province.[48]

The revolutionary movement was a significant force in Russian society in the 1880s but the government also greatly overestimated its strength. The specter of nihilism led government officials to joust with unreal problems, while leaving the important ones in abeyance. The targets, the pace, and the extent of the counterreforms were as often influenced by fear of nihilists as they were by reasoned, conservative arguments. In short, Russia was not merely undergoverned; it was badly governed. Even given the best of bureaucratic circumstances (in personnel, procedures, and lines of communication), the government of Alexander III was faced with an insuperable dilemma. With the resources of the state (in Plehve's words) "strained to the breaking point in the struggle against sedition" (both real and, more often, imagined), the Russian ministries could not focus their attention either on eliminating the revolutionary movement by police action or on rationalizing the system of government, education, or the judiciary by administrative order.[49]

Industrialization and Society

The assassination of Alexander II occurred at the end of the first year of the most severe Russian industrial depression in the second half of the nineteenth century. Prompted in part by a worldwide economic crisis following the American Civil War and in part by Russia's own tempo of industrialization, which accelerated spectacularly during the 1870s and dropped off precipitously after the Russo-Turkish War and the Congress of Berlin (1878), the Russian crisis lasted at least until the mid-1880s, and by some measures until 1887. To be sure, agricultural Russia responded much more slowly to the reinvigoration of the world economy in the early 1880s; a series of poor harvests at the end of the decade led to the 1891–92 famine that caused widespread death and misery. But from the middle of the 1880s until the end of Alexander III's reign, Russian industrial output grew at the unprecedented rate of 5 to 8 percent a year, setting the stage for Witte's industrialization plans and the emergence of Russia as a world economic power.[50]

Thus the Russia of Alexander III should be viewed as an industrializing nation. Already in the 1870s thirteen thousand versts of railway track had been built, compared to a mere thousand versts in the previous decades. Practically each year of Alexander III's reign witnessed the building of more track than the previous year. Just as the railways stimulated internal trade, foreign investment promoted the building of new factories. For the twelve years 1881–1892, 138 million rubles were invested in Russian industrial stocks, against 88 million for the previous twenty years. Between 1881 and 1894 the total foreign capital investment in Russian corporations and banks more than doubled. According to A. V. Pogozhev, the decade of the 1880s witnessed the building of some three thousand new factories, in comparison to twenty-one hundred in the previous decade.[51]

As a result of foreign investment, factory building, and the new railway lines, heavy industry recorded remarkable growth in the 1880s. Between 1880 and 1890 the amount of pig iron smelted more than doubled; petroleum output increased by twenty times; the extraction of coal and iron ore grew by 120 percent, iron and steel production by 30 percent. The textile and metal-working industries recorded similarly impressive growth rates, due in large measure to rapid advances in the use of mechanical looms and steam boilers and engines.[52]

The expansion of industry in the 1880s encouraged three continuing processes: urban growth, the increase in the size and concentration of the industrial proletariat, and the concentration of industry in larger and more mechanized factories. The urban population of European Russia rose from 6.1 million to 10.0 million between 1863 and 1885. From 1856 to 1885 the city of St. Petersburg grew from 491 thousand to 861 thousand; the city of Moscow from 369 to 753 thousand. Between 1850 and 1890, the population of both cities doubled, in part because of the influx of potential workers, but also because the death rate began to decline after the early 1880s.[53]

In thirty-four selected large industries in the 1880s, the number of workers increased only slightly, from 467 thousand to 493 thousand, but the number of factories and workshops in these same industries fell sharply. As a result, the concentration of workers increased, according to M. I. Tugan-Baranovskii, from twenty-eight per factory in 1865 to forty-one per factory in 1888.[54] The St. Petersburg and Moscow industrial regions contained most of the larger factories, and by the 1880s these regions together employed about 60 percent of all Russian workers. At the beginning of the 1880s, the St. Petersburg and Moscow regions had some 247 thousand workers each, with approximately 70 percent of the workers involved directly in industrial production. The process of industrialization also increased the concentration of workers in urban centers outside the St. Petersburg and Moscow regions. In 1879 eleven Russian industrial centers had populations of over five thousand workers, but by 1890 this number had grown to twenty-one.[55]

Despite the growth of industry and factory towns in the 1880s, Russia was still an overwhelmingly agricultural country; 90 percent of the population lived on the land and 85 percent were engaged in peasant agriculture. How did the peasants adapt to rapid industrialization? Was capitalism permeating the countryside? To Russian populist and Marxist intellectuals of the 1880s, these were the central questions of the day. The disastrous famine of 1891–92 sparked an especially intense debate about the impact of continued industrialization on peasant agriculture.

Even in the first years of Alexander III's reign, government officials recognized that the emancipation of 1861 had not provided the basis for peasant prosperity.[56] The nobles had received the best land. The peasants, in order to pay their excessively high debts (which consisted mostly of redemption payments), were forced to farm every bit of land available to them, a practice that exhausted the soil and destroyed pasture lands. There was no capital for investment in agriculture, and the rapidly growing rural population (from 58 to 86 million between 1871 and 1901) forced peasant communes to parcel out ever smaller plots of land during periodic repartitions. A precipitous decline in the world grain prices forced the price of domestic grain down by almost half between 1881 and 1894. As a result, the peasants' debts mounted and they were compelled to sell their animals at low prices while attempting to lease land at inflated costs. The loss of animals meant a shortage of draft power and a reduction in the supply of much needed fertilizer. The competition for new fields drove the prices of leasing land higher than the value of the grain raised on it.

The government tried to relieve the growing burden on the peasantry in 1881–1883 by reducing redemption payments, cancelling some altogether, and eliminating the "temporarily obligated" status that had plagued a segment of the peasantry since 1861. The government also set up the Peasant Bank in 1882 to aid in the leasing and, to a lesser extent, the purchase of land. The onerous poll tax, which had been levied on peasants since the time of Peter the Great, was first reduced and then eliminated altogether in January 1887.

But the government at the same time undermined even the limited effectiveness of these measures by its industrialization policy. Especially during the latter half of Alexander III's reign, Minister of Finance Vyshnegradskii's policy to export grain — no matter what the cost — ruined the Russian peasantry. Vyshnegradskii, and Sergei Witte after him, saw grain export as the primary means to balance Russian payments and build the country's gold reserves, thus bringing the ruble to convertible status. Since grain export was not enough to pay for the government's rapidly increasing railway building and industrial projects, Vyshnegradskii imposed a series of indirect taxes that destroyed the peasants' already limited ability to meet their financial obligations.

Equally detrimental for Russian agriculture was the continuation of communal control of the land, which discouraged individual initiative and perpetuated the antiquated three-field system of farming. The population explosion and land hunger in the villages during the 1880s only increased the frequency of land redistribution. In this sense the populists were correct; the Russian commune performed a vital function by distributing land to growing families and poor peasants. But the repartitions were so frequent and so harmful to overall peasant agriculture that in 1893 the government finally intervened, limiting repartitions to once every twelve years and subjecting them to strict administrative supervision. The frequent redistributions of land did not mean, as some Legal Populists asserted, that the influence of capitalism had been repelled by the Russian peasantry. On the contrary, it was the growing strength of capitalism in the villages that manifested itself in the repartitions, as well as in the peasantry's growing dependence on the grain markets, on supplementing their income by working in factories or on large latifundia, and on leasing and buying land. To be sure, the urban markets did not grow fast enough to prompt improvements in agriculture, though some specialization for these markets did occur. And the class divisions that might have developed in the countryside were blunted by communal redistribution and the vagaries of peasant farming, which often saw the rich get poorer and the poor get richer.[57] In sum, the countryside was neither completely absorbed by nor immune to the development of capitalism. The state, "the most powerful capitalist force in Russia" (in the words of the narodovol'tsy), both encouraged and hindered the development of capitalist relations in the villages.[58] Especially by supporting the continued existence of the commune, which it saw as a guarantee of social stability and a reliable source of revenue, the state condemned the peasantry to suffer many of the evils of the new and more modern Russia, while receiving few of its benefits.

For both the narodovol'tsy and the social democrats of the 1880s, the Russian peasants were simply too oppressed, too poor, and too ignorant (about 80 percent of them were illiterate) to contribute to revolutionary change. The peasants for the most part had ignored the propagandists of 1874, responded only sporadically to those of 1877–1880, and mourned the violent death of Alexander II. Later, during the famine relief efforts of 1891–92, they attacked and sometimes killed medical personnel who were trying to stem the cholera epidemic. Initially the narodovol'tsy had tried to interpret the anti-Jewish pogroms of 1881–82 as an outbreak of class war, as the beginning of a new Pugachevshchina, but soon they condemned them as more senseless violence.[59] There were isolated peasant revolutionaries, the narodovol'tsy contended, but they were too dispersed about the countryside to be of any use to the movement. The relatively few peasant uprisings that did occur in the period 1881–1894 failed to stir the radicals' imagination. These violent incidents, the narodovol'tsy concluded, did not increase the consciousness of the peasantry. Thus the party should take no steps to aid them or to incite others.[60] In short, the narodovol'tsy took a middle position, neither idealizing the peasants, as was the populist tendency, nor discounting them, as did many social democrats. Rather, they saw in the flickering remnants of communal self-government the possibility of peasant renewal. That possibility could become a reality only if the contemporary political system were changed from one that oppressed peasants to one that freed them and gave them all the land.

The effects of rapid industrialization under Alexander III tended to undermine the remaining illusions of those radicals who still believed in an imminent peasant revolution that would transform Russia into a land of federal socialist communes. At the same time, industrialization created new groups in society that demanded change, enforced these demands with action, and thus became central to the radicals' strategy for revolution. One of these groups was the emerging technical intelligentsia, educated by the tsarist system to design, build, and manage Russian industry. In addition, the new Russia demanded an expansion of its professional sector — doctors, lawyers, and teachers. Together these groups occupied a privileged position in Russian society; they were the harbingers and products of the new industrial age. By dint of their education and their professions, they were usually modernizers and Westernizers, sensitive to Russia's need for political and economic reform. In their student years these members of the intelligentsia were sometimes drawn to revolutionary circles, especially to those of the social democrats, who viewed themselves as the underground Westernizers. On the whole, however, the professional and technical intelligentsia of the 1880s can better be classified as politically progressive — parliamentarian and liberal by persuasion but unwilling to support revolutionary action, even in the name of a constitution. It was among the professionals and technological personnel that the program of "small deeds" found its greatest support. Developed initially by Ia. A. Abramov in his journal *Nedelia* (*The Week*), this program called for the intelligentsia to teach among the people, to carry out "modest humanitarian tasks in the service of the people."[61] This philosophy reflected the practical bent and training of the technical and professional intelligentsia, encouraging many of them to apply their talents as statisticians, teachers, doctors, agronomists, or veterinarians in the zemstvos, where they could be of immediate help to the peasantry.

Another segment of the intellectual elite of the 1880s might be called the cultural intelligentsia, generally wealthy and of noble birth, including the writers, artists, and intellectuals admired by educated society (*obshchestvo*). Theirs was a small and enclosed world, alienated both from the conservative government that closed down their presses and censored their works and from the underground radicals, whose crude violence they abhorred. Like their professional and technical counterpart, this group shared the view of the educated elite that the underground of the 1880s was a motley group of dropouts and thugs, misguided idealists and runaway girls. Their fear of engaging in revolutionary activity overlapped with loathing for those who did. The members of this cultural intelligentsia seldom aided the radicals directly, though some individuals did sympathize with them privately. For the most part they withdrew to their studies, continued to write, and waited for a better day. At the same time, the cultural intelligentsia's devotion to absolute justice was at odds with the slow-paced progressivist mentality of the technical and professional intelligentsia, a circumstance that isolated its members from the very obshchestvo that so admired them. This was the milieu of the "Legal Populists" Mikhailovskii, Zlatovratskii, Engel'hardt, Vorontsov, and Danielson (Nikolai-on), and later of the "Legal Marxists" Struve, Bulgakov, and Berdiaev. Though these labels fit many of the individuals within these two groups poorly, the fact that they were all radical thinkers and not political activists was an important common denominator. When they directed their very different messages to the revolutionaries, they couched them in the same sort of condescending and often irrelevant terms, though to be fair, the underground lived in a much more constricted, even ignorant, intellectual milieu than did the theorists in obshchestvo.

In terms of its social origins and social positions, the revolutionary intelligentsia occupied the lower stratum of educated society as a whole in the 1880s. Hundreds of these men and women were students or former students who had withdrawn from schools or been expelled for minor infractions; many of them were young, poor, children of commoners, and of non-Russian national origins. Some 20 percent of all the arrested radicals of the 1880s were *déclassé*. Jobless or drifting from job to job or school to school, they possessed at least a secondary education but were thoroughly isolated from the anchors of the Russian social · structure. The members of the revolutionary intelligentsia (as distinct from the professionals and technological personnel who entered the revolutionary movement, 11 percent of its ranks) were joined by a collective sense, or at least a collective psychology, that they were victims of the Russian social structure. They were Jews and Poles from the western provinces, educated in Russian schools, but discriminated against and, in the case of the Jews, forced to live under increasingly severe legal disabilities; some were children of nobles (25 percent of the total) who perhaps had lost or sold their estates; and sometimes they were educated women (12 percent of the total) who were frustrated by the limitations on their educational and professional lives.[62] The hopeful promises of social and political emancipation during the reign of Alexander II gave way to frustrated ambitions and bitter resentment, especially among women and the nationalities, in the reign of his heir.

The revolutionary movement of the 1880s also included a significant component of workers and artisans, 16 percent of the total arrested. In the last years of Alexander III's reign, 1890–1894, this component jumped to 28 percent, and by 1901–1903 to 47 percent.[63] Russian industrialization not only created a working class, but one which increasingly contributed to the development of the revolutionary movement.

Russian Workers

The living conditions of Russian workers varied widely and depended on such factors as location, type of industry, and the strength of rural ties. Official statistics taken from the reports of Russian factory inspectors from all over the empire in the mid-1880s placed the average working wage at 188 rubles a year, ranging from 606 rubles a year at the highest to 89 rubles at the lowest. Metal workers, located primarily in St. Petersburg, earned approximately twice the wages of the textile workers, located mostly in the Moscow and Vladimir regions. These averages include only the wages of adult male workers; generally, a woman earned half of a man's income, children a quarter.[64] Another significant variable complicating the picture of wages is the extent to which the individual worker was tied to the land. Miners who owned horses, for instance, were usually paid a bonus. A worker who lived on the land not only paid less rent, but was able to save on food and clothing costs. The much discussed Russian peasant-worker, who migrated to the cities in the fall after harvest and returned to the village in the spring for planting, was especially prevalent in the Moscow region. In this case, the worker left his (in some cases her) family in the village, lived in factory barracks under extremely primitive conditions, and sent a portion of his wages back to the commune. As a result of the scarcity of labor during the peak agricultural season, wages in the central industrial region were

10 to 20 percent higher during spring and summer. Even in St. Petersburg the population dropped significantly in the summer when about one-fifth of the city's inhabitants, 150,000 people, migrated to the countryside.[65] Some peasant-workers were so dependent on their factory income, however, that they chose to ignore their land altogether. The gendarme chief of Kolomenskii and Bronnitskii districts (Moscow province) reported that "from early spring, large parties of peasants trudge to Moscow and to Petersburg for various kinds of work, returning to the villages already in late fall, so that agriculture gets very little attention."[66]

The actual pay received by the Russian worker or peasant-worker ranged between one-third and one-half of his gross wage. According to a commission set up in March 1885 to review factory laws, chaired by Plehve, the workers sometimes lost close to 40 percent of their wages due to "the often completely arbitrary and extremely onerous [work] penalties." The company store also took a large percentage of the workers' earnings; in fact, Plehve directly blamed the factory owners for selling goods in the stores at a rate as high as 45 percent above market prices.[67] As one gendarme chief explained the system, the factory owners, in search of cheap labor, sent their agents to the countryside in the winter to negotiate with village elders for large contingents of laborers. Often the workers were not paid for two months after they began work in the spring, living off products in the factory store billed against future pay. "The products were worse than those on the market, and their prices higher. Thus the workers were always in debt to their masters," sometimes never receiving a single kopeck of pay.[68]

Low pay was complemented by long working hours, twelve to fourteen hours a day by official accounts, even after the promulgation of factory laws in the 1880s. Factory Inspector Ia. T. Mikhailovskii wrote that the twelve-hour workday actually involved thirteen and a half hours at the factory because of the long midday break. Without additional pay, the factory manager could demand overtime hours as well as lunchtime work from his laborers. Mikhailovskii noted that in the early 1880s neither the six-day week nor even religious holidays were consistently honored: "The Russian factory owner had the right to use the labor of workers of both sexes and various ages on all days of the year [and at any hour of the day], not excluding Sunday and other holidays."[69]

Youngsters from the age of six or seven, as well as females of all ages, were employed as laborers throughout Russia. Their pay was one-third to one-half that of adult men, and in time of economic difficulties they were the first to be laid off. Their jobs were as a rule less skilled and more taxing than those of the men. However, it should be noted that the Russian government made strenuous efforts in the early 1880s to eliminate night work for females as well as to pass a series of child-labor laws. Petersburg manufacturers argued that the elimination of night work by women would bolster the morale and improve the health and morals of the workers, whereas the Moscow section of the Council of Trade and Manufacturing insisted that it was better to have the workers in the factories at night rather than "debauching in the pubs and on the streets."[70] The high moral tone of arguments on both sides hardly concealed their real concerns, which were economic. Because of the plummeting market for their goods, Petersburg manufacturers pressed for the elimination of night work altogether. But Moscow manufacturers, anxious to maintain their edge against growing competition from the more mechanized Polish textile industry, fought against the proposed measures. Workers, too, often opposed the legislation, for they counted on their children's pitiful wages and their wives' night work to sustain their minimal living standards.[71]

Nevertheless the laws slowly came into being. According to the legislation of 1 June 1882, children under twelve were to be excluded from the labor force, day work of twelve- to fifteen-year-olds was limited to eight hours, and the post of factory inspector was created in the Ministry of Finance to enforce these laws. But the implementation of the laws was hindered by the small number of factory inspectors and the determined opposition of some factory owners. To some extent, the strike movement of 1884–85 forced the government to attempt to resolve the question of female labor. As of 1 October 1885, night work for youngsters under seventeen and for women was made illegal in the textile industry, and in other branches hours were negotiable between the factory owners and the factory inspectors, whose numbers were also increased by the legislation. Still, when Factory Inspector I. I. Ianzhul reviewed all the legislation on child labor and female night work, he noted that government measures hardly helped the condition of workers. Factory owners simply drove their workers harder, lengthening their workday, instituting double shifts, and engaging in secret violations of the law.[72]

Perhaps more decisive than the long workday and low real wages in shaping Russian workers' attitudes toward revolutionary propaganda-were the conditions in the factories. Here, Factory Inspector Mikhailovskii's reports of well-lighted, well-ventilated factory barracks, where workers made use of libraries, baths, medical clinics, and schools, were clearly fabrications and poorly disguised the truly appalling factory working conditions in the Russian Empire.[73] Ianzhul wrote that the aid of charitable institutions was seldom to be seen in Moscow factories; Sviatlovskii complained that there were no doctors in the overwhelming majority of Russian factories; and, in the words of the Moscow gendarme chief, "the sanitary conditions of the housing at factories are very unappealing and to change them would require measures very much opposed by the factory owners."[74] Measures to prevent industrial accidents were not implemented, despite appeals from the government, and even the newer factories rarely had proper hygiene or decent ventilation.

Conditions in workers' homes were often as bad if not worse than those in the factories. Besides sheer hunger, the lack of decent housing was probably the most difficult problem faced by the Russian workers. The rapid population growth of St. Petersburg and Moscow crowded industrial workers' quarters and swelled the number of families living in a single dwelling, abetting the fierce cholera epidemics and the outbreaks of syphilis characteristic of the early 1880s.[75] In factory barracks workers were crowded into small rooms on bunk beds with little more than sleeping space. At the Morozov factory, where twenty-five hundred workers lived in barracks, a small room, seven by nineteen feet, was inhabited by twenty-two workers.[76] Discipline in the barracks was often severely enforced. It was not unknown for the Russian worker to have his wages attached for singing or entertaining visitors in the barracks.

In Factory Inspector Ianzhul's pathbreaking studies of Russian and Polish workers, the former consistently suffered in comparison to their Polish comrades. The Russians lived under more miserable conditions, produced less despite longer working hours, and were more seriously undernourished and more prone to vagabondage. "Above all," Ianzhul wrote, "the Polish worker is, on the average, more intelligent and educated."[77] In the Moscow region about a third of the workers were literate; in the Polish region (like the St. Petersburg region), about half of the workers were literate. Generally in Russia literacy rates were higher among metal workers than textile workers, male workers than female workers, workers in the cities than those in the provinces.

Russian labor experienced particularly harsh privations during the depression of the early 1880s. In some of the largest factories in St. Petersburg between one-third and one-half the work force was laid off.[78] Many workers returned to their villages when factory management abandoned night shifts altogether. Those workers who had no villages to return to were arrested by the police for drunkenness or loitering and were sent to the town of Shlisselburg. Since there were no jobs there, the workers drifted illegally back to Petersburg, looking for work, where they were again picked up by the police. This process, according to the St. Petersburg police, was repeated five to ten times a year for thousands of workers.[79]

For the first time in its history Russia experienced massive industrial unemployment. According to official statistics for thirty-four industries in European Russia, slightly more than one-third of all workers — thirty thousand people in all — lost their jobs. In 1883 production in the most important industries of European Russia fell by 15 percent.[80] Officials were so worried that the layoffs would breed violence that they encouraged factory administrators to let workers go in small groups and to inform the police of the dates and numbers of those released.[81]

Reports of gendarmes from all over the empire described the economic situation of workers as bad to disastrous and, almost without exception, blamed the workers' problems on the factory owners and managers. In this description of the "falling spirits of the working people," an assistant chief of the Moscow gendarmes echoed the surprisingly widespread sympathy of the police officials for the workers:

> Drunkenness, promiscuity, and the direct consequence of the latter, syphilis, are rampant in the factories in the broadest measure. The combination of factory work and life in the barracks has created a brazen attitude among the female workers and a full rejection of feminine modesty. Following the example of parents and older children, youngsters from the earliest ages begin to drink from the cup of vice and there are already signs of degeneracy by the time they reach puberty. The factory owners and their closest subordinates not only do not stop the spread of vice, but by their examples serve directly as its partner.
>
> Having had the opportunity to examine closely the life of factory workers, I can find very little difference between their position and that of the earlier serfs; the same want, the same need, the same suppression of their rights; the same contempt for their spiritual needs. In one case the person was a yoked animal, in the other he is a senseless machine, differing very little from the machine at which he works.[82]

The political reliability of these workers, the St. Petersburg gendarme chief wrote (February 1884), cannot be taken for granted. Even the highly literate and more educated workers are "filled with shameful instincts." From early youth the worker "has learned drinking, widespread dissipation, not hesitating to do anything." This is the "dangerous element," the gendarme chief continued, on whom the "anarchists" can work the charms of "the socialist utopia." "During the present cutback in factory and industrial activities, wage-earning is made more difficult and poverty grows; to satisfy any needs becomes more difficult and he [the worker] searches for the reasons for . . . social inequality." So far, the gendarme chief concluded, the workers did not exhibit political interests, "but that evil day is coming closer and closer." Among the countermeasures he recommended (such as hiring factory priests, improving factory conditions, and so on) was a proposal strikingly similar to that of the radicals — "to publish books and organize lessons for workers in which a simple and basic understanding of political economy would be imparted."[83]

Even Minister of Internal Affairs Tolstoi viewed the growing number of conflicts between workers and management as fundamentally the fault of factory management. The absence of laws regulating the relations between workers and managers, Tolstoi wrote to Minister of Finance Bunge (4 February 1885), "opens a broad area for arbitrariness of the factory owners to the detriment of the workers and puts the latter in an extremely difficult position." Tolstoi added that the factory owners used high work penalties to lower "artificially" the real wages of the workers, "which causes justified anger and dissatisfaction among workers." Tolstoi concluded his letter to Bunge by insisting that the government could not call out the troops every time there was a workers' disturbance. Instead, he recommended that a special commission be formed from the Ministries of Internal Affairs, Justice, and Finance to review old factory laws and propose new ones.[84] Plehve, who shared Tolstoi's views, was assigned to head the commission. He confirmed the overwhelming financial debt of workers to the factory owners: "aware of their impossible situation," the workers sought "to protect themselves from further arbitrary behavior on the part of the owners. And because the right to complain in the courts is almost unavailable to workers — in their eyes the only means useful to protect their interests is the strike and every kind of willfulness."

Like Tolstoi, Plehve insisted that although the strikes were damaging to "social order and peace," it was "extremely unpropitious" to use soldiers to quell them, because in the minds of the workers, "exasperated by the contemporary conditions of factory life, military forces appear to support the arbitrariness of the factory owners." Indeed, in parts of his report, Plehve sounds very much like the propagandists he spent his life pursuing: "Before the rich capitalist, the individual factory worker is powerless and without influence, [especially] if the law, the worker's only savior, refuses to defend him.

But, gathered at the factory, those same workers are already a dangerous force, especially when there is cause for their dissatisfaction to feed on bad treatment."[85]

The Factory Law of 3 June 1886, adopted at the initiative of the Ministry of Internal Affairs and made urgent by the dangerous proportions of the 1884–85 strike movement, increased the numbers of factory inspectors and provided them with a larger role in adjudicating disputes between workers and management. The new law also ensured that the workers understood the cost of striking. Plehve and the State Council insisted on more severe penalties for workers on strike, especially for those who led them and those who refused to return to work after being ordered to do so by the police. Indeed, in the deliberations about the law, the Minister of Internal Affairs demanded that the local police retain primary responsibility for the maintenance of order at the factories, working in close collaboration with the factory inspectors.[86]

The Strike Movement

Despite their terrible working conditions and impoverishment, Russian workers were able to exert some pressure by means of strikes and disturbances. Intent on maintaining order, the Ministry of Internal Affairs refused to allow any private contracts between factory owners and labor that were drawn outside the jurisdiction of the state, continuing the paternalistic policies of the 1860s. Government paternalism also motivated the police to protect the rights of workers against owners, reflecting attitudes that dated back at least to the 1840s and continued into the twentieth century. Even the origins of many of the proposals for factory legislation can be found in the dozens of disbanded commissions to study factory conditions during the reign of Alexander II. But actual factory legislation in the 1880s was precipitated by worker action as well as paternalism, specifically by the strike movement in 1885, which saw close to twenty thousand workers participate in an estimated seventy-three strikes.[87]

Both the imperial police and Soviet historians correctly identify economic rather than political factors as the primary cause of the strikes in the 1880s.[88] But the police astutely added that the workers were developing a sense of their own power and that the seeds of political strikes had already been planted. Of the 331 workers' complaints received by Moscow Factory Inspector Ianzhul between November 1886 and January 1888, 153 were judged to be justified. Although the three most frequent categories of complaints dealt with such economic problems as being released before the end of a contract and not receiving full pay, the fourth highest category indicated "dissatisfaction with bad conditions, bad food, and the lack of hygiene facilities," and the fifth, "poor treatment at the hands of administrators or foremen." Strikes in the same period were called for economic causes pertaining to pay, penalties, and contracts. But the workers' sense of their dignity and rights as human beings also plays a role in the strike demands. Several strikes were caused by "the insulting treatment" of workers by factory administrators; in two cases the workers refused to return to work until the shop steward was fired. In another case, women demanded the same pay for identical work in the day as the men received at night. And in two more, workers protested when the owner used their food to feed pigs. Poor and restrictive conditions in the factory clinics aroused protests as did the overcrowding in factory barracks and the cavalier attitudes of managers, especially those of foreign origin.[89]

Police reports on strikes between 1885 and 1889 also demonstrate that Russian workers displayed a surprisingly high degree of organization and tactical acumen.[90] After walking off the job, the workers usually elected representatives to negotiate with the factory owners. Violence was rarely pointless; only after negotiations broke down were windows smashed, observers beaten, or factory machinery damaged. Indeed, in many strikes destruction of factory property seemed intended to invite the intervention of soldiers and of government officials. Often workers presented minimal demands and, as they were met, placed new ones in front of their employers. In some cases they raised money to hire liberal lawyers to defend their interests. The police also frequently noted the solidarity of workers, both within different areas of a single factory and among workers of neighboring factories. Although it was clear that socialist propagandists played little if any role in the strikes of the 1880s, workers expelled from other factories for striking often assumed the leadership of strikes in their new places of employment.

The largest labor disturbance of the decade, the January 1885 strike of textile workers at the Morozov Nikol'skoi factory complex in Orekhovo-Zuevo (Vladimir province), in many ways epitomized the new developments in the strike movement during that decade. Like its predecessors in the 1870s, the Morozov strike was economic in character and evolved into a violent expression of anger at the workers' harsh living and working conditions. However, the plans for the strike, its initial stages, and its overall organization reflected the generally high level of purpose among striking workers, aided by such veteran worker activists as Petr Moiseenko and Andrei Volkov. The underlying cause of the strike was a decline in both gross and real wages between 1881 and 1884; in November 1884 alone many

Morozov workers lost up to a quarter of their wages in penalties.[91] Worker discontent at Morozov was therefore directed against the factory owners and against those factory employees — the manager Lotarev and especially the weavers' foreman Shorin — who assessed the penalties.

The Morozov strike began on 7 January 1885, after almost two months of discussion among workers and agitation by Moiseenko, Volkov, and others. The weavers and spinners walked off the job, overpowered the factory police and the Tatar *chernye rabochie* (unskilled workers), who had been armed by the factory administration to maintain order, and forced the dyers to stop work. A crowd of about three thousand workers vandalized factory stores and set upon the homes of factory officials. The house of the weavers' foreman Shorin was thoroughly ransacked and looted. Even with the arrival of Cossacks and army regulars on January 8 and 9, the workers continued to attack factory buildings and clash with authorities. However, as soon as the Vladimir governor arrived to negotiate with the strikers, the prosecutor noted, they became very "well disciplined" and "did not allow themselves to engage in any further violent activities."[92] By January 14, with Morozov's promise to the governor and workers to fire Shorin and lower work penalties, the strike had ended, and the factory returned to normal.

The demands of the workers as articulated to the governor by their negotiator Volkov centered on the problem of low wages. Contemporary wages, the strikers stated, "do not provide the possibility to exist, to care for a family, and to pay state financial obligations." Therefore they demanded that no more than 5 percent of their salaries be subject to penalties, and that the level of wages return to what it was in 1881–82. In addition to a number of other demands (which would have regulated the assessment of penalties), the workers asked for state factory laws that would govern the reporting of factory accidents, injury compensation, the equalization of pay, and the amount of time required between giving notice and laying off workers.[93] Thus, though the demands of the workers were fundamentally economic, they constituted a call for the improvement of factory life as a whole. Rather than expressing any opposition to the state, the workers asked that the state act on their behalf against the interests of factory managers.

It is important not to overstate the differences between the Morozov strike and its predecessors. During the St. Petersburg Nevskii factory strike in 1870, the first major strike in Russian labor history, the workers also made demands for higher wages and better factory conditions, and they deftly negotiated with both management and the government.[94] It was not so much the program of the Morozov workers that was important to the labor history of Russia, but the sheer force of the strike, and the extent to which the violence on Orekhovo-Zuevo reverberated through Russia. In the end over six hundred workers were banished to their home villages for participation in the strike; thirty-three strike leaders were placed on trial for criminal offenses. A month later another large strike involving around a thousand workers broke out at the Morozov factory in Tver. In Orekhovo-Zuevo itself, the police were so worried about another workers' uprising that they kept two companies of Cossacks in the town until late spring and increased police surveillance.

After the trial of workers involved in the strike, Mikhail Katkov wrote in the *Moscow News*, "Yesterday in the sacred town of Vladimir [the location of the trial] a one-hundred-and-one gun salute was sounded in honor of the appearance of the workers' question in Russia." The country, mourned Katkov, was at a crossroads: "The uprising at the Nikol'skoi factory contained all the elements needed for Russia to seem possessed by the ailment of the proletariat and the workers' question; and what is more important, to represent in Russia the tragicomedy of a struggle between labor and capital."[95] From a very different point of view, Georgii Plekhanov, leader of the Emancipation of Labor group in Switzerland, also saw the Morozov strike as a turning-point in the history of Russian labor, the beginning, he wrote with great satisfaction, "of a new phase in the workers' movement."[96] Vera Zasulich, another member of the émigré social-democratic group, indicated (no doubt correctly) that it was not so much the workers' attitude toward the autocracy which had changed as a result of the strike, but that of the autocracy toward the workers: "After the trial of the Morozov strikers, factory workers must be added to the number of people whose interests contradicted the interests of the government. The government stopped trying them publicly and began to deal with them silently, as with enemies."[97]

During the last half of the 1880s, the government also curtailed the public reports of factory inspectors, and those who criticized factory management too harshly were relieved of their duties. New legislation in 1886 provided the bases both for censorship in reporting factory conditions and for establishing the illegality of strikes. Still the Ministry of Internal Affairs did not lose its fundamental sympathy with the workers' plight. Factory laws of 1886–87 finally regulated the assessment of work penalties, satisfying all of the workers' demands on that point. By using a mailed fist against strikers and passing legislation to alleviate some of the most severe conditions of factory labor, the government hoped to stop the strike movement in its infancy.

It is an especially difficult historical problem to establish a causal relationship between the development of the Russian labor movement in the 1880s and the contemporaneous emergence of social-democratic ideas among Russian radicals. No doubt, labor disturbances like the Morozov strike could not help but attract the notice of socialist revolutionaries who, by the middle of the 1880s, were in search of a new perspective from which to approach the problem of overthrowing the government. If rapid industrialization is necessary for social-democratic theories, especially Marxism, to flourish among radicals, then during the 1880s in Russia that essential precondition was beginning to be fulfilled. At the same time, the Russian workers' movement increasingly interacted with revolutionary currents. The immediate vision of an active labor force inspired social-democratic ideas among radicals as did the long-range hopes attached to the example of the Western European labor movement. Also, the interaction between intelligentsia activists and workers prompted further searching for worker-oriented theories of revolution, sometimes altering traditional narodovol'tsy thinking, at other times leading to social-democratic programs. Workers themselves were less interested in competing theories of revolutionary activity than in finding help to improve their economic and cultural circumstances. Usually it was the burning quest for literacy and knowledge that impelled them to join workers' circles, where the radicals—social democrats or narodovol'tsy—who were willing to teach often made converts to their causes.

The emergence of Russian social democracy in the 1880s was also influenced by government antirevolutionary policies and activities. Convinced that nihilists lurked everywhere in society, the government spread itself too thin to act effectively against them. Indeed, by attacking the universities, restricting the Polish and especially the Jewish populations, crushing the liberal press, and fostering suspicion and fear by its overreaction to minor crimes and insignificant political gatherings, the government created new radicals, far more than it could eliminate by police action.

All in all, the police failed to achieve its principal objective; too disorganized and understaffed, too beset by internal rivalries and multiple functions, it could not deal effectively with the underground. Still, the authorities managed to keep the narodovol'tsy on the run throughout the entire period, and hundreds of them were caught and exiled. Their circles were infiltrated by police spies and provocateurs, and they were hounded by police officials every bit as dedicated and wily as Sudeikin. For some of the narodovol'tsy, the answer to this intense pressure was increasing conspiracy and more terrorism. But for others, the answer lay in a rejection of terrorism, a turning away from conspiracy — anything to escape the repeated searches, arrests, and exiles that plagued their movement.

The radicals understood very well that no police official could make a career arresting worker-propagandists. They also understood that when these propagandists were caught their sentences were short and their treatment relatively mild. Social democrats, especially those who eschewed narodovol'tsy tactics and literature, were often not exiled at all, but simply placed under police surveillance in provincial towns. The relative tolerance that the authorities showed toward social democrats (compared to their overreaction to the slightest narodovol'tsy infraction) certainly assisted the development of the social-democratic movement in Russia. Similarly, the police sympathy for workers and their plight, apparent in their assessments of the labor movement in the 1880s, overlapped with their relatively lenient treatment of workers active in the revolutionary movement. The police considered both narodovol'tsy and social-democratic workers pawns of the intelligentsia, victims of their miserable circumstances, and consequently often excused their transgressions. But they tended to treat the social-democratic workers' circles with greater tolerance than those of the narodovol'tsy, thereby contributing to the success of the social democrats among workers.

Industrialization and the development of the labor movement were preconditions for the emergence of the Russian social-democratic movement, though neither eliminated the relevance of the narodovol'tsy program. Similarly, government policy and practice abetted the development of social democracy but could not eliminate terrorism or its proponents. Nevertheless, police successes and the failure of the March 1 assassination to spark an upheaval forced the narodovol'tsy to rethink their program, and in doing so set the stage for the revolutionary movement of the 1880s.

Narodnaia Volia After the First of March

2

Narodnaia Volia paid dearly for its March 1 success. The organizers of the assassination — Zheliabov, Rysakov, Mikhailov, Kibal'chich, and Gel'fman — were brought to trial on March 26 and condemned to hang. Only Gel'fman's sentence was not carried out because she was pregnant; and she died in prison soon after the birth of her child. The few remaining members of the Executive Committee fled to Moscow in the late spring and early summer of 1881, where they waited and hoped that the assassination would at least spur the government to grant a constitution. But the government's answer to Tikhomirov's counciliatory "Letter to Alexander III" (March 10), which came in the form of an Imperial Manifesto on April 29, made it abundantly clear that autocracy would remain the law of the land, consecrated by God and unfettered by any limitations. What is more, the government of Alexander III responded to what it saw as the continuing terrorist threat by declaring a state of siege in Russia. The acquiescence of liberals in the harsh police measures embodied in the Temporary Regulations of August 1881, the growing influence of the reactionary Holy Brotherhood in court circles, and the general indifference of the masses to the goals of the March 1 conspiracy cut short the period of the Executive Committee's suspension of terrorist activities and concessions to the constitutional struggle.

During the late summer of 1881, the new Moscow center of the party attempted to regroup for another attack on the autocracy. In addresses to the Russian working people (August 26) and to the Cossacks (September 3), as well as in issue number 6 of *Narodnaia Volia* (October 23), the narodovol'tsy — led by Lev Tikhomirov and

Mariia Oshanina — renewed the party's commitment to terrorism and the seizure of power. Vera Figner was sent to Kiev and Odessa to organize a new assault group; in St. Petersburg, the narodovol'tsy set up an explosives laboratory that was to prepare the bombs for an assassination attempt on the life of Alexander III.

This brief flurry of activity was brought to a close during the winter of 1881–82, when the authorities arrested the leaders of the Moscow organization and destroyed the laboratory. (The conspirators who managed to escape the winter arrests were seized the following June.) Oshanina fled the country in the spring of 1882; Tikhomirov followed in the early summer. Together they established the new headquarters of the Executive Committee in Paris. Only Vera Figner, out of the two dozen most influential leaders of the party, was still active in the underground.

Even with the leadership of Narodnaia Volia under arrest or in exile, radical circles, attracted by the seeming omnipotence of the party demonstrated by the assassination of Alexander II, rallied around narodovol'tsy-allied organizations and replenished their cadres. At the same time, the number of indictments of narodovol'tsy activists remained remarkably consistent throughout the 1880s, between 1500 and 1700 a year. Between March 1881 and 1894 a total of 5851 narodovol'tsy were actually convicted of political crimes and sentenced: 27 were executed, 342 were imprisoned or sent into hard labor, and 5482 received administrative sentences, usually of short periods of exile or banishment, combined with police surveillance.[1] Although Narodnaia Volia continued to function after March 1881, it did so more as the symbolic focus for a dispersed and only hazily defined movement than as a revolutionary party with the unified purpose and clear hierarchy of command that the Executive Committee had attempted to provide with some success prior to the assassination. In the immediate post-March period, the committee was in shambles, and despite the subsequent efforts of the "Parisians," it would never regain either its former status or competence. However, in some ways the break-up and emigration of the Executive Committee was actually good for the movement; the hundreds of new members who were attracted to local narodovol'tsy groups could carry on the work of socialist agitation and propaganda on their own, without sacrificing valuable financial and human resources to the center's demi-god of terrorism.

The Workers' Section
Before March 1, the leaders of Narodnaia Volia placed little emphasis on the development of a revolutionary working class in their

program or activities. Especially the Executive Committee was absorbed by the terrorist struggle and tended to view workers primarily as potential bomb-throwers and secondarily as future agitators for the countryside. Still, in contrast to their Land and Liberty forerunners, the narodovol'tsy did assign an independent political significance to the urban working class. Although the party's original 1879 program avoided the question of proletarian socialism, the later and more detailed pamphlet "Preparatory Work of the Party" (March-April 1880) explained that narodovol'tsy should propagandize among urban workers because these have an especially important significance for revolution and because they are "more highly developed" than the peasantry. The growing politicization of the party in the spring of 1880 demanded that one of its most significant tasks was to carry socialist propaganda to the Russian working class.

"Preparatory Work" also stressed the importance of forming a "mass organization" of workers, one that would bring "consciousness" and "solidarity" to the workers' movement. Indeed, the success of the revolution depended on the ability of narodovol'tsy to harness strikes and workers' demonstrations to the revolutionary cause: "If the party could develop ties with the workers before [the revolutionary situation], then the possibility exists of closing down the factories and the plants, of rousing the workers and moving them into the streets. This is already half the battle in ensuring the success of the cause." In addition, the extent of the workers' participation in the uprising would determine "the usefulness to the people of revolution" and the composition as well as the program of the "provisional government."[2]

During the spring and summer of 1880, narodovol'tsy propagandists transformed these principles of "Preparatory Work" into the program of the Workers' Section of Narodnaia Volia. By fall the core of the Workers' Section organization began operation in St. Petersburg under the patronage of Andrei Zheliabov and with a formal structure that was both complex and overweening.[3] The capital was divided into regions and each region was the independent charge of an agent of the party. Two levels of workers' circles were established along with a so-called teachers' circle, the task of which was to develop programs and lectures especially for the use of propagandists among the working class. The first level of these circles would conduct what was essentially elementary education — teaching arithmetic, reading, and basic geography. Only the second level would discuss the development of socialism, the program of Narodnaia Volia, and such underground revolutionary literature as the *Workers' Newspaper*.[4] Those who "accepted the program of Narodnaia Volia" would then be recruited to the "central" groups of each region. For the meetings of the central groups, "workers' apartments" were to be set up all over the city, in the homes of workers' families "committed to the revolutionary cause." The occupants would be student members of the party "obligated to read lectures to the assembled groups."[5]

In reality, however, the Workers' Section operated in a much more haphazard way. N. I. Rysakov admitted that the leadership could only maintain one or two workers' apartments in the entire city. He managed to hold only two meetings in his own apartment on Vasil'evskii Island, attended by as few as five or six workers.[6] I. I. Popov, another veteran of these St. Petersburg workers' circles of 1880–81, later noted that a "solid, regular, active workers' organization of Narodnaia Volia did not exist." According to Popov, some narodovol'tsy-organized circles simply lost contact with the intelligentsia and continued to meet independently of the party. Other circles, formed by workers themselves, never had contact with the party and became vague auxiliaries out of their interest in the narodovol'tsy program.[7] During the widespread arrests of spring 1881, the authorities broke up the initial organization of the St. Petersburg Workers' Section and arrested fifty-two *intelligenty* and workers, including Rysakov and the nineteen-year-old student leader of the group, Lev Kogan-Bernshtein. According to the St. Petersburg prosecutor, the workers who were arrested—about half the group—read revolutionary literature and attended meetings, but "did not take the most active roles in the work of agitation."[8]

The general disorganization of the narodovol'tsy effort among the St. Petersburg workers was an advantage during these spring arrests; it permitted many groups to remain undetected by the police. A workers' group that concentrated on the spread of literacy (led by Osip Nagornyi) was responsible for the killing of the suspected police agent Preim (27 June 1881), yet continued to function until January 1882. Several workers' circles under the leadership of warrant officer Anatolii Bulanov survived the spring arrests and met episodically throughout the summer of 1881, discussing "the necessity to rise against [factory] owners and administrations for the purpose of transferring the factories and plants into the hands of the workers."[9]

Corresponding to the sporadic emergence and subsequent suppression of narodovol'tsy-organized workers' circles in St. Petersburg, scattered groups of workers, students, and narodovol'tsy activists in other labor centers organized Workers' Sections in 1880–81. In Kiev, the Southern Russian Fighting Battalion took up the task of protecting such organizations from police spies. The workers, the battalion claimed, stand "in the first rank" of the "social-revolutionary struggle" but are the "least capable . . . of fighting espionage [*shpionstva.*]"[10] Southern workers' circles, partly in imitation of their protectors from the Fighting Battalion, often assumed more aggressively terrorist postures than their northern counterparts. A Southern Workers' Union demanded from the government freedom for workers' meetings, minimum wage laws, and reading rooms. If the government refused to meet these demands, the union would retaliate as the organization "taking upon itself the defense of all workers of the southern region who engage in the war against the capitalist enslavers."[11]

In Moscow, P. A. Tellalov organized a large circle of propagandists, which subsequently formed a Workers' Section among Moscow textile workers.[12] Anton Boreisha, another Moscow narodovolets worker-propagandist, traveled between Moscow and St. Petersburg maintaining contacts between the Workers' Sections of the two cities. In the fall of 1881, Boreisha was arrested carrying seven copies of the *Workers' Newspaper* and a manuscript entitled "The Exploitation of Workers at the [St. Petersburg] Baltic Works."[13] Before the assassination of Alexander II, workers and young *intelligenty* associated with Narodnaia Volia carried on propaganda among the workers in the name of the Workers' Section in Kharkov, Odessa, Rostov, and Ekaterinoslav, as well as in dozens of other factory towns around the empire.

The generally apathetic response among workers to the March assassination and the spring 1881 police roundups of narodovol'tsy activists forced the remaining leaders of the Petersburg Workers' Section (I. I. Popov, V. A. Bodaev, and N. M. Flerov) to reconsider their relationship with the Executive Committee. The winter of 1881–82 was a period of intense reevaluation, recalled Popov, and "we came to the conclusion that terror depleted revolutionary forces to no purpose." Not only did terrorism evoke no positive response among workers, Popov argued, but it demanded the kind of strict centralization that only facilitated the devastating mass arrests of spring 1881. Moreover, especially for the workers' groups, "such a strictly hierarchical centralized organization was impractical." Easily penetrated by police spies and incapable of rigid discipline, the Workers' Section also endangered a terrorist program. Workers' groups were, quite simply, "inimical" and "unnecessary" to a terrorist struggle.[14]

Among the leaders of the Workers' Section in the post-March period, tactical questions of maintaining a socialist workers' movement in Russia overlapped with theoretical divergencies from the program of the Executive Committee. The cornerstone of the Executive Committee's political thinking remained the eventual seizure of power by the party in the name of the people; the primary political weapon to accomplish this continued to be the terrorist struggle. To the Workers' Section propagandists, both terrorism and the concept of seizure of power seemed increasingly at odds with the building of a socialist movement. By the fall of 1882, Flerov dissociated himself from the program of Narodnaia Volia and claimed that he carried out "propaganda of socialist principles" among Petersburg workers "irrespective of the policies and actions of the Executive Committee."[15] In a statement of the fundamental post-March platform of the St. Petersburg Workers' Section, Popov implicitly rejected the leadership of the Executive Committee: "We ourselves must assume the organization of workers' groups and create the foundations for a systematic revolutionary struggle. This will be possible only when the matter of the liberation of the workers and working people is transferred into the hands of the people themselves."[16] The Workers' Section found itself thus in a perplexing dilemma. There was little question of completely abandoning the still glorious name of Narodnaia Volia — a name that continued to attract fresh young radical recruits and which had become, in the words of N. A. Troitskii, "a unique symbol of the revolutionary struggle" in Russia.[17] At the same time, the Paris Executive Committee appeared too distant and aloof to bend to the needs of the struggling workers' circles.

For its part, the Executive Committee only heightened opposition to its policies by resolutely opposing the effort of the Workers' Section to dissociate itself from terrorism and to disengage its circles from the centralized organization. Although after the assassination the Executive Committee devoted itself more intensively to the development of a socialist workers' movement as a crucial component in the struggle for its minimum program, the granting of a constitution, it was unwilling to loosen officially its organizational dictatorship. Plekhanov's accusations were correct; the Paris leadership was under the sway of Jacobinism and continued to demand a high degree of centralization, absolute leadership by the Executive Committee, and the persistent use of political terrorism. After the spring 1881 arrests, however, the argument became in part moot. The Paris centralists were in no position to determine the nature of the activities or the contents of the propaganda carried out by the Workers' Section. Ironically, it was precisely the inability of the Executive Committee to assert control over its network of workers' groups that allowed the Workers' Section to reestablish contacts with these scattered organizations and bring them back into Narodnaia Volia on a decentralized basis.

Just as the breakdown of the Executive Committee's organizational hierarchy abetted the growth of the Workers' Section so the blurring of ideological distinctions in the revolutionary movement as a whole during the post-March period prompted a fusion of earlier Black Repartition-organized workers with the Workers' Section. The federalist, *narodnik* (populist), and evolutionist Black Repartition, born "under an evil star" at the Lipetsk meeting in 1879, never achieved the dynamism or sizable following of its terrorist counterpart Narodnaia Volia.[18] Especially after the March 1881 assassination, radical Russia ignored the Plekhanov-dominated group. Black Repartition's other émigré leaders, Vera Zasulich and Lev Deich, now pressured Plekhanov to join the prestigious Executive Committee, encouraged by its temporary cessation of terrorist activities and its downplaying of the seizure-of-power concept.[19] In turn, the similarities between the two groups at home and abroad led the St. Petersburg Black Repartition leader, Iakov Stefanovich, to urge his colleagues to enter narodovol'tsy circles. According to the St. Petersburg prosecutor, it was at this point, the fall of 1881, that "Black Repartition, as an independent faction, ceased to exist."[20] A few Black Repartition workers' circles remained aloof from Narodnaia Volia, became known as *narodniki* (populists), and in 1884–85 helped build the social-democratic movement. But most workers' circles attached to Black Repartition responded to Stefanovich's call and painlessly shifted into the organization of the Worker's Section.

The dynamism of Workers' Section activities that resulted from these organizational and ideological breakdowns was especially notable in St. Petersburg, where in early 1882 several hundred workers were involved in the movement, and an increasingly large number of narodovol'tsy leaflets and brochures were confiscated by the police in the capital's factories. The Workers' Section movement also rapidly expanded in the South due to the efforts of the Kharkov, Odessa, and Kiev organizations. Kharkov narodovol'tsy organizers concentrated on propagandizing among Elizavetgrad workers. In March 1883, after a year and a half of patient legal and then semilegal propaganda work, one of these Elizavetgrad circles came into contact with illegal literature, became a part of the "revolutionary cause," and familiarized itself with the program of the Workers' Section. In the summer of 1883, additional worker-propagandists arrived in Elizavetgrad from Kiev and from Kharkov. Finally, in early 1884, an Elizavetgrad Workers' Section declared its organizational allegiance to the Kharkov branch of Narodnaia Volia.[21]

Similar to the attempts of Kharkov narodovol'tsy to organize subgroups in Elizavetgrad were the efforts made by Petr Antonov of the Odessa organization in Libiatin (on the Kharkov-Nikolaev railway line). Until April 1883, Antonov propagandized among railway workshop mechanics and formed a circle of eight worker-activists.[22] The railway workshops served as central targets of those narodovol'tsy propagandists who, like Antonov, knew various metal working trades, took up work in the workshops themselves, and began their activities as workers. The Rostov railway workshops attracted the attention of propagandists Sergei (Saul) Linitskii and Anton Ostroumov. In Nikolaev, in Kremenchug, and in Kiev, machinists attached to Narodnaia Volia carried out propaganda among railway workers.[23] Narodovol'tsy propagandists encountered particularly strong support in Ekaterinoslav, a growing center of metal-working factories and workshops associated with the transportation industry. Later, after the destruction of the party's organization because of the Lopatin disaster of November 1884, the entire narodovol'tsy headquarters moved to Ekaterinoslav and received sustenance from the locomotive workers' organizatons.[24]

In June 1883 the Poltava gendarmes uncovered an underground organization of about twenty-five local railway workers. Among the leaders of the organization was the twenty-seven-year-old lathe-turner Aleksei Tkachenko, who had come from Kharkov to organize train workers. An experienced narodovolets propagandist, Tkachenko used his apartment as an informal meeting place for interested workers, and would patiently explain anything that was not clear to them in the speeches of intelligentsia organizers. Tkachenko downplayed the terrorist struggle to the point of dissociating himself from the Executive Committee and its regicidal program, while emphasizing the necessity to prepare the people for the inevitable economic revolution that would lead to socialism.[25] However, not all Workers' Section activists shared the majority's negative view of terrorism. Student propagandists from Kiev University brought a commitment to localized terrorism directly into the workshops and factories. Two of these narodovol'tsy, Movsha-Leiba Zalkind and Nikolai Zabello, organized a half-dozen workers' circles in Kiev and constantly threatened the lives of policemen and provocateurs.[26]

It even happened sometimes that workers' groups themselves demanded localized terrorism as an immediate and vengeful response to what they thought were particularly flagrant cases of persecution on the part of the police, exploitation by factory administrations, or betrayal by their fellow conspirators. The workers' circles of the Shreder piano factory in Petersburg, for instance, demanded that their antiterrorist Workers' Section (earlier Black Repartition) propagandist, N. N. Lavrov, provide them with incendiary bombs. Angered by abuses of the factory management, they were also worried about being laid off because of the completed production of a large number of grand pianos. If the pianos were set on fire, the workers reasoned, then production would have to continue and they would have their proper revenge against the management. Lavrov was opposed to engaging in arson, but "out of fear of losing authority among them" — or so he claimed in his deposition — he prepared two bombs, neither of which (unbeknownst to the workers) was suitable for its purpose.[27]

The picture of interaction between the propagandists from the Workers' Section and the workers themselves is neither one of the intelligentsia forming, shaping, and molding workers' groups to do their bidding, nor one of workers' circles stolidly remaining aloof from intelligentsia leadership. Instead, a complex of varied interactions between these two extremes characterized the Workers' Section movement. In some workers' circles, relations between the intelligentsia and the workers were plainly antagonistic. One Rostov-on-Don organizer described these relations as "tense" and threatened the workers with withdrawing intelligentsia support and reclaiming the circles' illegal literature if the workers did not treat the leadership with more respect. In the train workshops of Rostov-on-Don, students from the local technological institute organized a number of workers' circles, formed a *kassa* (treasury) for the use of "workers of the Don," and initiated a boot-making *artel* (communal workshop). Soon, however, the workers and the students began quarreling about the organization of the artel, and finally, the students accused the workers of using the artel's "insignificant financial resources for their personal needs."[28]

The already problematic social and cultural differences between the propagandists (especially students) and the workers' groups were exacerbated by the interest of the former in creating a broad political movement and the concern of the workers for raising their own economic and cultural level. Even in the generally successful Elizavetgrad movement, one disgruntled student observed that "it was not worth it to spend much time with workers," while a worker noted that "the workers themselves were not interested in these [political] discussions." The student left his workers' circle concluding, "there is nothing to be done" in working-class circles.[29] This was also the judgment of Feofan Krylov, a propagandist who taught reading in several Moscow workers' circles and discussed working-class socialism in other more advanced groups. He left Moscow for Kazan in the hope of developing a more political workers' movement. In May 1882 he was the principal organizer of Workers' Section circles in Kazan until, again disenchanted with the results, he became convinced "that workers' circles were hardly conducive to revolutionary propaganda" and left Kazan to operate among student radical groups.[30]

Despite these periodic setbacks, the Workers' Section continued to expand its numbers and geographical base between 1881 and 1884. There were scattered attempts to discipline provocateurs as well as individual instances of teaching workers the ABCs of bomb making, but for the most part propagandists confined themselves to the much more modest activities of conducting primary education and discussing the most basic propaganda messages with urban workers. Often the workers' circles slipped in and out of contact with Narodnaia Volia through their Workers' Section propagandists. The propagandists themselves sometimes abandoned the circles for more substantial political work elsewhere. It was the fluidity and spontaneity of the Workers' Section movement that allowed it to survive despite police vigilance. The circles did not directly encourage or participate to a significant extent in the strikes of 1882–83, nor did they play a role in the major terrorist acts of Narodnaia Volia. Their great importance stems rather from the fact that they helped to perpetuate and strengthen the infant Russian socialist labor movement in a period of extremely difficult political circumstances.

Vera Figner in the South

It was characteristic of the dispersal of narodovol'tsy forces after March 1 that the development of the Workers' Section barely touched Vera Figner's concurrent efforts to reconstruct the Executive Committee in Kharkov and Odessa. Her immediate predecessor as head of the Odessa organization, Vladimir Zhebunev, had been a follower of the Workers' Section. He believed that urban workers constituted the sole support of the political struggle and thus had focused all the party's resources on developing more than thirty workers' circles.[31] Figner on the other hand was eager to revive an Executive Committee inside Russia and to shift the brunt of narodovol'tsy activities to the intelligentsia. Moving to Odessa in late spring of 1881, she quickly organized student circles at Novorossiiskii University and in local gymnasiums. Under her leadership a women's circle of intelligentsia was formed, which collected money for Narodnaia Volia's Red Cross group (devoted to supporting political exiles and their families) and met weekly to hear lectures on social and political questions.[32] Unhappy with the local leadership of the Odessa Executive Committee, Figner established contacts with the Kiev and Kharkov groups as well as with the leadership of the Military Organization in Nikolaev and Tiflis. Smaller groups in Rostov-on-Don, Poltava, Elizavetgrad, and other towns were also linked to her efforts. With little more than a few rubles in her treasury, Figner was forced to spend much of the summer of 1881 in search of funds from old contacts and friends. She managed to raise several thousand rubles by visiting wealthy acquaintances who had contributed to the populist movement of the seventies.

Figner also had to face what she considered to be the party's lackadaisical attitude toward the rules of conspiracy and organization, which caused, in her view, arrests that could have been avoided. But before she could move ahead in raising the party's conspiratorial norms, she realized that she must deal with Major-General V. S. Strel'nikov, the military-prosecutor of the entire southern region, who had been, in the words of one of his victims, "simply an artist as an investigator."[33] Sent to Kiev in August 1881 to clean the South of revolutionary activists, Strel'nikov operated under two firm principles, articulated in a 4 October 1881 letter to Plehve: that the leadership of workers' circles was composed almost exclusively of Jewish intellectuals and thus easily separable from the workers, and that the workers themselves joined the circles not because they were unhappy with their economic or political situations, but because they were desperate to learn, to read, and to discuss.[34] With the persistence of a "crazy misanthrope," Strel'nikov pushed the local gendarmes to the limit, breaking up dozens of groups and cleverly talking the workers into identifying the propagandists.[35] By releasing or failing to prosecute most of the worker participants he earned the confidence of many workers' groups and the hatred of his targeted victims from the ranks of the intelligentsia. Nor did Strel'nikov's behavior in court endear him to his antagonists. He was known to shout "you will hang" at the defendants and to describe graphically what would happen to their necks, tongues, and eyes when the verdict was carried out.[36]

Already in December 1881, Figner asked the still functioning Moscow center for a death sentence on Strel'nikov. The Moscow committee obliged her and immediately (December 31) sent to Odessa Stepan Khalturin, the former leader of the Northern Workers' Union, who was to carry out the sentence. After the March 1881 assassination Khalturin had taken over the leadership of the Moscow Workers' Section from P. A. Tellalov, who in turn had gone to St Petersburg in July 1881 to reorganize that city's worker-activists. At this point, however, Khalturin had little faith in propagandistic work and was eager to continue the terrorist struggle. His primary associate in the Strel'nikov assassination attempt was the quasi-demented N. A. Zhelvakov, a former St. Petersburg University auditor and Rostov-on-Don activist, who longed, according to his diary, to sacrifice his meaningless life for the cause.[37] Zhelvakov pestered the narodovol'tsy leaders for a terrorist assignment and was finally granted his wish when he was sent to Odessa to carry out Khalturin's plot.

On Figner's advice, Khalturin planned for the assassination attempt to take place in Odessa rather than the more closely policed Kiev. On 18 March 1882, Strel'nikov took his regular stroll and sat down on a bench overlooking the sea. While Khalturin waited nearby at the carriage, Zhelvakov walked up behind his victim and shot him in the back of the head, killing him almost instantly. After a wild chase, Khalturin and Zhelvakov were seized by the police and a group of irate citizens.[38] The following day Minister of Internal Affairs Ignat'ev telegraphed I. V. Gurko, the Odessa Governor-General: "His Majesty the Emperor commanded that the killers be tried before a military court and without any excuses be hanged within 24 hours."[39] A day later than he commanded, the Odessa courts fulfilled the tsar's wishes. With no members of the public admitted to the courtroom, no witnesses, and no defense lawyers, the military court sentenced and hanged Khalturin and Zhelvakov.

Although Figner realized that further terrorist actions were for the moment out of the question because of a lack of resources and personnel, government circles still feared an assassination attempt on Alexander III. Through the auspices of the Holy Brotherhood the famous radical publicist N. K. Mikhailovskii was urged to contact Figner and negotiate a cessation of narodovol'tsy terrorism. Naively hoping that the conditions of Tikhomirov's letter to Alexander III, which he helped to formulate, could still serve as a basis for negotiation, Mikhailovskii found Figner and suggested that since Narodnaia Volia lacked the resources to carry out terrorist acts, the party could lose nothing by entering into negotiations. But Figner refused and insisted that the party would continue its work as before. The gentle Mikhailovskii, caught again between his basically liberal humanistic nature and his sympathy for revolutionary heroes and heroines, silently took Figner's head in both his hands, kissed her, and returned dejected to St. Petersburg.[40]

With the lines clearly drawn for further battles, Figner decided to recruit leadership for the Executive Committee from the Military Organization, so she approached M. Iu. Ashenbrenner, N. M. Rogachev, N. D. Pokhitonov, F. I. Zavalishin, and B. A. Kraiskii. "I was motivated to follow this plan," she recalled in her memoirs, "because at that moment there was no source for the necessary manpower except for the military."[41] But Pokhitonov was too sick and Kraiskii and Zavalishin too committed to their military work to join the Odessa center. Ashenbrenner, an older, well-educated, and rather circumspect naval officer, agreed to join her, taking a year's leave of absence from his Nikolaev regiment. Ashenbrenner was given the assignment of returning to St. Petersburg in order to contact the military groups there, found an empire-wide Military Organization, and link it, through himself, to Figner's Odessa committee. On another point, Rogachev assumed the job of unifying military circles in the South while working directly with Figner in Odessa and

Kharkov. Figner was also able to establish a press in Odessa with the help of another military activist, Sergei Degaev. But Degaev was eventually arrested, interrogated, and subsequently recruited as a provocateur by the ambitious and effective secret police inspector G. D. Sudeikin. Degaev's treachery led directly to Figner's arrest (10 February 1883) and the destruction of the narodovol'tsy military group, and spelled the end of the radical circles Figner had managed to organize.

"The Degaevshchina"[42]

Sergei Petrovich Degaev came from a family of lower gentry radicals, and his mother, sister, and brother were involved in revolutionary politics. Certainly, young Sergei's activities before and after March 1 belie Lev Tikhomirov's assessment that Degaev "was never a revolutionary."[43] Trained as an artillery officer, Degaev became involved with a group of young narodovol'tsy army officers, first in Saratov and then in St. Petersburg. After the arrests that followed the assassination of Alexander II, Degaev rose rapidly in the ranks of the St. Petersburg party.

During the spring and summer of 1881, despite the decimation of its leadership, Narodnaia Volia actually increased in size.[44] The spectacular success of the assassination won hundreds of new members to the party, Degaev included, all swept along by what seemed the promise of imminent revolution. In the spring of 1882 Degaev moved to the south of Russia, where he joined Figner's efforts to reconstitute the party in its old image. Although Degaev was not asked to join the Executive Committee, he did become a member of Figner's administrative center. The military narodovol'tsy in the South, essentially untouched by the mass arrests of spring 1881, became his focus of operations. Degaev was also placed in charge of the reconstructed narodovol'tsy press in Odessa. Throughout the early fall of 1882 Degaev served as a trusted and capable operative in the revolutionary organization. It was at this point that secret police inspector Sudeikin, having purged St. Petersburg of the narodovol'tsy leadership, turned his attention to the South, especially to Vera Figner.

Sudeikin's very successful methods in St. Petersburg were well known to the revolutionaries.[45] First, he had hundreds of radicals imprisoned under the harsh conditions of preventive detention. Then he removed them to comfortable surroundings where he engaged them in political discussions. Insisting that he sympathized with many aspects of the populist program, Sudeikin explained that he felt terrorism to be counterproductive to the movement's goals. If his prisoners seemed willing to talk, and many were, Sudeikin then handed them some money for the purposes of "promoting our common goals," told them to return for further discussions at an appointed time and place, and released them. During the subsequent encounters Sudeikin provided more money to his recruits and asked them to report any terrorist plots, making it clear that there was no need to identify individuals. Sudeikin was unable to engage any first-class provocateurs until the recruitment of Degaev. Still, his methods created tremendous insecurity in the revolutionary movement. Everyone asked the question: who was reporting to Sudeikin?

The actual circumstances under which Sudeikin recruited Degaev are still somewhat obscure. Probably Sudeikin had been aware of the Degaev family since early 1882 and engaged in political discussions with Vladimir Degaev, Sergei's brother; through Vladimir Sudeikin made contact with Sergei before the actual moment of his arrest.[46] Sudeikin's methods and Degaev's known history as a radical make it unlikely that Degaev agreed immediately to become a full-time agent. In any case, in December 1882, the police arrested Degaev in Odessa and confiscated the party press. In the course of a three-day interview Degaev agreed to become Sudeikin's agent. During those three days, Sudeikin once again engaged his young subject in political discussions, extolling the virtues of reform and blaming terrorism for its obstruction. The police inspector also assured Degaev that he would make arrangements to assist his wife and family.

A fake escape was arranged for 14 January 1883.[47] Sergei was to be transported from Odessa to Kiev, guarded by two gendarmes. At the Odessa train station, according to plan, Degaev threw tobacco in the eyes of his guards and made his escape. For the next eleven months Degaev served as the direct agent of Sudeikin and the Russian secret police. With the help of the military narodovol'tsy, he made his way from the Odessa train station to Figner's Kharkov headquarters. This last of the "old" leaders of Narodnaia Volia was arrested as a result of the information that Degaev had provided the police.

Far from arousing suspicion in party ranks, Degaev's escape actually catapulted him to the forefront of party heroes.[48] Ironically, Degaev became a leader of the southern narodovol'tsy movement while the government used his information to arrest more than two hundred *militaristy* in the winter of 1883.[49] By the spring of 1883 the southern narodovol'tsy movement had been crushed, and the team of Sudeikin and Degaev could turn on St. Petersburg, where student circles and the Worker's Section of Narodnaia Volia had experienced a strong revival. Degaev became the virtual leader of the St. Petersburg underground, earning an excellent reputation for recruiting new members. Prominent among his recruits were Stanislaw Kunicki, the future leader of the Polish party Proletariat, and Petr Iakubovich, the foremost rebel of Young Narodnaia Volia.

Despite the fact that Sudeikin (and Degaev) handed over to the government the backbone of the *militaristy* movement (a movement that had caused considerable worry in government circles), there was no promotion in rank and no audience with the tsar. Simultaneously, Degaev found that despite his leadership role in the affairs of the capital's narodovol'tsy, he was not promoted to a more responsible position within the revolutionary organization. The Executive Committee, confused and self-absorbed in the aftermath of the assassination, did not invite Degaev or any other domestic narodovol'tsy to become members. The Executive Committee's indifference toward lower-echelon leaders and its distrust of spontaneous action closely resembled the attitudes that Sudeikin was encountering within the imperial bureaucracy.

In their common frustration, Sudeikin and Degaev discussed several schemes that would accelerate their climb to the summits of their respective organizations.[50] The initial discussions revolved around a fantastic scheme to stage an assassination attempt on Sudeikin.[51] The police inspector would take a walk in the park without his usual bodyguard. Degaev would intercept Sudeikin there, and shoot him in the arm, wounding him slightly. Sudeikin would then receive a medal, an audience with the tsar, and promotion to the rank of general. This scheme was abandoned, however, when a doctor told Sudeikin that such a wound could be dangerous. The second idea, dominating most of their discussions, called for a series of assassinations of high government officials. Tolstoi would be the first target, followed by Pobedonostsev and Orzhevskii.[52] Degaev was to arrange the assassinations and then turn over the terrorists to Sudeikin. The success of one plot would convince the tsar of the extent of the danger; the disclosure of a second plot (before its completion) would at last get Sudeikin due recognition as the true savior of Russia.

Before any definite plans could be drafted, Sudeikin sent Degaev and his wife abroad in late May 1882 to contact the emigration. (In this case, as in others, Sudeikin clearly usurped the functions of another police organization—the Foreign *Okhrana*. Degaev met Tikhomirov in Switzerland and after lengthy conversations admitted his role as Sudeikin's agent.[53] Tikhomirov claimed that Degaev had begun to realize that he would not make a career as a secret police agent and that his conscience was bothering him. Degaev returned to Russia with instructions to kill Sudeikin, but apparently had no opportunity to organize a plot that summer and in August went to explain his situation to Tikhomirov. During the second trip, Degaev was faced with a formal verdict from the Executive Committee: either he would assassinate Sudeikin or the narodovol'tsy would execute him. The committee forbade Degaev, on pain of death, to participate in any political activities once he had carried out the assassination. At the same time, it guaranteed him safe transport out of Russia.

Degaev's career as a double agent was even more bizarre than his service as a secret police agent. For six months, while ostensibly waiting for the right moment to kill Sudeikin, Degaev continued to earn his superior's trust by recruiting new members to the party, betraying prominent narodovol'tsy to the police, and infiltrating several St. Petersburg workers' circles.[54] Degaev's revolutionary colleagues knew only that he had returned from abroad with the Executive Committee's order to assassinate Sudeikin, a mandate that allayed any suspicions they might have had about his police role.[55] Tikhomirov later claimed that the narodovol'tsy in Russia could not be told about Degaev's role as a double agent without jeopardizing the whole plot.

One can only speculate about the reasons why Degaev delayed the assassination. First of all, he was not an experienced assassin and as events were to demonstrate, he was chary of bloodshed and ill-disposed to terrorism. It is possible that Degaev considered revealing the entire plot to Sudeikin, hoping that the police inspector would protect him against the terrorists and that he could remain a government agent. But given what we know of Degaev's character, it is likely that he was simply hesitant, hoping for some circumstance that would extricate him from an exceedingly difficult situation. Because of his delays, the Executive Committee sent the trusted revolutionary German Lopatin to St. Petersburg in late summer 1883 to enforce the demands of the narodovol'tsy emigration.[56]

On the urging of Lopatin to get on with the task, Degaev tried to revive Sudeikin's old idea of a fake assassination attempt, this time intending to turn it into a real one. Sudeikin, however, had by then lost interest in such terrorist schemes. Hearing rumors that Plehve would be promoted to deputy minister, Sudeikin hoped to replace him as director in the Department of Police. This development left Degaev no choice but to recruit two young narodovol'tsy activists (N. P. Starodvorskii and V. P. Konashevich) to carry out the assassination of Sudeikin.

Sudeikin maintained a number of apartments around the city where he surreptitiously met with his agents, and one of them, 93 Nevskii Prospect, was used by Degaev. The conspirators' plan was to lure Sudeikin to that apartment and to assassinate him there. One of

Lopatin's contributions to the plot was his insistence that an iron bar be used for the killing, "because a knife would be a hopeless weapon in a fight with such a powerful man as Sudeikin, and the party considered poison as a rather debased method."[57]

Degaev arranged a meeting with Sudeikin at the apartment on December 3. Arriving in his carriage, Sudeikin sent a watchman ahead to see if anyone were at home. Degaev lost his nerve and did not answer the door. A week later, Sudeikin was late for the second arranged meeting, whereupon Degaev panicked once again and sent Konashevich and Starodvorskii away. Only the third meeting, scheduled for December 16, began as planned. The half-hour-long battle that ensued can be reconstructed from the final indictment of the conspiracy and the minutes of Starodvorskii and Konashevich's confessions.[58] Konashevich waited for Sudeikin in the kitchen; Starodvorskii was in the bedroom. When Sudeikin arived with his kinsman and bodyguard Sudovskii, "Degaev opened the door to them and the three of them entered into the inner rooms." Degaev shot Sudeikin in the stomach, Konashevich attacked Sudovskii, and Starodvorskii moved in on Sudeikin to finish the job. According to Starodvorskii, Sudeikin fell to the floor "without any signs of life, but after a moment or two jumped up and ran into the watercloset, holding the door closed from inside." Starodvorskii "quickly put his foot between the door and the doorpost, trying to open the door with one hand and with the other he hit Sudeikin's hand with the iron bar. When the door was torn from Sudeikin's hand, the latter [Sudeikin] . . . lurched into the anteroom where Starodvorskii hit him again on the back of the head with the iron bar. From these blows, Sudeikin fell back into the watercloset; here he [Starodvorskii] hit Sudeikin again with the iron bar . . . and stopped hitting him only when he was convinced Sudeikin was dead."[59] Konashevich added that as soon as the fighting moved away from the door, "Degaev opened [it] and ran, without even closing it behind him."

After fleeing the scene of the murder, Degaev made his way to a prearranged meeting place. There he changed his clothes, grabbed his suitcase, and rushed to the Warsaw train station in the company of the conspirator Stepan Rossi. Starodvorskii just made the same train. Arriving in Vilna, Degaev was met by the Polish terrorist Kunicki, who provided him with a false passport and escorted him, "revolver in hand," to a ship in Riga bound for England.[60] The tsarist government immediately issued a poster offering the extraordinary sum of ten thousand rubles for information leading to Degaev's arrest. The police arrested Konashevich in Kiev on 3 January 1884, Starodvorskii in Moscow on March 16, and Stepan Rossi at Sudeikin's St. Petersburg funeral.[61] The narodovol'tsy issued a proclamation, written by Lopatin, which defended the killing of police oppressors.[62]

Only posthumously did Sudeikin receive the long-awaited recognition of the tsar. Tolstoi wrote that Alexander III, without any prompting from him, provided Sudeikin's wife with a generous pension of five thousand rubles and ensured state education for his children.[63] As for Degaev, he now attracted the attention of the Executive Committee, but not at all in the way he had hoped. Tikhomirov published an attack on Degaev in the English newspaper *Today*, describing him as a "scoundrel" who had never been a socialist.[64] As a result of the anathema that the Executive Committee placed on Degaev, Russian émigré radicals sent him anonymous threatening letters and insulted him whenever he tried to join their company. Degaev began to fear for his life as well as his reputation. His brother Vladimir, also an émigré, attempted to intercede for him. "I received a letter from Sergei," he wrote Tikhomirov, saying "that he was horribly tormented, that he could not sleep at night, and that when he fell asleep, he saw the faces of those in jail because of him."[65] In the end, probably in late 1884, Degaev emigrated to the United States and took the name of Alexander Pell. He studied mathematics, became a professor and a dean at the University of South Dakota, and died near Philadelphia soon after the 1917 Revolution.[66]

Though many unanswered questions remain, one crucial facet of the Degaev affair is indisputable: for six long months, while ostensibly waiting for the right moment to kill Sudeikin, Degaev continued to earn the police inspector's trust by recruiting new members to the party, turning over prominent narodovol'tsy to the police, and successfully infiltrating several St. Petersburg workers' circles while also enjoying the full trust of his revolutionary colleagues in Russia. What Degaev's treachery as a secret provocateur did not accomplish, his career as a double agent did: "the party suffered a complete defeat," wrote Ludwik Kulczycki.[67] V. I. Bogucharskii, the first historian of Narodnaia Volia, put it even more emphatically: the Degaevshchina ended the history of the party.[68]

It is certainly true that the first stage of the history of Narodnaia Volia after March 1 came to an abrupt conclusion when what was left of the central organization of the movement, painstakingly reconstructed by Figner, was devastated by the Degaev-related arrests. Yet at that point narodovol'tsy circles had already spread to sixty different cities and towns throughout the empire, often maintaining their autonomy and sometimes their total anonymity from the central organization.[69] Hundreds of new recruits had been drawn into these circles in 1882–83 and many of them were still at large at the time of Sudeikin's killing. While most narodovol'tsy activists lamented the tragic losses of the central organization, those groups that remained relatively untouched by the mass arrests, the Workers' Section and the informal student discussions groups, reached the conclusion, long inchoate in the party during the drama of political terrorism, that the old style Narodnaia Volia should not be revived.

Young Narodnaia Volia

The breakdown of classical narodovol'tsy thinking which occurred among student propagandists and worker-activists associated with labor circles contributed to a general sense, developing among the narodovol'tsy who had survived the Degaevshchina, that a new path to revolution must be found. There had been too much suffering in the underground and the accomplishments appeared to be nil. The Paris Executive Committee seemed aloof and unwilling to alter its fundamental precepts of centralized organization, political terrorism, and the seizure of power — all of which appeared increasingly irrelevant to those activists still at liberty in the underground in 1883–84. It was not that radicals questioned the revolutionary faith or the necessity for political struggle, but there was now grumbling and an openness to alternative solutions uncharacteristic of the narodovol'tsy prior to the March 1 assassination.

In the fall of 1883, Petr Filippovich Iakubovich, a poet and philosopher especially influential among St. Petersburg University students, organized the first serious intraparty opposition since the Voronezh meeting of 1879 had split Land and Liberty in two. Iakubovich received almost unanimous praise as a party organizer from his colleagues. His closest confederate, Mikhail Shebalin, wrote: "His ties to society and literary circles, his popularity among students at the university, and his charming personality made his work extraordinarily successful and fruitful."[70] Iakubovich testified later in his deposition that he had been recruited to the party in September 1883 by the provocateur Sergei Degaev. At that point, he was involved in the Student League, an organization formed the previous spring to advance student demands and to direct student protests. Iakubovich saw his task as that of transforming an organization concerned with purely student questions into one that would have a socialist content and could respond to revolutionary needs "outside the walls of the institutions of higher learning." He therefore organized the Union of Youth of Narodnaia Volia and sought recruits among the league's members, personally involving dozens of erstwhile activists from the student movement in narodovol'tsy propaganda. His ultimate goals, presumably approved by Degaev, were to join forces in the capital with the Worker's Section, establish an underground press, and publish a journal called *The Revolutionary (Revoliutsioner)*.[71]

Throughout the fall of 1883 and the winter and spring of 1884 Iakubovich carried his ideas of a revolutionary involvement of Russian students to meetings all over St. Petersburg. At these meetings, testified his supporter Aleksei Kirpishchikov, Iakubovich emphasized a decentralized approach to revolutionary activities. The central Petersburg circle was to consist of elected representatives from the local circles rather than of appointed agents as had previously been the case.[72] On 17 October 1883, at a meeting of twelve narodovol'tsy, including Konstantin Stepurin, Mikhail Shebalin, the provocateur Degaev, and several representatives from the Polish party Proletariat, Iakubovich also stressed that it was necessary to tie terrorism to the building of a mass movement and that terrorism should have a popular, factory-and-village (*fabrichno-agrarnyi*) rather than a strictly political character.[73] The assassination of government figures and police spies had little effect on the working people. Therefore, Iakubovich argued (not unlike Plekhanov in 1879), terror should be brought into the institutions that touched their lives directly — the factories, workshops, and farms.

When Degaev arranged the murder of Sudeikin in December 1883, the vast majority of Russian radicals had no idea that Degaev had been a provocateur. During the months following the killing, as the story of Degaev's police career gradually unfolded, narodovol'tsy throughout the empire expressed shock and dismay about being kept in the dark by the Executive Committee.[74] As Iakubovich noted, "The youth waited for some sort of clear and energetic word from the committee both about Degaev and about the revolutionary cause in general, which for the previous year and a half had found itself in some sort of strange and ambivalent situation. And the trustees of the center were either unable or didn't want to say anything about the past." It was the Executive Committee's poor handling of the Degaev affair, Iakubovich added, that led him into open rebellion.[75] The depositions of other Petersburg narodovol'tsy leaders — Mikhail Ovchinnikov, Petr Manuilov, and Fedor Grekov — confirmed Iakubovich's observation. Young narodovol'tsy were hurt, disgruntled, and angered by the performance of the Executive Committee on the Degaev issue.[76]

The Executive Committee delayed the planned departure from Russia of its Petersburg representative, Konstantin Stepurin, in the hope of keeping the organization intact. But Stepurin's efforts to hold back the growing rebellion and maintain party discipline were to no avail. While Mikhail Ovchinnikov attempted to keep peace between Stepurin on the side of the Executive Committee and Iakubovich on the other, Iakubovich led his Union of Youth into open confrontation with the program of Narodnaia Volia.

The dispute between the Youth and the Executive Committee, as Petr Manuilov correctly pointed out in his deposition, encompassed programmatic questions as well as the Degaev affair, the center's "fanaticism," and its inability to be more "attuned to the realities of local needs."[77] Iakubovich's program consisted of three components: (1) the revolutionary education of the mass of workers by means of oral and written propaganda; (2) the "systematization" of terror, which meant — in the radical jargon of the period — applying it on a level that was closer to factory and agricultural workers; and (3) the organization of local and regional workers' groups, which would operate independently of the central revolutionary institutions.[78] Terrorism cannot destroy the present system, the program of the Youth stated, and should be used only as "one of the weapons of agitation." Terrorism must be consistent with everyday needs of working people and must be understood by them.[79] Shebalin concluded that it was "the two points, 'autonomy' and 'factory-agrarian terror'," which set the Youth faction apart from the Executive Committee.[80]

In January 1884, draft program in hand and tailed by a police agent, Iakubovich traveled to Kiev in order to establish contact with southern narodovol'tsy and workers' circles. His purpose, in his own words, was "to rouse dissent in the party."[81] Iakubovich's program was sympathetically received in Kiev, but arrests in the Petersburg and Kiev organizations precluded effective union. Still, by the spring of 1884 the challenge of Young Narodnaia Volia was supported by numerous radical segments of Russian society. Student circles in St. Petersburg printed two underground newspapers, *Free Word* (*Svobodnoe slovo*), and *Students* (*Studenchestvo*), which attacked Narodnaia Volia's absolute politicism and underlined the need to return the emphasis of the struggle to revolutionary propaganda among the people. The remaining circles of the military narodovol'tsy, torn to shreds by Degaev's work of the previous year, also now supported the decentralization movement. The underground press experienced a revival, stimulated by the challenge of the Youth and by the many new recruits the group attracted to the party. The Workers' Section, wrote Popov, was more visible than ever before: "At that time, among all of us, the mood was magnificent. We thought that the hard years had passed." "Some kind of 'magic' befell us," Iakubovich wrote. The movement daily attracted new supporters. Life was worth living again. By slowing down the political struggle, Iakubovich hoped to recapture "the spirit of 1873" and develop a new form of "going-to-the-people" movement.[82] To a significant extent he succeeded.

When Iakubovich and the Youth first gained adherents among the new recruits to the party, the fragmented old leadership viewed the development with favor. Like the Workers' Section, Young Narodnaia Volia could serve "as a reservoir from which the party could draw material for replacing its thinning ranks and also as a school where future members of the party could be produced."[83] However, the leaders of the Paris Executive Committee, Lev Tikhomirov and Mariia Oshanina, in touch with Petersburg through their representative Stepurin, soon realized the challenge that Iakubovich represented and moved on the offensive against the young "red roosters."[84]

In the fall of 1883 the Executive Committee organized a series of meetings in Paris intended to resurrect its waning authority among various revolutionary groups, agreeing to dispatch an "administrative commission" to Russia to stifle the rebellion of the Youth. With the famous revolutionary hero German Lopatin at its head, the commission arrived in St. Petersburg in March 1884.[85] The position of the Executive Committee in the subsequent power struggle and negotiations was spelled out in its "Letter to the Comrades," which made certain concessions to Iakubovich's demands of the previous fall: "The center of the party should consist for the present time of the sum of the local centers, that is, of the representatives of the local groups." But in direct opposition to the Youth faction platform, these groups were to be centrally and hierarchically organized as before. "It is our conviction," the letter declared, "that strict centralism in revolutionary matters is absolutely necessary."[86] This statement, along with the reaffirmation of the supremacy of political terrorism in the editorial article of number 8–9 of Listok "Narodnoi voli", forced a showdown with the proponents of decentralization.[87] A struggle ensued which "occupied much precious time, much strength of will in vain."[88]

The commission's initial task was to reassert Narodnaia Volia's authority in the circles not directly tied to the Youth faction. Aleksei Kirpishchikov described several meetings in April and May 1884, in which commission member Vasilii Sukhomlin defended the Executive Committee's position among Workers' Section propagandists. At these meetings Sukhomlin "polemicized against the appropriateness of factory terror and asserted that such terror could only discredit the party in the eyes of society." As a result of Sukhomlin's presentation, Kirpishchikov's group of worker propagandists decided to join "neither the old, nor the young parties of Narodnaia Volia, in order to preserve for itself full freedom of action."[89]

The first round of negotiations between Lopatin and Iakubovich took place at the end of March and the beginning of April 1884. Iakubovich claimed that initially the differences between the two were almost insuperable. "Several organizational questions" and "the theoretical side of revolutionary activities in Russia" were vigorously debated. In addition, the Degaev issue threatened to disrupt the talks. The question to which Iakubovich repeatedly returned was how could the Executive Committee—without informing the party youth and local revolutionary groups—allow such a provocateur to function within the party, especially after his treacherous role had been revealed. "We were ready to understand," wrote Iakubovich, "to accept apologies and to discuss ways of avoiding such catastrophes in the future. But the committee for its part was unable to provide us with a detailed and fully truthful explanation." As a result, Iakubovich added, "our groups were completely cut off from one another for a very long time by the personality of Degaev."

The dispute between the Youth and the commission also involved a historical evaluation of the crisis of 1881: "The committee wanted to leave the program in exactly the same form as it had been in the flowering period of the activities of Narodnaia Volia, 1879–1882. And that meant to direct all forces, all branches of the revolutionary cause, to the struggle against the political system existing in Russia." The Youth faction, on the other hand, believed that since 1881 the party had experienced "a kind of intellectual crisis." Narodnaia Volia's program of political struggle and centralized terrorism had nearly destroyed the revolutionary movement. Fanaticism could not take the place of a genuine movement of the people. Therefore, the task of the party was to slow down the political struggle, to involve the urban work force in socialist propaganda, and to rebuild the movement in the name of a popular revolution.[90]

Despite these differences, negotiations were resumed in May 1884 in St. Petersburg and Moscow. The discussions were increasingly dominated by German Lopatin, whose revolutionary credentials impressed all the rebels. Even Iakubovich, who had prepared himself for an all-out struggle, found himself enthralled by the "extremely likable and talented people" sent from Paris.[91] The Moscow organization of the Youth was almost immediately won over to Lopatin's plea for unity. To split the party at this point over tactical divergencies, Lopatin argued, would destroy rather than benefit the revolutionary movement. This argument and its advocate proved so persuasive that Iakubovich too succumbed in June 1884. According to the police, "Iakubovich fell under the influence of Lopatin" and the two earlier opponents reached an "understanding" whereby Iakubovich would work "under the direction of Lopatin."[92]

In the summer of 1884, Lopatin, Sukhomlin, Salova, and Iakubovich (who was now practically a member of the commission) traveled to various urban centers, setting up several new narodovol'tsy circles and subordinating old ones to the leadership of the administrative commission. During this period, Lopatin also picked up crucial supplies and illegally imported publications through Riga and distributed them in Odessa, Kremenchug, Poltava, Rostov-on-Don, Kharkov, and Moscow. As a result of the joint efforts of Lopatin and Iakubovich, an underground press was set up in Derpt, run by activists from both the Youth faction and the Worker's Section.[93]

The Derpt press managed to publish the tenth number of *Narodnaia Volia* (September 1884), the first to appear in two-and-a-half years. Its publication elicited an enthusiastic response among radicals and liberals alike, restoring some of the old party's prestige.[94] The paper was so conciliatory on issues of centralization, and even more on the issue of political terrorism, that Iakubovich and Lopatin hoped that a new "compromise" unity program could be drawn up between them. Although Iakubovich had leaned toward Lopatin's earlier calls for unity, it was with the publication of number 10, he emphasized, that he became a full supporter of the Executive Committee. In a letter to Salova Iakubovich wrote: "I recognize that while being correct about much, I personally made many mistakes . . . I don't fault myself and am not sorry because at that time I believed in the correctness of each of my steps and all of them were sincere. But I admit that enthusiasm and passion carried me further than I would have gone at an earlier time and at the present. G. P. [Lopatin] and I still disagree about a great deal, but the divergencies are not such that they need to be aired in public."[95]

Before the two could put together a new program that would reconcile their own remaining differences and placate the recalcitrant Workers' Section propagandists, Lopatin was arrested in St. Petersburg (4 October 1884). When the police seized the normally careful Lopatin, he was carrying dynamite caps, revolutionary proclamations, and, worst of all, a list of revolutionary organizations and personnel which he had systematically collected during the summer. The police authorities were ecstatic; using these "notes and addresses" they could track down organizations and circles in thirty-one different centers throughout the empire. In fact, as a result of Lopatin's list, the police were able to arrest approximately five hundred narodovol'tsy in October and November of 1884 — a blow equal in scale to the mass arrests caused by Degaev's treachery.[96]

Salova, Sukhomlin, and Ovchinnikov fell in the first October wave of arrests. "A storm cloud hangs over us all," Iakubovich wrote.[97] Yet he managed to escape arrest until late November and for six weeks found himself alone at the head of the shattered commission. Iakubovich attempted to carry out general party directives as "the Executive Committee's agent" in Russia. In his deposition he described his task with characteristic bravado: he would collect the "forgotten and dispersed," stand hard and fast at his post, and provide party members with some continuity in leadership.[98] According to the reports of agents in Paris, however, Iakubovich felt his position to be much more tenuous. He sent three panicky letters in code to Tikhomirov (dated October 31 and November 3 and 10) in which he "complained about the difficulty of his position" and claimed that he could no longer lead the revolutionary movement alone. New leaders would have to be recruited because he sensed (accurately) that his arrest was imminent.[99]

The ties between Iakubovich in St. Petersburg and the provincial centers were almost completely broken by the October and November arrests, and there was little hope of reestablishing them. In December 1884 Vladimir Burtsev wrote a number of desperate letters from Kazan to St. Petersburg outlining the situation of local narodovol'tsy: "There are no letters, there are no packages, I don't understand how that can be. The tie with the center is broken. Everyone turns to me; [they] forget that you and those [others] on whom I had counted are silent. Last year there was a growing local revolutionary group here. Fifteen people were arrested and there were close to fifty searches. Now the provinces are neglected. Time is slipping by."[100] Much could be done in Kazan, Burtsev added, but the center needed to show some life and make new efforts immediately. Understandably, Burtsev's pleas went unheeded. Iakubovich did make one major effort to reestablish contact with the provinces when he sent Vasilii Moiseev to Tula, Voronezh, and Saratov, but the envoy got no farther than Tula. There the police seized him carrying a hundred copies of *Narodnaia Volia*, as well as a letter from Iakubovich begging the provinces for financial help. ("Our finances are in very, very bad shape.")[101]

The workers' groups, dispersed all over the empire and having refused to join the administrative commission's reorganization efforts, remained relatively unscathed by the Lopatin-list arrests. Iakubovich seized the initiative as the top remaining functionary of the Executive Committee in Russia to enlist the workers' movement, once and for all, into the narodovol'tsy ranks. St. Petersburg worker-propagandists Mikhail Orlov and Vasilii Golovkin received a letter from Iakubovich in which he, "in the name of the Executive Committee of the party," invited the Workers' Section to "united (*edinodushnyi*) activity on the field of revolutionary struggle against the government."[102] Iakubovich realized that the task of convincing the workers' groups was not going to be easy, explaining that "when . . . the young party joined together with the Committee, a part of the workers' groups also joined up with it, but the majority held on to their earlier views, among them 'Ivan Ivanovich' [Popov] with whom I carried on negotiations in the fall of 1884."[103] Iakubovich's official letter to the Workers' Section, dated 14 November 1884 and intended for Popov, was the final effort of the narodovol'tsy in this period to harness the workers to their movement. The letter outlined the issues that concerned the workers' groups, referred to Iakubovich's own past in the Youth faction to support his position as arbiter, and tried to convince the Workers' Section that the interests of the Executive Committee and the workers were not so far apart that unity in the movement should be sacrificed. Iakubovich claimed, for instance, that "in principle" the Executive Committee "had nothing against [terrorist] acts of a factory character." Indeed, number 10 of *Narodnaia Volia* recognized factory terror as a legitimate form of revolutionary action. Certainly the question was "not so deep or so essential that we have to pursue it so much and with *such sacrifices*." The Executive Committee hoped, continued Iakubovich, that the Workers' Section would be extremely careful and circumspect in propagandizing the idea of factory terror among workers. And, of course, terrorism should be carried out in a highly secret and well-organized fashion—something which could only be assured by turning over the terrorist activity to the professionals of the Executive Committee.

In direct reference to the growing interest among worker-propagandists in a purely labor party Iakubovich assured the Workers' Section that the Executive Committee would recognize its rights to organizational autonomy. It would be damaging to the movement, however, to raise the banner of a "new party," as the Workers' Section apparently planned to do "in the near future." Examining his own history as a party rebel, Iakubovich concluded that as a result of his "crime (yes, crime!) . . . how much strength was wasted, how many dear, pure souls died as a result of this internal war of brother against brother! . . . Don't say that they were lost as a result of external conditions. No, we ourselves eliminated each other." Clearly overdramatizing his case, Iakubovich blamed the series of "pogroms" of party members on internal narodovol'tsy squabbling.

Iakubovich concluded his pleas for unity by encouraging the Workers' Section to look at Narodnaia Volia as its party. Tikhomirov "is our common theoretical leader [*vozhd*]." Not all narodovol'tsy by far "are narrow terrorists!" To be sure, the program of the "narodniki" (referring here to the followers of Plekhanov) claims to support the cause of the workers, but their program will take "all in all ten thousand years" to be realized. Since our idea is the same, let us not allow factional, organizational infighting to deter the advancement of that idea — the social revolution.[104]

Almost immediately after sending the letter, Iakubovich was apprehended by the police. The banner of revolt within the party, which he himself had raised, had been cut down. By the time of his arrest the members of the Youth were on the side of the Executive Committee. As Popov noted, only the workers' groups continued to express their independence from the Executive Committee and proceeded to formulate their own program, "which denied the necessity of political terror." The remaining narodovol'tsy were in a state of shock as a result of the mass arrests of October and November and the loss of both Lopatin and Iakubovich. The party "as an organizational whole ceased to exist."[105] There remained "uncoordinated small subgroups," but they completely lost contact with the Paris center and often remained independent from the Petersburg and Moscow primary organizations.[106]

Vera Zasulich, a member of Plekhanov's Emancipation of Labor group, had been elated by the challenge of the Youth, interpreting it as a break in Narodnaia Volia's stranglehold on the Russian revolutionary movement. In a 2 March 1884 letter to Engels — at the beginning of Iakubovich's rebellion — she asked permission to publish Marx's *Poverty of Philosophy* and expressed the conviction that this work would lead to a wider acceptance of Marxism among young intelligentsia members: "You perhaps know that . . . our young narodovol'tsy as well as narodniki circles are beginning to be interested . . . in theoretical questions. For this they need serious books . . . The reception which greeted the beginning of our propaganda attack of scientific socialism promises even greater success than we could have hoped for."[107] In an undated letter to Engels after the appearance of Plekhanov's *Our Differences* in Russia in 1885, Zasulich attacked the reassertion of narodovol'tsy centralism and predicted the imminent fall of the Executive Committee. Everything Narodnaia Volia says, wrote Zasulich, "they already said ten years ago. They have only strength enough to repeat phrases." In her opinion, the party was a relic due to pass into historical oblivion. "The intellectual standard of the party is falling; the youth who think, who attempt to understand what they are doing, have stopped joining these narodovol'tsy circles."[108]

Zasulich's estimate of the state of the revolutionary movement inside Russia was partially correct. The challenge of the Youth to the dictates of the Executive Committee and the consistent defiance of the Workers' Section expressed the desire of the radical intelligentsia for a new formula to deal with the problem of revolutionary action in an autocratic society. Political terrorism and its concomitant, centralized, hierarchical, and conspiratorial organization, was no longer quite so compelling. More than their Paris superiors, both the Youth and the Workers' Section recognized the potential revolutionary importance of Russian labor and both concluded that the tactics and the organization of the revolutionary movement must be determined by the requirements of successful agitation among urban workers.

Despite these fissures in the narodovol'tsy movement, Narodnaia Volia, as an idea and even as an organizational entity, did not disappear as Zasulich had predicted, nor did Marxism immediately take possession of the radical intelligentsia. From late 1884 until the aftermath of the 1891 famine, when the popularity of Marxism among the Russian intelligentsia increased spectacularly, narodovol'tsy tactics and programs continued to be relevant to the revolutionary movement, though much less influenced by the Executive Committee and in much more diverse forms.

Social Democrats in
St. Petersburg, 1884–1888

3

The tumultous years of revolutionary Russia — years of confusion and tactical uncertainty following the assassination of Alexander II — gave birth to the first Russian social-democratic movement. Russian radicals had had to endure constant arrests and weather their own internal strife. In the process they had become disenchanted with the Paris leadership's theoretical and practical directives, and began to seek alternatives to strategies that had failed to produce a revolution in Russia. Turning to the urban work force for inspiration, they came to see the workers as revolutionary allies, as the "people" who could help bring a successful revolution in Russia.

Some young radicals were actually moving in a direction that Plekhanov had charted four years earlier at Voronezh. In walking out of the 1879 Land and Liberty meeting, Plekhanov had taken the first step toward depriving revolutionary populism of its monolithic hold on radical Russia. Four years later, as head of the Emancipation of Labor group in Switzerland, Plekhanov used the ideas of European Marxism to attack the narodovol'tsy's Jacobin and terrorist orientation. The attack proved timely, for a group of St. Petersburg students, calling themselves the Party of Social Democrats, was just beginning to apply the tenets of Lassalle and Marx to the Russian political situation. Equally important, small groups of Russian workers, usually already exposed to populist and narodovol'tsy propaganda, became acquainted with Marxist literature and were increasingly attracted to social-democratic ideas. But like other Russian radicals in the 1880s, the social democrats borrowed liberally from Western (including Polish) socialist works and combined these ideas with those of the narodovol'tsy and populists, perpetually shifting their programs to adjust to the realities of propaganda among the Russian working class.

Marx and Russia

By the early 1880s the works of Marx had become standard fare in the revolutionary socialist libraries that dotted the Russian Empire from Siberia to Poland. The *Communist Manifesto* had been translated into Russian as early as 1869, and the Russian translation of *Das Kapital* (the first in any language) was distributed in 1872. During the 1870s the Russian economist N. I. Ziber's lectures and articles popularized Marx's economic theories, which provided the fuel for the debates over Russia's newest "accursed question": would the empire fall prey to the menace of capitalism? The Russian populists were generally well acquainted with Marx's ideas; hence the Executive Committee of Narodnaia Volia did not exaggerate when it wrote to Marx in autumn 1880 that *Das Kapital* had already become "the basic book of educated people" in Russia, as well as in Western Europe.[1]

Marx's own views of the narodovol'tsy were just as complimentary, in part because of his visceral admiration for revolutionary zeal and action. While privately he doubted that these terrorists could be termed socialists, he publicly praised their courage, their stamina, and their cause. His indifference to the ideologically more compatible Plekhanov and his paeans to the narodovol'tsy are surprising only if one overlooks the fact that Marx frequently sacrificed theoretical purity to political expediency on issues concerning the coming of revolution to Europe. In the case of Russia, he believed that the narodovol'tsy, not Plekhanov and his followers, were best equipped to defeat the autocracy which, in Marx's view, was the most formidable enemy of the European proletariat. Typical of Marx's approach was his famous 8 March 1881 (n.s.) response to Vera Zasulich's pleas for a clarification of his position on the Russian commune. Blessing the continuing terrorist struggle of Narodnaia Volia, Marx stated that the commune could serve as the basis for the regeneration of Russia, but only if the autocracy were overthrown and replaced by a government that could guarantee the commune "normal conditions of unfettered development."[2] The March 1 assassination of Alexander II only intensified Marx's admiration for the narodovol'tsy, while further deflating his opinion of Plekhanov's group. Marx wrote to Jenny Longuet, 11 April 1881 (n.s.): "The Geneva crowd [Plekhanov and his group] have actually been trying for a long time to convince Europe that *they* in fact direct the movement in Russia; now that this lie which they themselves have spread has been picked up by Bismarck and Co. and has become dangerous for them, they assert the opposite and try in vain to convince the world of their innocence. In fact, they are nothing but doctrinaires, confused Anarchist-socialists, and their influence on the Russian 'theater of war' is zero."[3] Until his death in 1883, Marx continued to place his hopes for a Russian revolution on the narodovol'tsy terrorists.

Neither Marx's rebuffs nor those of the Western socialist community deterred Plekhanov. While his comrades Vera Zasulich and Lev Deich used Marx's statements in their own attempts to unify the divided ranks of émigré revolutionaries, Plekhanov doggedly worked on his translation of the *Communist Manifesto*. "I was intoxicated by the *Manifesto*," Plekhanov later wrote; it constituted "an epoch in my life."[4] By the time he had published the translation in spring 1882, Plekhanov was well on his way to adopting Western social-democratic ideas.

Plekhanov adamantly opposed his colleagues' efforts to unify the radical emigration, especially those involving Tikhomirov and the Executive Committee. Yet under constant pressure from Zasulich and Deich, as well as from Petr Lavrov, the unofficial leader of the Russian emigration, Plekhanov reluctantly agreed in April 1882 to join the editorial board of the proposed common journal, *Vestnik "Narodnoi voli"*. But negotiations broke down, not so much over the ideological questions of political terrorism and the seizure of power, but over the practical matter of who would control the editorial policy of *Vestnik*. Plekhanov was understandably piqued when informed that Tikhomirov would hold ultimate editorial control, and Zasulich and Deich finally gave up trying to bring the two rivals together.[5] In late 1883 Plekhanov, Deich, Zasulich, Iakov Stefanovich, and Nikolai Ignatov formed their own group, Emancipation of Labor, dedicated to the spread of social-democratic literature in Russia. Over the next decade, Plekhanov's group supplied underground Russia with pamphlets, translations, and original works that popularized the "science" of Marx and Engels in radical circles throughout the empire.

The émigrés did not, however, have a monopoly on the printing of social-democratic literature; the *legal* Russian press also distributed thousands of copies of Marx's works, including several editions of *Das Kapital*. Repeatedly, the imperial committees for censorship concluded that *Das Kapital* "is a serious [piece of] research, accessible, both in its contents and conclusions, only to specialists."[6] The censors were correct in their evaluation of the book's economic complexity, but they probably did not realize that it could be popularized by specialists and thus made available to the broader audiences of the progressive journals. N. S. Rusanov, a writer for the journals *Russkoe bogatstvo (Russian Wealth)* and *Delo (The Cause)*, and N. V.

Shelgunov, the editor of *Delo*, wrote treatises that digested the complexities of Marx's economic thought and thereby made possible its more general dissemination in intelligentsia and workers' circles. *A Catalogue of Systematic Study*, a seventeen-page, legally printed brochure listing all the works of Marx legally available in Russia, circulated in underground circles. In some of the copies found by police, the illegal works had been penciled in by hand.[7]

Determined to spread the fundamentals of Marxist political economy and workers' organization among their scattered circles, Workers' Section propagandists armed themselves with Rusanov's articles, handwritten summaries of Marx's thought, precious copies of the Polish Marxist Szymon Diksztajn's *Who Lives From What?*, and stacks of *Tsar-Hunger* by the narodovolets Abram Bakh. The Ekaterinoslav railroad worker Andrei Karpenko told his circle that capitalism contained inherent contradictions that would lead inevitably to the victory of the proletariat. The workers received starvation wages because of the collusion between the capitalist factory owners and the government.[8] This simplified message was carried by narodovol'tsy propagandists who played a crucial role in preparing the ground for the popularity of the social democrats. Some gave lectures on Lassalle's "iron law of labor wages," while others concentrated their efforts on agitating for labor unions. Almost as soon as Plekhanov's translation of the *Communist Manifesto* was published, narodovol'tsy propagandists brought handwritten and hectographed copies to Moscow and St. Petersburg workers' circles.[9]

Not the least important network for the spread of Marxist literature and social-democratic ideas in Russia was the Polish Marxist party, Proletariat (1882–1886). Circulating easily in the Russian underground, Proletariat members carried hundreds of publications that police later discovered in narodovol'tsy circles all across the empire. Some Russian radicals even learned Polish in order to read the works printed by the Warsaw and Polish émigré presses. The Workers' Section leaders Popov and Flerov were so impressed by the social-democratic arguments of the Proletariat leader Tadeusz Rechniewski (whom they called "little Marx"), that they imported several Polish workers to propagandize in Workers' Section circles. Not only did Workers' Section members contemplate forming their own Marxist party, as indicated in one of Iakubovich's letters, but they also considered merging with the Proletariat.[10]

Thus Marxist and social-democratic texts had become an integral part of the Russian revolutionary liturgy before Plekhanov's attacks on the narodovol'tsy and before the Party of Social Democrats was established as a radical organization in St. Petersburg. First the populists in the 1870s and then Narodnaia Volia and the Proletariat in the 1880s planted the new ideological seeds in the Russian revolutionary movement.

The Party of Social Democrats

While social-democratic thinking made striking inroads within the narodovol'tsy movement, those who became social democrats came from a new generation of students—younger, poorer, and more isolated from the mainstream of St. Petersburg student life than their narodovol'tsy predecessors. These students often belonged to the *zemliachestvo* circles, groups of young people from the same home regions of the empire who joined together in order to share their material and intellectual resources. The zemliachestvo circles set up dozens of self-help apartments and common kitchens—known as *kommunaly*—which also served as centers for discussions of radical ideas. It was in one of these kitchens that Dimitr Blagoev, a poor Bulgarian student, received his political education.[11]

Blagoev arrrived in Petersburg at the beginning of October 1880 without a clear idea of his course of study. After some hesitation he entered the aesthetics faculty and in early 1882 joined Vasilii Kharitonov's communal kitchen in order to reduce his living expenses.[12] Like many St. Petersburg student groups, Kharitonov's circle discussed philosophical and political texts from the legal and the illegal press. In his letters Blagoev recalled that from the spring of 1881 until mid-1882, the students searched for new solutions to the problems of social and political action under an autocratic government. The terror and repression of the times, the mass arrests and retreat from liberalism, had robbed the old answers of their meaning: "The arguments at these assemblies and meetings, the reading of general literature on social questions, and especially on the revolutionary movements, convinced me that neither *narodnichestvo* [populism] nor *narodovol'chestvo* in all their variants could be demonstrated scientifically, and therefore, nothing came from the controversies. Then I turned to studying Marx's *Das Kapital* and the writings of Lassalle."[13]

At Kharitonov's Blagoev became acquainted with members of the Circle of the Don and Kuban, one of the most cohesive and radical organizations in Petersburg. His contacts in this group included the Cossacks Nikolai Borodin and Orest Govorukhin, both future members of the Terrorist Fraction. Blagoev's student world also encompassed groups with antiterrorist and populist leanings, including a circle of students from Perm province (the Perm zemliachestvo), who unconditionally opposed terrorism.[14]

The Russian authorities first became aware of Blagoev's radicalism in 1883, when they discovered that he was peripherally involved in the printing of number 10 of the illegal newspaper *Narodnaia Volia* in Derpt. The police were also aware of Blagoev's contacts with Mariia Emel'ianova (Kostiurina), a Workers' Section propagandist involved in negotiations with Iakubovich.[15] By 1884 Blagoev, Kharitonov, and several of their university friends had developed what the Bulgarian termed a consistent social-democratic world view, and in early 1885, this group of fifteen or sixteen St. Petersburg students proclaimed itself the Party of Russian Social Democrats.[16]

Propaganda lectures dominated the early months of the new party's existence. M. S. Ol'minskii, a narodovolets in 1885, later recalled that Blagoev's St. Petersburg lectures spoke "in defense of Marxist ideas." The Bulgarian polemicized "against the petty-bourgeois narodovol'tsy views" and "demonstrated that the intelligentsia did not compose a separate class."[17] Orest Govorukhin remembered listening to "a lively social-democratic speech" by Blagoev. "He talked of Karl Marx and Ferdinand Lassalle, of the enormous importance of the workers' question in all progressive countries of the world." The famous Soviet writer A. Popov (A. S. Serafimovich), veteran of the Circle of the Don and Kuban, was asked in 1926 if he recalled one of Blagoev's early speeches: "Indeed, indeed, is such a speech ever to be forgotten!"[18] Yet Blagoev looked back on his early formulations more realistically, admitting that they combined a variety of ideologies and failed to offer a definitive social-democratic doctrine: "There cannot be any doubt whatsoever that our views and program differed greatly from contemporary social-democratic views and programs. They represented a mixture of scientific socialism with Lassallism, and, if you like, with Lavrism."[19]

The activities of these social democrats can be divided into three general periods. The first period lasted from late 1883, when the group was no more than a collection of students brought together by their common poverty and radicalism, until February 1885, when Blagoev was expelled from Russia because of his contacts with the Paris Executive Committee. During this period, the group devoted most of its energy to the first number of *Rabochii* (*The Worker*), a newspaper for and about workers. Instead of using their resources to organize new workers' circles, the early social democrats carried their propaganda to groups that had already been organized by Black Repartition or the Workers' Section.[20] P. A. Latyshev and V. F. Blagoslavov of Black Repartition and Emel'ianova of the Workers' Section facilitated these contacts. Some workers' circles merged with the new party; others retained their affiliations with Black Repartition or the Worker's Section; most avoided any formal political affiliation whatsoever.

Kharitonov and Latyshev dominated the second period of the group's activities, which began with Blagoev's expulsion from the country and ended with the first in a series of arrests that marked the winter of 1885–86. Bolstered by the news of the 1885 Morozov strike, the publication of number 2 of *Rabochii*, and the appearance of Plekhanov's *Our Differences*, the social democrats enjoyed a brief period of success that raised their hopes for the future. According to the secret police, more than sixty students at the St. Petersburg Technological Institute alone were suspected of political activities at the time of Kharitonov's arrest in November 1885; half of them were associated with the social democrats.[21]

The third period witnessed the dispersal of the social-democratic forces. From early 1886 until the mass arrests brought about by police infiltration and destruction of the Terrorist Fraction in March 1887, the group disintegrated into a loose association of like-minded radicals who met at the apartment of the Andreev brothers (Petr and Nikolai). Plans for a third number of *Rabochii* collapsed with Kharitonov's arrest, and the Andreevs had to content themselves with the collection of funds to support workers' propaganda.

Even though they were not backed by a tight organization, the Andreevs' efforts were not in vain. In September 1886, a "ten kopeck" collection campaign for worker and intelligentsia propaganda reaped a total of sixty-four rubles from 564 individuals.[22] The students also succeeded in channeling dozens of imported social-democratic brochures, each in hundreds of copies, through narodovol'tsy circles in Vilna.[23] With less success, the students recruited sympathizers from the ranks of workers' groups outside St. Petersburg, finding their most enthusiastic responses among railroad workers on the Vladimir-Rostov line and among laborers in Kazan.

Pavel Shat'ko was one of the social democrats' most effective propagandists during this period. He graduated from the Technological Institute in 1886 and went to work as a draftsman in the Davydov factory, where he immediately contacted existing workers' circles. At Davydov as well as at other factories in the city, Shat'ko urged the workers to join together to protect their interests. In his view, informal workers' circles should be transformed into a "workers' party"—a party that would include only individuals who were truly "committed to changing the present structure." The "Rules of the Kassa," a pamphlet that Shat'ko was carrying at the time of his arrest, explains his strategy for recruiting workers to the social-democratic cause: "Our most immediate goal is the union of the largest number of workers in a workers' party, which might be able to change the existing order of things to the benefit of the working class; we think that the success of the cause will only be assured when workers will be strong and knowledgeable and conscious of their moral and material unity." In the fall of 1886 Shat'ko joined forces with the former Workers' Section propagandist Apollinarii Gerasimov (a worker himself) and with Petr Latyshev, who had just returned from Bessarabia to take his medical examinations. According to the secret police, Latyshev "rarely visited the clinic" and instead spent his time at St. Petersburg factories distributing revolutionary publications to workers.[24]

While no first-hand account of actual intelligentsia-worker interaction in social-democratic circles is available, the handwritten materials and pamphlets found by the police at the home of G. N. Lavrov, a Mining Institute social democrat in contact with Latyshev's propaganda efforts, include a variety of documents intended to persuade workers to support the social-democratic cause.[25] One long, handwritten treatise, which attempted to disabuse the workers of their faith in the tsar as a reformer, concluded that only a "union of workers in an organization" could improve the life of Russian workers. The police also confiscated a plan for workers' education which instructed teachers to prepare students for more difficult lectures by beginning lessons with simple stories from the daily lives of workers. As for the lectures themselves, "first—provide the workers with the bases of political economy," and "then acquaint them with the situation of workers in Western Europe and Russia." These lessons were to be accompanied by a review of the accomplishments of the workers' movement. Next, "the meaning of socialism" should be brought to the workers' attention: while clarifying the short- and long-term programs of the two revolutionary parties—Narodnaia Volia and the social democrats—the teacher should point out that "the demands and the hopes of workers are part of the program of the latter party." Lavrov's plan for workers' education went beyond classroom instruction to include the establishment of funds, libraries, and unions of families. Once these organizations were firmly rooted in their lives, the workers would be prepared to press for such political freedoms as the right of assembly and the right to strike. The goal of the workers' movement, one which Lavrov indicated lay "in the far future," was a government that defended the interests of workers.[26]

This propaganda message, as the social democrats themselves recognized, did not differ substantially from that of the Workers' Section. In a letter to Emancipation of Labor, the social democrats wrote that the main difference between them and the narodovol'tsy was that the narodovol'tsy saw everything in the context of political terror whereas the social democrats attended "to the organization and the

spreading of local groups." As far as the Workers' Section was concerned, the letter continued, "in [our] views of activities among
workers there are positively no differences."[27] One of the social
democrats' outstanding propagandists, V. A. Kugushev, wrote to
Kharitonov in 1924 that his workers' circle distributed a proclamation
that "expressed solidarity with the narodovol'tsy." There were tactical
differences, to be sure, wrote Kugushev, but we "got along with them,"
"helped one another," and "shared the experiences of underground
work."[28] Even the notes of Lavrov, which attempt to draw distinctions
between Narodnaia Volia and the Party of Social Democrats, conclude that the parties shared the goal of improving the workers' position, but differed as to means: the narodovol'tsy sought to use terror,
whereas the social democrats preferred to explain to workers their "interests and goals" while pressuring the government for reforms.[29]

Similarly, the narodovol'tsy found little to object to in the formation of the social-democratic movement. As Ol'minskii recalled: "As
far as I remember, we saw no real harm in the propaganda of Blagoev
and his circle. Therefore, during the entire time, discussions were held
about the unification of narodovol'tsy circles carrying on activities
among the workers, since in this specialized area, there were no apparent differences between us. The Blagoevtsy did not refuse to
negotiate, but avoided unification."[30] During the mid-1880s there were
even several attempts to unite the various groups carrying out worker
propaganda. But the ideological distinctions among the groups were
so vague that a united-front mentality had developed spontaneously,
rendering formal alliances unnecessary. Furthermore, the fresh
memory of the Degaev disaster made intelligentsia radicals reluctant
to formalize bonds that might lead to their arrest.

The ease with which many individuals continued to move among
the various circles demonstrates the ideological blurring characteristic
of this period. Latyshev and Blagoslavov remained close to former
Black Repartitionists; Blagoev and Kharitonov were on intimate terms
with the remaining populists. Some terrorists joined the social
democrats, and members of the Youth had few ideological
disagreements with the social democrats. In stark contrast to the snip-
ing and bitterness that increasingly characterized relations between
Plekhanov's Emancipation of Labor and Tikhomirov's Executive
Committee, an antagonism based as much on personal rivalry as on
ideological differences, social democrats and narodovol'tsy inside the
empire worked harmoniously, even though they generally maintained
separate circles.

The emergence of the Party of Social Democrats did not drain
narodovol'tsy membership, although, as Popov has noted, the first

number of *Rabochii* and the arrests of Iakubovich and Lopatin stimulated "a part of the circles of young narodovol'tsy" to join the "Blagoevtsy."[31] Historians have also offered a variety of explanations for the continuity between the social democrats and the 1887 Terrorist Fraction of Narodnaia Volia, but what really determined continuity between these groups was their common platform vis-a-vis the Russian workers. By mid-1880, the groups that constituted revolutionary Russia—the Workers' Section, Young Narodnaia Volia, the social democrats, and the narodovol'tsy—had become united in their devotion to propaganda among the working class and in their awareness of the necessity for political struggle. That struggle might take the form of political terrorism, of "factory-agrarian" terrorism, of political strikes, or of agitation for a constitution. But Russian radicals agreed that propaganda among the working class would promote the political struggle in the forms they preferred. Although they disagreed about the details of present and future political action, they shared an infatuation with Marxism and an awareness of the revolutionary significance of the industrial proletariat.

Plekhanov and the Ideology of the Social Democrats

In his memoirs, Blagoev emphasizes that the ideology of the Party of Social Democrats evolved without the assistance of other radical organizations inside or outside Russia.[32] In spite of this claim, Soviet historiography has long attributed the decisive role in the evolution of Russian Marxism, the social democrats included, to Plekhanov's émigré Emancipation of Labor group. The nearly unanimous view of both Russian and Western historiography is summarized by Iu. Z. Polevoi: "It was precisely under the influence of the group 'Emancipation of Labor' that the Blagoev group, as well as Blagoev himself, became liberated from the vestiges of narodnichestvo and Lassallism." Plekhanov's group, continues Polevoi, was "the first Russian Marxist organization," controlling the ideological formations of all Russian Marxist groups until V. I. Lenin arrived on the scene in 1892–93.[33] Samuel Baron, the American biographer of Plekhanov, states in even more emphatic terms that Emancipation of Labor was "not only prominent" in the social-democratic movement between 1883 and 1893, "it *was* the movement."[34]

One of the few voices to counter the chorus of Plekhanov partisans is that of N. L. Sergievskii, a controversial Soviet historian of the 1920s, whose arguments about the rise of social democracy in Russia deserve to be revived. In Sergievskii's view, Blagoev and the social democrats were already Marxists in 1884, a year before Emancipation of Labor had articulated a coherent Marxist outlook, and in fact it was the social democrats who influenced Plekhanov's move toward Marxism. Even if Plekhanov's *Socialism and the Political Struggle* (1883) and the draft "Program of Emancipation of Labor" (1884) can be considered Marxist (and Sergievskii thinks they cannot), he argues that there is still no evidence that the social democrats were influenced by them. The only identifiable source of Plekhanov's influence on the social democrats, he concludes, was their reception of his 1885 pamphlet, *Our Differences*, which simply bolstered their already Marxist orientation and served as an important recruitment device for the movement.[35]

There is no doubt that *Our Differences* was welcomed with joy by the Party of Social Democrats. In the name of his group, Blagoev wrote a letter to Emancipation of Labor thanking them for the pamphlet and expressing the hope that it would encourage dissatisfied narodovol'tsy either to form a dissident organization or to join the ranks of the social democrats:

> The period of 1883–1884 . . . was a period of complete anarchy of thought in the midst of the dominant party of narodovol'tsy. The majority waited for a resolution from no. 1 of *Vestnik "Narodnoi voli "* or from abroad. But an answer to the agonizing questions did not come at all . . . Finally, this impossible situation was solved by a split, the falling away of the "youth" party. This was a cry of desperation, a protest against the weakened, suffocating conditions of the old narodovol'tsy . . . The division in the party was formally healed, but the fanaticism of the old and the dissatisfaction of the youth remained.
>
> In this case a radical means was necessary which would lift the fog from the eyes of the youth, which would, like it or not, force an examination of those ideals that are not argued but worshipped . . . Such a powerful means appears to be the brochure *Our Differences*. Even if this book does not make them completely join sides with the opinions of our group (although such a phenomenon is already observable), then it is undoubtedly [the case] that it provides them with material for a criticism of the narodovol'tsy program, and makes the reworking of the program positively necessary in the interests of the struggle.[36]

Two years later Nikolai Andreev, the librarian of the social democrats, told Plekhanov that *Our Differences* enjoyed great success in Russia, "raising the spirits of Russian social democrats" and gradually inducing the narodovol'tsy to join the social-democratic movement.[37] Even the secret police greeted *Our Differences* with enthusiasm, because "it strongly challenged the belief in the wisdom of the means of action and of the program of the party Narodnaia Volia "[38]

Despite the praise that they lavished upon *Our Differences*, social democrats never regarded Plekhanov's Emancipation of Labor group as their mentor, and the two groups continued to exist as equals throughout the mid-1880s. What intellectual influences there were proved mutual, and to the émigrés such an exchange of ideas meant an end to their painful isolation. Upon receiving Blagoev's letter, Plekhanov wrote to Aksel'rod, "you can see that we have not suffered in vain."[39] Saul Grinfest, also writing to Aksel'rod in a rush of elation, proclaimed, "Russians themselves have begun at last to seek us out."[40] The emotional tone of these letters underscores the gratitude of men who had at last found the moral support that could counterbalance both their geographical isolation and a long series of rebuffs at the hands of Marx and the entire Western socialist community.

In return the émigrés offered to help their new home-based allies with their propaganda efforts. In an encoded letter to Kharitonov, the "Specialist" (Emancipation of Labor's V. N. Ignatov) affirmed his group's friendship with the social democrats and assured them: "you may count on us to be of service to you in any way we can." But in response to the social democrats' request for more copies of *Our Differences* (it had arrived in Russia in very modest numbers), Ignatov insisted that no shipment could be sent until "the rest of the money" was received. "The more money you send," he added, "the easier it will be to build our cause and the more real will be its success."[41]

This theme of mutual assistance permeates the entire correspondence. Emancipation of Labor provided the propaganda materials the social democrats needed to bolster their library, to recruit new members, and to pressure Narodnaia Volia to adopt a more social-democratic program. For Emancipation of Labor, the social democrats brought an end to political isolation and provided a crucial source of funds. The further development of social-democratic propaganda was itself a reflection of this mutual relationship. To gain wider appeal Plekhanov's orthodox and somewhat pedantic statements of Marxist theory needed to be simplified and popularized, a service that the social democrats were eager and well equipped to provide.

The social democrats read the program of Emancipation of Labor for the first time in mid-1884. Agreeing with its essence, they wrote a letter to Plekhanov and comrades expressing the desire to formulate a common program. The social democrats anticipated some difficulties in drawing one up, for they recognized that the two groups differed on several issues. In the correspondence that followed, Latyshev and Kharitonov of the social democrats agreed to Plekhanov's request to postpone publicizing a final version of the program until the negotiations were completed.[42] In return Plekhanov agreed to withdraw his own 1884 draft program in the hope of formulating a new, mutually satisfactory document.[43] Despite this exchange, the social democrats printed two articles that were essentially programmatic in content: "What Do the Working People Need?" and "What Do the Working People Strive For?," both written by Blagoev, appeared in number 1 of *Rabochii* (January 1885).[44]

Central to both articles was an emphasis on the movement's need to develop class consciousness among the workers. "If there were knowledge," wrote Blagoev, "then everything would be [possible] . . . Knowledge is the bright force which alone can bring about justice. Without knowledge there is no happiness." Class consciousness was an essential prerequisite to self-liberation, but the workers would be unable to liberate themselves until they had joined forces with the peasantry. This union of the conscious elements in both classes would be "the force . . . which could be capable of transforming the state for the benefit of the people." Since this remained a distant goal, Blagoev argued that the intelligentsia should concentrate at first on building workers' consciousness by formulating "a program of minimal demands for people's rights and interests." This program was more a call for the democratization of Russia than a plea for working-class rights: "Until there is freedom of speech, the press, assembly, education, there can be no security of his [the worker's] personal sanctity — the matter cannot go much further . . . The final demands are understood in and of themselves." The 1885 articles in *Rabochii* provided workers only with hazy Lavrist slogans about "knowledge," "unity," and "democracy"; they failed to articulate a theory of revolution and to elucidate the role of the working class in the political struggle.[45]

The group's unpublished draft program, written by Blagoev and Kharitonov in 1884, conveys a sharper picture of the social democrats' ideology.[46] Here, more clearly than in *Rabochii*, the social democrats revealed their differences with populist ideology. Instead of portraying capitalism as an evil to be eliminated at all costs, this program characterized it as an economic stage that would lead inevitably to socialism, the peak of mankind's development. Capitalism was not yet triumphant in Russia, but it "had already been established and is growing." Blagoev and Kharitonov also reiterated the social democrats' commitment to the growth of democracy in Russia: "In order for the state authorities to serve the real interests of the people, it is necessary that it [the state] becomes the expression of the people's desires, which can be achieved only by a general election without regard to sex, nationality, or religion." The creation of a people's state would depend on "gradual democratization" and "the transfer of economic and political influence from the hands of the privileged classes to the hands of the people." This shift could be accomplished "only by the active unity" of the people welded together "by means of a whole line of people's movements."[47] For the moment, securing a constitution was a low-priority goal. As Blagoev later explained, constitutionalism would remain an illusion "until a strong workers' party appeared with aims independent of the bourgeoisie."[48]

The social democrats, then, conceived their work to be that of "political educators," either forming or joining groups that brought together conscious workers and conscious peasants. In addition to maintaining that the party's goals could be realized only by "tying the peasant revolution to the political movement of the workers," the program asserted that the intelligentsia should use its own social position to push for the civil rights mentioned in the *Rabochii* articles and to promote the spread of capitalism in Russia. Railway building and state credit institutions were to be supported as measures to stimulate the growth of capitalism.[49]

The social democrats' views on terrorism reflect especially clearly their ability to synthesize a broad range of political ideologies. They flatly rejected the use of terrorism as a principal form of struggle, but in certain situations they approved of its use as a short-term expedient.[50] The St. Petersburg secret police believed that the party's willingness to admit the possibility of a terrorist struggle was not simply a theoretical point but a practical decision. A 27 October 1886 police report revealed that narodovol'tsy explosives experts were in demand among social democratic tacticians, and it was known that party circles had discussed extending the range of targets to include government officials, as well as undercover agents and factory owners.[51] This attachment to the terrorist tradition was not unique to the indigenous social democrats. Plekhanov's 1884 émigré program similarly stated that it "recognized the necessity of the terrorist struggle against the absolutist government," disagreeing with Narodnaia Volia "only on the questions of the so-called seizure of power by the revolutionary party" and on the actual goals of socialist propaganda among the working class.[52]

Emancipation of Labor took a stance somewhere between the narodovol'tsy's militant seizure-of-power plans and the social democrats' emphasis on the gradual development of worker consciousness. Striking a compromise between spontaneity and organization, Emancipation of Labor suggested that outsiders could aid workers in their struggle to overthrow the autocracy, but advised the social democrats to forget about the peasants, who "could only become useful for the revolution at the point when they ceased to be peasants."[53] Unlike the social democrats, who believed that preparation for the revolution was the exclusive task of a union of conscious workers and conscious peasants, Plekhanov and his followers were willing to allot the intelligentsia a role in the political struggle. In an article entitled "The Contemporary Goals of Russian Workers," published in number 2 of *Rabochii*, Plekhanov expressed his support for the kind of intelligentsia-led party that the social democrats had pointedly criticized. "Calling itself primarily a workers' party, I would only say that our revolutionary intelligentsia should travel alongside the workers, and [that] our peasantry should follow behind them. With such a statement of the question, our social-democratic party can preserve its workers' character without at all falling into harmful exclusiveness."[54]

Plekhanov translated his political outlook, which militated against the slow-paced, long-range propaganda efforts of the Party of Social Democrats, into practical policy—the use of agitation to speed workers along the path to revolution. An offshoot of Plekhanov's faith in the proximity of the revolution was his belief that a social-democratic party could seize state power in the name of the revolution. Although Plekhanov carefully distinguished this seizure of power, which was dependent upon the "objective" conditions of socioeconomic development, from what he considered the Jacobinism of Narodnaia Volia, the social democrats were not to be placated by his fine distinctions. Stubbornly, they wrote to Emancipation of Labor, "We will not touch here on the obvious difference [between us] on the role of the state in the attainment of a socialist structure, since this is a question of the distant future." But in fact the letter did touch on the "obvious difference": the social democrats disagreed with the significance that Plekhanov had attributed to the use of state power in the construction of socialism.[55]

Blagoev's letters to Plekhanov in the spring and summer of 1885 revealed that the passing of time and the influence of *Our Differences* had neither shaken his faith in the positive revolutionary potential of the masses nor reduced his skepticism about the political potential of a revolutionary party. Blagoev continued to insist that an actual socialist party could be formed only in the future, when Russia had reached a higher stage of capitalist development.[56] Emancipation of Labor, on the other hand, urged the immediate formation of such a party to push the development of capitalism and to be ready to assume the powers of the state when the proper moment arrived, when capitalism and the proletariat had reached their mature stage of development. Though he never admitted it, Plekhanov's view of the role of the party in advancing the cause of socialism was influenced by the narodovol'tsy, whereas the social democrats linked themselves to the anarchism of Black Repartition and the earlier populist movement.

The Society of St. Petersburg Craftsmen

In the last months of 1885 there appeared in St. Petersburg an organization of activists who, unlike the Party of Social Democrats or Emancipation of Labor, were only marginally interested in devising a broad strategy of revolution. Devoting their efforts to the concrete demands of the workers' circles, these predominantly working-class radicals rarely engaged in the types of action that the Russian authorities regarded as politically dangerous. It is clear that members of the intelligentsia had little to do with these socialist workers' groups, whose lack of political involvement made them strangers to both the radical intelligentsia and the imperial police.[57] Initially calling themselves the Society to Assist in the Raising of the Material, Intellectual, and Moral Level of the Working Class in Russia, these radicals were brought together in the winter of 1885-86 under the leadership of the Polish metal worker Pavel Varfolomeevich Tochiskii.[58]

Tochiskii, the son of a French woman and a Polish officer in the Russian army, was born 3 May 1864 in Ekaterinburg, Perm province. He dropped out of the Ekaterinburg classical gymnasium (where he was known as a poor student, constantly in trouble with the school authorities), took a job in the Ekaterinburg railroad workshops, and in 1884 settled in St. Petersburg with his sister Mariia. While working as an apprentice in the Gano gun works, Tochiskii also enrolled in a metal-working course at the Technical Society's Evening Artisan School, completing his training in January 1887.

The sources of Tochiskii's social-democratic outlook are obscure. Soviet historians argue that he was connected with the Party of Social Democrats and influenced by Plekhanov's theoretical writings — both questionable assertions in light of the historical evidence.[59] Scattered sources suggest that Tochiskii first encountered radical literature through the narodovol'tsy, but it is more likely that his radical views were shaped by the new milieu of young worker-*intelligenty* to which he belonged — often sons and daughters of nobility forced into the working class by economic necessity. Like Tochiskii, the iron worker Dmitrii Lazarev was the son of a nobleman; after failing the entrance examinations for the Technical Artillery School, he entered the urban work force while studying at the Technical Society's Evening School.[60] Together with Egor Klimanov-Afanas'ev (known in police records as "Klim"), one of Lazarev's fellow iron workers at the Baird works in St. Petersburg, Lazarev and Tochiskii formally launched the activities of the Society to Assist in the Raising of the Material, Intellectual, and Moral Level of the Working Class in Russia in the spring of 1886. A man of working-class background and a gifted speaker, Klimanov (later a founding member of the Central Workers' Circle of 1889–90) proved to be one of the society's most effective liaisons with the informal network of workers' circles in the capital.

In fall 1886 Tochiskii renamed the group the Society of St. Petersburg Craftsmen to emphasize its elite worker character. The society included students from the Bestuzhev Women's School, such as Mariia Tochiskaia and Elizaveta Danilova; leaders from the St. Petersburg workers' circles, most notably Egor Klimanov and Nil Vasil'ev; and the Prussian brothers Ludwig (Leonid), Genrikh (Andrei), and Eduard Breitfus. With the exception of the nearly fifty-year-old Vasil'ev, a veteran of the populist movement, the group was extraordinarily young. Tochiskii (as "elder") and Ludwig Breitfus were twenty-two; Lazarev and Eduard Breitfus were only eighteen.

From 1886 until February 1888, the society, dominated by Tochiskii, committed itself to "the raising of the intellectual level and material conditions of workers."[61] The Russian police wrote that the group was less interested in "the struggle against capital" than in building a "union of workers similar to those existing in England and America."[62] In her memoirs Mariia Tochiskaia declared that her brother Pavel was not a revolutionary: "My brother definitely stood for action among the workers, for organizing them on economic interests, not participating in the political struggle. The most important thing was to create a mass movement, to draw in the masses, to give them a single, clear . . . common language of economic interests."[63] The police took the same view concluding that there was no evidence that members of the society either espoused revolutionary principles or spread revolutionary propaganda among the working class of the capital.[64]

Some members of the group, including the Breitfus brothers, clearly sympathized with the broad platform that constituted the narodovol'tsy cause. For instance, the police found at Elizaveta Danilova's flat extensive notes in which she threatens the tsar, talks of his imminent assassination, exalts in the coming revolution, praises Russian women for their heroic role in the terrorist struggle, and polemicizes against those who oppose swift and merciless violence.[65] But Tochiskii abhorred violence and was indifferent to the concerns of the peasantry and of the intelligentsia, viewing the latter as merely "a chance guest" in the historical process leading to revolution.[66] Indeed, his first draft of the society's rules went so far as to exclude any other members of the intelligentsia from membership in his circle. Andrei

Breitfus, who maintained extensive contacts with the narodovol'tsy intelligentsia, was "surprised and intrigued" by Tochiskii's "severe criticism" of populism and of the radical intelligentsia. Tochiskii's "total and uncompromising rejection of terrorism staggered me," Breitfus wrote. Still, Breitfus considered Tochiskii a committed revolutionary, a true believer in the working class's power to transform Russia.[67]

Sympathy for the intelligentsia within the society, coupled with the inevitable need to solicit funds from them, eventually forced Tochiskii to modify his views. He allowed several non-workers to enter the society in a "passive" or "auxiliary" status, permitting them to pay dues and listen to society debates but forbidding them to participate in the group's activities.[68]

During the period of its existence, from fall 1885 until winter 1888, the society did little more than hold periodic meetings and catalogue socialist materials for its library. By binding its own volumes or copying the pages of other radicals' books, the group built a collection of approximately six hundred titles (most of them related to the conditions of workers in Western Europe) to supplement the radical literature housed in the Breitfus brothers' private library.[69] Despite the brothers' objections, Tochiskii, who controlled the circulation of illegal books, was reluctant to distribute books of a revolutionary character, even among workers who were full-time members of the society. Most of the illegal works that he kept under his scrutiny were by narodovol'tsy authors.[70] Tochiskii himself, who was an avid reader of Saltykov-Shchedrin and Mikhailovskii, remarked that his favorite propaganda piece was Szymon Diksztajn's *Who Lives from What?*[71] The society's librarian, Andrei Breitfus, spent most of his time reproducing and binding *Kalendar "Narodnoi voli "*. Not a single copy of the Emancipation of Labor program and only one copy of *Rabochii* could be found in the library.

The rules of the society called for the establishment of a collection fund (kassa) to lend money to workers in financial straits.[72] While never amounting to much more than a formal statement of intention and a modest source of funds for the society's library, this kassa nevertheless remained an important theme in the society's propaganda campaign.

Tochiskii's activities among workers included monthly lectures to the leaders of several workers' circles, most notably Egor Klimanov-Afanas'ev and I. I. Timofeev of the Baltic works and Vasilii Buianov of the Putilov works, all of whom would in a few years be among the most influential labor activists in Russia. Known only by their code names, these workers (with the exception of Nil Vasil'ev) were never identified by the police.[73]

Tochiskii's propaganda work among the capital's labor elite constituted his most significant contribution to the development of Russian social democracy. He encouraged leaders of workers' circles to develop their own activities, lent them legally printed books, and helped them financially. Tochiskii also reduced the working-class leaders' chances of being arrested by keeping them away from illegal pamphlets and potential spies. Nevertheless, he frequently disagreed with the ideological approaches of the labor intelligentsia and even refused to meet with Vasil'ev's circles because of its leader's populist leanings.[74] Also, his "narrow" labor approach tended to exclude the vast majority of workers from the society's activities. Still, Tochiskii's actions were generally consistent with his goal — the development of a group of worker intelligentsia which would lead the working class to its own liberation.

Tensions between Tochiskii's purely labor-defined views and the Breitfus brothers' narodovol'tsy-oriented outlook nearly led to a schism in January and February 1888. At a meeting in the village of Karlovka, Tochiskii introduced a plan to restrict all intelligentsia members of the society to an inactive status. As could be predicted, the Breitfuses rejected the plan.[75] Rumors suggesting Tochiskii's imminent arrest impelled him to announce at Karlovka that he planned to flee Russia. On hearing this, the society elected Ludwig Breitfus "elder" in Tochiskii's place. Before Tochiskii could escape, he was arrested (21 February 1888) and, along with Dmitrii Lazarev, banished under police surveillance to Zhitomir in the Ukraine.

At the next meeting of the society, April 1888, L. Breitfus passed some of the reforms that Tochiskii had blocked, eliminating the distinction between actual and "auxiliary" (intelligentsia) members of the society. He also instituted a separate kassa to benefit political prisoners and exiles, and at last won permission to open the illegal library, allowing its materials to circulate among workers' circles. With this last measure Breitfus hoped to broaden the society's contacts in the working class, to move beyond the leaders of the workers' circles and "get acquainted" with the workers themselves, "who could then be drawn into the circle."[76] According to Mariia Tochiskaia, Andrei Breitfus, who succeeded his brother as "elder," even hoped to include the peasantry in the society's propaganda efforts.[77] Despite the Breitfus brothers' ambitions, the society's activities continued to be limited after Tochiskii's departure from Petersburg. The distribution of a few illegal books among workers' circles and the collection of modest funds to benefit the library were among its few accomplishments during the period.

Upon receiving his sister's copy of the society's new rules in May 1888, Tochiskii wrote a formal letter of protest to the Petersburg group in the name of Lazarev, Danilova, and himself. The new rules would destroy the group he had helped to build: "The intelligentsia cannot possibly care about the goals of the circle as much as the workers do." Implementing a separate treasury for political purposes, opening up the illegal library, and contacting uninitiated workers were foolhardy and dangerous actions, sure to bring down the wrath of the police.[78] Breitfus tried to persuade Tochiskii that his fears were unfounded, but the arrests of fall 1888 proved Breitfus wrong. The minister of justice, upon uncovering the underground library and the political kassa, concluded that the society was "also not adverse at times to antigovernment activity" and recommended jail sentences for the group's leaders.[79]

The year 1886 was a quiet one in the St. Petersburg underground. Narodnaia Volia had moved most of its activities to the south, and the only excitement in radical circles was stimulated by demonstrations of working-class discontent. Examining this nonterrorist, labor-dominated radical landscape, the social democrat Debora Pozner speculated that hegemony in the radical movement might well pass to the Party of Social Democrats.[80] Although the social democrats did not seize the revolutionary movement from the hands of the narodovol'tsy, they did succeed in popularizing the thought of Marx and Lassalle as the basis for a new and potentially viable political strategy. Continuity with St. Petersburg social-democratic groups of the period 1889–1893 is difficult to establish, since the authorities destroyed their party and sentenced twenty leading social democrats to jail terms of up to five years. But many of the workers' groups they contacted remained undetected and served as important elements of the growing socialist labor movement at the beginning of the 1890s.

At least three distinct variants of the social-democratic world view emerged during this initial phase of its popularity among Russian radicals. First, but of least immediate importance to revolutionary developments within Russia, was the variation of Marxist thought popularized by Plekhanov and Emancipation of Labor. Plekhanov's writings, emphasizing the role of the party in implementing the revolution, provided a prototype for a radical organization that did not yet exist in Russia. Although he was not adverse to terrorism, Plekhanov believed that the workers' movement should be strengthened to assure that workers would ally with the social-democratic party in the coming revolutionary situation, which would be dictated by the inexorable advances of capitalism. Deich was not without justification when he argued that unless Emancipation of Labor could develop a subsidiary inside Russia, the Zurich group would be "stillborn."[81] But in saying this, he overlooked the role played by the Party of Social Democrats in keeping Emancipation of Labor's ultimate cause alive in Russia.

This second variant of Russian social democracy showed less concern with organizational purity than did Emancipation of Labor and, like the narodovol'tsy, sought to bring the peasantry into the revolutionary struggle. Like Plekhanov's group and the narodovol'tsy, the social democrats tolerated terrorism, but their primary concern was the development of a broadly based revolutionary consciousness. In many ways their program was closer to that of the émigré Lavrov (who had begun to call himself a Marxist by the mid-1880s) than it was to Plekhanov's platform. As one example, the social democrats' willingness to work with the narodovol'tsy in the underground was strikingly similar to Lavrov's consistent efforts to unify émigré radicals, and noticeably different from Plekhanov's testy polemics against all such efforts.

Distrusting the intelligentsia and discarding terrorism, the third group of Russian social democrats made the most complete break with narodovol'tsy tradition. Tochiskii's strain of social democracy, interested only in the workers' movement, anticipated the Economism that was to become a force in Russia at the end of the century. Tochiskii's goals, the organization of workers by workers for the benefit of workers alone, were those of the union activist he later became.[82] The political struggle that unified other Russian radical groups had little allure for Tochiskii, a man independent of party ties and political ideology.

When one turns from theory to revolutionary practice, it becomes more difficult to draw clear distinctions among the radicals active during this period. Members of all three social-democratic groups, as well as the narodovol'tsy propagandists, shared a devotion to the development of working-class consciousness. The most important distinction may well have been symbolic; a small group of Russian radicals conspicuously departed along a new path in the history of the revolutionary movement by calling themselves social *democrats* instead of social *revolutionaries*, the latter being an appellation which was used even by the Polish Proletariat and Plekhanov's Emancipation of Labor group. The change in nomenclature reflected a new self-image that was to dictate the specifications of a Russian workers' party: tied to similar parties in the West, modeled on them, and devoted to the goals of obtaining for workers their legitimate place in government and society.

Narodnaia Volia
in the South, 1884–1887

4

The emergence of social democracy in the mid-1880s reflected in part the growing militancy of Russian workers in a rapidly industrializing society. But the popularity of social-democratic thinking was also advanced by the failure of terrorist attempts by the narodovol'tsy to deflect the government from its reactionary course. Moreover, narodovol'tsy demands for the centralization of revolutionary forces backfired when the combination of Degaev's guile and Lopatin's carelessness dealt the final blow to Narodnaia Volia as a party. With these failures in mind, it is all the more striking that the magic of the name Narodnaia Volia, which had been associated for six years with a program of terrorism, socialism, and conspiracy, continued to appeal to underground groups of diverse intellectual persuasions and social origins.

From the point of view of radical Russia, Narodnaia Volia was still the only party that had come close to eliminating the nightmare of autocracy. For this reason alone, many young revolutionaries decided that it would be foolhardy, especially in this moment of weakness, to abandon the name that evoked strength. The party's glorious past thus retained its power as symbol but it was also partially preserved in fact, for the organizational efforts of the years 1878–1884 were not totally undone in the years that followed. To be sure, the central party headquarters in St. Petersburg and Moscow had been destroyed, and its provincial centers, so meticulously fostered by Lopatin and Iakubovich, languished without a central press or a steady source of funds. Still, new shoots sprang from the severed roots. These groups were certainly not as impressive as those which had confronted the autocracy in 1880 and 1881, but were still able to engage new members in the activities of narodovol'tsy propaganda, agitation, and even terrorism.

These later efforts to reproduce the formula that had brought glory to Narodnaia Volia comprise one of the least known chapters in the history of the Russian revolutionary movement. This lacuna is in part a consequence of Soviet historians' myopically exclusive attention to the development of social democracy and their lack of interest in the origins of the Socialist-Revolutionary party. There are also certain practical problems in reconstructing the history of the revolutionary movement during this period. For one thing, few of its survivors ended their lives in a style befitting Bolshevik notions of revolutionary heroism; a number joined the Socialist-Revolutionary party, played a role in its anti-Bolshevik efforts, and then lived out their last years in obscurity. Others, like Khaim Lev Shternberg and Natan (Vladimir) Bogoraz, banished to the reaches of Siberia, developed an interest in the native peoples and geography of these regions and made important contributions to Soviet anthropology and geography. One corollary of these biographical patterns was a reluctance to communicate to posterity their experiences as revolutionaries. Furthermore, the papers of Tikhomirov are of little use to the historian of underground Russia in the late 1880s because he and the Paris emigration had lost faith in and were not really in touch with the internal movement by 1884–85. Finally, there was no central radical organization to coordinate and record the activities of the scattered groups that had risen to predominance in the South and Southwest of Russia after the Lopatin-related arrests, and the local police kept less complete accounts of the underground than did the police of Moscow and St. Petersburg.

The dramatic displacement of the radical movement was largely the consequence of the growing efficiency of the police in the major urban centers of central and northern Russia, and the government's practice of banishing arrested narodovol'tsy to the provincial centers of the South and Southwest. (One can even speak of a Siberian revolutionary movement in the late 1880s, which can also be traced to exiled narodovol'tsy.) This policy of banishment also contributed to a significant change in the complexion of the revolutionary movement: an increase in working-class participation. Narodovol'tsy not already forced into the working class by economic necessity were brought close to it as a result of the government's banishment practices. With the closing of opportunities in the government, the local universities, and the (legal) literary world, banished narodovol'tsy had little choice but to work in the factories and workshops of their new homes. There they developed contacts with workers' circles and brought countless workers into the movement.

The narodovol'tsy of 1884–1887 included many more Jews and other minorities than did the old party. Of the movement's seven major leaders during these years (Sergei Ivanov, Abram Bakh, Boris Orzhikh, Natan Bogoraz, Zakharii Kogan, Khaim Lev Shternberg, and Leon Jacewicz), the last was a Pole, the first a Russian, and the others Jews or converted Jews. However, there is no evidence that radicals of Jewish descent altered the focus of revolutionary activities or thought in this period *because* they were Jews. Their ancestry was much more significant for the police, who were nearly unanimous in their conviction that the Jews were the most dangerous component of the revolutionary movement. Moscow's chief of police articulated the sentiments of many of his colleagues when he wrote in February 1887: "The very people who resist a transition to a peaceful program are the Jews, who recently have been quietly attempting to grasp the initiative of the revolutionary movement into their hands."[1] The police went so far as to estimate that in 1886 Jews constituted about 80 percent of the narodovol'tsy membership in the South and Southwest.[2] While this estimate is clearly too high (a more accurate figure would be approximately 35 percent for 1886 and 20–25 percent for the period 1885–1890) it is nevertheless true that by the mid-1880s minority peoples and especially Jews provided the critical force behind the continuation of the movement.[3]

Keeping the Movement Alive

Number 10 of *Narodnaia Volia*, printed in Derpt in September 1884, symbolized the unification of the circles of the "old" and the "young" in the narodovol'tsy movement. Although its appearance roused hopes at home and in emigration that a new phase of party history had begun, it more accurately signified the end of a reasonably uniform program of narodovol'tsy activity. The so-called compromise achieved by Iakubovich and Lopatin was little more than a potpourri of the most disparate and even self-contradictory elements of populist, narodovol'tsy, and social-democratic theory, and its unifying ideology was simply too broad to be meaningful. Even the two old rallying points of the party — the necessity of terrorism and the value of political struggle — were now subjected to bitter debate. Tikhomirov, for example, had changed his stance on terrorism, declaring flatly that he refused to support any such actions by the party in the future. The best advice he could offer the domestic narodovol'tsy, he wrote to Lopatin in late 1884, was "to emigrate and wait for better times."[4]

Not only was ideological unity collapsing; the old feeling of revolutionary optimism was also wearing thin among the émigrés. The Paris branch of the Okhrana observed that there was an almost "total collapse of spirit" in the emigration; Tikhomirov and friends had "lost all confidence" in the movement's potential.[5] To make matters worse, the home movement was badly fragmented. Saul Grinfest, surveying the revolutionary movement inside Russia for social-democratic opportunities, wrote to Plekhanov in 1884 that the dozens of narodovol'tsy circles represented a bewildering display of opinions:

> Revol[utionary] Moscow, and even also Peter[sburg], are nothing but kasha; even the devil himself would break his teeth before finding something to bite into. In general, the narodovol'tsy orientation prevails, though that's not correct — it is not an orientation, but a tradition, in which — despite all my hopes — I couldn't grab onto an orientation: every narodovol'[tsy] circle and each individual narodovolets pushes its own distinct program, and almost every member of one and the same circle understands it [the program] and advocates the goals of N[arodnaia] V[olia] in a diametrically opposed way, agreeing only on one thing — that they are narodovol'tsy.[6]

Considering the lack of a firm program of action, not to mention the destruction of a central narodovol'tsy organization, the resilience of the movement during the mid-1880s is all the more remarkable. Certainly the conditions of Russian political life which gave rise to the party in the first place had not vanished; they had only become more extreme. When old party leaders disappeared, new ones repeatedly came to the fore. The most important of these was Sergei Ivanov, a former student in the St. Petersburg Medical Surgery Academy exiled to Siberia in 1881 for spreading propaganda among workers. In December 1882 Ivanov escaped from Siberia and reentered underground circles, working close with Vera Figner in the South before her arrest. Then, early in 1883, Ivanov returned to St. Petersburg where he played a role in defending the Executive Committee against Young Narodnaia Volia. Like most of the narodovol'tsy radicals in the provinces, Ivanov remained loyal to the old concepts of party activity but felt no animosity against Iakubovich and his fellow rebels. Popov remembered him during this period as a handsome, well-dressed man, who stuttered a bit; he had a "lovely face . . . with warm blue eyes, from which, when necessary, shone decisiveness and courage." Ivanov's main goal was to keep everyone in the movement satisfied and to avoid internal strife. Similarly, in his Petersburg negotiations with the Polish Proletariat party, Ivanov did not insist on organizational or ideological uniformity, but instead encouraged the Poles to go their own way in the Congress Kingdom, while cooperating with the Russian revolutionaries whenever possible.[7]

When Lopatin assumed leadership of the narodovol'tsy effort in St. Petersburg in the fall of 1883, Ivanov turned his attention to the South. There, after Figner's arrest in February, revolutionary affairs had drifted under the uninspired leadership of Vsevolod Goncharov. Ivanov resurrected the party centers in Kharkov and Ekaterinoslav and acquired new type for an underground printing press in Rostov-on-Don. Ivanov himself worked on the press, printing several hundred copies of number 10 *Narodnaia Volia* to supplement the Derpt edition. However, each of Ivanov's accomplishments in the South was hampered by one unrelenting problem — the lack of funds. Liberal Russia had reacted to the hardening of autocracy by withdrawing altogether from the political battlefield, and even those who had once contributed generously to the movement were now unwilling to aid the heirs of its heroic period. Perhaps even more detrimental to the movement's financial condition was the poverty of the heirs themselves. The era of the rich gentry revolutionary was past; not only did the revolutionaries themselves have little to contribute to the cause, but the party had lost contact with those few sympathizers who might have provided financial support.

Ivanov found himself in a financial bind. Luka Kalegaev, son of a rich Eisk merchant, had donated funds to set up an explosives center in Lugansk, and upon receiving them Ivanov had filled the center with up-to-date revolvers and eqiupment for the manufacture of better and safer attack bombs. But Abram Bakh, Ivanov's main coworker in the South and his contact with Kalegaev, could not convince the donor to continue his contributions.[8] Following this disappointment, Ivanov turned to organized robbery as a solution, in partial imitation of Figner's earlier plans. The narodovol'tsy claimed they would rob only government money, not banks that held private savings. The Nikolaev worker and propagandist Petr Antonov, well known as an articulate defender of working-class rights, was Ivanov's main recruit for these holdups. Antonov was a small, powerful man, who was always armed with an American Smith and Wesson revolver and a small dagger, and he proved the perfect choice to lead the new stage of narodovol'tsy banditry.[9] On 17 October 1883, Antonov led a gang, including Petr El'ko, Iakov Berdichevskii, and Vsevolod Goncharov, in an unsuccessful attack on a group of postal carriers on the Kharkov-Chuguev road. The next attempt occurred only a week later, the target being a heavily guarded shipment containing some thirty thousand rubles. Unlike the first group, these carriers put up armed resistance; in the gun battle which followed, Berdichevskii was shot to death by one of the postal guards.[10]

Robbery and shootings dominated narodovol'tsy activities in the South. The Kiev organization's brother-and-sister team, Genrietta and Eduard Kosarzhetskii, was seized while waiting in ambush for a Kiev to Chernigov postal shipment.[11] The Kharkov narodovolets Evelina Ulanovskaia was sentenced to five years in Eastern Siberia for allegedly stealing gold and silver jewelry for the party's treasury.[12] When the police showed up at Saul Lisianskii's apartment (2 May 1885) in conjunction with her heist, Lisianskii opened fire with two revolvers, killing the chief investigator and wounding his assistant.[13] In addition to the violence entailed by the search for operating funds, the Ivanov-led narodovol'tsy movement assassinated the police spy Fedor Shkrioba. Ivanov sent Petr El'ko to Kharkov to supervise the operation, and El'ko recruited Antonov to be the assassin. "I met Shkrioba on the morning of the day of the assassination," Antonov later admitted to the police, "and finding out from him that he was going to the Saburov dacha, I told him that I also had to go there, so we went together. When we entered a field, I let him walk in front of me and I shot him, apparently directly in the head . . . I returned to town and told him [El'ko] that I had finished off Shkrioba."[14] The victim's body was found on 9 January 1884, and two days later a printed proclamation was distributed which justified the murder on the grounds that Shkrioba was "a turncoat and a spy."[15] Ivanov also ordered the assassination of the Kharkov gendarme colonel Sazonov, but the plan had to be abandoned due to the many arrests resulting from the Shkrioba investigation.[16]

With the Kharkov organization under extreme pressure from the police, the bulk of narodovol'tsy activities shifted to the Odessa group led by Khaim Lev Shternberg. Shternberg had grown up in Zhitomir in a thoroughly Jewish milieu, but like Moisei Krol', his neighbor and boyhood friend, he quickly moved from studying the Talmud to reading Chernyshevskii and Lavrov. In an often repeated pattern, the boys joined with other young Jews to form a circle sympathetic to the narodovol'tsy.[17] Then Shternberg and Krol' enrolled in St. Petersburg University where they joined narodovol'tsy circles. In January 1882 both were arrested for student-oriented activities and sent back to Zhitomir under police surveillance, but in the summer of 1882 they were allowed to enroll in Odessa's Novorossiiskii University, where their commitment to Narodnaia Volia intensified. In the winter of 1883–84, Shternberg wrote the influential pamphlet "Political Terror in Russia," which advocated "systematic" terror, a constant theme of narodovol'tsy "theory" until the end of the decade: "The *goal* of terror—is to overthrow tsarism and to win the sympathy of the masses; the *means*—the systematic killing of the tsar and the most important of the prominent enemies of the people and the intelligentsia. On the one hand, the isolation of the government, its reduction to the status of a small group of personalities, and on the other hand the selfless devotion of the followers of terror—guarantees the success [of terror]. And the sympathy of society for those who seek freedom guarantees its enduring success."[18]

At Novorossiiskii University, Shternberg—"the soul of the group"—assembled a new core of narodovol'tsy activists dedicated both to terrorism and to unifying workers' circles throughout Odessa.[19] Iakov Grinstsev, Moisei Krol', and Saul Piker initiated narodovol'tsy workers' circles in Odessa itself; and Adolf Levit and Ivan Khmelevtsev, who were assigned to organize workers in nearby Nikolaev, used already established underground crafts artels as building blocks for an expanded narodovol'tsy workers' organization. Altogether, the police estimated that the "hard-core" of the Odessa group consisted of about thirty-five propagandists, many of whom were seized during the arrests of the sixty Odessa narodovol'tsy in the summer of 1884.[20] As a result of these arrests, the Odessa group decided to retaliate by killing the chief of the local gendarmes, Colonel Katanskii. At eleven in the morning, 8 August 1884, Mariia Kaliuzhnaia showed up at Katanskii's apartment. She chatted with him for about an hour and then made some joke about shooting him. She pulled a handkerchief out of her pocket, unnerving the colonel at first but then calming his fears of being shot. Then she quickly pulled out a gun and fired, but the bullet missed him. Katanskii disarmed her and immediately reported the incident to government authorities. As a result, she was quickly tried by a military court (August 29) and sentenced to twenty years hard labor.[21]

Neither police pressure in Kharkov and Odessa nor growing opposition in narodovol'tsy ranks to open battles with the government dissuaded Ivanov from planning yet another attack on a postal money carrier—this time near Voronezh on 17 November 1884.[22] Once again, the man whom Pobedonostsev called "the sworn enemy of the government" took no direct part in the assault, leaving its leadership to Antonov.[23] The attack provoked a bloody gun battle in which Antonov killed a postman and escaped with a small sum of money. Ivanov remained unsatisfied; the postal raids had cost the party more than they had reaped. In response to these costly failures he began to draft plans for a more profitable robbery, and Lisianskii supported the plan: "It would be stupid to confine ourselves to thousands when the matter smells of millions."[24] The planned robbery involved seizing the large sums of money carried on the Saratov and Riazan railway line. For his "inside connection" Ivanov recruited the railway clerk Ivan Benevol'skii and turned over the details of the operation to the seemingly unstoppable Antonov.[25]

But the killing of the police agent Shkrioba had caught up with the party. Petr El'ko had been arrested and was turning over enough information to cause the arrests of dozens of narodovol'tsy leaders, including Antonov. Barely eluding the police, Ivanov fled to Paris. On hearing from his captors that his former intimate El'ko had betrayed him, Antonov tried to slash his wrists, but was stopped.[26]

The Bogoraz-Orzhikh Group

Ivanov later confessed to the police that he left Russia in January 1885 because he was disheartened by the state of the revolutionary movement. "Not even the most simple ties between outlying localities could be regularized," he complained, bitterly concluding that his ultimate goal — "the further unification of revolutionary Russia" — was impossible at the present time.[27] His confederate Abram Bakh came to the same conclusion and emigrated only two months later. Despite the potential "reserves" in the South and in the Caucasus, Bakh wrote in his memoirs, "it became clear to me that Narodnaia Volia had outlived its era." Ivanov, Bakh added, "was very depressed and felt a great weariness of spirit."[28] Yet once again new leaders came forward to replace the old, and new centers of party activity achieved prominence. This time, in the beginning of 1885, the efforts of Leon Jacewicz, Natan Bogoraz, Boris Orzhikh, and Zakharii Kogan revived the narodovol'tsy movement.

Bogoraz, the acknowledged leader of the four, had been a student at St. Petersburg University until he was expelled in November 1882 for participating in a student protest. In 1883 and 1884 the police sought him primarily for his connections with the Ekaterinoslav organizing activities, but they were also suspicious of his alleged ties with a newly formed press in Tula. In the winter of 1884–85 Bogoraz propagandized among Taganrog workers, setting up tightly organized circles that in future years could constitute the bases for expanding the movement. During 1885 and 1886 Bogoraz ("Natan the Wise" as he was called by his comrades) traveled around southern Russia, periodically going to Moscow to pick up supplies and funds for his newly founded Novocherkassk press.[29]

Boris Orzhikh, Bogoraz's friend and admirer, was the "contact man" of the hastily assembled narodovol'tsy organization in Novocherkassk. He had attended school in Odessa and moved to Tomsk in 1878. There, as a sixteen-year-old, he participated in an organization to aid escaping political exiles. One of his main confederates in the Tomsk Red Cross was the narodovolets Petr Orlov, whose subsequent arrest, mental derangement, and suicide weighed heavily on Orzhikh. After leaving Tomsk, Orzhikh enrolled in the university at Odessa in the fall of 1882, joined a communal kitchen shortly thereafter, and became an official member of the party in late 1882. In fall 1883 he joined other Jewish students under the leadership of Samuil Fel'dman to try to organize Odessa workers. One year later, having helped to smuggle literature through Podolia, he went underground in the Elizavetgrad-Kharkov organization, where he played an important role in the construction of the Rostov-on-Don press. Orzhikh's agenda for 1885–86 was two-fold: to recruit funds for the party from sympathetic liberals and to take charge of the Novocherkassk group's distribution of propaganda and storage of explosives.[30]

The Novocherkassk explosives warehouse was assembled by Leon Jacewicz, one of the most interesting though obscure figures in the 1880s movement. An active supporter of the Polish party Proletariat, Jacewicz, like many of his Polish narodovol'tsy compatriots, had received his radical education at the St. Petersburg Technological Institute. Within the next few years he became the guiding force of the Ekaterinoslav organization, which, despite the city's small population (about thirty-five thousand), was the best organized and most effective of all the narodovol'tsy groups in 1884.[31] Here, the experienced propagandist's efforts to win over the Ekaterinoslav railroad mechanics resulted in the building of a underground library and the completion of a series of handwritten primers for workers on the subject of political economy. During these months Jacewicz also helped Orzhikh and his cousin Zakharii Kogan to establish the Rostov-on-Don press. When the police moved in on the Ekaterinoslav organization at the end of 1884, Jacewicz transferred his operations to Moscow, where he organized a bomb-manufacturing workshop for the local narodovol'tsy. With a new organization under Bogoraz and Orzhikh emerging in Taganrog, Jacewicz moved south again and spread propaganda among Sevastopol dock workers. In fall 1885, fearing arrest, Jacewicz fled the country and proceeded to serve as the main contact between the home movement and the Swiss and Paris emigrations.[32]

The question of finances was extremely serious for these narodovol'tsy. "We didn't have a dime for a meal," Bogoraz recalled, and there was no money even to buy winter coats.[33] Consequently, the first major joint activity of the Bogoraz and Orzhikh groups revolved around a plan to rob the post between Mariupol and Berdiansk in the spring of 1885. Orzhikh, Antonov (by now an experienced Robin Hood), the Dmitrii Bartenev (a former Kharkov worker and propagandist) advanced this plan as the only way to obtain the necessary funds. But Bogoraz questioned the validity of robbery in the overall strategy of building narodovol'tsy prestige, and Jacewicz advised caution; in the end intervening events cancelled the plans. On May 1 Antonov was arrested in Kharkov after a shoot-out with the police. Jacewicz went into emigration, and the Mariupol conspiratorial center was abandoned.[34]

Despite its constant complaints about a shortage of funds, the new southern narodovol'tsy group managed to operate two presses during the spring of 1885, one in Novocherkassk and the other in Rostov-on-Don. (Rostov was a particularly active revolutionary center during this period, consisting of approximately seventy committed intelligentsia and worker narodovol'tsy.) Zakharii Kogan, who had worked in various émigré revolutionary presses, returned to Russia in late 1884 to supervise these operations, routinely traveling between Rostov and Novocherkassk with a suitcase full of tools, spare type, and underground publications.[35] With the police closing in on both presses, Orzhikh dismantled the Novocherkassk operation in June and moved it to Taganrog, a town known both for its weak police force and its tight-knit narodovol'tsy circles. The Rostov-on-Don press was closed down shortly thereafter. In Taganrog, again under Kogan's expert supervision, the most sophisticated underground printing operation in Narodnaia Volia's history was assembled. By early fall of 1885, according to Orzhikh's deposition, the press could "quickly print brochures and other recommended materials."[36]

The new Taganrog press breathed hope into the badly demoralized narodovol'tsy activists; in July Bogoraz wrote Petr Lavrov that he believed a virtual flood of publications would soon wash away the autocracy. Backed by this feeling of renewal, Bogoraz announced that the time had come to rebuild the central party inside Russia, and for this purpose he called for a September 1885 meeting of narodovol'tsy leaders in southern Russia.[37] Jacewicz, Orzhikh, Shternberg, S. Turskii, A. Shekhter (later Minor), A. Makarevskii, and several others responded to his call. In a forest dacha outside Ekaterinoslav, Bogoraz and Orzhikh spent a week presenting their views of a reconstructed party. The group read and discussed an upcoming *Narodnaia Volia* editorial on the future of the party, as well as the précis of Bogoraz's forthcoming "The Struggle of Social Forces in Russia"; both articles were soon printed by the Taganrog press.[38]

The debates at the September 1885 meeting focused on the two issues that had troubled the party since its inception — terrorism and organization. Perhaps making a virtue of necessity, the new leadership neatly resolved the organizational question. Instead of reconstituting itself as a centralized and hierarchical party, Narodnaia Volia would be a confederation, each group autonomously carrying out the general mandates of propaganda and organization. The issue of terrorism proved more difficult to resolve. Representing the majority, Orzhikh and Shternberg argued in favor of the use of "systematic" terrorism, which they defined as "an uninterrupted repetition of terrorist acts": revolutionary groups should kill and bomb whenever and wherever the possibility arose.[39] As Shternberg had argued in his earlier pamphlet, "Political Terror in Russia," there was no limit to the usefulness of assassinating government officials—the only problem was that the killings had been too sporadic, allowing the government too much time to catch its breath before the next attempt. Jacewicz and Makarevskii presented the minority position, arguing that since terrorism injured the cause of workers' propaganda, it should be used only when carefully prepared and clearly justified. For the most part, the participants amicably recognized their differences. "A split did not occur," recalled Makarevskii; "the meeting went on [in a tone of] friendly mutual respect for our differences, and all of us were ready to carry out the work that fell to each of us."[40] The debate on terrorism, unresolved by the meeting, was later settled when the antiterrorist Jacewicz left Russia in November and the proterrorist Sergei Ivanov arrived unexpectedly from Paris in October. From the moment of his return, the movement followed the general compromise policy of applying terrorism only when it could be justified as a positive agitational weapon for local groups in response to local needs, a revival of Young Narodnaia Volia's notion of propagandistic terrorism.

Ivanov arrived in Russia with bad tidings from his comrades in Paris. They had no books, no materials, no news, and no money, and "without immediate help from Russia" the emigration "was in no condition to carry on."[41] Bogoraz took this information in stride. In his view, the September meeting in Ekaterinoslav had been a great success, as evidenced by the revival of the Ekaterinoslav movement itself under the leadership of Anastasiia Shekhter (Minor) and Vera Gassokh (later Gots). In October 1885 the Taganrog press began printing number 11–12 of *Narodnaia Volia*, and by December copies had been distributed all over southern Russia. With a new sense of optimism, Bogoraz sought to rekindle a common feeling of purpose within the party in Russia and abroad.

Much like Iakubovich before him, Bogoraz intended to change the very structure of narodovol'tsy activity, envisioning especially important modifications in the role of terror. He was particularly opposed to centralized terror, feeling that it "compromised the party in the eyes of the masses," but, as he told the police informant Ivan Benevol'skii, he did not intend to exclude terrorism altogether. Indeed, his organizational plans called for the establishment of a Fighting Battalion (*Boevaia Druzhina*) to "consider assassinating" Tolstoi, Pobedonostsev, and selected factory owners. Still, despite these important concessions to terrorism, Bogoraz believed that the leadership of the party should remain firmly in the hands of the literary circle around the Taganrog press, a group already responsible for supervising the activities of eight to ten large groups of narodovol'tsy in southern Russia. In short, the role of terrorism was to be a limited one in a reconstructed party; publishing and propaganda would constitute the party's primary activities until the advent of the revolutionary situation.[42]

Although Bogoraz's thoughts on organization and terror were reminiscent of the Young Narodnaia Volia, his concept of revolution did not depart from the mainstream of Executive Committee ideology. For the revolution to be victorious, he wrote in "The Struggle of Social Forces in Russia," its planning must remain "in the hands of the revolutionary intelligentsia and the people." Still, it was possible that the revolutionary party itself could seize power by "skillfully delivering its blows and exploiting the demoralization of the government." In replying to the "Don Quixotes" who criticized any seizure of power independent of a revolution made by the people, Bogoraz reaffirmed the essential Jacobinism of Tikhomirov and the Executive Committee: "No less than they do we honor the principle of people's government; nevertheless we think that if the revolutionary party achieves power, then it should not hand it over prematurely to the masses."[43]

Bogoraz's group also shared the Executive Committee's apparent immunity to the inroads social-democratic thinking was making in the narodovol'tsy movement. Writing in number 11–12 of *Narodnaia Volia*, Bogoraz attacked social democracy as vacillating between a "sentimental drive to unite with the people and the German social-democratic strain," both of which he considered synonymous with the politics of "social defeatism" because they avoided the centrality of revolution.[44] There were few copies of Marx's works in the narodovol'tsy libraries, and not once did the propaganda of Bogoraz's group refer to urban workers as an independent political force.[45] In a typical pamphlet, "Provincial Activities of School Youth, no. 194," students, officers, and educated society were identified as proper targets of propaganda; workers and peasants were not even mentioned.[46] The Odessa student David Koberman epitomized the attitude of many southern narodovol'tsy who, unlike Bogoraz, felt some sympathy for the social-democratic program; in a response to one of Ple-

khanov's questionnaires, he wrote that the social democrats might
well be the party of the future, but the present belonged to the social
revolutionaries. Time was not to be wasted worrying about the
future—the present crisis demanded action and confirmed the
necessity of the terrorist struggle.[47] A phrase from one of the handwritten documents that circulated among the group pithily
summarized the sentiments of the narodovol'tsy in the South: "time is
short, every delay is a step backwards."[48] There was a sense among the
Bogoraz narodovol'tsy that they were witnessing the most crucial
period in the history of the revolutionary movement, an epoch that
might well conclude with a sudden change "in the course of national
life, for a long time determining the fate of the people."[49] Russia was
steeped in a well-publicized financial crisis; annual deficits had
strained the state budget to the breaking point; and the ruble's worth
on foreign markets had never been lower. Therefore any deviation
from basic narodovol'tsy principles at this point was completely unnecessary.

While Bogoraz supervised operations in the South, Orzhikh and
Ivanov traveled the length of Russia in the winter of 1885–86 attempting to reestablish contacts between the new party center and the scattered circles of central and northern Russia. In Kursk Orzhikh raised
money among local intelligentsia involved in setting up a legal peasant
bank. In Moscow, using the Kapger Group as his base, Ivanov
managed to contact thirty young narodovol'tsy who committed
themselves to the new southern center. At the end of 1885, with remaining ties to St. Petersburg in jeopardy, both Orzhikh and Ivanov
hurried to the capital. There they met with student narodovol'tsy
circles and in Derpt with Lev Kogan-Bernshtein, the Workers' Section
leader who had just escaped from Siberian exile. "Within several days
of my arrival in Petersburg," Orzhikh wrote in his memoirs,"I formed
a circle of personal acquaintances . . . I dreamed of uniting many of
them later on in one or two closely tied active groups." On a more
practical note, he explained that "it would take only a month or two to
succeed in putting into effect the plan for an organization in the
North."[50]

Orzhikh's optimism was based in part on the presence of a strong
and cooperative organization of Jewish students in Petersburg led by
Boris Ginzburg. In addition, the Petersburg Party of Social Democrats
appeared more than willing to work with the new Narodnaia Volia.
Kharitonov, whom Orzhikh characterized as a "worker-oriented anar-
chist," responded with enthusiasm to Orzhikh's suggestion for a joint
press in either the South or North of Russia.[51] A. Aleksandrin, the
leader of the Circle of the Don and Kuban, met Orzhikh at the train

station and put his circle's resources at the southern leader's disposal. With the Kapger group in Moscow, the Jewish narodovol'tsy circle in Odessa, circles in Minsk, Ufa, and Orenburg, the organizations in Taganrog, Ekaterinoslav, Novocherkassk, Kiev, and Rostov-on-Don, and the radical community in St. Petersburg all sympathetic to his cause, Orzhikh therefore could claim that at least through its contacts Narodnaia Volia was finally a nationwide party. Still, he was astute enough to recognize that narodovol'tsy "lived and worked as if on a volcano," and "the word 'center' became almost chimerical because it was spilled over such an enormous territory."[52]

Narodnaia Volia and the Emigration

The relationship between the Bogoraz-Orzhikh Narodnaia Volia party and Tikhomirov's émigré group closely resembled that between the domestic social democrats and Plekhanov's Emancipation of Labor. In both cases the emigrants, although demoralized and poverty-stricken, assumed a superior, sometimes arrogant stance toward their "little brothers" inside Russia. Each of these émigré groups was dominated by an outstanding publicist, the narodovol'tsy by Tikhomirov and Emancipation of Labor by Plekhanov. Thus, for the home groups, the revolutionaries in exile wielded the power of the pen; they were a source of fresh ideas and new books which were eagerly awaited by their colleagues within the empire. Such similarities in organization and attitude did not, however, prevent the two émigré groups from feuding with one another, whereas the two home groups cooperated in the spirit of a popular front. In both cases the domestic group was stronger and more realistic than the one abroad, less prone either to overwrought dejection or foolish optimism.

In 1885–86 conflicting attitudes toward the new movement at home sparked the most bitter of the arguments between the Executive Committee and Emancipation of Labor. Plekhanov and friends, though poorer, fewer, and more isolated than Tikhomirov's Paris group, nevertheless responded to the developments in Russia with rapturous enthusiasm. In stark contrast, Tikhomirov was depressed and openly defeatist. In his view, the great days of the party were over, the movement was dead, and he even began to feel that conservative monarchism might be the best solution to Russia's problems. Shortly after declaring his new-found conservatism in 1888, Tikhomirov received permission from the tsar to return to Russia.[53]

The gloom surrounding the Paris Executive Committee was apparent to the revolutionaries at home. One activist wrote from abroad: "the devil knows what condition the movement is in . . . about

Vestnik nothing is said . . . In a word—complete ruin! . . . Maybe something will manage to get accomplished, although I admit that I have little hope."[54]

While in Paris, Ivanov had begged Tikhomirov to make some gesture of support to the growing narodovol'tsy movement in the South, and the increasingly reluctant leader finally responded on 5 December 1885. In the letter Tikhomirov expressed his willingness to reestablish contact with the internal movement and named Sergei Ivanov his representative inside Russia. But the real message of this communication, and of all his correspondence to Russia during this period, was that the narodovol'tsy at home must abandon their hopes of reconstituting the party. "How nice it was for me to hear [presumably from Ivanov] that people are not losing heart and not giving up," he wrote. "Still, in regard to the general organization of the cause, I cannot say that it seems satisfactory to me." The party had chosen a false path and "all forces were expended on terror, not on revolution." To be sure, this was "pardonable in the beginning," but later, especially after the first of March, this preoccupation with "mechanics" (organization) and "terror" served no purpose and deserved no excuse. "Mechanics and terror" had become Narodnaia Volia's *raison d'être* at the expense of the party's true purpose, the struggle for freedom. As a consequence of this abandonment of earlier ideals, the Russian people could no longer view Narodnaia Volia as a faithful ally and spokesman for their needs. This is a crucial matter, Tikhomirov wrote the southern narodovol'tsy, and here "I do not see any improvement even in you." He also advised them to abandon "the pleasure of terror"; otherwise, the movement would "eternally remain at zero." There was no sense in forming any special central organization; the only thing to do was to build units slowly, in diverse locations, and wait. "I will not enter into any organization of forces," Tikhomirov stated flatly at the end of his letter, but "I will do everything I can for those who ask."[55]

Tikhomirov's unwitting analysis of his own failings as the leader of Narodnaia Volia made little impact on the internal movement. Zakharii Kogan answered the émigré leader's defeatism with a largely conciliatory letter (June 1886) that attempted to prop up Tikhomirov's failing spirits and replace the mantle of leadership firmly on his shoulders. The letter opened with an ebullient description of the great advances made by the narodovol'tsy movement ("great joy over-whelms my entire being; my heart is pounding with joy and my soul abounds with energy and strength"). Although Kogan did concede the need to alter the "means of struggle" and admitted that a central party was no longer the most "enlightened way to organize narodovol'tsy affairs," he stressed that such concessions were made only because the old ways were responsible for "turning up traitors and spies with incredible regularity." On an even more conciliatory note, he assured Tikhomirov that the party inside Russia followed "the correct principles of the Executive Committee, not losing its common cause with the émigré leadership." Despite these assurances, Kogan ignored the leader's plea to abandon organizational work, maintaining that the terrorist/antiterrorist split at the Ekaterinoslav meeting had "disappeared, like fog, and among us there appeared a marvelous unity, despite the fact that we find ourselves far from one another in various corners of Russia." Kogan wrote that the party was very much alive, had survived serious internal crises, and had never lost sight of its "guiding star" — the principle of "people's will, [expressed] by means of a political overthrow followed by a social revolution."[56]

Orzhikh did not share Kogan's conciliatory attitude. Incensed by what he considered to be the émigrés' meddling in a movement of which they knew and cared little, he viewed Tikhomirov's letter as another example of such interference.[57] Orzhikh also considered the emigration a security risk and insisted that Tikhomirov not be informed of the location of the Taganrog press or even of the planned printing of number 11–12 of *Narodnaia Volia*. In contrast to Kogan, Orzhikh did share Tikhomirov's negative evaluation of the movement's status, but firmly opposed the émigré leader's views on terrorism. In his private notes on the development of the radical intelligentsia, Orzhikh lamented the lack of revolutionary involvement on the part of Russian youth, especially regrettable because the government was weak internationally and had insurmountable financial problems. The best way to exploit these weaknesses and to revive the revolutionary movement, he contended, was through terrorism.[58]

In an openly defiant tone, Orzhikh wrote to Tikhomirov: "We will use all [our] strength in order to carry out . . . systematic terror . . . If the party is turned over to purely cultural-literary activities, then it would be a thoroughly fruitless effort, for the government daily would tear our new ranks to pieces. And the sympathy of the populace, not seeing any clear displays of strength by the party, would lessen. Besides that, every terrorist act is a step forward . . . The public craves terror." Even when propaganda efforts are successful, Orzhikh noted, people expect words to be followed by assassinations. The decline of the party was due not to the terrorist campaign but "precisely to the rejection of terror." Orzhikh argued that because of the conditions of reactionary Russia, it was simply "unthinkable" to create a broad movement of propagandists. Arrests were too common. But the material for a revitalized movement was there, and a "terrorist act at the first opportunity" would serve as the spark to ignite radical Russia. Other activities are certainly important, Orzhikh continued, but "terror will be our immediate goal."[59]

Orzhikh's thoughts in 1886 were very similar to those of Tikhomirov six years earlier. The conditions in Russia which had fostered narodovol'tsy terrorism in the first place had not changed significantly. Even the repeated disappointments and the hundreds of arrests each year had not altered the logic of the radicals. Just as the structure of radical activities in Russia apparently demanded a program of terror, so too did the internal movement need the blessings of the revolutionary apostles in the emigration. With Tikhomirov lost to defeatism and depression, the southern group turned to Petr Lavrov, the aging but still active leader of the Russian emigration.

Lavrov's patronage was easily obtained; his own views in the 1880s centered on the need to foster unity and harmony among all camps of the Russian opposition. This desire for unity was coupled with ideological flexibililty: he was always ready to encourage the formation of any new party, terrorist or not, narodovol'tsy or social democrat, as long as it expressed a devotion to the revolution. Lavrov's reception of the narodovol'tsy Jacewicz and Makarevskii, who visited him in late 1885, was typical. Whereas Tikhomirov treated the two as strangers, at Lavrov's "it seemed that a father was meeting his sons who had returned from a far-off land."[60] In a letter to Aleksandr Tseitlin of the Rostov-on-Don group, Lavrov explained that the various segments of the opposition shared one common purpose: "We will continue to work together for the common cause, knowing that on the banks of the Don and on the banks of the Seine, our hearts, young and old, beat with love for the same Russian people."[61]

While in Western Europe, Sergei Ivanov had met with Lavrov and promised financial help for the publication of a "Lavrov Jubilee Collection." Ivanov then wrote back to Bogoraz that Lavrov was behind their efforts and that, in compensation for the lack of literary activities abroad, he supported their attempt to publish number 11–12 of *Narodnaia Volia*. [62] The Bogoraz group was greatly encouraged, especially given Tikhomirov's bleak letters. Particularly disappointing had been Tikhomirov's advice that they form small, independent circles, joined perhaps by the name Union of Narodnaia Volia — advice that contrasted vividly with Lavrov's statements favoring the "reconstruction of the Executive Committee." To change the committee's name or to alter the traditional concepts of the movement, Lavrov wrote, would mean "the suicide of the party."[63] Lavrov had expressed precisely the view of the Bogoraz-Orzhikh group, and they in turn voiced their appreciation by joyously celebrating on 2 July 1885 Lavrov's twenty-fifth year as a revolutionary leader, "our dear teacher, Petr Lavrovich," and "the best of the friends of the Russian people."[64]

Lavrov's popularity, however, was not limited to the Bogoraz-Orzhikh group. Circles from all over Russia turned to him for support and in each case he provided moral encouragement while steering clear of programmatic issues, much to Orzhikh's liking. Appropriately, his response to the Bogoraz greetings (13 December 1885) remained general though warm. He expressed his deep gratitude for the honors "reaching me from the most dispersed localities of our land" and told of his lasting respect "for all those fighters of all generations" who courageously continued to struggle in the name of political and economic freedom against "the hateful order of things in Russia."[65]

The End of the Southern Narodovol'tsy

The Bogoraz-Orzhikh group carried out few of the revolutionary activities promised in their letters to Tikhomirov and Lavrov and none of the major terrorist acts that Orzhikh and Shternberg considered so indispensable. Instead, their primary contribution to the revolutionary movement was in the field of propaganda. Before the police destroyed the Taganrog press on the night of 23 January 1886, the group had managed to print and distribute thousands of revolutionary brochures, pamphlets, newspapers, and proclamations – a fund of materials that would shape the objectives of young revolutionaries until 1905. Bogoraz's "The Struggle of Social Forces in Russia" was printed in five hundred copies as was Tikhomirov's "What Do We Expect from Revolution?" (from number 2 of Vestnik "Narodnoi voli "). Under Kogan's expert direction, the Taganrog and Novocherkassk presses also hectographed a number of longer works, mostly by Tikhomirov and Lavrov. Two of the most technically impressive pieces were Marx's The Civil War in France and Alphonse Thun's History of the Revolutionary Movement, both of which became standard works in underground libraries.[66] Of the approximately twenty hectographed proclamations produced by the southern narodovol'tsy, one of the most interesting was issued by the Women's Revolutionary Committee (6 February 1886). The committee attacked a professor at the Bestuzhev Women's School for expelling Vera Sokolova, "one of the countless instances of outrageous violence of government lackeys against our women friends [podrugi]." The proclamation declared that a new stage in the struggle for "women's thought and emancipation" had arrived and warned the government "that among us, Zasulich, Perovskaia and Figner are still not dead."[67]

Taganrog was also the site of the party's impressive supply of false passports, forged signatures, and counterfeit official stamps. Fake government pronouncements could be manufactured by the Taganrog operation as could diverse paraphernalia for the training of professional propagandists and terrorists. Among the wide-ranging collection of materials found by the police was a large, highly sophisticated poster detailing the steps and picturing the actual-sized pieces involved in assembling a homemade bomb.[68]

In their efforts to reconstruct the party, the Bogoraz-Orzhikh group also established ties with auxiliary circles of Saratov printers, young Tiflis officers, Kharkov populists, and students at the Demidov Juridical School in Iaroslavl.[69] With the assistance of the young Jewish narodovol'tsy Movsha (Mikhail) Gots, Morits Solomonov, and Matvei Fundaminskii, Bogoraz and Orzhikh set up a headquarters for their empire-wide Red Cross (Society to Aid Political Prisoners and Exiles) activities in Moscow.[70] The authorities estimated that the monthly income of the Red Cross group was between four and seven hundred rubles. Altogether, the Bogoraz-Orzhikh narodovol'tsy collected close to ten thousand rubles in the period 1885–86, most of which was used to send revolutionary literature, warm clothing, and forged documents (for escape) to Siberian exiles.[71]

On 13 January 1886 the police arrested Sergei Ivanov after following him for several days. Ivanov, like Lopatin a year earlier, was seized while carrying a list of addresses of fellow revolutionaries.[72] Orzhikh was arrested five weeks later (on 22 February 1886), but the police waited eleven months before seizing Bogoraz (9 December 1886) and Kogan (27 January 1887). During this period the police had the group under strict surveillance, and before completing their arrests, they destroyed the Taganrog press (23 January 1887) and then closely observed the formation of a new press in Kremenchug under the leadership of the former cavalry lieutenant Nikolai Perlashkevich.[73]

The government treated the arrested narodovol'tsy harshly, following the Department of Police's order doubling the maximum length of administrative exile for all radicals and confining those of Jewish origin to a dangerously underprovisioned area of northern Iakutsk province. It was in the town of Iakutsk that a group of mistreated Jewish administrative exiles, primarily associated with the southern narodovol'tsy, staged an uprising in March 1889 which resulted only in increased government repression. After standing trial before a military tribunal for their role in the uprising, Kogan-Bernshtein and

Albert Gausman were hanged; Movsha Gots, Anastasiia Shekter, and Iosif Minor received long terms of hard labor.[74]

Mikhail Kancher committed suicide in exile (1891) as did Mariia Kaliuzhnaia (1889). Boris Orzhikh, after unsuccessfully resisting arrest, was locked in the Petropavlovsk Fortress and sentenced to hang, though the sentence was later commuted. In confinement he suffered psychological problems, writing pitiful letters to his sister about seeing corpses in his sleep. On 19 July 1886 Orzhikh tried to hang himself with his nightshirt, but his guards cut him down in time.[75] The police finally caught up with Jacewicz in Vienna, and in October 1887, after "the energetic intervention" of the Russian ambassador, Jacewicz was handed over to the Russian authorities. In jail in St. Petersburg, he was tormented by dreams of being buried alive by Russian customs agents and eventually died in an insane asylum.[76] Bogoraz fared somewhat better in a Moscow prison, where he jotted down thoughts in a notebook eventually confiscated by his wardens. He lamented that his own life would not end as nobly as that of Warynski (of the Polish Proletariat) or Zundelevich (of the first Executive Committee). Fittingly closing his own first chapter in the history of the revolutionary movement—he later became a member of the "Trudovik" party—Bogoraz wrote: "Yes, all has been destroyed, all the great plans, all the grandiose dreams. The attempt to transform the program and the party, the hope to revive the party of the revolution, to produce a broad and carefully thought-out literature, to resume the political struggle in its earlier dimension,—everything is gone . . . One can only curse the structure where you cannot even die in the struggle."[77]

If the arrests caused by Lopatin's capture and the list of radicals he carried had signaled the end of the Narodnaia Volia as an organization, the internment and exile of the Bogoraz-Orzhikh group entailed the psychological collapse of the narodovol'tsy movement. The suicides, the attempted suicides, and the hopeless uprisings in prison and in exile demonstrated the terrible isolation that separated these radicals from autocratic and liberal Russia, as well as from the classic Russian intelligentsia of noble and *raznochintsy* origins. They were extremely poor and sometimes social misfits before they entered radical circles. Perhaps even more devastating, they were clearly outmatched by the tsarist police and judicial administration. Rejected by educated society, infiltrated by police agents, sent into Siberian exile for ten years without judicial process, the revolutionaries of the Bogoraz-Orzhikh group rarely aroused sympathy or respect from their contemporaries. The peasant masses, for whom the revolution was intended, remained docile; systematic terrorism, the starting point of revolutionary action, seemed chimerical if not completely absurd under these conditions.

Nevertheless, the historical significance of the narodovol'tsy in the South during the mid-1880s should not be underestimated. The government's "nihilist" phobia continued without interruption, in part because of the narodovol'tsy's ability to replace their depleted ranks, form new circles, publish revolutionary literature, and plan assassinations. Many of the arguments within the Bogoraz-Orzhikh group resurfaced during the 1890s among those terrorists who eventually formed the Battle Organization of the Socialist-Revolutionary party in April 1902, when the program of systematic terror resulted in a spectacular series of assassinations of government ministers. Continuity between the narodovol'tsy of the mid-1880s and the Socialist-Revolutionary party is evident in personnel as well as in programs. Of the twenty-five most important leaders of that party at its founding during the winter of 1901–1902, five — Abram Bakh, Aleksandr Gedeonovskii, Movsha (Mikhail) Gots, Pavel Kraft, and Iosif Minor — had been important figures in the southern narodovol'tsy movement.[78] Dozens of other narodovol'tsy from this period, including Khaim Lev Shternberg and Sergei Ivanov, also later were associated with the socialist revolutionaries.

That Narodnaia Volia did not totally disappear despite the destruction of its organization in 1883–84 and the terrible fate suffered by the members of its Bogoraz-Orzhikh group, attests to the ability of tsarist Russia to produce desperate young men and women who continued, with frightening regularity, to hurl themselves against the brick wall of autocracy. And these radicals came not only from the ranks of frustrated Jewish students or angry workers, but from the very heart of the autocratic system itself, the Russian military.

Russian Radicals and the Military

5

The Russian government viewed its military forces as a bulwark of stability. The army was ultimately responsible for domestic tranquillity and, in return, it was granted an elevated station in the Russian social hierarchy. Hence, of the hundreds of radical circles in the 1880s, those that angered the government the most were the groups associated with military officers. Tsar Alexander III considered it above all "disgraceful" that the Russian military could involve itself in revolutionary activities, especially after the horror of the first of March.[1] Police reports of "notable decline in morals and cases of political unreliability" among young army and navy officers enraged Minister of War P. S. Vannovskii.[2] Like other high officials of the imperial bureaucracy, he was convinced that radical thought took root during the reform period, when elements of the "lower classes" had been allowed to infiltrate the officers' ranks. In the true spirit of the reaction, Vannovskii wanted to turn the clock back to the day when only nobles and officers' sons could become officers. Similar conclusions were reached by an imperial commission (chaired by Grand Prince Nikolai Nikolaevich the elder) that was hastily assembled on 20 June 1884 and instructed to formulate "special measures to defend the army and navy against the spread of revolutionary propaganda."[3] The only tangible result of the commission's work was a special agreement between the chief of the Naval Ministry and the Ministers of War, Justice, and Internal Affairs to increase the investigative and penal authority of military prosecutors. Proposals advanced by Minister of Internal Affairs Tolstoi and Minister of Education Delianov to draft student radicals into the army were opposed by the commission and rejected by Vannovskii as dangerous to the political reliability of the army.[4]

Despite periodic government concern, the military remained for the most part immune both to counterreform and to significant inroads by radical organizations. However, it is going too far to say, in the words of P. A. Zaionchkovskii, that "the Russian officer corps was absolutely uninformed about the political life of the country, and all social questions that moved the intelligentsia youth of that time went right by them."[5] Zaionchkovskii does note that there was a greater degree of radical activity among officers between 1881 and 1883 than in the previous or following decades. But whereas he indicates that only forty-two officers were involved in political activities between 1881 and 1883, L. N. Godunova and L. T. Senchakova demonstrate that one hundred ninety-two officers belonged to the Military Organization of Narodnaia Volia in that period.[6] In addition, Zaionchkovskii ignores the forty-eight officers who were indicted for political crimes in the case of the Central Military Circle (1886–87), as well as the scores of military officers associated with the Moscow *militaristy* (1884), the Dushevskii-Chizhevskii group (1888–89), and the several military narodovol'tsy groups located at virtually every major station of the Russian army in the empire.[7]

Certainly, when viewed rationally from the perspective of the autocracy, the Russian officer corps posed no immediate or potential political danger; at most, military activists were an embarrassment and an irritation. After all, in the 1880s the radicals comprised a minute fraction of an army of some 800,000 men and an officer corps of 30,000. Yet as we know, the view from the heights was not always rational, and the military narodovol'tsy evoked among the leaders of tsarist Russia unwarranted nightmares of another Decembrist uprising. More important to the history of Russian radicals, the involvement of military officers, both as participants and as objects of revolutionary propaganda, exerted an important influence on the organizational and ideological development of the revolutionary movement.

Radical officers also shared the general characteristics of the movement's participants. Often they acquired their initial radical orientation in St. Petersburg schools, in this case, the several military specialty schools in St. Petersburg and Kronstadt. (Generally, the radicals were not associated with the elite guards regiments, whose members tended to be recruited exclusively from the upper nobility.) They were usually young army lieutenants or naval ensigns, and many were part of the growing technical intelligentsia, with specialties in engineering, ordnance, artillery mechanics, or shipbuilding. Some joined Narodnaia Volia while others associated themselves with social-democratic organizations. Like other radical groups in the 1880s, most military circles mixed elements of social-democratic and narodovol'tsy thinking. And by the end of the 1880s, military circles, like many narodovol'tsy, rejected their early Jacobinism and turned to a broader strategy of uniting radicals and educated society in a campaign for a constitution.

The members of the military circles were called *militaristy*, a confusing and misleading term because it included both military officers who were radicals and civilian radicals who devoted themselves to propaganda among the ranks of the army and navy. Both kinds of militaristy shared the goal of organizing "a military conspiracy to overthrow the autocracy," either in the near or distant future.[8] Some circles of militaristy saw themselves as heirs to the Decembrists, capable of organizing a strictly military solution to Russia's political problems without the aid of the radical underground parties; other civilian militaristy groups never came into contact with officers at all and devoted their energies to the spread of radical thought in educated society as a whole, still aiming, however, for a military overthrow. Thus except for their *militarizm*, a general devotion to the use of the military in bringing down the government, the militaristy, both civilians and men in uniform, represented a microcosm of Russian radicalism in the 1880s, responding to the same pressures and expressing similar aspirations as their counterparts active among workers or intelligentsia groups.

The Military Organization

The populists of the 1870s had paid little attention to the military, and few officers participated in the revolutionary movement. This changed soon after the widely criticized performance of the Russian army in the 1877–78 Russo-Turkish War and the humiliating settlement at the Congress of Berlin (1878), where Russia was forced by the European powers to relinquish its gains from the war. As a result, young military officers began to form their own "self-development" circles which addressed social and political issues. At the same time, Russian populism had also changed from a peasant-oriented to a political movement, culminating in the 1879 formation of Narodnaia Volia. From the beginning, Narodnaia Volia was interested in winning over the officers' circles, because, as its program stated, "the military and the administration are especially important in connection with the overthrow."[9] "Preparatory Work of the Party," written in the spring of 1880, placed even greater emphasis on the role of the military: "The significance of the army during a revolution is enormous. One can say that having the army with us we can overthrow the government even without the help of the people, but having the army against us there is no doubt that nothing could be accomplished even with the support of the people."[10]

Active recruitment of army officers paid off for Narodnaia Volia. In early 1880, several dozen officers from the Petersburg military district who had joined the party organized their own Central Military Group, dedicated to spreading revolutionary propaganda among officers in the army and navy. By the end of the year they had decided to form an auxiliary to Narodnaia Volia. This new Military Organization (sometimes called Section) was supposed to involve military officers directly in the struggle to seize state power. The goals of the new organization were elaborated at a series of meetings in Nikolai Sukhanov's apartment. Lieutenants Sukhanov, N. M. Rogachev, and A. P. Shtromberg spoke for the officers, while Zheliabov and Kolodkevich represented the Executive Committee. By mid-December, the "rules" and the "instructions" of the new group had been completed.

The Military Organization was to be "strictly centralized" and would be headed by a central committee named by the Executive Committee of Narodnaia Volia. For security reasons, it was decided that the Military Organization and the party would remain separate, except for an organizational tie at the top between the central committee of the Military Organization and the Executive Committee — an astute decision, given the arrests that soon rocked Narodnaia Volia. The "instructions" encouraged officers to prepare for the coming revolution by placing their most able members in critical positions in the military, as "adjutants, paymasters, commanders of armories, and so on."[11]

The first central committee of the Military Organization was composed of its founders — Rogachev, Sukhanov, and Shtromberg from the military, and Zheliabov and Kolodkevich from the party. Month by month the organization grew in size, and by the spring of 1881 it consisted of one hundred and fifty officers, the majority from St. Petersburg and the surrounding areas, including substantial groups in Kronstadt (led by N. D. Pokhitonov and E. A. Serebriakov) and in Helsinki (led by Rogachev).[12] With Zheliabov increasingly involved in preparations for regicide, Sukhanov became the moving force of the organization. He was the kind of person, Figner recalled, "whom it was impossible not to love . . . the more you knew him the more you loved him."[13] But Sukhanov also lent his aid to the March 1 conspirators and as a result was arrested in April 1881 and executed the following March. The talented young naval lieutenant Aleksandr

Butsevich took Sukhanov's place as leader of the central committee.

Butsevich was typical of the young, idealistic generation of officers who joined the narodovol'tsy movement. As he later explained to the police, "he considered himself obligated, as a Russian officer, to defend the interests of Russia and of its representative the SOVEREIGN EMPEROR as long as the interests of Russia and its SOVEREIGN are at one with each other, but when these interests reveal themselves to be no longer mutual, then he, Butsevich, considers it his duty to stand on the side of the people."[14] Butsevich had graduated from the Naval School, the Petersburg Naval Academy, and the Institute of Communications, and soon after his joining the central committee, the Minister of Communications commissioned him as a senior consultant for the construction of port facilities in Nikolaev. Butsevich was a gifted propagandist as well as a trained naval engineer, and his placement in Nikolaev offered the party an opportunity for large-scale activities in that Black Sea city.[15] In the meantime the Military Organization sent Rogachev, who had been so successful in disseminating propaganda among Helsinki artillery officers, to the Southwest to form new military circles and draw them, together with existing ones, into the organization. While in Kiev, he contacted Lieutenant Colonel M. Iu. Ashenbrenner, who had for three years led an army officers' circle dedicated to the study of radical thought. The well-educated, thoughtful Ashenbrenner, one of the few senior officers in the movement, remained neutral in the struggle between Narodnaia Volia and Black Repartition but after the assassination of Alexander II he agreed to attach his group to the terrorist party.[16] Rogachev also contacted Vera Figner, at that point reorganizing the party in Odessa, and she agreed to coordinate her activities with those of Ashenbrenner to organize various narodovol'tsy circles in the South.

Determined to strike again at the autocracy as soon as possible, Figner sent Rogachev back to St. Petersburg with instructions to set the stage for an uprising by preparing an elite group of military terrorists.[17] This group would then assassinate the tsar and selected civilian officials and also attack and hold government buildings during a revolution. When family problems prevented Rogachev from carrying out Figner's instructions, they were taken up by a new central committee whose members included lieutenants Butsevich, N. D. Pokhitonov, V. A. Papin, and Sergei Degaev (who had come to Petersburg from the Saratov military circles), as well as Figner herself, S. S. Zlatopol'skii, and Anna Korba, the representatives of the Executive Committee. Papin later confessed that in 1882–83 the activities of the Petersburg Military Organization focused on constructing a "fighting arm" of the party "with the goal of temporarily seizing power and paralyzing the administration of government functions."[18]

As was so often the case in the 1880s, the efforts to found a terrorist attack group were less successful than the spread of circles' work. The police constantly monitored the political situation in Kronstadt and learned that the naval circle and the artillery detachment circle met regularly, collected funds for the party, organized illegal libraries, and prepared for what was thought to be an inevitable revolutionary upheaval. Similarly, almost every military school in the St. Petersburg district, including the Artillery Academy, the Konstantinovskii Military School, the Engineers Academy, the Bombardiers School, and the civilian Institute of Communications, contained at least one circle tied to the Military Organization. The Kronstadt naval circle, led at this point by Midshipman V. P. Druzhinin, even published several revolutionary tracts, and in the spring of 1882 planned to publish a military-revolutionary journal.[19]

The organizational efforts of the military narodovol'tsy outside the St. Petersburg region lent a note of realism to these hopes for revolution. Mikhail Iul'evich was able to coordinate the activities of military circles located in Pskov, Minsk, Riga, and Smolensk. Even more important was Ensign I. P. Iuvachev's work in the South. In the spring of 1882, Iuvachev accompanied Ashenbrenner to Nikolaev, where he set up a circle among fellow naval officers and tied it to Ashenbrenner's circles of army officers in the nearby Prague Regiment.[20] By the fall of 1882 Ashenbrenner had united all the circles in Odessa and Nikolaev on the understanding that their members "were obliged to stand on the side of the revolutionaries in the case of an uprising against the government."[21] Ashenbrenner's transfer to Odessa's Lublin Regiment in October 1882 added yet another link to the growing chain of military circles in the South. The final link was the consolidation of officers' circles in the Mingrelian Regiment stationed in Tiflis. Anna Korba ("Varvara Stepanovna") and Galina Cherniavskaia had worked incessantly among Tiflis officers (as well as among local Georgian narodovol'tsy), trying to persuade them to join Narodnaia Volia as part of the Military Organization.[22]

When Degaev traveled to St. Petersburg and Kronstadt in October 1882, he could report to the army and navy circles he visited that a powerful network of military circles had been formed in Odessa, Nikolaev, and Tiflis.[23] Similarly, Mikhail Ovchinnikov tied military circles in the western towns and cities (Vilna, Minsk, Grodno, Dinaburg, Riga, Bobruisk, and Mogilev) to the central committee in Petersburg.[24] By the end of 1882, close to four hundred officers in twenty-five cities and towns all over the empire could be counted as members, associates, or sympathizers of the Military Organization.

At the head of this broad effort stood Vera Figner, who directed the Military Organization and coordinated all narodovol'tsy activities during this period. Despite its apparent size and strength, the organization suffered from a number of glaring weaknesses, not the least of which was a shortage of funds, which prompted numerous discussions about possible bank robberies. It was also partly Figner's responsibility that there was no clear vision of the Military Organization's role in the revolutionary process; the Executive Committee demanded only that the military "cannot remain neutral during the revolution" but must stand at the side of the people during the "open struggle against tyranny."[25] With several notable exceptions, the military officers themselves, as Sergei Ivanov wrote, "were people without a clearly defined political ideology . . . but ready, out of straightforward political decency, in the name of comradeship, friendship, or that unique knightly-military spirit, to offer their help."[26] There had been suggestions that military narodovol'tsy would make particularly adept terrorists, but few officers seemed willing to elect that role.[27] In the absence of talented civilian narodovol'tsy leadership and lacking a well-defined task for the Military Organization, Figner decided to coopt the best military leaders into her own executive committee.

It is important to point out that the Military Organization did not attempt to recruit or propagandize among the enlisted soldiers and sailors. Of course there were exceptions, such as the Kronstadt naval officers, who (in the words of the police) demonstrated "a reprehensible familiarity with the lower ranks."[28] Also, earlier military adherents of Black Repartition, A. P. Bulanov, A. E. Skvortsov, and Druzhinin (from the Kronstadt naval circle), tried to conduct propaganda among the lower ranks. But Ashenbrenner's point of view, apparently supported by the Military Organization as a whole, was that officers could not carry out such propaganda because the common soldiers, "under the influence of discipline, will always relate to the latter [officers] with mistrust." For this reason, Iuvachev reported to the police, Ashenbrenner and Figner sent "worker-intelligentsia" rather than officers to try to contact regular soldiers and sailors in Nikolaev and Odessa.[29]

No doubt the greatest weakness of the Military Organization was that its liaison with Figner and the Executive Committee was Sergei Degaev. By divulging the whereabouts of Figner and facilitating the arrests of countless officers, including Rogachev, Pokhitonov, and Ashenbrenner, Degaev precipitated the complete destruction of the southern circles (some two hundred military narodovol'tsy were arrested) and crippled the Petersburg and Kronstadt groups. After the arrests of 1884 related to Lopatin's capture, the few remaining circles of the Military Organization were broken up by the police. Yet some government officials interpreted these arrests to mean widespread narodovol'tsy support in the military. Even Valuev panicked when he heard about the scale of militaristy activity: "I am afraid I do not err in sensing the fall of the Russian Empire."[30]

Moscow Students, *Militarizm*, and the Society of Translators

The arrests of early 1883, resulting from the treachery of Degaev, demolished the revolutionary movement among Russian officers. Because Degaev knew nearly every circle in every town and city, few officer-activists escaped imprisonment or exile. The mass arrests, combined with the enhanced powers of the military prosecutors to investigate and prosecute political crimes in the army and navy, constituted a major victory for the government; indeed, after the spring of 1883, there would be no serious radical organization of military officers. Chronic problems among officers and enlisted men at the Kronstadt garrison continued to arouse the concern of the authorities, and radical young officers and students retained their interest in organizing circles among the military. But with the destruction of the Military Organization, the narodovol'tsy no longer dominated these developments.

Within the Moscow student movement during late 1882 and early 1883, a new and very different form of *militarizm* emerged, defined by its adherents simply as a devotion to spreading radical propaganda among military officers.[31] Like their comrades at other universities throughout the empire, the Moscow students organized regional associations, the zemliachestvos. Each zemliachestvo had its particular political orientation; some were very radical but most went no further than sponsoring a few "self-education" circles, which discussed political questions only in the most general way. All the circles advocated educating young military officers to some extent; if not to overthrow the regime or to remain neutral during a revolution, at least to recruit the military to the progressive camp. One can only speculate why radical Moscow students centered more of their efforts on the military than did their counterparts in St. Petersburg. Certainly they were far fewer and their ties with the workers' movement, which attracted the attention of Petersburg students, were scattered and unsystematic. Because of the students' isolation and numerical weakness, they saw no help for radical causes in the social movements, while at the same time they idealized the revolutionary potential of the military.

As in the Petersburg student movement, the most radical students from the various zemliachestvos attempted to unite all the circles into an All-Student Union, which could coordinate educational activities among the military. But the radicals intended that the union "not count itself as a component of any of the active parties," rather a "schooling battalion" that could constantly supply new cadres for the "fighting circles."[32] And the students' lithographed journal *Union* (*Soiuz*) pledged in its columns to help the young people make the transition from "the realm of thought" to courageous political activity.[33]

Those circles which joined the union or were associated with it mixed political concerns with the original regional interests of the zemliachestvos and the vague *militarizm* current among Moscow students. One of the most active of the Moscow groups was led by Aleksandr Aleksandrov, who set up an underground press in 1884 and subsequently organized the lithographing and distribution of illegal works. When Aleksandrov died in an accident in April 1885, his place was taken by Ivan Sotnikov, who had been treasurer of the Moscow circle of narodovol'tsy. From this point on, the Aleksandrov group assumed a more political orientation, leading Sergei Ivanov to count it as part of his renewed Narodnaia Volia organization.[34] The largest of the Moscow circles associated with the All-Student Union and with the militaristy movement was composed primarily of women and was led by Sofia Lazerova. The Lazerova circle organized fund-raising evenings and other special functions to collect money for the Red Cross and contact progressive military officers. Among the circles tied most directly to the zemliachestvo movement was one whose members called themselves the Voronezhtsy, which met for purposes of self-education. In February 1885 one of its members, the former Petrovskii Academy student Sergei Kapger, returned from Paris and convinced his circle to engage in propaganda outside the student milieu. Police reports claim that between February 1885 and May 1885, when the circle was broken up by the authorities, the Voronezhtsy devoted themselves "to anti-government agitation among the workers with the idea of forming circles among them." Another of the members, Apollinarii Borodzich, recruited the worker Ivan Sokolov and, again in the words of the police, "visited factories and workers . . . [and] passed out banned books and brochures." Borodzich in particular leaned toward the social-democratic program — the police found on him a manuscript that described the fundamentals of Marxist political economy and spoke of the need to form workers' circles.[35]

Among the circles allied to the All-Student Union and intertwined with the Aleksandrov, Lazerova, and Voronezhtsy groups were those that formally took the name "militaristy." Formed in early 1883, these

military circles attempted to carry out propaganda among the
Moscow region officers, who had not been approached by the revolutionary movement. The most active of these military circles was
closely tied to the Siberian zemliachestvo. Vasilii Trifonovich
Raspopin, a Moscow University student from Siberia, led the group,
and, as far as can be determined, its initial membership was
exclusively Siberian.[36]

Militarizm reflected the students' expectation that the military
would play a critical role in the eventual overthrow of the autocracy,
their own task therefore being to spread propaganda among the
military. The Moscow prosecutor reported that at a meeting of
Raspopin's group in the summer of 1883 the proposition was raised
and unanimously accepted that there should be a change in the existing state structure "by means of a military revolution," and that the
goal of their society should be to propagandize among military youth
toward this end.[37] P. Argunov, a veteran of Raspopin's circle,
remembered that among some students the notion of a military overthrow suggested "memories of the Decembrists" more strongly than it
denoted any kind of narodovol'tsy concept of the seizure of power. In
fact, Raspopin's circle expressed two rather contradictory aims. They
wanted to produce a revolutionary "strongman" (*kulak*), an officer
who would think in terms of "the leading Decembrists — of military
terror," and also to engage in "peaceful cultural work" (*kul'tur-
nichestvo*), which would lay the intellectual foundations for revolutionary activity.[38]

Although Raspopin's circle explicitly rejected the program of
Narodnaia Volia as being "too unscientific," they did not do so because
of an inclination toward social democracy. Rather, they mixed
elements of social democracy, narodovolt'sy thinking, and Moscow
student *militarizm,* as did most of the groups associated with the All-
Student Union. Tikhomirov could justifiably refer to the militaristy as
"our Siberians" when he wrote Lopatin (27 September 1884) asking
him to treat them kindly.[39] (Typically, Tikhomirov was anxious to
receive more funds from them.) At the same time, Argunov, with
equal justification, identified Raspopin as "one of the leading early
propagandists of the works of Marx and Engels in Russia."[40]

When he arrived in Moscow in the early fall of 1884, Lopatin immediately contacted the Raspopin group, but found that the "party"
that professed "the ideology of so-called *militarizm*" had very little
strength. The group's contacts with military officers were sporadic and
completely disorganized. (Apparently, Raspopin was the only
member to carry out systematic propaganda among military officers.)
Both Lopatin and Mikhail Sabunaev attempted to channel the

militaristy into more directly political activity, but they failed and left the group to its largely peaceful work.[41]

All but forgetting its initial goal of preparing strong military leaders, the Raspopin group turned increasingly to the second goal of disseminating an ideology which called for revolutionary action. The central circle of the militaristy soon adopted the name "editorial committee," which in turn became known as the Society of Translators and Publishers.[42] The society inaugurated its work with a series of meetings in which the classics of European positivism, especially the work of John Stuart Mill, were read and debated. From Mill the militaristy turned to Marx and Engels and devoted several sessions to discussing the first volume of *Das Kapital*. But the students ran into a serious problem; the military officers, who at least formally were still the objects of their work, as well as many of the students themselves, could not read foreign-language works. Therefore, in Argunov's words, "our circle quickly came to the idea of organizing the underground publication [in Russian] primarily of Marxist literature, but also of several of the most important publications of socialists of other schools."[43]

In the introduction to its first publication, Louis Blanc's "On Monarchies and Republics," the society affirmed that it "does not present narrow party aims in its choice of material, but is dedicated to works of a scientific character."[44] "Science" soon became equated with the writings of Marx and Engels, and the society supplied underground Russia with publications of the Marxist classics. Each of these works was translated by members of the society, without the help of any other translations, and they were impressively lithographed in fifty to one hundred copies at an underground student printshop. Ludwik Janowicz, a Polish narodovolets, raised funds for publication costs at evening parties sponsored by "self-development" circles around Moscow. Janowicz also played an important role in the distribution of the publications in Kharkov, St. Petersburg, and even in Warsaw, where he had excellent connections with the Proletariat party.[45]

The society's limited activities among the military soon ceased altogether, while its publishing and translating ventures exceeded all expectations. Encouraged by the success of their earlier publications, the students decided to issue Russia's first "thick journal" of scientific socialism, entitled *Socialist Knowledge*. Again, the members of the society translated parts of socialist works — Louis Blanc's *Organization of Work*, Engels's *Position of the Working Class in England* and *Socialism: Utopian and Scientific* — and presented them as chapters of their journal. The first (and only) issue of *Socialist Knowledge* (February 1884) also demonstrated that the society had adopted much of the world view of the works it was translating. In contrast to earlier statements, the introduction to *Socialist Knowledge* insisted on the centrality of "the question of the position of the working masses in Russia," and stressed the fact that "in a capitalist society workers represent the class of hired slaves."[46] In addition, Argunov claims that the society welcomed the program of Emancipation of Labor, which it received through Janowicz's good contacts with Aksel'rod and Deich.[47] But shortly before it was broken up by the police in the summer of 1884, the society was engaged in negotiations to become the Moscow branch of a revived Military Organization of Narodnaia Volia; thus it is rather unlikely that the group immediately became followers or even allies of Plekhanov.

The Moscow militaristy's contacts with Lopatin alerted the police to their circle's existence and by the end of 1884 the entire organization had been destroyed; most of the members of the Society of Translators and Publishers were locked up in Moscow prisons. Although they never abandoned the name of militaristy, it is quite clear that by the end of the group's existence the new and for them more powerful ideology of "scientific" socialism attracted and held their interest. They were certainly not social democrats, nor did they break completely with narodovol'tsy thinking. Rather, they encouraged a shift in focus of civilian militaristy away from the seizure of power and on to the centrality of the working class, a shift that soon took place among young military officers themselves.

The Central Military Group

The Moscow militaristy emerged completely independently of the activities of the Military Organization. No ties between them are mentioned in the archives, and Vera Figner recalls explicitly that the Military Organization's extensive contacts did not include the Moscow group.[48] Similarly, the new military movement that arose in St. Petersburg in late 1884 and early 1885 had no documented links either to the Moscow militaristy or, what is even more remarkable, to established Petersburg military circles.

The St. Petersburg prosecutor traced the origins of this new movement among local officers to a circle of Military School Junkers who, in late 1884, met in private quarters around the city "to read . . . in the main, socio-economic works."[49] By early 1885, the student Mark Braginskii, Lieutenant Dmitrii Bruevich, and the Bestuzhev student Nadezhda Sleptsova attended sessions of the circle, bringing with them a raft of illegal publications. Although all three had been sympathizers of Narodnaia Volia, they were interested in developing new forms of revolutionary action that would directly involve military officers.[50]

At the same time that the Junkers' circle formed, a group of midshipmen from the Kronstadt Naval School also joined in a circle to study social questions and examine the tactics of Narodnaia Volia. Among its members were the midshipmen N. N. Shelgunov, A. I. Dolivo-Dobrovol'skii, N. I. Chernevskii, L. S. Bobrovskii, and N. N. Khodovskii. Shelgunov (1861–1909), the circle's leader, should be considered one of the most important Russian social democrats of the 1880s. He was the illegitimate son of L. N. Shelgunova and A. A. Serno-Solov'evich, the famous Russian radical of the 1860s. N. V. Shelgunov, the radical publicist and darling of the intelligentsia, agreed to take over the education of N. N. Shelgunov and cared for the youngster as his own. As a midshipman at the Naval School, the young Shelgunov became involved in radical circles and quickly came to the conclusion that the Blanquist tactics of Narodnaia Volia could not lead to a genuine revolution in Russia. Basing his ideas on his study of Marx, Engels, and Lassalle, Shelgunov became an advocate of a workers' revolution.[51]

In addition to Shelgunov's circle of midshipmen and the Junkers' circle, a third military group, led by Vera Gurari, operated in St. Petersburg in late 1884. Much like the Moscow militaristy, this group studied social-democratic materials (including Marx, Lassalle, and I. I. Ivaniukov) and also held discussions of how best to carry out the military overthrow of the government. Gurari's circle was one of the few military groups of the 1880s which actually laid plans to assassinate Alexander III.[52] Although Gurari was soon forced to leave St. Petersburg and her circle split up, the idea of overt political action by the military spurred Braginskii (of the Junkers) and Shelgunov (of the midshipmen) to join forces. The two circles merged at the end of 1885, and by February 1886, they had established firm contacts with both the former members of the Gurari circle and the other military circles in the city.[53] At this point Braginskii and Shelgunov decided to leave the phase of self-education and form an exclusively revolutionary organization that would propagandize among the military and formulate a revolutionary program.

During a series of meetings in March, April, and May 1886, the combined group formulated and discussed its draft program, assembled an underground library, and collected money for its treasury. The discussions about the proposed program were heated, reflecting the diverse political opinions of the day. With several other members, O. P. Kuchin withdrew from the group—he sympathized with terror and wanted the new organization to join with Narodnaia Volia, which was unacceptable to the majority. A. M. Red'ko, the group's librarian, opposed terrorism in any form, and was a proponent of peaceful propaganda among the military.[54] Bruevich, Luka

Gaevskii, and Nadezhda Sleptsova (who had been associated with the Gurari circle) insisted that the program be directed exclusively at revolutionary work among the military, whereas Shelgunov and Braginskii argued that the group should spread revolutionary ideas among other classes of society: "the people themselves should recognize their oppression and present demands for the betterment of their existence."[55]

The majority adopted the Shelgunov-Braginskii view, and, as a result, Bruevich, Gaevskii, and Sleptsova left the group to follow their own policy. Arguing that the government must "be deprived of its only support," the military, they formed a circle that included several recent graduates of the Konstantinovskii Military School, among them Lieutenants Ostashevich and Belkeshov.[56] Sometimes called simply the militaristy or the *lukisty* (after Luka Gaevskii), Bruevich's group continued to support the old militaristy formula of action: intense study of all schools of revolutionary literature combined with propaganda efforts among military officers.

Meanwhile, the Braginskii-Shelgunov group, which took the name Central Military Circle, intensified its own commitment to a revolutionary theory based on the aspirations of the working class. Among the groups of the 1880s which inclined toward social democracy, the Central Military Circle was one of the most conversant in the works published by the Emancipation of Labor group. Pavel Shat'ko, a member of the Petersburg Party of Social Democrats, obtained these publications for Shelgunov through his contacts in Vilna, and Shelgunov passed them on to members of his circle. One of the members, Lieutenant N. A. Semashko of the Petrozavodsk Regiment, reported that he and Lieutenant V. I. Sheidevandt of the Kursk Regiment received from Shelgunov copies of Plekhanov's *Our Differences*, Aksel'rod's "The Hegemony of Capital and the Struggle against It," and Plekhanov's translations of Engels's *Scientific Socialism*, Marx's "Wage-Labor and Capital," and Marx's "Discussion of Free Trade," among others. In fact, the police eventually seized from the arrested members of the Central Military Circle at least one copy of every work published by Emancipation of Labor, including several copies of its 1884 program.[57]

Having struggled to acquire a solid background in the social-democratic classics, the Central Military Circle completed its program, which combined a deep devotion to the military's role in the revolutionary process and Shelgunov's social-democratic ideas. "We are socialists," the program began, "and our final goal is the creation of a socialistic society." Revolutionary actions have two components, "destructive and constructive activity," and the military was "especially important in the former." But, the program added, even in the "destructive" aspects of revolutionary work, the military, important as it was, could not accomplish its goals alone; it required the "participation of other classes," especially those "interested in the new society," that is, "the people, the workers, and the worker-intelligentsia." The program admitted that the moment had not yet arrived for the formation of a fighting organization among the people. However, since the worsening economic situation in the country would inevitably lead to an uprising, the primary task of the Central Military Circle was to prepare for its outbreak by ensuring that the army would stand on the side of the people and that there would be leaders among the people who could point to "the true reasons" for its poverty and exploitation. Just as the military was part of the people, not a "separate caste," so should the Central Military Circle be a part of the all-Russian revolutionary party. The circle should continue to conduct propaganda among the military, but at the same time it must help the "more exploited" class of society develop its own "conscious" leadership.[58]

The influence of social democracy on the young military officers can be seen in their generalized devotion to the working class and in their rejection (by omission) of the use of terrorism. In more concrete terms, the program denied the possibility, even the desirability, of a purely military takeover, and expressed complete confidence in the inevitability of a people's revolution that would be led by the most advanced, politically conscious elements of the people. Like the entreaties of the social democrats in the mid-1880s, the program of the Central Military Circle warned that the revolution would not accomplish its proper ends, not be a true social revolution, without the participation of tribunes from the people. It is typical of the military groups of the 1880s that the ideological bonds between the young officers and the workers expressed in the Central Military Circle's program did not extend to the common soldiers and sailors. The program did not mention them at all, and the circle itself, as far as we know, made no attempt to propagandize among them.

In its attempt to develop a social-democratic program the Central Military Circle resembled the St. Petersburg Party of Social Democrats, founded by Kharitonov, Blagoev, and Govorukhin, and during the spring 1886 meetings of the circle, Shelgunov and Braginskii decided to find ways to cooperate with the social democrats. Shelgunov himself already had ample contacts with one of the party's members, N. G. Grigor'ev, who provided him with social-democratic publications, including copies of the party's newspaper, *Rabochii*. In addition, a number of the social democrats were associated with the military circles when they did their service, the most notable of whom was Nikolai Andreev. P. A. Alekseev was a member of both groups; Pavel Shat'ko and David Gofman served as formal liaisons between them.[59]

During the summer of 1886 the Military Circle and the Party of Social Democrats decided to hold a series of joint meetings, the first at F. M. Pol'skii's apartment in the Academy of Sciences building. In addition to an exchange of views, the Military Circle received a number of new publications from a group of engineer-technologists among the social democrats.[60] At a second meeting at Alekseev's apartment, the social democrats explained their program in great detail to various groups from the military schools allied with the Central Military Circle. Although the two programs did not diverge significantly, it is unlikely that either group significantly influenced the other.[61] Cooperation between them consisted of an exchange of programs and of views as well as a more regularized system of passing social-democratic literature to the Military Circle. While the Party of Social Democrats apparently found the officers a willing audience for their views, Shelgunov made it quite clear that the Military Circle, though delighted to receive the literature, would remain completely independent in its program and in its activities.[62]

Rather than join forces with the social democrats, Shelgunov attempted to spread his circle's program to other military groups in Russia. When eight Junkers from the Bombardiers School in St. Petersburg were transferred in late summer 1886 to the Kiev Artillery Arsenal, the Central Military Circle used the opportunity to spread its organization to the South. These young officers already had contacts with Shelgunov and the central circle, and in Kiev they joined forces with the military group under Lieutenant I. I. Aksentovich of the Kiev Engineering Battalion. Through Aleksandr Red'ko, Shelgunov passed his group's program to the Kiev circle and, in the late fall of 1886, both Shelgunov and Chernevskii met personally with Aksentovich's group. (Shelgunov had been assigned to the Black Sea fleet in Sevastopol.)

Meanwhile, three other members of the Central Military Circle were also transferred to active duty outside St. Petersburg: Mikhail Mauer was sent to the Bessarabian regiment in Kiev; Semashko was assigned to Grodno, and Sheidevandt to Zhitomir. Before they left Petersburg, the officers agreed to spread their organization wherever they were assigned, to propagandize among military officers, and to send funds back to the Central Military Circle, which would coordinate all the provincial activities.[63] Lieutenant Mauer became the pivotal figure of the renewed effort at military organization in the South. He and Aksentovich even went beyond the narrow military confines of the St. Petersburg organization and established an underground circle among skilled workers at the arsenal.[64] Chernevskii propagandized incessantly in this worker's circle, while Shelgunov, when ashore, involved himself in Aksentovich's military circle.

On 13 December 1886, shortly after Shelgunov, Mauer, and the others had been assigned to the South, the police picked up Mauer, searched his apartment, and found an extraordinarily large quantity of social-democratic literature. Other materials found there led them to Aksentovich and Vladimir Essen, one of the Petersburg Junkers transferred to Kiev. Through Essen's well-informed confession, the police were able to destroy the arsenal circle and to establish the connections to the Petersburg Military Circle. Within a month, fifty-eight members of the Kiev and St. Petersburg groups were under indictment, among them eighteen active officers and thirty Junkers.[65] Most of the officers were demoted and sent back into service in the ranks. The civilians were administratively sentenced to four or five years of Siberian exile. The Jews Bramson and Braginskii suffered the worst fate. Sent to the far reaches of Iakutsk province for ten years, the pair participated in an 1889 uprising during transit, for which they were sentenced to hard labor for life.

Military Circles, 1886–1892

Between the December 1886 destruction of the Central Military Circle and its branches in Kiev and St. Petersburg and the end of the reign of Alexander III, radical circles in the military continued to function sporadically, but never on the scale or with the formal organization that had characterized the groups during the period 1881–1886. The officers of the Kronstadt garrison remained an intermittent problem for the authorities, and the Revel Regiment, stationed in Kazan, contained a number of radical circles throughout the 1880s. One of these, led by the reserve officer and narodovolets I. N. Smirnov and the reserve noncommissioned officer V. A. Muratov, hectographed a large number of illegal narodovol'tsy and social-democratic materials. In 1886–87, the Revel warrant officer S. F. Arkhangel'skii led a circle that studied various revolutionary theories and even attempted to introduce radical thought to the rank-and-file soldiers. In Suwalki, an officers' circle of the Third Cavalry Regiment under A. S. Kholopov, which was indirectly tied to the activities of the Terrorist Fraction, also engaged in theoretical studies. The irrepressible Petr Zaichnevskii, a famed radical Jacobin of the 1860s, assembled a student group in Kostroma devoted to building a hard core of intelligentsia and officers who could seize power. Along with Zaichnevskii, M. P. Iasenev and Aleksandr Orlov attempted with some success to carry their propaganda to the Junkers of the Moscow Infantry School and to establish contacts with circles at the Academy of Military Medicine, also in Moscow.[66]

From the point of view of the government, the most dangerous military circle of the late 1880s and early 1890s was, predictably, a narodovol'tsy group, tied to the reappearance of Sofia Ginsburg in St. Petersburg in 1888. Ginsburg had worked with Nadezhda Sleptsova and Vera Gurari of the Bestuzhev women's circle, which carried out revolutionary propaganda among military circles in 1884–85. Among her contacts were two Junkers, Ivan Chizhevskii and Petr Dushevskii, who had sided with Sleptsova during the confrontation with the Shelgunov-Braginskii group and withdrew from the Central Military Circle, but continued to carry out narodovol'tsy propaganda when they were commissioned and assigned to the Kronstadt artillery detachment.[67] While Ginsburg went abroad in late 1885, Chizhevskii and Dushevskii built up a sizable Kronstadt following. In August 1888 the two decided to return to St. Petersburg, with the specific goal of organizing circles in the military schools around the city and tying them to the Kronstadt circle. After spending three years in Western Europe, Ginsburg too returned to St. Petersburg with the idea of using her military contacts, specifically Dushevskii and Chizhevskii, to reconstruct Narodnaia Volia and assassinate Alexander III. But Dushevskii and Chizhevskii rejected her plans; their goals were much more modest. Along with the other members of their small circle — artillery lieutenants E. A. Selunskii, N. Sokol'skii, and S. Egorov — they were not interested "in organizing any kind of revolutionary party, but had in mind only the spread of revolutionary views" among the military.[68]

Shortly before Christmas 1888, the Chizhevskii-Dushevskii circle adopted a program that even criticized all the contemporary approaches to revolutionary activity ("narodovol'tsy, social-democratic, and others") and concluded that its main task was to see to "the necessity of spreading enlightenment among the people, as well as military-revolutionary propaganda."[69] In stating these broad aims, the Chizhevskii-Dushevskii group reflected the ideas of a growing number of radical activists at the end of the 1880s — the notion that specific ideologies hampered the development of a general revolutionary consciousness, and that what was needed was an all-Russian liberation movement dedicated to propaganda among all interested groups in society. This, it was hoped, would pressure the government into conceding democratic reforms.

In reviewing the history of the military circles during the reign of Alexander III it is immediately obvious that it did not diverge significantly from the general lines of the movements among students or workers. Perhaps the Military Organization clung longer to the classical ideology of Narodnaia Volia, but that can be explained by the substantial number of pre-March 1881 activists who remained in the group after the assassination of Alexander II. Certainly, the formation and ideology of the Moscow militaristy circles and Shelgunov's Central Military Circle reflected the increasing attention that Russian radicals paid to social-democratic teachings in the period 1883–1886. The Society of Translators and Publishers served an extremely important function by providing the movement as a whole with a large and professionally produced body of social-democratic literature. The Shelgunov-led Central Military Circle, with its peculiar mix of *militarizm* and social democracy, was one of the few groups of the 1880s that was clearly influenced by Plekhanov's works.

Like their fellow intelligentsia activists of the 1880s, the radical military officers were unable to establish meaningful contacts with the elusive "people," the proclaimed object of their revolutionary devotion. Even more remarkable, they made few attempts to organize their own men. By the end of the decade, again reflecting the general trends in the revolutionary movement, the officers chose a broad strategy of bringing about a revolution. They rejected the notion of a military conspiracy to seize power, as did most radicals of the day, and advocated instead an empire-wide, all-class approach to bringing down the autocracy.

The St. Petersburg Student Movement and the Terrorist Fraction

6

By mid-1886 there were signs that the tense atmosphere of assassination, intrigue, and arbitrary arrest which had gripped St. Petersburg for more than seven years was giving way to a new period of calm. The mood of the intelligentsia in the capital was decisively antiterrorist; for nearly a year-and-a-half the police had faced no serious narodovol'tsy conspiracy in the city. For the most part, even underground Russia greeted this new tranquility with enthusiasm, relieved that pitched battles with the government were a thing of the past. Substantial numbers of narodovol'tsy deserted their circles to join the Party of Social Democrats in its program of peaceful long-range propaganda work among the working class, and few St. Petersburg radicals contributed either financially or morally to the organization of terrorist plots in the South. This outward calm was shattered on 9 May 1887, when the *Government Gazette* confirmed that on March 1 the police had foiled a plot to assassinate the tsar. Six conspirators had been seized as they mingled with crowds on Nevskii Prospect; three of the terrorists were carrying concealed bombs, while the other three were supposed to signal the approach of the tsar.[1] The final signal had never been given, however, and the uncovering of this plot of the Terrorist Fraction of Narodnaia Volia sent shivers of relief through goverment circles, soon followed by anger and exasperation.

Despite its failure, this conspiracy has become renowned as the most important event in the history of Russian radicalism during the reign of Alexander III. Its almost legendary status is largely a consequence of the participation of Aleksandr Il'ich Ul'ianov, Lenin's older brother. A gifted member of that now enshrined family, Aleksandr

Ul'ianov has been the subject of several Soviet biographies, document collections, and memoirs—all of which have vastly expanded our knowledge of the intricacies of the "Second first of March."[2] Another factor that enhances the symbolic dimension of the plot is the participation of the Pilsudski brothers, Bronislaw and the younger Joseph, who was to become the architect of post-Versailles Poland.

Even without the participation of Ul'ianov and Pilsudski, the Terrorist Fraction would constitute a legitimate focus for historical research. The group clearly articulated the same mixture of Marxist and narodovol'tsy thinking which dominated the revolutionary movement during the 1880s. Its participants—Poles, Russians, Jews, and Cossacks—reflected the increasingly multinational character of the Russian underground. And perhaps most important for the historian, the conspiracy expressed the prevailing ideology of radical students at St. Petersburg University. Integrally tied to the Russian student movement, the Terrorist Fraction took a significant step toward realizing what had become, seemingly overnight, the conscious wish of a majority of the university's radical students—the assassination of Alexander III.

The Government and the Universities

During the 1880s the autocratic counterreform was directed most relentlessly and vengefully against one particular target, the Russian university system. It was the almost unanimous opinion of the tsar's advisers that the universities themselves were responsible for the proliferation of "student bomb-throwers." By nourishing free-thinkers, admitting students from the lower classes, and failing to supervise student activities closely, the universities were thought to encourage students to take up the cause of revolution.[3] Although government leaders were not united on the best means to develop loyal institutions of higher learning, they did agree that counterreform was essential. The result was the 1884 charter to the universities.

Intended to eliminate all vestiges of faculty autonomy in university affairs, the charter gave the Minister of Education and the curators appointed by him exclusive control over the content of faculty lectures and empowered the minister to appoint the rectors, who had previously been elected by the faculties. All student affairs were now to be monitored by the curators, who quickly became the object of student derision. The government also sought to dampen student radicalism by eliminating lower-class students from the student bodies. Even the secondary schools came under this attack; according to the famous 18 June 1887 circular of the Ministry of Education, "gymnasia and progymnasia are dispensed from receiving the children of coachmen, lackeys, cooks, washerwomen, small tradespeople, and the like."[4] The 1884 charter also raised student fees from forty to sixty rubles a year, and in 1887 the ministry increased them to a staggering one hundred rubles a year. Also in 1887, the government placed stricter quotas on Jewish students, a group that was perceived as the source of "nihilist" doctrines. Jewish students were to compose no more than 10 percent of the total enrollment in the universities of the Pale, 3 percent in St. Petersburg and Moscow universities, and 5 percent in the remaining institutions of higher learning. Moreover, the new charter called for the strict enforcement of such unpopular rules as the mandatory wearing of student uniforms and the ban on student-organized meetings.[5]

As with so many of the counterreforms, the 1884 charter accomplished few of its original goals. The social composition of the universities was not significantly altered by the increased fees; instead, students simply became more impoverished. Control of the content of lectures did not eliminate free-thinking; it merely forced it deeper underground. Professors who remained in the universities were increasingly distrusted by the students, whereas those who were attacked and expelled for their lectures quickly became heroes. Indeed, the overwhelming supervision of university life did little more than increase student resentment, provoking serious disorders in 1884 and 1887 and culminating in a genuine political challenge to the government—the student riots and strikes of 1899–1902.

It is no exaggeration to argue that the government was indirectly responsible for the birth of the Terrorist Fraction. Its origins can be traced directly to student reactions to the government's mounting intervention in the affairs of St. Petersburg University; its ideology, organization, and contacts with other student groups grew out of the immediate experiences of the St. Petersburg University radicals.

The Petersburg Student Corporation

The repeated defeats of Narodnaia Volia between 1881 and 1883 left an organizational void in the St. Petersburg underground—a void soon to be filled by various illegal student organizations. These new circles, the most important of which was the St. Petersburg Student Corporation, attracted students whose political interests exceeded the narrow bounds of the mutual-help societies but failed to conform to the program of Narodnaia Volia.

The Student Corporation began with fewer than a dozen students in October 1883 and immediately established a small treasury to maintain a library of legal and illegal works. The original library held about 150 legal titles, and the corporation more than doubled this number in the next year by combining its own collection with the 217 titles in the zemliachestvo library. By 1884 the corporation was operating a lending library that carried virtually all the major works — European and Russian — dealing with political economy and social theory. Within its first year its membership had expanded to fifty regular and twenty "candidate" members, all pledged to the "material, moral, and spiritual support" of their colleagues. In addition, all members were obliged to give one-fiftieth of their monthly income to the group: of this sum, 50 percent went to the assistance of poorer students, 20 percent to the library, and 15 percent to the publication of student periodicals. As stated in the "rules," the corporation sought "peaceful goals," but accepted "conspiratorial means" as a tactic essential to the group's survival as a secret and illegal society.[6]

As revealed in the subsequent testimony of its members, the corporation comprised students from two distinct ideological groups: one, a small radical faction, saw the corporation as a preparatory school for participation in the anxiously awaited Russian revolution; the other, a majority, was interested primarily in the study of social theory, thus continuing the tradition of the self-education circles of the 1870s. In December 1883 the radicals (some of whom were tied to Narodnaia Volia) tried to impose a new set of rules, which would broaden the entire corporation's efforts to include both cooperation with "the revolutionary parties" and propaganda activities among the workers. The proposed rules also limited membership to those in sympathy with "the emancipation of the people by means of the realization of social theory."[7] The moderates were able to defeat this attempt to implement a new program, and the original self-education principles remained in force until the corporation, first shaken by arrests in the fall of 1884, finally disappeared in early 1886.

The relationship between the corporation and its newspaper *Students* (*Studenchestvo*), renamed *Free Word* (*Svobodone Slovo*) in 1884, remains undetermined. The police were able to establish only that the student group and its newspaper were somehow connected. The rules of the corporation had indeed called for the complete autonomy of its publishing ventures, but common personnel probably linked the two groups. The Soviet historian G. S. Zhuikov singles out a group of students from Perm as playing an especially important role in both ventures and identifies V. Barybin, later to become a member of the Party of Social Democrats, as the crucial figure in the formulation of the ideology expressed in *Free Word*. Three other prominent associates of the social democrats — V. V. Blagoslavov (who carried out propaganda among workers in the Nevskii district of the city),

Kharitonov, and G. V. Khlopin—were also influential in the corporation and its publications. Because all these students were involved in the Party of Social Democrats, Zhuikov maintains that the Student Corporation was a proto-Marxist organization reflecting the intellectual influence of Plekhanov's writings and disaffection with traditional narodovol'tsy thinking.[8]

Zhuikov's assertion is impossible to substantiate. What is certain is that the newspapers were supported by the corporation and publicized the standard arguments of Western European and Russian Marxists. As was constantly reiterated in the editorial notes of the newspapers (and in the rules of the corporation), these students were devoted to promoting the development of student organizations and creating a comprehensive social theory. Despite the demoralization of Russian society as a whole, *Students* insisted that the majority of students remained democratic and committed to the interests of the people. In order to channel the healthy instincts of students into constructive activities, the corporation urged the strengthening of circle life at the university, emphasizing especially the importance of cooperation among the various circles.[9] Only through cooperation could ideas and books be exchanged, common programs of study implemented, and commitment to a common purpose, the social movement, developed. As future leaders of society, the students must be prepared to struggle for the rights of the people, in government service, in the zemstvos, indeed, "in whatever political institutions possible." This task was just as important as propagating socialism among the people: both would serve the end of developing what *Free Word* called "the independent people's movement."[10]

Although these underground publications consistently expressed admiration for the heroes of Narodnaia Volia and applauded the assassination of Sudeikin as "the natural response to government terror," the students remained less than enthusiastic about the program of the narodovol'tsy.[11] In fact, *Free Word* accused the narodovol'tsy of failing to have any program at all and of lacking a coherent political outlook. It was said that Narodnaia Volia not only failed to provide norms for revolutionary activity, but that the party also remained indifferent to the students' central concern: "a political analysis of our lives—our existence." In short, because the narodovol'tsy spoke about the necessity of terror only in a general way, they failed to satisfy the students' need for a systematic justification of revolutionary activity.[12]

Narodnaia Volia's general lack of interest in ideological questions, not to mention the overall lull in its activities during 1883–84, prompted radical students to search for a more comprehensive theoretical basis for revolutionary activity. Even before Plekhanov and Emancipation of Labor began sending publications into Russia, many students had recognized the importance of Marxism as a revolutionary theory. In its April 1883 issue, *Students* published a long explanation of Marx's ideas on political economy, concluding that anyone seriously interested in economic questions must study *Das Kapital*, the work that contained the seeds of the future. For the writers of *Students*, Marx linked economic analysis with a telling social critique that guaranteed the demise of the contemporary order. As part of their commitment to a discussion of Marxist ideas, the students also reprinted Engels's *Scientific Socialism*, the program and a proclamation of the Polish Marxist Proletariat, and a long review of Plekhanov's *Socialism and the Political Struggle*.[13]

The editorial comment of *Students* on the work of Engels demonstrated that the newspaper was not exclusively Marxist but instead reflected its program's commitment to discuss "the question of the day"—the development of socialism—from a variety of perspectives. Reviewing their group's past, the writers of *Students* criticized themselves for having been too easily influenced by onesided arguments and inconsistent interpretations of socialism. They resolved that thereafter, "in one form or another, each of us will differ about socialism." Their goal was not unanimity, but the responsibility of each member to define precisely his concept of socialism.[14]

The St. Petersburg students thus decided to reopen the "accursed questions" and to fill their publications with discussions of new ways to grapple with old dilemmas. One suggestion, reiterated at the end of the decade by the Group of Narodovol'tsy, was to unify the liberation movement by rejecting any form of sectarianism. Narodnaia Volia was criticized for "having degenerated into impatience, into a narrow fixation on its own doctrines (*partiinost'*), and suspiciousness."[15] Echoing the objections of Young Narodnaia Volia, the student publicists attacked Narodnaia Volia for being exclusively concerned with political terror and suggested that agrarian and factory terror might be more consistent with the needs of the people.

The student newspapers were equally critical of Plekhanov's brand of Marxism, which, in the name of "objective conditions," forbade mapping out a plan of action on behalf of the people. *Free Word* complained that Plekhanov wanted the socialist intelligentsia to ignore the possibility of changing rural Russia's traditional social order. "Plekhanov," the writer charged, "thinks that only the industrial workers can join the intelligentsia in its struggle against the autocracy—but what about the peasants?" *Free Word* concluded that Plekhanov's weakness as a theoretician derived from his ignorance of statistical studies of social change in the countryside and of works detailing the real conditions of Russian society. The students branded Plekhanov as "simply a 'Marxist'," that is, a man who had failed to apply the ideas of Marx to the dynamics of Russian reality.[16]

For the students, then, Plekhanov's Marxism was just as narrow and poorly informed about the conditions of contemporary Russia as the terrorist program of Narodnaia Volia. Propagandists and agitators should concern themselves with the peasantry as well as with the urban workers; indeed, "no one should be left out."[17] The intelligentsia, the military, the national minorities, and the religious dissenters could and should be drawn into the revolutionary struggle. This pansocietal enthusiasm was also reflected in the activities of the corporation. Members raised money for the Narodnaia Volia's Red Cross organization and helped the Moscow student Society of Translators and Publishers reprint hectographed West European social-democratic works.[18] They maintained contacts with the Warsaw-based Proletariat, as well as with diverse student groups in the provinces. Their ties with Young Narodnaia Volia and with the Petersburg Party of Social Democrats indicated that the students too were dissatisfied with the traditional forms of revolutionary action. They were not really proto-Marxists in the way that Zhuikov has suggested; however, they were open to Marx's approach and were willing to use his ideas to acquire a comprehensive understanding of revolution. In this way the St. Petersburg Student Corporation developed an ideology that student radicals were to borrow in the decade to come.

The Zemliachestvos and the Circle of the Don and Kuban

While the Student Corporation and its newspapers forged the ideology of St. Petersburg University student radicals after 1883, the organization of students centered on the zemliachestvo circles, associations of students of common geographical and national origins. Of the approximately twenty-seven hundred students enrolled in the university, close to 10 percent were of Polish origin and about one thousand came from the Perm, Don, Kuban, or Western Siberian regions of Russia. Only about eight hundred had been born in the capital itself.[19] Student poverty also contributed to banding together and pooling resources. Despite government measures to restrict Russian universities to the nobility, students from the noble estate constituted less than one-fifth of the enrollment of St. Petersburg University in the mid-1880s, and even some of them were in need of financial help. In the early and mid-1870s, students had relied primarily on the self-education circles to provide for their social and economic needs. But with the arrests resulting from the activities of Narodnaia Volia in the late 1870s and early 1880s, especially widespread in St. Petersburg, the self-education circles attracted constant police attention. Thus for their psychological, social, and economic well-being, the students turned increasingly to the less suspect zemliachestvo circles. By the end of 1881 there were already sixty-five zemliachestvo circles in the major university cities of the empire: sixteen were located in Moscow and fifteen in St. Petersburg.[20]

With the exception of the large and influential Siberian zemliachestvo, which was known to have contacts with radical circles in the capital, the regional associations stayed clear of any political involvement and protected themselves from police harassment by limiting the size of their meetings and focusing their attention on the tasks at hand—providing housing, food, and small loans for their poorest members. For the police, however, these seemingly apolitical functions appeared to be based on suspiciously socialist principles of comradeship rather than on pragmatic economic concerns. One police report warned that a dangerous "moral element" characterized the relations between members of the zemliachestvos, enabling a circle to gain control over its members' activities.[21] Also, by early 1885, the police began reporting that several zemliachestvo circles met with radicals, offered them food and shelter, and provided a source of comfort for radical cadres. The dilemma for the government, which perceived conspiracy in cooperation and danger in autonomous organization, was that the zemliachestvo circles were perfectly legal. Although the 1884 charter could be used to justify the expulsion of eighteen members of the St. Petersburg University Student Corporation in the fall of 1886, it offered no rationale for taking such punitive action against the zemliachestvo circles.[22]

Despite the concerns voiced by his subordinates, Viachislav Plehve, the director of the Department of Police, recommended to Minister of Internal Affairs Tolstoi that the government not interfere in the zemliachestvo circles. Plehve's attitude toward these circles was clearly articulated in his letter to Tolstoi (January 1887): "as long as they are not dangerous in the political sense of the word," that is, "as long as they do not move away from their announced goal—mutual material help—it is impossible to take any kind of direct actions against them." Although Plehve recognized that the revolutionaries attempted to use the groups for their own purposes, sometimes successfully, he believed that it would be unwise to suppress them. Even if the government succeeded in completely eliminating them from the universities, there would be no guarantee that the zemliachestvo circles "would not reemerge in another still more dangerous organization."

Tolstoi was frustrated and angered by his police director's report, scribbling in the margins, "that's right," "exactly," and "yes," wherever Plehve suggested that the zemliachestvo circles might be dangerous. In response to Plehve's perceptive and, as it turned out, prophetic observation that the repression of the circles could lead to the emergence of an even more dangerous group, Tolstoi wrote, "then it will be necessary to destroy it too."[23] In February 1885 Tolstoi attempted to pressure Minister of Education Delianov to take "some kind of extraordinary measures for the struggle against this evil," but Delianov demurred, claiming that the circles were police business.[24] By January 1887 Tolstoi was so convinced of the zemliachestvo circles' perfidy that he overruled Plehve and insisted that Delianov destroy them, "beginning with the most dangerous in the political sense."[25] Delianov finally capitulated; as justification, he stated that the Charter of 1884 could be interpreted to prevent any student organization without university (thus government) authorization from collecting funds to promote its activities. He then instructed the university councils to deny the zemliachestvo circles the right to collect money or hold meetings. As a final measure, Delianov proclaimed that all students who participated in zemliachestvo activities be expelled immediately from the universities; those who remained were forced to sign a promise not to participate in the zemliachestvos.[26]

The government's timing was characteristically inept. In the main, the zemliachestvo circles had eschewed politics. But by January 1887, when the government outlawed them at the universities, enough radicals had been operating in their midst to turn the former zemliachestvo activists into exactly the kind of dangerous revolutionaries that Plehve feared. The suppression of the zemliachestvos occurred precisely at the time when angry and vengeful students could merge into the underground Terrorist Fraction.

The zemliachestvo group that led most directly to the creation of the Fraction was the Circle of the Don and Kuban. As early as 1881–82 the circle, under the leadership of Sergei Peshkerov, had established ties with the Workers' Section of Narodnaia Volia, and within the next few years had begun to share resources and activities with the Party of Social Democrats. Kharitonov and Orlov of the social democrats lived in the same quarters as A. Aleksandrin and Orest Govorukhin of the circle.[27] In fact, Soviet historian V. P. Krikunov concludes that the social democrats and the Circle of the Don and Kuban "overlapped" so closely that they represented "one trend"—the development of Marxism.[28] Despite the personal ties between members of the circle and the Party of Social Democrats, Krikunov overstates his case. The circle also maintained a network of communication with the remnants of Narodnaia Volia and even came to the aid of Boris Orzhikh, the narodovol'tsy terrorist, when he asked for their help. Like the Student Corporation, the Circle of the Don and Kuban sought a comprehensive radical ideology, and its members studied the social-democratic doctrine. For them, the social democrats and narodovol'tsy provided two components — sometimes indistinguishable, sometimes complementary — of a single ideology of revolution.

Until the end of 1885 the circle, like the other zemliachestvo groups, concerned itself primarily with helping its poorest members. Its communal kitchen served as a meeting place for its own members as well as for students from other circles. At the end of 1885, the Circle of the Don and Kuban (now under the leadership of Petr Shevyrev) began to involve itself in more explicitly political activities. Indeed, with a membership of approximately one hundred, the Circle of the Don and Kuban had become one of the most potentially dangerous radical groups in Russia. Its actual political debut, prompted by the government's dismissal of the popular historian V. I. Semevskii, occurred in December 1885. The Ministry of Education had charged that Semevskii violated the spirit of the 1884 Charter by delivering a series of lectures on the development of Russian serfdom which encouraged antigovernment thinking. Under Shevyrev's leadership, the members of the Circle of the Don and Kuban collected signatures for a petition that the student organizer S. Ashetkov had drafted to protest the government's action. Prince V. P. Meshcherskii, who was personally overseeing the government's efforts against "nihilism" at the university, recommended that Ashetkov be arrested; the police promptly complied with this request.[29]

The petition campaign produced more than three hundred signatures, including those of the future Terrorist Fraction leaders Shevyrev, Ul'ianov, and Orest Govorukhin. More important than the number of signatures collected, however, was the spirit of cooperation that developed as various St. Petersburg University circles joined to protest the banning of Semevskii's lectures. Shevyrev used these contacts to organize a Union of Zemliachestvos, formally established in March-April 1886. As the union was an illegal organization, Shevyrev and the other leaders (including Ul'ianov from the Volga Circle, Govorukhin from the Don and Kuban, I. D. Lukashevich from the Polish, S. A. Nikonov, the son of an admiral, from the Tavrida, and M. Novorusskii from the Novgorod) were forced to meet in conspiratorial circumstances. By the end of 1886, the union was operating a small underground printing shop and had prepared the first number of a new student newspaper.[30]

But Shevyrev's goals went beyond this simple unification of

zemliachestvo circles. He hoped to organize all student groups into one broad front which, by legally maintaining a central library and a large mutual-help fund, could serve as a basis for the transition to revolutionary activities. All that was needed was an institution to serve as a legal cover for Shevyrev's student front, and the prestigious Scientific-Literary Society was quickly chosen for this purpose. Founded in early 1882 by leading antirevolutionary students and faculty, the Scientific-Literary Society had acquired a more liberal character under the influence of the literary historian Orest Miller. Nevertheless, the society steered clear of political issues, preferring to concentrate on purely scientific and literary problems. For the radical students, the society had two great advantages — its library of three thousand volumes, and its good reputation; because its members were elected by a committee of faculty and students, the society remained beyond government reproach.[31]

Aleksandr Ul'ianov's extraordinary achievements in the field of zoology (he received a university gold medal in February 1886 for his academic work on a family of worms) won him election to the society in March, and Shevyrev's invitation came only one month later. By October, when Ul'ianov was made a member of the society's council and secretary of its scientific section, a large number of zemliachestvo radicals (including Govorukhin, Lukashevich, Nikonov, Popov, and S. Khlebnikov) had joined the group. The society's membership expanded rapidly, and at the beginning of 1887 more than a third of the organization's 287 members consisted of new recruits.[32] As could have been predicted, a high proportion of the new members were zemliachestvo activists, and their views came to play a role in shaping society policy. Shevyrev and Ul'ianov worked closely with Vasilii Vodovozov, the student leader of the society, and tried to persuade him of the benefits of joining its treasury and library with those of the Union of Zemliachestvos.[33]

During 1886, as the discussions of the society shifted from purely academic issues to general social questions, the police became more and more anxious about its activities. At the same time, the police grew increasingly convinced that there was a real political threat from the still legal Circle of the Don and Kuban. A demonstration at Volkovo Cemetery on 19 February 1886 confirmed their suspicions that the circle was more than a mutual aid society. Organized by Shevyrev and Ul'ianov, the meeting commemorated the twenty-fifth anniversary of the emancipation of the serfs. After brief speeches at the graves of Turgenev, Pisarev, and other heroes, the approximately four hundred students (representing thirteen zemliachestvo circles) marched around the city and dispersed.[34]

Even more serious from the point of view of the police was the 17 November 1886 demonstration commemorating the death of the radical literary critic Nikolai Dobroliubov.[35] When approximately one thousand students gathered at the Volkovo Cemetery to lay wreaths on Dobroliubov's grave, their entry was blocked by a cordon of police. After brief negotiations determined that no speeches would be delivered at the gravesite, thirty students at a time were permitted into the cemetery to place their wreaths. About five hundred students decided then to march to Kazan Cathedral to hold an assembly, but they were stopped and surrounded by a detachment of Cossacks at Ligovskii Canal. St. Petersburg Police Chief Gresser arrived at the scene and after two hours of questioning released most of the students. But close to forty were arrested and exiled to their provincial homes, among them three men who later became well-known Marxists: M. I. Tugan-Baranovskii, M. Mandel'shtam, and Eduard Abramovich. The zemliachestvo circles immediately published a leaflet entitled "To Society," in which the author, undoubtedly Ul'ianov, condemned police interference and political repression. "To Society" also made a plea to members of the Russian intelligentsia to remember their revolutionary forebears — and to emulate them.

The Terrorist Fraction

The police interference in the demonstration of November 1886 and the Ministry of Education's suppression of the zemliachestvo movement in December 1886 and January 1887 gave the impetus to Shevyrev and the Circle of the Don and Kuban to begin preparations for more serious political activities. Up to that time regicide had been mentioned only in passing by some circle members. In the winter of 1886–87, however, several radical student groups in St. Petersburg independently came to the same conclusion; the only political activity that made any sense was the assassination of the tsar, followed by the murder of his chief officials — Tolstoi, Pobedonostsev, Katkov, and Prince Vladimir Aleksandrovich. The St. Petersburg students were not alone in this assessment. From Kharkov and Moscow in January 1887 came programs that complained about the "lack of leadership and organization," about too much time spent on trying to develop common theoretical programs. The only viable means of struggle, the Moscow "narodovol'tsy terrorists" concluded, was assassination.[36]

Vasilii Osipanov, a Kazan student who had been involved in narodovol'tsy activites since 1882, had moved to St. Petersburg in 1886 with the intention of killing the tsar singlehandedly.[37] Pakhomii Andreiushkin of the Circle of the Don and Kuban similarly decided that he would shoot the tsar.[38] But in December 1886 Shevyrev managed to convince them both to be patient and wait for him to organize a conspiracy that had a good chance of succeeding. Shevyrev's closest fellow conspirator was the Vilna zemliachestvo student Iosif Lukashevich. Lukashevich had enrolled at St. Petersburg University in the fall of 1883 and participated in Polish self-education circles during 1884–85. He searched out narodovol'tsy circles but could find none that appealed to him. Meeting Shevyrev at the Scientific-Literary Society, he worked with him in the zemliachestvo organization and agreed to prepare explosives for the growing conspiracy. By mid-December the conspiracy had taken the name Terrorist Fraction of Narodnaia Volia, and by the first of January the details of the plot had been worked out. Soviet accounts contend that Aleksandr Ul'ianov was the unchallenged leader of the conspiracy, but in fact the more prominent leader was Petr Shevyrev. Despite his somewhat "choleric" appearance and generally poor health, Shevyrev was an "energetic, enterprising, and talented organizer."[39] His activities, the police wrote, "run like a red thread throughout this entire affair."[40] It was Shevyrev who recruited Vasilii Generalov of the Don and Kuban Circle to join Osipanov and Andreiushkin as one of the bomb-throwers. Similarly, Shevyrev convinced Mikhail Kancher, Petr Gorkun, and Stepan Volokhov, all from the circle, to serve as the spotters. Preparation of the Terrorist Fraction's program was left to Ul'ianov and Govorukhin. Shevyrev was careful to keep the conspirators from knowing each other's roles until the last moment: Lukashevich, who was preparing the explosives, did not know of Andreiushkin's or Generalov's participation; Ul'ianov and Generalov knew nothing of Ospinov's role in the plot.

Ul'ianov was only twenty at the time of the conspiracy but his "erudition and the broadness of his world view" had already earned him considerable respect among his fellow students.[41] By all accounts he was a talented and gifted student, easy to get along with and altruistic.[42] It was said that Ul'ianov even pawned the gold medal he had won for his research to provide funds for the cause. Lukashevich, who had worked with Ul'ianov for four years in the university, characterized his student politics as a blend of narodovol'tsy and social-democratic thinking; he "highly valued political freedom as a blessing in and of itself" as well as a means to promote "the struggle of the working people for a better future."[43]

Given the contradictory evidence of memoir sources, it is difficult to establish the pattern of Ul'ianov's ideological develpment. Govorukhin claims that Ul'ianov was a fervent admirer of Marx, a young man "entranced by Marxist dialectics."[44] According to him Ul'ianov had fully accepted Blagoev's social-democratic teachings in

1883–84 and by late 1886 had read Marx's *Das Kapital* and Plekhanov's *Our Differences*, as well as *Socialism and the Political Struggle*. Both Khlebnikov and Nikonov, however, remember Ul'ianov as a follower of Narodnaia Volia.[45] It is probably most accurate to conclude that Ul'ianov's ideology was a blend of narodovol'tsy and Marxist thought; for him (as for several members of the Terrorist Fraction) the two traditions were complementary, sometimes even indistinguishable world views. One of the reasons why these two ideologies could be so easily reconciled in Ul'ianov's time was that the hostility between social democrats and narodovol'tsy in emigration barely touched the internal movement. Even when disagreements arose within the domestic movement, the arguments, as Smirnov recalled, "had the most comradely character."[46] Generally, the mania for theoretical purity, so prevalent in the works of the younger V. I. Ul'ianov fifteen years later, was not characteristic of the revolutionary movement in the late 1880s.

Still, Ul'ianov and Govorukhin confronted a real challenge in drafting a program for the Terrorist Fraction, and Ul'ianov complicated the task by attempting to unify all of the various revolutionary circles under one umbrella program. Within the Terrorist Fraction alone, ideological leanings were so diverse as to seem irreconcilable, ranging from what one observer called "the purest narodovol'tsy to the most extreme social democrats."[47] Andreiushkin, at the narodovol'tsy end of the spectrum, expressed contempt for the social democrats and advocated "relentless terror."[48] Nikonov, who also had strong terrorist sympathies, had been a member of Narodnaia Volia groups until Shevyrev recruited him to the new group in the spring of 1886. Although he read and appreciated Marx, Nikonov continued to think of himself as a narodovolets.[49] For another member, Generalov, terrorism became an obsession that ruled out his earlier devotion to propagandizing socialist ideas among the working class.[50] The leader of the Vilna associates of the Fraction, Isaak Dembo, likewise belonged to the narodovol'tsy camp. For Dembo, the program of the Party of Social Democrats was "inimical to the cause of revolution."[51]

At the other end of the ideological spectrum were Govorukhin and Lukashevich. "It was clear to us," Lukashevich wrote, "that capitalism would develop in Russia, that a capitalist structure represented a step forward . . . and that soon the revolutionary movement would take on a more peaceful social-democratic character."[52] Shevyrev, who stood closer to the center of the spectrum, spoke of the necessity of a terrorist plot but expressed an interest in the eventual participation of workers in the Fraction's activities. Another view was represented by Bronislaw Pilsudski, who echoed the program of the Polish Marxist Proletariat in his call for the formation of a social-revolutionary party which would join the international socialist movement.[53]

The program that Ul'ianov coauthored provides an explanation for the Terrorist Fraction's ideological diversity: the group had to weigh two concerns — its long-term goals and its short-term tactics. The Terrorist Fraction wanted "to devote its primary forces to organizing and teaching the working class, and preparing them for their coming social role," but, for the moment, terror was the necessary means to this end. Ul'ianov recognized that common goals already existed to unify the various groups that constituted the revolutionary movement and stated in his program that the Terrorist Fraction's differences with the social democrats "seem to us very insignificant *and only theoretical.*" Disunity in the revolutionary movement had persisted because Narodnaia Volia had failed to offer the "scientific" explanations that revolutionary circles had longed for. By correcting these shortcomings, Ul'ianov believed that the Terrorist Fraction would be able to eliminate disagreements over revolutionary principles. Once principles had been agreed upon, terrorist actions could be carried out to infuse the revolutionary movement with a new, positive spirit. "We are all socialists," Ul'ianov declared at the outset of his program. By this he meant that each of the revolutionary groups hoped to establish a society in which "the social organization of labor provides the workers with the opportunity to use all their products and in which the economic independence of the individual guarantees his freedom in all relations."

This classic narodovol'tsy formulation of the socialist future was complemented in the Fraction's program by the equally classic social-democratic analysis of the historical process — economic advancement inevitably leads to society's adoption of a socialist structure of organization. In the view of the Fraction, indeed in the programs of almost all narodovol'tsy groups in the late 1880s, socialism was the necessary result of class conflicts in a capitalist society. The program conceded that the inevitability of a transition from capitalism to socialism did not rule out the possibility of skipping the capitalist phase of development altogether, but such a direct transition could not occur until the working class had gained in strength and consciousness. Only through the strengthening of the working class could changes in the relations of social forces in Russia be brought about. As for the economic transformation of Russia — that was to be promoted by the political struggle.

Ul'ianov's program reflected his belief in general laws of history, but he made sure to apply these laws to the specific social and political conditions of his own society. Of the social groups in late nineteenth-century Russia, he singled out the peasantry as being the most important for the ultimate development of socialism. Despite the emergence of a "petite bourgeoisie" in its ranks, the peasantry clung to its traditional principles of democracy and socialism. Ul'ianov believed that it was realistic and appropriate "to hope for the direct transition of the peasant economy to the socialist," because the communal organization of rural Russia had inclined the peasantry "toward collective labor." Like the programs of later social democrats, the Terrorist Fraction's program called for the eventual nationalization of the land. But the final goal was classically populist, calling for the independence of the commune as an economic and administrative unit. The Terrorist Fraction recognized what the narodovol'tsy had claimed for a long time: the peasants were the most important social force in the country and would play the dominant role in the eventual social revolution, but for the moment they were of little political consequence.

Of greater political significance was the working class. In many ways the Terrorist Fraction's program echoed the faith that the Workers' Section expressed in the revolutionary role of Russian labor. Not only was the working class capable of thoroughly understanding socialist ideas; it was also the group that could best carry these ideas to the peasantry. Through their struggle for economic improvements, the urban workers would exert "the decisive influence" in bringing the revolution to its final stages — the transformation of Russia's social structure. But the working class also had an important role to play in the present. Unlike the peasantry, workers showed an interest in the political struggle and could be recruited for support in political activities. Consequently, the crucial immediate task of the Fraction was to organize the active ranks of the working class.

The program's treatment of the role of the intelligentsia in the revolutionary process was a typical compromise between traditional narodovol'tsy and social-democratic views. Lacking a class character, the Russian intelligentsia could not play an independent role in the social-revolutionary struggle, but it could assume leadership in the political struggle. By refusing to allow the intelligentsia to express its political opposition legally, the government had driven this group to take a terrorist position. That the political struggle must take the form of terrorism was therefore a conclusion based on an "objective" and "scientific" analysis of contemporary Russia's economic and social conditions.

According to its program, then, the Terrorist Fraction had adopted the terrorist struggle out of frustration — a feeling that could be appeased if the government were to grant basic political rights. Perhaps the strongest message of the Terrorist Fraction was its call for intelligentsia radicals all over Russia to embark on terrorist deeds wherever and whenever they could contribute to the general cause of disorganizing the government. Terrorism was not to be a means of seizing power, as it was for the Executive Committee of Narodnaia Volia. Instead, it was to be a way of forcing the government into political reform. But like the program of the Bogoraz-Orzhikh group, Ul'ianov also provided a second rationale for the adoption of terror: by providing continuous proof (through the "systematic" killing of officials) of ongoing political struggle, it was hoped that terror would raise "the revolutionary spirit of the people."[54]

It would be a mistake to make too much out of the Terrorist Fraction's program. No doubt Rudevich was correct when he wrote Lavrov (fall 1887) that the actual participants in the assassination attempt, the bomb-throwers and the spotters, cared little for ideology and were motivated simply by "extreme hatred" for the government, typical of many Russian students.[55] Yet Rudevich added that there were four or five serious socialists in the group — among them Ul'ianov, Govorukhin, and Shevyrev. Their thinking and their program reflected the basic compatibility of narodovol'tsy and social-democratic ideologies during the 1880s. If some radicals found the social democracy of Plekhanov too passive and insufficiently attuned to the uniqueness of Russian historical and social development, others found the narodovol'tsy program too wedded to principles of terror, seizure of power, and conspiracy, and oblivious to the growing political importance of the working class and of the science of revolutionary theory. The attempt by the Terrorist Fraction to unite these two radical world views under a single program mirrored the general course of ideological developments in the 1880s: a search for the right combination of the Russian revolutionary tradition, represented by Narodnaia Volia, and the "scientific" revolutionary theory of social democracy.

1 March 1887

Shevyrev recruited his Terrorist Fraction comrades Lukashevich and Govorukhin to help elaborate the assassination plot. As the central group of the Fraction, the three men worked feverishly to transform their dreams of regicide into a detailed plan of action. Since Shevyrev's instinctive caution militated against involving other groups in the conspiratorial plans, he was not terribly disappointed when Narodnaia Volia failed to give official sanction to the plot. Even though the Fraction had decided by acclamation to "join" Narodnaia Volia, the narodovol'tsy made no effort to rally behind Shevyrev's scheme. By the beginning of January 1887, the central group realized that it did not have the resources to carry out its plans alone and turned for support to the Vilna narodovol'tsy circle, a well-organized group composed primarily of Jews and Poles. The Vilna group more than obliged, providing the conspirators with nearly all the materials they needed to stage their plot.[56] For technical assistance, the central group again turned to Ul'ianov, and it was not long before the young zoologist mastered the complex art of preparing explosives.

In mid-January Shevyrev sent Mikhail Kancher to Vilna to pick up an order of chemicals for the explosives, and after speaking with the Vilna leaders Dembo, Boleslaw Pilsudski, and Gnatovskii, Kancher spent the night at Joseph Pilsudski's apartment. Having obtained a suitcase full of chemicals, a pistol, and 110 rubles, Kancher wired Ul'ianov's sister Anna that he was taking the train back to St. Petersburg the next day. Ul'ianov met Kancher at the station and took the explosives to Generalov's apartment. Finding that these were not the correct materials, he and Lukashevich dumped them into the Neva, and sent Kancher back to Vilna for a new shipment.[57] When he returned with proper chemicals, Ul'ianov set up a laboratory at a dacha in Pargolovo, outside St. Petersburg. Lukashevich, who had already explained to Ul'ianov the process of turning nitroglycerine into dynamite and had designed the bombs, left the final work to him and remained in St. Petersburg to supervise the plot. Ul'ianov worked furiously on the explosives, knowing that the tsar planned to leave St. Petersburg on March 28 for the holidays.

Finishing his job on February 14, Ul'ianov concealed the bombs and the laboratory and returned to St. Petersburg. In the meantime, Shevyrev's health had deteriorated. He was about to leave St. Petersburg for a cure in the Crimea, but first wanted to be sure that the plot was organized to the last detail. Shevyrev therefore invited Ul'ianov to take his place in the central group and introduced him to Osipanov, the leader of the bomb-throwers. Simultaneously, Shevyrev arranged for Petr Gorkun and Stepan Volokhov to join Kancher as spotters. Finally, he made arrangements with the Vilna circle to smuggle Govorukhin and Nikolai Rudevich out of Russia; neither was crucial to the implementation of the plot, and both had long radical histories that made them susceptible to police surveillance.[58] With his work done, Shevyrev designated Lukashevich as his successor and left for the Crimea on February 17.

On February 20 Ul'ianov (who from this point on assumed the most active role in the plot) called a meeting of the participants at Kancher's apartment. He explained in detail to Osipanov, Andreiushkin, and Generalov the construction of their bombs and read to them the program of the Terrorist Fraction. One bomb was concealed in a hollowed-out book (ironically enough, the *Digest of Laws*) in keeping with Lukashevich's design, while the others were contained in easily concealed cylindrical tubes. Ul'ianov demonstrated how to activate a bomb, explaining that on the day of the plot it would be Kancher's responsibility to be sure that the bombs had been activated before the group went out on the street. At a second meeting at Kancher's on the evening of February 25, the details of the plot were reviewed. The tsar was expected to go to St. Isaac's Cathedral on the following day. At eleven in the morning the spotters and the bomb-throwers would scatter on Nevskii Prospect between the Public Library and the Admiralty, there awaiting the tsar's carriage. The signal for his approach would be a handkerchief raised to the nose. Once again Ul'ianov went over the construction of the bombs and took Osipanov aside to read him the program of Narodnaia Volia so that he could prepare himself for the possibility of an appearance in court.[59]

On February 26, as planned, the six terrorists roamed Nevskii between eleven and two in the afternoon, but the tsar's procession never appeared. On February 28 the terrorists again walked through the crowds futilely searching for the tsar. Though advised by his comrades to leave, Lukashevich stayed in Petersburg in case the first group failed. Explosive bombs had already been constructed and hidden at Pargolovo for a second group, which Shevyrev had determined would be composed of workers. Meanwhile, Ul'ianov worked with Bronislaw Pilsudski on the printing of the Fraction's program.

On March 1 the bomb-throwers and the spotters once again went out to Nevskii Prospect to await their target, this time bolstered by rumors that the tsar was sure to pass in his carriage. As soon as they began mingling with the crowds, they were seized by the police. Although still unaware of the assassination plot, the police had intercepted a letter from Andreiushkin to a Kharkov narodovolets and while following the former they picked up the trail of Osipanov.[60] Osipanov's suspicious behavior on that day prompted the police to bring him in with his friends. When Osipanov was hauled into the office of the chief of police for questioning, he threw the bomb, still concealed in the book, at the official, but it did not explode. Apparently Kancher had not appeared at the rendezvous point on time, and Osipanov, who was not well versed in the technology of bombs, had made a mistake when he tried to activate the weapon.[61] Only at this point did the police realize that they had stumbled on a terrorist plot, whereupon they quickly arrested the other conspirators. On the same day, police agents seized Ul'ianov, who was on his way to Generalov's apartment. Bronislaw Pilsudski and Lukashevich were apprehended on the evening of the third and the police finally caught up with Shevyrev in Yalta on March 7 and transported him back to

Petersburg. Unfortunately for the Fraction, Kancher told the police everything he knew, even accompanying police agents to Vilna, pointing out where he had gotten the explosives and where he had stayed.[62]

By March 12 the new director of the Department of Police, P. N. Durnovo, had arrested all the primary conspirators and submitted his summary report to Tolstoi. The report suggested that the terrorists be tried by the Senate rather than by a military tribunal — both alternatives were permissible under the law. Durnovo preferred the Senate because the views of its chief justice, Senator P. A. Dreier, insured that "correct and harsh decisions" would be made concerning the accused.[63] On April 15, with the concurrence of Tolstoi, the Senate met behind closed doors to try the fifteen conspirators. The prosecution's argument was straightforward: because the plot could have resulted in the death of the tsar, anyone who was even peripherally involved should be sentenced to hang.

The conspirators had agreed beforehand that Aleksandr Ul'ianov should speak for all if their plot was uncovered by the authorities. Lukashevich, the only other logical choice because of his thorough knowledge of the revolutionary movement's history, was a Pole, and the group did not want him to be the focus of attention.[64] Ul'ianov's speech at the trial, one observer wrote, "created an extraordinarily strong impression."[65] There can be no doubt that it was a careful, reasoned, and broad-ranging defense of terrorism. The speaker's constant references to the "scientific-objective" basis of the intelligentsia's use of terrorism forced the chair to interrupt him several times, demanding that he stick to the details of the plot. From Ul'ianov's confessions to the police and his speech at the trial, it is apparent that he attempted to take most of the blame for the conspiracy. Chief Prosecutor Nekliudov even stated at the trial that "Ul'ianov is probably also accepting guilt for what he did not do."[66] Although Nekliudov soon realized that Shevyrev (not Ul'ianov) "was the heart of the evil deed, its originator and its leader," Ul'ianov was able to convince his listeners that he, rather than Lukashevich, organized the construction of the bombs.[67] Lukashevich later recalled this fact with some remorse, explaining that he had remained silent at the trial only because Ul'ianov had whispered to him to admit nothing, to let all guilt fall on his, Ul'ianov's, shoulders.[68]

During Ul'ianov's trial and imprisonment his mother sent numerous petitions to the tsar and to Tolstoi begging for clemency. The widowed and impoverished Mariia Ul'ianova promised that if the tsar would pardon and release Aleksandr, she would turn him over to the judicial authorities and be a witness against him if he ever committed the least crime.[69] Aleksandr resisted his mother's advice to petition for a pardon until shortly before his hanging, when he realized just how frail her health was. His curt petition did ask for a pardon, but coupled it with an admission that he had no "moral basis or right" to be forgiven for his actions.[70] Although Ul'ianov's sentence was not changed, Tolstoi at last allowed Mariia Ul'ianova to visit her son in prison. The minister was still convinced that the Terrorist Fraction was a front for Narodnaia Volia, and he hoped that Ul'ianov's final words with his mother would reveal the crucial link between the two groups. After failing to learn of any new underground connections, Tolstoi showed clemency to Ul'ianov's sister Anna, exiled because of her minor involvement in the plot, and sent her home to Kazan under police surveillance ("in view of the poverty of the mother").[71]

Accepting Nekliudov's recommendation, the Senate on April 25 condemned all fifteen Terrorists Fraction defendants to death. The sentences of the spotters Kancher, Gorkun, and Volokhov were reduced by imperial clemency to life at hard labor, and those of Novorusskii and Lukashevich were also commuted to life imprisonment. Bronislaw Pilsudski and Mariia Anan'ina (who along with Novorusskii had arranged for the Pargolovo laboratory), had their sentences altered to twenty years at hard labor.[72] The bomb-throwers Generalov, Andreiushkin, and Osipanov were the first members of the conspiracy to die by hanging on 8 May 1887. According to Tolstoi's official report, the three revolutionaries shouted "Long live Narodnaia Volia!" from their places on the scaffold; Ul'ianov and Shevyrev silently followed their comrades to the gallows.[73]

During the investigation and trial of the Terrorist Fraction, the police launched a roundup of all radical activists in the capital as well as in Vilna and Kharkov. Altogether, some fifty students (including Joseph Pilsudski) were exiled by administrative order to Siberia.[74] Dembo and Gnatovskii from Vilna managed to follow Govorukhin and Rudevich to freedom in Switzerland. The Kharkov narodovol'tsy, a group not even involved in the plot, were not so lucky. During the spring of 1887 the police seized M. A. Ufliand, S. M. Ratin, and V. P. Brazhnikov.[75] In St. Petersburg the police conducted hundreds of searches of student apartments. The Scientific-Literary Society was banned and Orest Miller was relieved of his teaching post. Eventually, over two hundred students from various institutions of higher learning (most of whom had nothing to do with the plot) were expelled from St. Petersburg and exiled to their homes.[76] The Circle of the Don and Kuban was completely destroyed by these arrests. Also, the Party of Social Democrats, led in early 1887 by Petr Latyshev, was eliminated in the aftermath of the assassination attempt because

Tolstoi had concluded that the ties between them and the Terrorist Fraction were more than personal.

The Aftermath of March 1

Alexander III officially commended the police for their actions in preventing the assassination. Still, he and his officials were shocked and terrified that the conspiracy had developed as far as it had. Senator N. A. Khvostov expressed the government's trepidations when he wrote that the history of the Terrorist Fraction proved that the investigative department left "much to be desired."[77] Shortly after the plot was uncovered, Deputy Minister Orzhevskii, responsible for the gendarmes, was forced to resign because of his department's alleged lack of vigilance.[78] Rumors circulated around the capital that this was only the first of a series of bombing attempts. The police, appalled that so few "nihilists" could have organized a plot of such proportions in so short a time, drew their own conclusions from the nearly successful assassination plot. The only way to prevent an assassination attempt from being carried out in the future was to subject each piece of intercepted correspondence to thorough investigation; even punctuation marks were to be analyzed under the microscope.[79] Ironically, the reaction of Petr Lavrov was quite similar to that of the police. From his headquarters in Switzerland, he expressed surprise that such a major assassination attempt could have been organized by such a motley group as the Terrorist Fraction.[80]

The rector of St. Petersburg University, I. E. Andreevskii, gathered students and professors in the university auditorium on March 6 and read them his address to Alexander III—an address that expressed mortification at the assassination attempt and begged the tsar for forgiveness. That St. Petersburg students were capable of participating in such "hellish thoughts and criminal society" was an unbearable black mark on the university's good name, but the institution would atone for its sins by demonstrating to the tsar its "loyal obedience and passionate love." The tsar commented in the margins of the address that he hoped this loyalty would manifest itself "not only on paper, but in reality" and would be demonstrated by a "harsh countenance" against those students who harbored "illegal thoughts."[81]

The tsar's skepticism was well founded. In a March 13 report to Tolstoi, the Department of Police stated that not all students shared Andreevskii's sentiments. "The students have still not settled down," the police wrote, and as examples cited the beating of a pro-government student and the vandalizing of the rector's office by a small group of radical students.[82] More serious in the government's eyes were the secret meetings at which students expressed support for their imprisoned comrades. One group, under the name of The Union of United St. Petersburg Students, issued a proclamation on 7 March 1887 to counteract the rector's speech. The hectographed proclamation, sent by post to various university centers in the empire, stated that "the best part of the students" protested against the address to the tsar, but they protested quietly because the government threatened to remove the "liberal" rector if any sympathy for the first of March conspirators was detected. Nevertheless the members of the union wanted to inform Russian society that they had not and would not stray from the traditions of revolution. They would neither renounce nor criticize their comrades, whose attempt to assassinate the tsar had represented the highest plane of morality. Instead, they pledged themselves to carry on the goals of their "brothers of the heart," the "realization of truth in its social forms," and teach others "how necessary it is to love and to struggle."[83]

In early April 1887 the police had received information that members of the union were preparing a program for their own organization; in early May, they found a proclamation protesting the sentences of the Terrorist Fraction. Aleksei Pavlovskii, Evgenii Iakovenko, and Boleslav Motts, all St. Petersburg University students, constituted the central circle of this fledgling organization.[84] The penciled draft of the proclamation found by the police began, "Friends, yesterday the 8th of May, the government murdered five more of our comrades," and continued by denouncing the government's action as "idiocy" and "perfidy," urging all students who shared the "deeply moral feeling of sacred hate for the despicable enemy" to act quickly. "To the cause! We cannot waste any time; otherwise, all honest people will be massacred."[85]

A draft of the union's program, formulated during a May 12 meeting on Krestovskii Island, offered a more sober analysis of the events of March 1. With the founding of the Terrorist Fraction, it was argued, a new phase in the history of Narodnaia Volia had begun. The assassination attempt was the first terrorist act to be carried out without the official authorization of the Executive Committee, and it was an act that signified the weakness of Narodnaia Volia. Not only had the strength of Narodnaia Volia diminished; the group was actually struggling for its very existence. Its hegemony in the revolutionary movement had been shaken by the entrance of a new, more "scientific" revolutionary group, a group that had learned how to use the terrorist victories won by Narodnaia Volia in the past to promote a revolutionary future. In short, the organization of Narodnaia Volia had disappeared, yet its spirit still permeated the ranks of the revolutionary movement.[86]

The union was unable to accomplish much more than hold a few meetings and draft a program and a proclamation; the police had infiltrated the group as early as the middle of March. Convinced (though lacking proof), that the union was tied to the central Narodnaia Volia organization, the authorities arrested its members and exiled them to Siberia.

The short, two-month history of the union reaffirms our general conclusions about the St. Petersburg student movement between 1883 and 1887. First of all, there was little difference between the narodovol'tsy and social-democratic radicals. A draft program for Russian social democrats, found among the union's papers, even called for terrorist actions, among other tactics, to "overthrow absolutism in Russia."[87] Second, though the peasantry was destined to play the decisive role in the social revolution, for the moment the revolutionary vanguard would consist of a decentralized "union of the proletariat and the intelligentsia."[88] Finally, terrorism was by no means a discredited form of struggle. Instead, the youthful St. Petersburg radicals intended to update terrorism by placing it in a more "scientific" context and combining it with peaceful means of political struggle. The goal, no doubt difficult to achieve, was to form a broad political movement under the banner of liberation, to create an ideology and organization that would unite radical Russia.

Social Democracy in St. Petersburg and Moscow, 1889–1893

7

The arrests following the destruction of the Terrorist Fraction in the spring of 1887 also engulfed the vestiges of the Party of Social Democrats, founded by Kharitonov and Blagoev in 1883, and the Society of St. Petersburg Craftsmen, led by Tochiskii. After the spring of 1888, the only veterans of the social-democratic movement who remained at liberty inside Russia were the leaders of the workers' circles that had been associated with the society: among them were I. I. Timofeev, K. M. Norinskii, G. Mefodiev, V. A. Shelgunov, and E. A. Afanas'ev-Klimanov. These propagandists and others like them met in small circles, and, much as they had done during the Tochiskii era, carried out oral propaganda urging their fellow workers to join in labor associations for the betterment of their working lives. The politics of these labor leaders varied widely; among them were narodovol'tsy, social democrats, incipient trade unionists, and some who combined all three elements in various ways. Their attitude towards the intelligentsia also covered the full spectrum from complete distrust to deep attachment.

Between 1887 and 1889, the views of labor leaders on cooperation with the intelligentsia were of little consequence – in the wake of the Terrorist Fraction arrests, no intelligentsia propagandists could be found for the workers' circles, some of which may have desired the funds and the literature that association with the intelligentsia sometimes brought. But this situation changed rapidly at the end of the eighties and the beginning of the nineties as large numbers of Petersburg students from the technical institutes, organized initially in small, politically innocuous self-education circles, sought out workers' groups and established a network of contacts which could legitimately be called a social-democratic movement.

Much like their contemporaries in St. Petersburg, the Moscow self-education groups at the technical schools and the university confronted the ideas of Marx and the realities of the Russian labor movement in 1888–1890. There were differences between the social-democratic movements in the two cities, however, perhaps the most striking being the absence of worker involvement in Moscow. In St. Petersburg experienced propagandists from the ranks of the workers themselves, most of whom were *slesari* (skilled metal workers and machinists) in the capital's large factories, formed the Central Workers' Circle and provided the force behind the Workers' Union. These worker-propagandists were primarily responsible for forging the links with intelligentsia social democrats. The workers of Moscow were poorer, less literate, more often employed in the textile industry, and tied more closely to the countryside than their fellows in St. Petersburg; they neither sought help from the intelligentsia nor, as far as we know, formed their own social-democratic organizations. Instead, the Moscow social democrats turned to the workers in Tula, Russia's arms and ammunition factory center 110 miles south of Moscow. But even the machinist-dominated Tula workers' circles were led by two banished St. Petersburg Workers' Union veterans, Gavril Mefodiev and N. N. Rudelev.

In both Moscow and Petersburg Polish activists contributed their knowledge of social-democratic theory and practice to the developing Russian movement. In Petersburg, the involvement of individual Polish students aided the growth and sophistication of the movement; in Moscow, the history of social democracy in this period cannot be understood without considering the direct influence of Warsaw-based Marxist groups. Even many of the Russian students who led the Moscow social democrats received their first radical training in the Kingdom of Poland while attending the Novo-Aleksandriisk Institute for Agronomy in Pulawy (near Lublin). To be sure, Plekhanov and the Emancipation of Labor group contributed to the development of social democracy in both cities but this influence was much more direct in Moscow than in St. Petersburg, and much less significant in either case than Soviet historians claim.

The scholar must be grateful to the tsarist authorities for the fact that the development of Moscow social democracy (1889–1892) is perhaps the best-documented aspect of the revolutionary movement between 1881 and 1894. In May 1891 the police first picked up the trail of Mikhail Egupov, one of the main organizers of the new group. Rather than arrest Egupov immediately, the authorities monitored his every move, and even succeeded in planting an agent, Mikhail Petrov, as his Moscow roommate. Since Egupov related his peripatetic activities in detail to Petrov, agents were able to remain close on his heels during his trips outside the city. After he was finally arrested on 13 April 1892, Egupov himself provided a detailed account for posterity. Desperately anxious to save himself and continue his education, he gave the police a full description of his activities and those of every of every radical he knew.[1] Minister of Justice N. V. Murav'ev rightly questioned the veracity of some of Egupov's testimony, but much of it is substantiated by secret police reports.[2] The sum of these revelations provides the kind of detailed and nonpartisan information on the origins of Moscow social democracy that we must distill from memoirs published in the Soviet Union in the 1920s and 1930s when trying to reconstruct the parallel movement in St. Petersburg. On the other hand, because St. Petersburg was so central to the development of the Union of Struggle (1895–96) and the eventual formation of the Russian Social-Democratic party (1898), the origins of its social-democratic movement have been the subject of much more concerted historical investigation.[3]

Petersburg Technologists

There is no evidence of any continuity between the Petersburg students who carried out social-democratic propaganda under the aegis of the Party of Social Democrats and those who, in early 1887, formed circles to contact and educate workers. Certainly, part of the reason for a lack of continuity is that the former group consisted primarily of St. Petersburg University students, whereas the latter came almost exclusively from the several technical schools in the city, especially from the St. Petersburg Technological Institute. After the events of 1 March 1887, university students dropped out of the movement almost entirely; the government declared war on the university, even closing it altogether for a period in the fall of 1887. The police reacted quickly and mercilessly to the least sign of political activities in the ranks of university students. Despite a long history of involvement in the revolutionary movement, the students of the Technological Institute were considered less dangerous, and the police treated the social-democratic circles that formed among them in early 1887 as by far the lesser evil in comparison to the narodovol'tsy activities of the university students.

That Technological Institute students became so heavily involved in the social-democratic movement at the end of the 1880s can be attributed to other factors besides the relative tolerance of the authorities. Perhaps most important, the institute attracted a large number of Poles (almost 25 percent of its student body), and they, more than any other group, gave the impetus to the St. Petersburg social-democratic movement in this period.[4] Poles were an embattled minority in the 1880s, subjected to intensifying discrimination by the government of Alexander III and thus generally hostile to the autocratic system. Avoiding Warsaw University, which they saw as an instrument of Russianization, and facing quotas at other Russian universities, the young Poles hoped to gain access to good positions in industry and government by acquiring a technical education. But two important barriers stood in the way of advancement of the Polish technologists: the increasingly virulent nationalism expressed by Alexander III and his advisors made careers in the bureaucracy difficult for Poles, and the general depression that engulfed the Russian economy in the 1880s made jobs in industry hard to get and far from attractive. In addition, there was a tradition of Polish social-democratic groups at the Technological Institute, where as early as 1878 Poles had formed circles that read Marx and advocated the building of a workers' party.[5] Although many moved their efforts to the Kingdom of Poland and eventually established the Marxist party Proletariat, the work continued with other Polish students at the Institute, who received social-democratic literature from the Warsaw-based party and continued to dream of an empire-wide workers' revolutionary movement. They were able to stay up-to-date in the latest Marxist literature and ideas, and were aware that in Warsaw revolutionary groups had succeeded in tying their aspirations to those of the workers.

The inclination of Technological Institute students toward the social-democratic movement also derived from the Institute's educational program. Trained to be engineers, mechanics, and designers of a new Russia, these students from all backgrounds generally felt little attachment to the populist remnants in the narodovol'tsy platform. Instead, Marx's analysis of the growth of capitalism, which, in the minds of a majority of the students, would lead to the inexorable dominance of their new world over the old, held their undivided attention, much as it would most of educated Russian society by the mid-1890s. In addition, Technological Institute students, unlike those in other institutions of higher learning, had direct ties to the working class. Sometimes they worked part-time in the machine shops of the capital or dropped out of school to occupy lower management positions in the factories; on the whole they knew and understood the life of Russian labor much better than did the university students. They felt at ease and acted naturally among workers in the factories, and as a rule their contacts with workers were less laden with the mutual suspicions and antagonisms that characterized earlier contacts between workers and members of the intelligentsia.

At the end of 1887 and the beginning of 1888, a small circle of technologists, led by the institute's Gury Pietrowski, began to seek contact with workers' circles at the giant Putilov mechanized works. Among the circle's leaders were the Poles Boleslaw Lelewel, Gabriel Rodziewicz, and Waclaw Cywinski. Rodziewicz had been a student at the Military Medical Academy and had carried out agitation among Petersburg workers with members of Vera Gurari's narodovol'tsy circle. Cywinski and Lelewel were students at the Technological Institute. The circle quickly absorbed a number of other Polish and Russian students interested in propaganda among the working class: Jozef Buraczewski, Czeslaw Bankowski, Waclaw Iwanicki, Vasilii Ivanov, Antoni Kosinski, and Anatolii Perfil'ev. Petr Golubev from the Mining Institute joined the circle as did Julja Rodziewicz, Gabriel's wife, who had participated in the narodovol'tsy-oriented Revolutionary Cadres at the Bestuzhev Women's School.[6]

There were no rules for the group, nor was there any kind of program. They called themselves "social democrats" only to distinguish themselves from the narodovol'tsy.[7] As the narodovol'tsy leader Nionila Istomina reported to the police, the new circle was exclusively concerned with "the peaceful propaganda of socialist ideas, primarily among workers."[8] Istomina, who had known and worked with both Gabriel and Julja Rodziewicz, further indicated that the new social-democratic circle severed all contact and common activities with the narodovol'tsy by the winter of 1888–89.

The student circle therefore served primarily as a loosely knit association of propagandists among Petersburg workers, sharing materials and experiences with their circle confederates. About two-thirds of them were Poles, and initially they carried out their propaganda primarily among Polish workers in the city.[9] Lelewel did visit a group of mechanics at the Baltic ship and machine building works, where he met and worked with I. I. Timofeev, an associate of the St. Petersburg Craftsmen. In the fall of 1888, Lelewel also attended meetings of workers at the Obukhovskii factory. Gabriel Rodziewicz propagandized among workers at the harbor, while Vasilii Ivanov and Petr Golubev continued Pietrowski's efforts at the Putilov works. Especially effective among the Putilov workers was Buraczewski, who convinced the workers to establish a small strike fund.[10] From the material found by the police on the Rodziewiczes, it is clear that the goals of the propagandists were very modest. They separated "prepared" workers from the "unprepared" and attempted to introduce appropriate subjects for each. They collected information on industrial accidents, workers' salaries, employer-worker relations, and workers' insurance, attempting to compare the situation in Russia with that in Western Europe.[11]

In the fall of 1889, three additional students from the Technological Institute joined the circle—Mikhail Brusnev, Vasilii Golubev, and Leonid Krasin, all of whom had already engaged in some form of propaganda among the workers and were self-proclaimed social democrats. Brusnev had been watched by the police since 1886 for "taking part in secret meetings, propaganda among workers, and student disturbances."[12] The initial successes of the student circle were halted by arrests in the spring of 1890. Despite their efforts to avoid police harassment by ceasing any contact with the narodovol'tsy, it was too late for the Rodziewiczes. Because of their earlier collaboration with Istomina's circle, they were seized by the police. In addition, many Technological Institute students were exiled from the city because of disturbances at the institute. Altogether, according to Vasilii Golubev, only about twenty social-democratic students remained from an original complement of fifty to sixty.[13] Pietrowski had already been arrested in the summer of 1889 and committed suicide in jail; the Rodziewiczes were gone; and the leadership of the group fell to Brusnev, Golubev, and Cywinski.

The Central Workers' Circle

During the winter of 1889–90, Brusnev's goal had been to unite the student circle of technologists with the workers' circles around the capital. Ignited initially by the Society of St. Petersburg Craftsmen, the circles' movement among workers in the city grew quickly at the end of the eighties. The job of the student circle of propagandists, Brusnev had concluded, "was to stand at the head of these organizations and lead the entire movement."[14] But Brusnev's goal was frustrated by the inherent weaknesses of a predominantly student circle, not the least of which was that its members left the city during summer vacation and returned to their provincial homes. In addition, the police watched the activities of students much more closely than those of the workers and student arrests and deportations, like the series of arrests in the spring of 1890, repeatedly interrupted the continuity of the circle's activities. The students' outlook was predominantly social-democratic, which meant, almost by definition, that they harbored an aversion to conspiracy and the precautions built into the narodovol'tsy world view. Therefore, though Brusnev wanted the student circle to organize the workers, it was the workers themselves who took the initiative in early 1890, forming their own Central Workers' Circle and tying it to the efforts of the students.

The Central Workers' Circle was the product of five to six years' involvement of workers in the world of radical propaganda. Eight experienced worker-propagandists, each of whom led his own circle, constituted the initial membership of the central circle: Egor Afanas'-ev-Klimanov (from the Franco-Russian works), Gavril Mefodiev (then at the Warsaw railway works), V. V. Fomin (of the Baltic works), F. A. Afanas'ev (from the Vasil'evskii Island circles), P. E. Evgrafov (from the New Admiralty shipbuilding factory), and N. D. Bogdanov (from the Putilov works). Afanas'ev-Klimanov, Mefodiev, and Fomin had already worked directly with Tochiskii and the Society of St. Petersburg Craftsmen. Bogdanov had received his initial radical training in narodovol'tsy circles. Several additional worker associates of the group, including A. Filimonov and I. I. Keizer, earlier were supporters of the narodovol'tsy program.

The structure of the Central Workers' Circle was based on an ostensibly democratic principle of organization. Each circle, headed by one of these experienced workers, was to run its own activities, and the circles of each region would elect a representative to the central circle. By the spring of 1890, approximately twenty workers' circles, each with six or seven members, were represented in the Central Workers' Circle by the eight worker-propagandists.[15] The central circle also invited a representative of the social-democratic student circle to join its ranks. Vasilii Golubev served this function until his arrest; Brusnev replaced him. The representative of the student circle was to supply money, literature, and most important, propagandists for those workers' circles which requested them.[16]

Altogether, the Central Workers' Circle got off to a very good start. It inherited a library of approximately one thousand titles from I. I. Timofeev, a worker associate of the St. Petersburg Craftsmen who has organized the first workers' circle at the Baltic works mechanics shop in early 1887 and had cooperated closely with Lelewel. The size of the library soon doubled with the addition of Golubev's collections of clippings for workers from the legal press and the "thick" journals. Workers themselves contributed books that they bought at the Sunday flea markets. Every Saturday, the central circle met at an apartment outfitted with all the trappings of a name-day celebration, just in case the police showed up. Usually, the meetings started in the late afternoon and did not end until early morning. The worker-propagandists and the student representative drank tea, discussed their problems, and the workers asked theoretical questions of the student. Sometimes, when they received news of victories in the West European workers' movement, they celebrated by drinking vodka and delivering impassioned toasts.[17]

The ideology of these labor leaders was clearly social-democratic, as can be seen from the papers of Nikolai Bogdanov and Aleksandr Filimonov, a pair of twenty-one-year-old machinists who carried on sophisticated discussions with the workers in the Nevskii district. After his arrest, Filimonov told the police that his sole interest was to develop the strike as a weapon to advance the economic and political position of workers. "I sympathize not with the revolutionary movement," Filimonov stated, "but with the workers' movement."[18] In fact, Filimonov, like Bogdanov, Mefodiev, and the Afanas'evs, was already a potential "Russian Bebel," well aware of the importance of the labor movement to the economic and political advancement of Russian workers. He is reported to have told workers: "It is time for the Russian worker to try to develop himself, organize, set up strikes, gain broader rights, shorter working hours, an increase in pay; by means of the strike also to attempt to gain for himself political rights — the establishment of a constitution, based on general electoral laws so that every worker can elect deputies from his own numbers to the governing body and so that these deputies can have the opportunity to represent the interests of their electors when laws are passed."[19]

Though sharing the general views of his friend Filimonov, Bogdanov was more interested in the cultural tasks at hand. The main difference between the Russian worker and the Western worker, he declared in a handwritten propaganda piece, is "intellectual development." Both suffer under "the yoke of the capitalist structure." Yet it is especially incumbent upon advanced Russian workers to help their less developed brethren since the latter, unlike the Western workers, are unaware of the possibilities of action because of ignorance, illiteracy, and lack of leadership.[20]

For Filimonov, Bogdanov, and the rest of the Central Workers' Circle, the primary task was to create new circles at factories all over the city. But they faced formidable problems, not the least of which was police surveillance. Also, like university students, urban workers divided themselves into zemliachestvos, many of which had their special allies and special enemies. These regional associations of workers sometimes dominated whole factories and were instantly suspicious of any outsiders.[21] In many factories, as well, evangelists were at work, often enjoying much greater success than the preachers of social democracy. Even the so-called labor intelligentsia avoided the social democrats. Most of these educated workers were gradualists, interested in current events or in discussing belles-lettres, but unwilling to engage in anything that resembled illegal activities. However, Fomin remembered, they did provide some financial help for the Central Workers' Circle and now and again concealed worker-activists in trouble with the authorities.[22] In addition, many workers' circles continued to be loyal to narodovol'tsy or populist thinking. At the Baltic Works, for instance, one of the most respected workers was Ivan Vasil'evich Krutov, known as *Starik* — the old-timer. Born and raised in the factory and now in his mid-forties, Krutov peppered his speech with foreign words and wore a German top-hat, even while working at his lathe. Like so many worker-activists of the period, Krutov hungered for knowledge, loved books, but used his knowledge and his prestige to counter social-democratic ideas. Still, Fomin recalled, "our relations with him were always most friendly."[23] Other members of the Central Workers' Circle also acknowledged Krutov's hostility, yet maintained that his services were indispensable to the labor movement because he was able to attract young people to workers' circles through his "cheerfulness, jokes, and commitment — with all his soul — to the workers' cause."[24]

In addition to apathy, religiosity, and even hostile radical opinions among workers, the activists faced difficulties of a much more prosaic nature: how to find the time to talk to workers. Much of the propagandizing, in the end, took place in the "clubs," the toilets of the factories where workers smoked and sometimes ate. Often late night work was useful, because at 11:30 or midnight the offices would close, the supervisors would go home, and the workers could talk freely. At early morning tea, before the start of the work day, it was also possible for the social democrats to present their ideas to the workers at their home; when they did they sometimes met with stern opposition from wives and even children. This did not mean that all the women workers lacked interest in political questions, only that the hold of religion seemed to be stronger over them.[25]

In fact, the Central Workers' Circle made impressive inroads among women workers. One of the founders of the social-democratic women's circle was A. G. Boldyreva, who started working in a textile plant at the age of nine. In 1888, Boldyreva worked at the K. Ia. Pal' textile factory in the Nevskii district and began to attend the local Sunday school, which taught urban workers elementary reading and writing. She, like so many other social-democratic workers, experienced an overwhelming desire to learn and to educate herself. As A. P. Il'in wrote, characterizing an entire generation of worker-activists, "At the time, my love for the printed word was not comparable [to my attachment] to anything else."[26] Through the Sunday school, Boldyreva met Dorofei Nikitich, who in turn introduced her to the respected weaver Fedor Afanas'ev, a member of the central circle. Afanas'ev encouraged Boldyreva in her self-education efforts, while suggesting that she attend meetings at the New Cotton Mill factory. Both Afanas'ev and Nikitich were peasants from the same locality of St. Petersburg province, and their circle at the New Cotton Mill was as much a zemliachestvo group as it was an organization designed to promote self-development. Boldyreva soon joined the factory as a worker and became one of the circle's leading members.[27]

A second source of membership for the social-democratic women's circle came through Nikolai Bogdanov's contacts with group of young women raised in a St. Petersburg home for children born out of wedlock. Once these girls were of age (usually thirteen or fourteen), they were forced to serve a mandatory period of menial labor at schools for noblewomen. At one such institute for noblewomen, on Vasil'evskii Island, Vera Karelina, Varia Nikolaeva, and Masha Makhlakova protested in 1887 against their very difficult working conditions, encouraged by the narodovol'tsy women's activist, Natalia Aleksandrova. When Karelina went to work at a lying-in hospital, she was already receptive to the radical books she received from a circle of midwife students at the hospital, and in the winter of 1888–89 she met Bogdanov, who helped her start a circle of female hospital workers. Karelina recalled that her reading – Chernyshevskii, Pisarev, and others – went "very slowly," but that "we did not regret the amount of time it took, two-three hours, or five or six, it did not matter, just so we could learn."[28] At the suggestion of Fedor Afanas'ev, Karelina then went to work at the New Cotton Mill factory, joined the circle of weavers, and along with Anna Boldyreva (now Egorova) and Nikitich organized an exclusively women's circle.[29] There is no evidence that the circle pursued any specifically feminist goals. Rather, the women devoted themselves to propagandizing among other female workers; they read and discussed social-democratic and narodovol'tsy literature, and Boldyreva and Karelina, as the circle's leaders, attended the meetings of the Central Workers' Circle, becoming important labor leaders in their own right.

Despite the difficulties of organizing in the factories, there was no dearth of new recruits for the circles' movement in the city. Unexpectedly, a large group of prospective worker-propagandists from the Ecclesiastical Academy contacted the Central Workers' circle and several meetings were held in academy buildings.[30] A group of workers at the Tolstoyan newspaper store Posrednik, led by the young worker Mikhail Iakovlev, also contacted the circle and eventually provided material for other circles' reading needs. Bogdanov became the organizer, "the soul," of a series of circles, some engaged in no more than teaching workers to read. However, the overall effort was very impressive indeed. Workers' circles operated at all the major factories in the capital, and though few, if any, could be called revolutionary, a Russian socialist labor movement, organized by Russian workers, had emerged. Even the gendarmes began to realize that urban workers were "most susceptible" to social-democratic ideas. "Despite periodic arrests the activities in this [worker propaganda] continue uninteruptedly; and in place of the old leaders come new [ones], arousing among workers dissatisfaction with their position."[31]

The Worker's Union

By the winter of 1890–91, the Central Workers' Circle and the circle of students operated in tandem in what can certainly be called Russia's first social-democratic organization, the Workers' Union.[32] Vasilii Golubev served as the representative of the intelligentsia in the Central Workers' Circle and was responsible for coordinating the activities of the two groups, providing propagandists for workers' circles that requested them, and helping students make contacts with workers' circles. During December and January, 1890–91, the revamped social-democratic organization participated for the first time in the labor movement as a whole when strikes broke out at the Thornton cloth factory and at the New Admiralty factory. The worker members of the union wanted to join the strikers, but, as Golubev recalled, the "intelligentsia decisively opposed the fighting mood of the workers."[33] In the end, the workers were placated by the establishment of a strike fund. Three hundred rubles were collected by the Workers' Union and distributed to the striking workers. In addition, Vasilii Golubev and Leonid Krasin wrote and distributed what Brusnev called "very lively" proclamations supporting the strikers' demands.[34] However, no further action was taken.

At a meeting of the Central Workers' Circle in March 1891, Golubev suggested that the workers might want to visit the radical writer N. V. Shelgunov, who was gravely ill. The workers agreed and decided to write an address to Shelgunov, with the help of Golubev. "You were the first to recognize the miserable condition of the working class in Russia," the address stated; "you always tried and to this moment continue to try to explain to us why we are held in this enslaved position and what keeps us intellectually underdeveloped."[35] The weaver Fedor Afanas'ev was chosen to head the delegation because of his age (about forty), his wisdom, and the general respect accorded him by his fellow workers.[36] Shortly before the delegation was to deliver the address, Golubev was arrested (March 20). With his arrest, Bogdanov wrote, "we lost a wise and careful leader of our organization."[37] The visit to Shelgunov was postponed.

Just as Brusnev had inherited Rodziewicz's circle of harbor workers when the latter was arrested, Brusnev now moved into Golubev's place as the intelligentsia representative in the central circle. It was thus only for the few months between Golubev's arrest in March and June 1891, when Brusnev left St. Petersburg for Moscow, that the Workers' Union could justifiably be called the Brusnevtsy, although this is the term applied to it by Soviet historiography for the entire period 1888–1892. Concentrating on economic rather than political issues, Brusnev accurately characterized his own efforts in the well-known statement: "We wanted to make future Russian Bebels out of our worker-listeners."[38] The German social democrats were his ideal, but for the moment he was concerned simply with teaching workers the importance of developing "an organized and conscious labor force."[39] However, Brusnev also tightened the conspiratorial regulations of the intelligentsia circle. "When I entered," recalled Leonid Krasin (later Soviet ambassador to London and Paris), "the organization of the circle was so tightly conspiratorial that very little was imparted to me about the full extent of its activities." Pseudonyms were always used, and addresses were kept secret.[40] V. V. Sviatlovskii, another student who joined the circle at this time, wrote, "virtually all matters touching immediately on the organization were observed with the strictest secrecy."[41]

Brusnev also reorganized the workers' circles themselves, dividing them into two categories. The lower-level circles, headed usually by a member of the student circle, engaged in primary education; the more advanced circles, about twenty altogether, were headed by worker-propagandists, who at the same time comprised the membership of the Central Workers' Circle. Brusnev's "Program for Activities among Workers" traced a ten-step series of lessons, which would be introduced to the lower-level circles to aid them in the transition to the higher level:

I.   Read, write, and count.
II.   Chemistry, physics, botany, zoology, physiology, anatomy, hygiene — briefly: geology, cosmology, and astronomy. Various theories about the formation of the earth and the origins of the universe.
III.   Theory of Darwin. Theory of the origins and development of organisms and of the origins of man.
IV.   History of culture . . . Periods of civilization . . . Histories of science, philosophy, discoveries, and inventions.
V.   Political economy . . .
VI.   Condition and history of the peasants in Russia and

This list circulated among the propagandists of the intelligentsia circle and they attempted to follow it as best they could. Brusnev helped them by writing some thirty pages of lectures on the fundamentals of political economy, which he himself used in workers' circles in Petersburg and later in Moscow.

On 12 April 1891 Shelgunov died, and the workers decided to participate in the funeral procession and lay wreaths on his grave. Both Brusnev and Cywinski attempted to dissuade them from their plan, fearing police suppression of the newly organized union. But the workers prevailed and close to one hundred of them marched in the procession, holding high their six wreaths on which were written, "Shelgunov — a signpost on the path to freedom and brotherhood."[43] The police duly noted the names of thirty to forty workers who had participated in the demonstration, and the venerable Krutov and the brothers Ivan and Gavril Mefodiev were arrested and given a warning.[44] The student participants in the procession were not so lucky. The Krasin brothers, Leonid and German, were banished from the capital, as were the more famous figures of the intelligentsia, Nikolai Mikhailovskii and Gleb Uspenskii. Undetected by the police, the young student Iulii Tsederbaum, later Martov, carried one of the wreaths part of the way to the cemetery in his first act of participation in the labor movement.

With the approach of 1 May 1891, the workers began to discuss the possibility of commemorating the holiday, first celebrated by American workers in Chicago in 1888, with another demonstration. One such May-day demonstration had already taken place in Warsaw in 1890, and the legal press reported parades and marches all across Europe. Again, Brusnev and some of the workers opposed a demonstration because of possible police repression. In the end, a compromise was found; an illegal assembly would be held, and only members of the fully committed circles represented in the Central Workers' Circle would be invited. The speeches were to be delivered by Bogdanov, Fedor Afanas'ev, and V. Proshin, and drafts were discussed and revised by members of the Central Workers' Circle, including Brusnev, who later claimed that he edited them, "in a programmatic sense."[45] The actual May 1 meetings were held at several locations in and around St. Petersburg. Bogdanov, F. Afanas'ev and Proshin delivered their addresses to about seventy-five workers gathered on the banks of the Ekateringof River; a second, smaller assembly met at Afanas'ev-Klimanov's apartment to hear speeches by him, Bogdanov, and Egorov.[46]

Although Brusnev departed St. Petersburg for Moscow in June, the activities of the Workers' Union intensified, especially in the fall and winter of 1891–92. Dmitrii Stranden, who had worked with Cywinski in Technological Institute student groups in 1886 and was later influenced by Petr Struve, took a leading role in circle propaganda.[47] He often visited the workers' circle of about seventy members, run by Petr Lopatin and Vasilii Gall (who later turned in Stranden, as well as every other activist he knew, to the police) and lectured on the principles of physical geography, the structure of the earth, and the movement of the planets. "At subsequent meetings," Gall testified, "Stranden explained the basics of labor, capital, and production, and then began to discuss the position and the life of workers in Western countries in comparison to Russia."[48] Cywinski's presentations followed a similar format. First, he would quote from Darwin and then go on to explain the fundamentals of his theory of evolution and natural selection. In later meetings, Cywinski moved from a discussion of the origins of man to the question of how workers lived in Western Europe and Russia. The police reported that Cywinski's meetings were also attended by about sixty workers.[49]

Egor Afanas'ev-Klimanov, a participant in Cywinski's group and a long-time worker-activist, reported to the police that the workers at the Baird iron works had organized their own circles to study socialist literature. But they constantly experienced problems of theory that required intelligentsia help. "No one could explain this or that difficult thought," Afanas'ev told the police. "That is why they wanted to invite into the circle a person who could direct their studies." The "person" was Cywinski, and his message was similar to other social democrats of the period: "Thanks to their development, Western workers themselves achieved many political rights, which in turn resulted in their material position becoming considerably better than that of our own workers."[50]

The St. Petersburg prosecutor's investigation of the growing number of local workers' circles in 1891–92 uncovered a repeated pattern of workers in search of intelligentsia help. Afanas'ev-

Klimanov told the police that the seamstress Natalia Aleksandrova sought out his advice on which socialist publications her newly formed circle should read and asked him to assign a student propagandist to her circle. He, in turn, looked to the social democrats, because, as he explained, the workers "knew nothing" about the narodovol'tsy.[51] Nikolai Sivokhin, a friend of Brusnev's and a student at the Forestry Institute, agreed to take on the job. His methods followed those of the other successful social-democratic propagandists of the period, Cywinski, Stranden, and V. V. Sviatlovskii. He began by presenting the workers with "some information about physical geography; thereafter I acquainted them with the theories of Darwin; and finally, I moved to the explanation of the laws of political economy and began to read to them Diksztajn's brochure *Who Lives From What?*"[52] But Sivokhin's goal, unlike that of Sviatlovskii or Cywinski, was to prompt workers into labor disturbances.

During the spring and early summer of 1892, new workers' circles continued to be formed throughout the city. Sviatlovskii, perhaps the most popular and respected social democrat in the city during this period, met with Vladimir Fomin's circle at the Baltic works and with those of Aleksandr Iakovlev at the Baird works.[53] Echoing the widespread admiration for Sviatlovskii among workers, Karelina wrote: "he lived together with workers in a communal apartment on Riga Prospect, and was distinguished by his great simplicity [and by the fact] that he very much liked workers."[54] When Stranden left the country in the spring of 1892, the worker Petr Evgrafov took over the leadership of the circles at the New Admiralty. Cywinski continued to operate a number of circles, the largest at the home of the worker G. N. Lunegov, and both Cywinski and Sviatlovskii met with the Central Worker's Circle as intelligentsia representatives.

At the end of April 1892 strikes erupted in Lodz, one of the largest and most important industrial centers in the Russian Empire. Over twenty factories were struck, several tens of thousands of workers were involved, and violent street battles erupted between workers and the police. The Workers' Union maintained good contacts with the more advanced Polish movement, in part because of Sviatlovskii's periodic trips to Warsaw to get radical literature and in part because several workers in the organization moved back and forth from factories in Petersburg to those in the Kingdom of Poland.[55] Fedor Pashin, who had met with a representative of the Lodz workers and who now led the circles of the Baltic works, urged his colleagues to stage a May 1 demonstration that would simultaneously express solidarity with the Lodz workers and provide an occasion to unify their own efforts in Petersburg.[56] Once again, fearing police intervention, the intelligentsia circle, this time led by Cywinski, tried to dissuade the workers from an open demonstration. The police were indeed watching closely for a May 1 demonstration, and the workers were well advised not to hold it. The leadership of the Workers' Union then scheduled a meeting for the 24th of May, the day of the Holy Trinity, on Krestovskii Island. Assembling in small groups, workers made their way by boat and ferry to the island. Altogether, approximately one hundred workers gathered; Cywinski and Sviatlovskii attended dressed in peasant garb. Just as the meeting began to hear speeches prepared by Cywinski, Afanas'ev-Klimanov, Proshin, and Fomin, police and forest watchmen, alerted to the meeting time and place, moved in and forced the workers to disperse. Many of the workers left in the small boats they had come in, singing and playing harmonicas, jeering at the police on the banks of the island.[57]

Ever-increasing police vigilance did not seem to discourage the workers' circles from engaging in political activities. Pashin's circle distributed an "Open Letter to Polish Workers" among Petersburg workers, expressing sympathy for the Lodz strikers. His circle also passed around the "First Letter to Starving Peasants," published by the Group of Narodovol'tsy in 1892. Evgrafov's New Admiralty circle, as well as a new Franco-Russian factory workers' circle led by Petr Lopatin and Petr Raskol'nikov, was also implicated in the distribution of the letters.[58] The letter to the Polish workers, probably written by Stranden shortly before his departure from Russia, congratulated the Polish comrades for having "openly joined the ranks of the world-wide social-democratic army . . . You are hounded terribly, but you are happier than we, you have already entered into the open struggle — we only prepare for it, but soon we also will enter into the struggle against the common enemy: the tsar, the barons, the factory owners, the priests."[59]

Even as the members of the Central Workers' Circle were distributing the letter to the Poles, they realized the limitations of their ability to influence the city's labor movement. On 1 June 1892, about seven hundred workers at the Mitrofan'evskii textile plant stopped work in protest against a quality directive that would in effect have lowered their wages. The director of the plant, a foreigner named Johnson, ordered the workers back to their stations, but the strike continued. The police moved quickly, arresting twelve alleged "instigators" and banishing them to their home towns and villages for a year. By June 3 operations at the plant were back to normal.[60] The Workers' Union did not participate in the strike, nor did it try to push the Mitrofan'evskii workers into more radical activity. Instead, it called special meetings of its own organization to discuss the events and to solicit funds for the arrested, raising altogether about one hundred rubles, which were distributed among the families of the banished workers.[61]

Rather than attempt to participate in the increasingly militant activities of the St. Petersburg labor movement, the Workers' Union concentrated on bolstering the morale of its twenty or so workers' circles. As part of this effort, Cywinski, Sviatlovskii, and Fomin from the Baltic works and Iakovlev from the Baird works organized a large meeting, attended by some hundred workers representing the circles, in the Volkov-Iamskii forest five miles outside the city.[62] The detailed police reports on the meeting (held on Sunday, July 28), as well as the increased attention the police paid to the Workers' Union, suggest that the authorities probably let the meeting go ahead in the hope of gaining enough information to prosecute the entire group. As the police reported, "antigovernment" speeches were delivered by eight worker activists: Fomin and Petr Kaizo from the Baltic works, Petr Kozhevnikov from the Shlisselburg circle, the unskilled ("black") worker Ivan Egorov and his wife Anna Boldyreva (Egorova), the machinist Grigorii Lunegov of the State Paper factory, and the New Admiralty worker Mikhail Stepanenkov. Lunegov's opening speech (which the police later discovered was written by Afanas'ev-Klimanov, the veteran activist and leader of the Central Workers' Circle), set the tone for the rest of the meeting. He traced the accomplishments of West European workers and asked, "who are we, Russian workers, to be worse than they!" Everyone must struggle together, "not only the less developed classes, but also the representatives of literature, the school youth, the zemstvos, and all those who strive for justice." But Russian labor should not forget that "our salvation is in ourselves, in the united and strict organization of workers." At the same time the workers' organization must reach out to the intelligentsia, "of whom thousands have been lost to Alexander III and his barbaric administration. Only force can answer force." The other speeches at the meeting carried the same message; Russian workers should unite in a strong organization like those of their Western brethren. The tsar and the ruling classes combined to exploit Russian workers, and in order to achieve the same political rights and material gains as Western workers, the Russian labor movement must cooperate with other forces of the liberation movement.[63]

The blatantly political tone of the July 28 speeches gave the authorities all the justification they needed to suppress the Workers' Union. According to the St. Petersburg Prosecutor, Cywinski, Sivokhin, and Stranden had done their work well; "in a comparatively short time," they had involved the workers in political questions.[64]

Stranden was seized by the police when he tried to return to Petersburg in September with a packet of social-democratic writings. Cywinski and Sivokhin managed to leave Petersburg before a series of mass arrests. Twenty-five workers who could be identified as attending the July 28 meeting were arrested and sentenced.[65] Despite the amount and the sophistication of the social-democratic materials found in the workers' quarters during the investigation, it is apparent from the indictment and sentences that the authorities still believed that the workers were innocent pawns in the hands of the intelligentsia, and that social democrats were less of a threat to the government than the narodovol'tsy.[66] The most severe sentences were meted out to Petr Evgrafov, who after Stranden's departure led several workers' circles, and to Grigorii Lunegov, who delivered the opening address to the July 28 meeting. Both received a year in jail and three more in exile, a sharp contrast with the almost mandatory five-year sentences for the most innocuous narodovol'tsy propagandists.

The prosecutor could not conceive of a union of intelligentsia and workers' circles without direction from the emigration, in this instance from Plekhanov and the Emancipation of Labor group.[67] The evidence, however, did not support his allegation that the Workers' Union members were followers of Emancipation of Labor. Not once in the testimony, correspondence, or writings of the members of the union collected by the police is Plekhanov or his group mentioned. In fact, as Golubev later wrote, "we somehow forgot about the group Emancipation of Labor."[68] Even Aksel'rod bemoaned the fact that the homegrown social democrats paid no attention to Plekhanov's émigré organization.[69]

After the Workers' Union

The regenerative powers of the Russian movement, especially of the workers' circles, were once again apparent in the summer and fall of 1892 and in early 1893. The destruction of the St. Peterburg Workers' Union only temporarily broke the ties between the workers' circles and the intelligentsia social democrats. Vasilii Shelgunov, who had been involved in the St. Petersburg Masters as well as in the Workers' Union, assembled the remaining leaders of the workers' circles in 1882–93 (K. M. Norinskii, G. M. Fisher, and I. I. Kaizer) and reestablished the Central Workers' Circle. Shelgunov, like Bogdanov during the previous period, earned the respect of numerous workers' circle leaders around the city. He had studied at the Sunday and evening schools of the Technical Society and had been recruited to the Central Workers' Circle by Afanas'ev-Klimanov. Using the reconstructed Central Workers' Circle as his base, Shelgunov led the fight in the winter of 1893 to rebuild a strike fund, the United Fund of St. Petersburg Workers.[70] Through these efforts Shelgunov was also able to contact intelligentsia circles in the capital sympathetic to the labor movement but heretofore out of contact with the city's social-democratic organizations.

By the beginning of the new school year, October–November 1893, the intelligentsia circle was also able to regroup and again engage in social-democratic activities. Two Technological Institute students, Nikolai Aliushkevich and Gavril Kulev, had organized circles among workers as early as the fall of 1891. One of their most gifted associates, the metal worker Vasilii Platonov from the Franco-Russian factory, engaged in diverse propagandistic activities, collecting money for strike funds and translating pamphlets from the Polish for use in the workers' circles.[71] Aliushkevich (known as the "chemist" to the workers, because he taught chemistry in their circles), Kulev, and Platonov survived the summer 1892 arrests because their association with the Workers' Union was only informal. One of their associates at the Technological Institute, Stepan Radchenko, took no part at all in the Workers' Union, confining himself instead to propaganda work among the intelligentsia. Though a member of the Aliushkevich group, Radchenko believed in strict conspiracy and avoided any contact with the workers' movement, which he considered too susceptible to police infiltration and arrest.[72] In the summer of 1893 the police broke up the Aliushkevich group, leaving only Radchenko at large. The workers' circles' leaders Afanas'ev-Klimanov, Vladimir Proshin and Platonov (along with some thirty other workers) were also seized in the police dragnet, as was Cywinski, who had earlier moved to Saratov.[73] Thus in August 1893, when V. I. Ul'ianov (Lenin) arrived in St. Petersburg, it was Radchenko's still extant circle of intelligentsia social democrats which he sought out and joined.

Between the summers of 1892 and 1893, in the period of the reconstitution of the Central Workers' Circle under Shelgunov and Norinskii and their new intelligentsia associates led by Aliushkevich, one notices the first serious indication that ideological differences between the social democrats and the narodovol'tsy could become important. In the formative period 1888–1891, few workers' circles really cared whether the propagandists who taught them were narodovol'tsy or social democrats. Even in the Central Workers' Circle there had been no disputes, not even any discussions concerning the participation of a narodovol'tsy group headed by M. Aleksandrov (Ol'minskii) and his wife Ekaterina. However, the resurgence of narodovol'tsy strength in 1892–93, in the form of the Group of Narodovol'tsy, and the polemics between Legal Marxists and Legal Populists over the causes and implications of the great famine of 1891–92, precipitated the first ideological conflicts within the Central Workers' Circle. As a result, the workers invited representatives of both groups to present their programs. A. A. Fedulov and M. Ia. Sushchinskii from the Group of Narodovol'tsy debated with the social democrats V. V. Starkov and German Krasin in a series of sessions held at Shelgunov's apartment.[74] Despite the lively debates and sharp differences expressed at the meetings, attended sometimes by Aleksandrov from the narodovol'tsy and perhaps by Stepan Radchenko from the social democrats, cooperation rather than conflict characterized the resolutions of the Central Workers' Circle. Generally, the circle expressed sympathy for the narodovol'tsy efforts, though Keizer was the only member of the circle to prefer their program to that of the social democrats.[75] The circle did insist, however, that the narodovol'tsy visit only those workers' circles to which they were directly invited, and to report all their activities among Petersburg workers to the Central Workers' Circle. Even though the circle was careful of contacts with the narodovol'tsy, when the police caught up with the Group of Narodovol'tsy in the spring and early summer of 1894 they destroyed the new Central Workers' Circle because of its association with the group.

Outside the activities of the Central Workers' Circle and the Workers' Union, Marxism had also made inroads into circles of the St. Petersburg intelligentsia. Especially important to the later development of the theories of Russian Marxism was a small circle at St. Petersburg University, which consisted of the students Iulii Tsederbaum (Martov), S. A. Gofman, and Ivan Stavskii. After the famine of 1891–92, the circle, now joined by a half-dozen other students, including some who had been involved in narodovol'tsy activities, took on a more consciously Marxist orientation. When one of its members, Aleksandr Potresov, returned from abroad in the fall of 1892 with a package of Emancipation of Labor materials, the group even renamed itself the Petersburg Emancipation of Labor group.[76] Although the circle had some contacts with Stranden, it did not participate directly in the city's social-democratic movement. Like the young and powerful intellectual Petr Struve, who impressed the circle with his lectures on Marxist theory, the members of the Petersburg Emancipation of Labor group soon became actively involved in shaping a new generation of revolutionary social democrats.

Moscow Student Circles

The destruction of the Society of Translators and Publishers in 1886 and the government's attack on the Moscow zemliachestvo circles in

1887 and 1888 did not purge student radicals as thoroughly as did the post-March 1887 arrests in St. Petersburg. One of the most influential and interesting of the circles that continued to function was that of Grigorii Mandel'shtam and Girsh Krukovskii, whose sole purpose was to study Marx's *Das Kapital*.[77] Both Mandel'shtam and Krukovskii were practicing engineers, and they soon attracted other young members of the technical intelligentsia to their circle. The brothers A. N. Vinokurov and P. N. Vinokurov, S. Mitskevich, M. Liadov (Mandel'shtam's brother), and the others met every Saturday "for the study of Marx and other books on the social sciences."[78] The group's studies became particularly sophisticated after Mandel'shtam returned from a brief trip to Europe in 1889. There he attended the first congress of the Second Internatonal and brought back a fairly complete library of the publications of Emancipation of Labor. Mandel'shtam also led the polemics against Mikhailovskii's Legal Populist views, which had become popular in some Moscow circles, but neither he nor Krukovskii propagandized their views among Moscow workers before they were arrested in 1894.

Soviet historians are unanimous in maintaining that Krukovskii and Mandel'shtam were "pure Marxists," but the evidence is ambiguous. Mandel'shtam certainly spoke out against Mikhailovskii and the populists, but not against the narodovol'tsy. Similarly, Egupov's characterization of Krukovskii suggests that his circle, while undoubtedly entranced by Marx, did not necessarily see his work as incompatible with narodovol'tsy doctrine. "According to his [Krukovskii's] way of thinking he closely resembled the narodovol'tsy orientation, combined with the goal that reigned supreme in him, to propagandize the teachings of Marx among the intelligentsia . . . He not only mastered them, but he began to use as his own . . . the modes and methods of [Marxist] argument."[79] Even the Moscow circles that explicitly called themselves narodovol'tsy, such as that of Pavel Kraft and A. I. Gukovskii at Moscow University, 1888–89, propagandized Marxist works and incorporated some of his ideas into their own world view. One member of the Kraft-Gukovskii circle, V. K. Kurnatovskii, actively sought out social-democratic contacts and eventually became a leading Bolshevik. Similarly, the Moscow narodovolets, Petr Kashinskii, became more committed to the development of a workers' movement, spread propaganda within a few Moscow workers' circles, and in the spring of 1891 went to St. Petersburg to learn about the Workers' Union. There he met with Leonid Krasin, who later claimed that Kashinskii was extremely well informed about Marxism and the tenets of Western social democracy.[80] Still, it is apparent from the arguments which later erupted in Moscow social-democratic circles that elements of narodovol'tsy thinking, especially the advocacy of terrorism to bring about political freedom, remained central to Kashinskii's outlook, just as they were to Kurnatovskii and Krukovskii.

Kashinskii maintained constant communications with the Workers' Union in St. Petersburg through his friend and fellow radical, Boleslaw Kwiatkowski. When Leonid Krasin was expelled from Petersburg because of his participation in the Shelgunov funeral, he went into exile in Nizhnii Novgorod by way of Moscow in order to carry on discussions with Kashinskii. In the absence of any indigenous worker social democrats in Moscow, Krasin and Kashinskii agreed that the worker-propagandist Fedor Afanas'ev should be brought to the city to contact local workers' circles.[81] Kashinskii raised the money for Afanas'ev's trip, consulted further with Krasin in Nizhnii Novgorod, and agreed that Mikhail Brusnev, who was eager to spread the organization of the Workers' Union throughout Russia, should begin his task in Moscow. By bringing Afanas'ev to Moscow by late summer and Brusnev by late fall 1891, Kashinskii had formed the nucleus of a new Moscow social-democratic organization. But the real impetus behind the group was Mikhail Egupov.

Egupov and the Moscow Social Democrats

Soviet historians have severely underestimated Egupov's role in the development of Russian social democracy. Like Kashinskii, Egupov came to social democracy through circles that shared the narodovol'tsy philosophy of revolution. In 1887 he entered the Novo-Aleksandriisk Institute of Agronomy and Forestry in Pulawy, where he joined a narodovol'tsy-oriented circle that included Georgii Psalty, Mikhail Kalinin, and Stepan Dandurov. The last two defended both the tactics and the program of Narodnaia Volia, whereas Egupov, especially after reading Engels's *Scientific Socialism*, began to doubt the ability of a party to seize power in Russia without a social revolution. During 1888 and the first half of 1889, Egupov contacted social-democratic circles in Warsaw and obtained several works by Marx and Lassalle for the Pulawy group. Egupov's organizational activities betweern 1887 and July 1889 (when he left Pulawy for military duty at Kronstadt) were charaterized by enormous energy and persistence, but lacked any clearly articulated ideology. Interested above all in the success of the revolutionary movement in Russia, Egupov indiscriminately adopted elements of both narodovol'tsy and social-democratic thinking.

Prompted by the arrest of Pavel Nemtsov, one of his St. Petersburg friends who had also been at Pulawy, Egupov went to Moscow at the end of May 1891.[82] Another of his Pulawy associates, Viktor Vanovskii, put him in contact with a Moscow revolutionary circle that was also composed of former Pulawyites (including A. N. Novosil'tsev and the police spy M. M. Petrov) and had established a network for the transportation of illegal propaganda materials from Odessa and Kharkov in the South to Riga in the North.

Egupov made his first contacts outside the narrow group of Pulawy graduates when he encountered what the police called the Russian-Caucasian circle. This circle was actually an alliance of two groups — V. V. Avaliani's circle of Petrovskii Academy students and a circle at the Technical School led by Boris Groman, among others. Groman and Avaliani were interested primarily in developing self-education circles for students, but helped Egupov in his plan to contact workers' circles in Tula.[83] According to a December 1891 secret police report, two circles were active among Tula workers, the most popular of which was "terrorist" and "had a completely satisfactory library." The second, so-called democratic circle had just been formed and therefore asked the Moscow intelligentsia (Avaliani) to "send them books and a leader."[84] Avaliani told the circle to contact Egupov, who, after learning of the workers' decision to set up an artel workshop, decided to begin extensive propaganda among them.

Arriving in Tula in late October 1891, Egupov held a series of discussions with the workers' leaders, the former Petersburg activists Medofiev and Rudelev. Although the members of the Tula group were anxious to receive massive financial help from Egupov, they wanted first to find out about his views on terror. Egupov responded that "in my view, there are still not the forces for it, which would decide the question in a practical sense. And in theory, it was impossible to decide definitively [for terror]." Rudelev agreed with Egupov and added that the most important task at the moment was "propaganda among workers."[85]

Egupov worked with the Tula circle throughout the fall of 1891, bringing funds (raised by Vanovskii) and literature from Moscow. In late November, on his second visit to Tula, Rudelev and Mefodiev again gave him "something on the order of an examination" and then revealed their connection with the Petersburg Workers' Union. Mefodiev took the lead in their new conversations, convincing his comrades to give up the idea of forming an artel workshop, and arguing that they should instead devote their energies to worker organization. "Only an organization of circles can be of use," Mefodiev said, citing Petr Alekseev's widely read 1877 trial speech: "only workers can accomplish the political revolution in Russia." Egupov was undoubtedly correct in concluding that "Mefodiev was a fanatic about workers' organization and propaganda." As Egupov departed Tula, Rudelev told him that the workers "counted on" him, because intelligentsia assistance, even from Petersburg, was not forthcoming. In return Rudelev promised that he would come to Moscow to acquaint Egupov with local workers.[86]

Back in Moscow, Egupov decided to travel to Warsaw where he intended to stock an illegal library for Moscow and Tula workers and to contact Warsaw underground circles in the hope of forming a Warsaw-Moscow axis of worker-oriented organizations. The money for the trip and for purchasing illegal literature was raised by one of Vanovskii's lotteries. Arriving in Warsaw, Egupov contacted Polish radicals from various branches of the socialist movement, but his most important contact was Sergei Ivanitskii, another old Pulawy friend. Egupov described Ivanitskii as "a follower of Plekhanov, that is, an advocate of exclusive propaganda among workers in order to form a social-democratic union."[87] It was Ivanitskii who collected a large stock of social-democratic literature, printed by Emancipation of Labor and by the Poles, which Egupov took back to Moscow in mid-December.

Upon his return Egupov moved quickly to consolidate the various radical circles into a more tightly knit organization. During his absence Vanovskii had joined the circle of Krukovskii and Mandel'shtam and at the end of December 1891 this circle formally allied itself to Egupov and Vanovskii. Even more important, in the course of that month Egupov finally met Kashinskii, and through him, Brusnev. Having established firm contacts with the Tula workers, the Russian-Caucasian circle of Avaliani, and the Krukovskii-Mandel'shtam group, Egupov now moved to absorb Kashinskii's circle.

In January 1892 Kashinskii and Egupov met almost weekly. "We agreed," Egupov wrote, "that it was necessary for us to unite in common work, because theoretically we were in accord, that is he [Kashinskii], Vanovskii, and I were disposed to the narodovol'tsy program but with a significant admixture of social-democratic ideas."[88] Kashinskii and Egupov also agreed that seeking to overthrow the government would be premature — there were not sufficient forces for a revolution. Instead, they would unite their circles, pool their financial resources, and attempt to contact the many similar but unknown circles in Moscow and throughout Russia as a whole.

In his memoirs, Brusnev recalls that he and Afanas'ev opposed the union of the circles, convinced that it would mean lowering the ideological level of the group.[89] However, the available archival sources provide no evidence that Brusnev either opposed unification or manifested an unusual degree of ideological purity. On the contrary, the prosecutor notes that Brusnev became, along with Egupov, Kashinskii, and Vanovskii, an important leader of the new organization.[90] Egupov, who certainly would have reacted negatively to Brusnev's opposition, says only that Brusnev "made a positive impression."[91] To be sure, Brusnev was the most careful and thoughtful member of the new group, in most ways the direct opposite of Egupov. He constantly reminded his colleagues about the importance of Marxist theory. His idea of being a revolutionary, he wrote to Sivokhin, was to aid the "inevitable" historical advance of the proletariat, and he opposed initiating either political terrorism or workers disturbances that did not conform to a theoretical framework.[92]

In February 1892, Egupov went once again to Warsaw to contact Ivanitskii and pick up a new batch of illegal literature. He met several members of the Union of Polish Workers and was fascinated by their theories of agitation, which had been firmly established among Polish labor during the period of the Proletariat (1882–1886): "They said that in the beginning it was necessary to rally the workers by means of struggle against the owners, by initiating strikes and strike funds in order to educate them politically, or better, to get them to arrive at political conclusions themselves. For this, it is necessary to organize protests, meetings, processions, in addition to, of course, propaganda and the spread of illegal literature, as well as the presentation of petitions about the improvement of workers' lives." The purpose of supporting the daily demands of better conditions for workers, the Poles told Egupov, was "to raise the sense among workers of their personal human worth," the key to a successful social-democratic movement.[93] After Warsaw Egupov went to Riga, where he contacted a small, highly sophisticated circle of Marxists at the Polytechnic School. Having received printed materials, including the controversial second number of Plekhanov's *Social Democrat*, from both the Riga group and the Poles, Egupov returned home to Moscow at the end of February.

On his return, he discussed what he had learned in Riga and in Warsaw at a meeting at Brusnev's. "At this meeting," he later told the authorities, "we spoke about the émigrés, Plekhanov and Lavrov, and about their differences." Brusnev immediately identified himself as a Marxist. Afanas'ev complained bitterly about the difficulty he was having organizing workers at a textile factory where he had begun to work, claiming that "among the workers there is no interest at all." He doubted whether a purely workers' party could exist at all. Instead, there should be "an intelligentsia organization whose single goal would be to form a workers' party." Brusnev, Kashinskii, and others disagreed, citing the relative leniency with which the government treated arrested workers. In addition, they argued that the workers' movement was "more lively when it is conducted by the workers themselves, as, for example, in Petersburg." There were numerous complaints about the lack of intelligentsia help in organizing workers and the meeting then dispersed.[94]

This odd situation, in which workers called for an intelligentsia organization while members of the intelligentsia called for a workers' organization, was repeated at a second meeting in early March. It had been convened to read and discuss Zasulich's "Revolutionaries from the Bourgeois Ranks," printed in the second number of *Social Democrat*. Again, the discussion focused on the lack of intelligentsia involvement in the workers' movement. Brusnev concluded that the old intelligentsia type was passing, and that the future belonged exclusively to the involved and conscious workers. "Today's working class activists," he stated, "are the future revolutionary leaders." As we have seen, his memoirs indicate that his primary goal was to create "Russian Bebels." Kashinskii insisted, however, that there was a future role for the intelligentsia—the granting of a constitution was necessary, and this would come only through the application of intelligentsia terrorism. Egupov added that such a development was certainly desirable, and the others agreed—save for Brusnev, who "said nothing." [95]

The meeting's most important resolution was the decision that Kashinskii, Brusnev, Terent'ev, Kwiatkowski, Egupov, and Vanovskii should constitute an "organizing committee" to lay the foundation for a united Russian social-revolutionary party. Egupov hoped to draw other elements into the new party, including the Russian-Caucasian circle and his various Pulawy contacts, who now led circles in Kharkov and Moscow.[96] The Riga Marxists and Warsaw University social democrats might also be persuaded to join the fledgling party, and Brusnev would draw in the Petersburg Workers' Union, in which he counted about sixty members. Kashinskii "sadly" could muster only himself, Kwiatkowski, and Terent'ev, but the latter two suggested that they could bring in large numbers of Moscow University students and perhaps even some of the textile-worker circles among which they were conducting propaganda.[97]

The discussions in late April and May 1892 about the program of the new organization once again reflected the willingness and ability of the participants to unite around a common "liberation" platform. There was no question of simply adopting the programs of either Emancipation of Labor or Narodnaia Volia. Instead, the committee agreed that a fresh program would have to be developed around the real work of the organization, "which would have its roots sunk deep into all classes of society, but mainly among the workers of industrial centers."[98] The only differences in the programmatic discussions came over the issue of how quickly the new organization should be formed. Brusnev in particular advocated great care and patience, while Kashinskii wanted to move immediately. Altogether, though, the participants in the organizing committee expressed great enthusiasm about their prospects. Egupov wrote in an April 12 letter to Kashinskii that the organizational efforts "are going great. They are leaving the phase of circles work."[99]

The Moscow Committee and Emancipation of Labor

Whenever news of successful Russian social-democratic organizations reached him in Switzerland, Plekhanov turned his attention to the home front, hoping to tap a new source of funds for his publishing ventures. Therefore it was no accident that in April 1892 Stepan (Simkha) Raichin arrived in Moscow as a representative of Emancipation of Labor and its Polish ally, the (second) Proletariat.[100] Although he brought from Warsaw a packet of illegal materials for Egupov, the organizing committee was suspicious of Raichin's plan to involve the émigrés in the Moscow movement. Egupov refused to give him any addresses and set several conditions for further discussions, the most crucial being that Raichin leave Russia immediately after negotiations were concluded.

Undoubtedly because his Warsaw contacts exaggerated Egupov's importance to the Moscow movement, Raichin accepted these conditions, and Egupov introduced him to Kashinskii and Brusnev. For hours the three questioned Raichin about the émigré group and its intentions, taking care that Raichin never learn the real names of his interlocutors. Raichin told them (as Egupov stressed in his later confession to the police) that "many Jews have gathered around the émigré Plekhanov—thus in Paris the group Emancipation of Labor is called 'the group of Jews'." The envoy also reported that Plekhanov's group was more careful and less dogmatic that it used to be. Although Plekhanov still wanted "to transfer the program of the German social democrats to Russia letter for letter," he now considered terrorism a possible means of legitimate political struggle.

Raichin impressed Egupov, Brusnev, and Kashinskii. He had demonstrated considerable patience with their conditions for negotiations and had generally been willing to compromise. They therefore concluded that they would work out an agreement with Emancipation of Labor through Raichin. Kashinskii, who spoke for the group, agreed to send immediately to Plekhanov two hundred rubles. In exchange, the organizing committee would obtain exclusive rights to distribute Emancipation of Labor literature in Russia, a monopoly that would facilitate the committee's ability to contact and unite other social-democratic groups. Kashinskii also agreed to send further funds to Plekhanov if the émigrés would agree to print reports and articles written by the committee's members. Finally, Raichin and the committee agreed on the joint publication of a newspaper-journal, named *Proletariat* at Kashinskii's suggestion. The committee would assume responsibility for articles directed at workers, while Emancipation of Labor would write those intended for the intelligentsia. Before leaving Moscow, Raichin asked for a written agreement on the all-important question of finances and suggested that members of the committee consult with Plekhanov personally in Switzerland. Kashinskii agreed, and Brusnev added that a delegation of Russian workers would call on Plekhanov on its way to the meeting of the International.[101]

Later in April 1892 Raichin left Moscow for Warsaw as agreed, and the organizing committee continued its task of forming a party. [102] Even while Raichin was in Moscow, meetings were taking place on programmatic questions. At one such meeting on April 4, to which the Tula leaders Mefodiev and Rudelev were invited, Brusnev, Egupov, and Kashinskii clashed openly on the question of precisely what kind of party should be formed.[103] Egupov, impressed both by the hundreds of arrests that recently had plagued the Polish Union of Workers and by the destruction of the Moscow narodovol'tsy circle led by I. D. Miagkov, argued that it would be too easy for the police to infiltrate a workers' party. His notion of a party closely resembled that of the Petersburg Terrorist Fraction: an intelligentsia group of conspirators carrying out the terrorist struggle against the government in order to achieve political freedom and a constitution. At the same time, this elite group should maintain enough ties to workers' circles to be able to join with them in a social-democratic party once a modicum of political freedom had been attained.[104]

In his memoirs, Brusnev accused Egupov of being a "terrorist and conspirator of the clearest sort."[105] This characterization, fully shared by Soviet historians, is not complete enough; like so many of his contemporaries, Kashinskii among them, Egupov combined narodovol'tsy tactics with social-democratic theory. He may have been a terrorist and a conspirator, but he was also a social democrat, and he saw no inherent contradictions between the two. Kashinskii, whom both Brusnev and Soviet historians are willing to label a social democrat, suggested at the April 4 meeting that the committee should develop its skills in making bombs in order to accelerate the revolutionary process.[106]

Brusnev was clearly in the minority at that April meeting, arguing once again for an exclusively workers' party. The job of the intelligentsia, Brusenv continued to assert, was to create cadres of workers who could lead the proposed party themselves. Quoting Marx, Brusnev insisted that political freedom could result only from a change in the economic structure; terrorism could not substitute for fundamental social and economic progress. The arguments continued late into the night. Finally, in the early morning, a compromise was reached: the committee should proceed with preparations for an organization to struggle against the government, while at the same time making more concerted efforts to develop the social-democratic movement among workers. The committee also agreed to purchase additional books for its library and, taking proper conspiratorial precautions, planned to have Egupov and Brusnev visit Tula in the summer to discuss questions of Russian labor with the circles of Mefodiev and Rudelev.[107] (Later, the committee decided to place Leonid Krasin, already in charge of the Nizhnii Novgorod circles, at the head of the new Tula organization.)

In order to set the new party on a firm foundation, the leaders of the committee decided to send Egupov to Warsaw again to contact Ivanitskii, charging him with three main tasks: to gather information about explosives for the terrorist struggle, to obtain illegal materials, and to recruit Polish social-democratic students for the Moscow movement. The organizing committee's intention was to bolster the very slim ranks of Moscow social democrats by importing Polish propagandists. Having completed their studies in Warsaw, the Poles would settle in Moscow, work in the city's factories, and help to develop workers' circles.[108] On his return to Moscow on April 16, Egupov once again held a series of meetings with Kashinskii and Brusnev. At the first meeting, the committee decided to send Kashinskii to Kiev and Kharkov to contact revolutionary groups. Brusnev would go to St. Petersburg to draw the Workers' Union into the organization and to borrow two hundred rubles from its treasury. Egupov would return to Warsaw via Riga.

The committee assigned Kashinskii to write a draft program for the group, a task that he had completed before his planned trip to the South.[109] Brusnev could not have been particularly happy with the document, for it clearly demonstrated that the organizing committee still held strong narodovol'tsy convictions. Point one of the program stated that as convinced social revolutionaries (not social democrats), "we will attempt to form in the near future a fighting social-revolutionary organization." Point five maintained that "the tsar and the state remain the primary enemies of the people." Political terrorism of a "systematic" sort, carried out by a "strictly centralized and disciplined" party, was depicted as the only viable means to accomplish revolutionary aims. In order to support the terrorist struggle, the program argued that the party must undertake to propagandize socialism "among the democratic intelligentsia of all social categories." However, in accordance with earlier discussions, the committee promised to direct its energies chiefly to the development "of propaganda and agitation among factory workers," and the workers' organization was seen as the main component of the revolutionary movement. But even the workers should involve themselves in the terrorist struggle: "We maintain that the worker proletariat, going hand in hand with the intelligentsia, can and must in the near future fight for its liberation by means of political terror."

There is no evidence that Brusnev opposed the program, though it is certain that he neither wrote it nor reacted enthusiastically to it. Certainly, the program's strong narodovol'tsy tone undermines the thesis of some Soviet historians that the Moscow social democrats were, through Brusnev and Afanas'ev, directed by the St. Petersburg Workers' Union.[110] The program was a compromise, apparently accepted by Brusnev, and as such, it united both narodovol'tsy and social democrats. Radicals like Egupov and Kashinskii could claim they were social democrats in the future and narodovol'tsy for the moment, whereas Brusnev and Mefodiev could prepare for the future by developing conscious worker-activists. *All* defined themselves as social democrats; *all* considered themselves part of the social-revolutionary movement.

The final meetings of the Moscow committee, held to prepare for a 1 May 1892 celebration among Tula workers, when the existence of an all-empire social-revolutionary organization would be announced, were interrupted by the police decision to break up the group. On 26 April 1892, Brusnev was arrested in Moscow. On the same day the police seized Egupov at the train station, about to leave for Tula with a large package of revolutionary materials.[111] Kashinskii was arrested upon his arrival in Kiev, and with Egupov's testimony, the rest of the committee was arrested and the circles associated with them were quickly destroyed by the police. It is noteworthy that Brusnev received the harshest sentence of any member of the group (four years in prison and ten years in exile in Eastern Siberia), not because he was a committed social democrat and labor organizer, but because the prosecutor found some evidence that he may have held explosives for the Terrorist Fraction in 1887.[112]

The first and most obvious conclusion in reviewing the history of the initial stage of the St. Petersburg and Moscow social-democratic movements is that the former was in part influenced and led by Russian workers themselves whereas the latter, with the exception of the Tula connection, consisted almost entirely of intelligentsia radicals. Robert Johnson offers considerable help in understanding this phenomenon when he describes the "insularity" and "homogeneity," the geographical and psychological "isolation" of Moscow workers.[113] They lived in a culturally rich world of their own that spanned the city and countryside, but proved, at least in the period 1888–1892, impervious to new ideas introduced from the outside or from their own ranks. The situation of St. Petersburg workers, though certainly similar in many instances to that of their Moscow brethren, at least allowed room for some workers to satisfy their desire for an education and at most provided an audience for worker-intelligentsia to spread the message of social democracy. Certainly the history of circles in the ranks of Petersburg workers went back at least to the 1860s and early 1870s and they grew steadily in the 1880s (due in good measure to the narodovol'tsy), encouraging both radical workers and intelligentsia in the capital to continue the attempt "to contact and build workers' circles" – a conditioned reflex to the question, "What is to be Done?" In other words, it was the history of relative success among workers in St. Petersburg as much as the structural impediments to propaganda among Moscow workers that determined the important role of Petersburg worker-activists in the 1888–1895 movement.

Second, although Russian workers did not reject outright the narodovol'tsy program as ideologically opposed to their genuine interests, they did demonstrate a preference for social democracy. Primarily, the preference was tactical. Like the Workers' Section of Narodnaia Volia, the activists of the Central Workers' Circle preferred propaganda to terrorism, decentralization to conspiracy, and education to the seizure of power. However, unlike the intelligentsia activists, especially those in Moscow who attempted to achieve a synthesis of narodovol'tsy and social-democratic thinking, the worker leaders of the movement reflected a blend of trade-unionism and social democracy, which interchangeably (and indiscriminately) called on the thought of Marx and Lassalle, even Louis Blanc or the populist tribune of the 1870s Petr Alekseev, to justify their actions ideologically. If the narodovol'tsy were willing to aid the working class in increasing its economic, intellectual, and political powers, without endangering the livelihood of individual workers, then the worker-activists had no objection to cooperating with them, even joining their circles. Still, it was the Petersburg social democrats –

Rodziewicz, Pietrowski, Brusnev, Golubev, Sviatlovskii, Krasin, Stranden, Cywinski, and dozens of others — who were willing to bring their interests in line with those of the workers' circles, which meant patient propaganda, teaching, and often simple lessons in reading and writing. For this reason, as much as any other, the experienced worker-propagandists became committed social democrats. Certainly, too, the example of West European labor successes, and closer to home, the strike movement in the Kingdom of Poland, contributed to the Russian workers' attachment to social democracy. Finally, the goals of Western social democracy appealed to the workers. There is no evidence that workers were moved by the idea of seizing the means of production from the bourgeoisie. The inspiring vision was rather that of Germany, where they saw a powerful workers' party increasingly able to participate in the affairs of state, defending the interest of workers, and providing them with their fair share of economic and social power.

The third and final conclusion concerns the general issue of conflict between members of the intelligentsia and worker activists, ably analyzed in the work of Reginald Zelnik.[114] From the perspective of the period 1888–1893, one can question whether there was a genuine "conflict" at all. The predominant antagonisms were not between workers and intelligentsia, but between intelligentsia leaders like Egupov and Kashinskii, who advocated a more political, broad approach to the social-democratic movement, and men like Brusnev or Krasin, whose goal was to downplay politics in favor of developing Russian Bebels. Among the "Bebels," the worker-activists in the social-democratic camp, most sided with Brusnev's orientation, but some leaned toward Egupov. In both cases there was more strife between the worker-intelligentsia and their opponents in the factories, whether the evangelists or the worker-activists holding liberal, populist, or narodovol'tsy views, than between the worker-activists and the intelligentsia.

Yet areas of disagreement did exist between the worker-activists and the intelligentsia, though given the evidence, it is impossible to attribute them either to "structural" differences between workers and intelligentsia or to a "malaise" in their interrelationship.[115] First of all, the worker-activists pushed for more involvement in the strike movement and in political demonstrations, whereas the intelligentsia, especially in St. Petersburg, attempted to confine social-democratic activities to education and organization of circles. The Petersburg social democrats from the intelligentsia were more wary of police intervention than the workers, more protective of the small gains that had been made, and less eager to demonstrate the limited influence of their fledgling organization. The worker-activists were quite simply

more open and spontaneous than their comrades from the intelligentsia, and this characteristic influenced other areas of differences as well.
For instance, the workers were more willing to cede a role to
narodovol'tsy propagandists than were the intelligentsia, though it
must be emphasized again that ideological conflicts were rare among
the intelligentsia and among workers. The workers were also much
less concerned with the rules of conspiracy than were the intelligentsia
social democrats, which led isolated members of the latter group (Radchenko is the best known example) to shun workers' circles altogether.
In fact, the Petersburg worker-activists complained incessantly that
there were too few members of the intelligentsia willing to sate their
peers' hunger for knowledge and radical literature, though of course in
Moscow the situation was the opposite; few workers' circles were willing to adopt intelligentsia propagandists.

It would be unwise to overestimate the importance of these areas of
conflict — for the spirit of the period 1888–1893 was one of cooperation
and mutual discovery, not unlike the heady atmosphere of the going-
to-the-people movement. The social-democratic intelligentsia had
discovered the people, went among them, taught and nurtured them,
and sometimes tried to merge with them, living and dressing in their
fashion. But the people, in this case the worker-activists, learned
about the intelligentsia, in their own way merged with them, and lived
and dressed like them. Certainly there was some resentment and envy
that derived from the social distance between them. But at least at the
inception of the Russian social-democratic movement, the relationship
between worker and intelligentsia leaders was characterized for the
most part by trust, cooperation, and mutual respect.

Social Democrats in the Provinces, 1887–1892

8

The Revolution of 1917 was not simply a tale of two cities — St. Petersburg and Moscow. Nor was the emergence of Russian social democracy confined only to these centers. At the end of the 1880s and early 1890s, social democratic circles functioned in the most diverse and sometimes unlikely provincial towns of the Russian Empire. The university centers of Kharkov, Odessa, Kazan, Kiev, and Riga spawned social-democratic groups, as did the industrial towns of Ivanovo-Voznesensk and Orekhovo-Zuevo. Social democracy also had a following in such backwaters as Belgorod, Nezhin, and Tobolsk. Traveling along the Volga, stopping in the hamlets and villages that dotted its banks, Gorky describes in his memoirs, *My Universities*, the dozens of circles that met for discussions in the back room of a store, in a gymnasium student's flat, or even in an open field. Provincial Russia trained many outstanding Marxist revolutionaries, among them young Vladimir Il'ich Ul'ianov (Lenin), who was born in Simbirsk, was involved in Kazan narodovol'tsy circles in the late 1880s, and "converted" to Marxism as a practicing lawyer in Samara in 1892–93.

The geographical spread of social-democratic circles was matched by the variety of national origins of their participants. As we have seen, Poles were instrumental in the formation of social-democratic groups in St. Petersburg and Moscow. While Poles, Ukrainians, and other nationalities were important to the development of social democracy in the provinces, Jewish radicals often played the key roles in the western and southern provinces of Russia, in such towns as

Odessa, Ekaterinoslav, Kiev, Minsk, and Vilna. With considerable irritation, Lenin complained that at the Second Congress of the Russian Democratic Party (1903) a third of the participants were Jews.[1] The leader of the Bolshevik faction did not speak out of appreciation; yet his rough count reflected the highly disproportionate contribution of Jews to the development of Russian social democracy in light of the fact that Jews comprised only 4 percent of the Russian Empire's population.

Tiflis and Riga

Police and judicial reports of antigovernment activities in the provinces in the period 1888–1892 demonstrate that narodovol'tsy circles continued to function, but that social-democratic ideas had permeated the revolutionary movement as a whole. Much as in St. Petersburg and Moscow, the radicals in the provinces viewed social democracy not in contradistinction to the ideology of the narodovol'tsy, but rather as a necessary modernization of a somewhat outdated formula for revolutionary activity. In the provincial cities, as in St. Petersburg and Moscow, social-democratic groups emerged among workers as well as within intelligentsia circles. Sometimes the two groups intersected and combined in joint efforts; as a rule, however, social-democratic circles among workers in the provinces remained isolated from those among the intelligentsia, and thus were often not detected by the police.

At the end of the 1880s the police found proclamations, notes, printed and hand-written propaganda tracts, and even underground libraries at factories all over the empire. In Ivanovo-Voznesensk, a group called the Workers' Battalion issued a hectographed proclamation (1890) that urged the workers to join together in an organization defending the interests of Russian labor.[2] During a 1888 strike at the Pavlov textile factory in Shuia, a worker spoke to the strikers in the name of a circle of weavers, urging them to support common demands and form a joint organization. During the investigation of the circle, the police turned up a rich library of social-democratic literature located at the plant itself.[3] Even in the small centers of craftsmen in Siberia, social-democratic literature had an impact. In Tobolsk province, for example, the police uncovered in 1888 a widespread organization of circles, devoted to the printing and distribution of illegal social-democratic literature.[4]

From the point of view of the authorities, one of the most dangerous groups in Russia in late 1887–early 1888 ("more serious," the gendarmes noted, than the Society of St. Petersburg Craftsmen) was the Tiflis social-democratic circle.[5] At the city's Transcaucasus railway workshop, two senior metal workers, Fedor Guzenko and Vasilii

Gerasimov, conducted meetings in which "books were read, the contents of which seemed to be intended exclusively for the working people, with an explanation for the reasons for their poor economic situation." According to one of the circle's participants, Petr Kalosh, workers from local factories as well as metal workers from the railway workshop went beyond the discussion of purely economic issues. The idea of the meetings, he testified, "was to prepare the workers for an open protest against the government . . . and to demand the changing of the existing state order."[6]

Guzenko had come to Tiflis in April 1887 from Rostov-on-Don with another worker-activist, Petr Shafranov. Guzenko was widely known as a talented orator, and from all the evidence he was also an energetic organizer. He contacted Nikolai Ermolaev, the former student and Workers' Section leader who had been banished to Tiflis, and Ermolaev provided him and Kalosh with illegal literature. Guzenko also seemed to fit the general ideological description of working class radicals of the period. He was committed to raising the intellectual level of workers, while at the same time he blamed the poor conditions of workers on the government and demanded from it "freedom of speech, the press, and a constitutional form of government."[7] In July 1888, Guzenko and Shafranov left Tiflis for Batum, where they continued their propaganda among workers. The lathe-turner Ivan Chepurno took over direction of the Tiflis circle until its destruction in early 1889.

While the Tiflis circle is an example of social-democratic groups composed exclusively of workers, the Riga social-democratic circle, formed by students at the Polytechnical Institute at the end of 1889, was confined exclusively to intelligentsia radicals. Not only did the Riga circle have no contacts with workers (because they considered themselves "theoreticians" rather then "practitioners"), but they also completely rejected cooperation with the narodovol'tsy and demonstrated a genuine distaste for narodovol'tsy theory and practice. Similarly, the narodovol'tsy circle at the Riga Institute, led by the veteran Polish radical Stanislaw Gorbaczewski, had little interest in the Marxists. Indeed, the Riga case was the only example of pure antagonism and ideological feuding between narodovol'tsy and social democrats, even though Soviet historians claim that conflict was the rule rather than the exception during the 1880s. The police, accustomed to cooperation between the two movements, were incredulous about that situation: "not only did [these groups] not pursue common goals together nor have any organic ties between themselves, but on the contrary, [they] viewed one another with . . . distrust and even animosity."[8]

Led by Vasilii D'iakov and Vasilii Ul'rikh, the Riga "Marxists," as the circle was called, consisted of seventeen members, all of whom were thoroughly familiar with the works of Marx and Plekhanov. Although they thought of themselves primarily as a discussion group, they also set up a lithograph operation to copy and distribute social-democratic literature. "The Marxists," Egupov noted, "were more Marxist than Marx himself," a statement that was often applied to Plekhanov as well. Like them, but unlike most narodovol'tsy circles since the beginning of the 1880s, the narodovol'tsy circle in Riga completely rejected "the usefulness of propaganda among workers" because "they could not play a major role as weapons in the hands of an intelligentsia organization."[9] In Riga, then, workers were ignored by both Marxists and narodovol'tsy, in the former case because capitalism had not advanced far enough for the workers to have achieved a conscious role in their own liberation, in the latter (related) case because they were considered to be too concerned with their own economic needs to pay attention to the political struggle.

Except for printing literature, financing some activities of the Moscow social democrats, and providing a forum for the discussion of Marxist ideas, the Riga circle accomplished little in the way of spreading its organizational network or contacting other social-democratic circles in Russia or in the emigration. Just as the members claimed in their depositions, the circle was intended exclusively for self-education. Its members read and discussed *Das Kapital* and held lengthy sessions devoted to refuting Mikhailovskii's articles in *Russian Treasury*. With Egupov's arrest and subsequent testimony, which implicated the circle in the financial support of Moscow social democrats, the police arrested all the members of the Riga Marxists in the summer of 1892 and banished them from university towns for five years.[10]

Kharkov and Rostov-on-Don

The Tiflis and Riga social-democratic movements represent two extremes — a workers' movement independent of intelligentsia and an intelligentsia movement independent of workers. The case of the Kharkov social democrats is much more typical of the empire as a whole. To be sure, in Kharkov, as in Tiflis, it was the workers who initiated the movement, but they then turned to intelligentsia activists for help. Dr. Dmitrii Bekariukov, the primary intellectual in the Kharkov movement, came from an organization, the Conspirators, which, not unlike the Riga Marxists, was composed exclusively of intelligentsia, only in this case members were encouraged to bring workers' circles under the aegis of their own group.

The Kharkov prosecutor traced the origins of the social-democratic circles to late 1885, when a number of craftsmen, mostly tailors, formed a secret circle for the purposes of "self-development."[11] However, most of the workers had benefited from experience in narodovol'tsy and Black Repartition circles in 1882–1885, among them Vasilii Sokolov, Ivan Veden'ev, Andrei Kondratenko, Iakov Riabokon, Aleksandr and Solomon Bronshtein, Semen Chaichenko, and Iakov Alekseev.[12] By February 1886, the leaders of the narodovol'tsy workers (Kondratenko, Riabokon, and Reshetnikova) and of the Black Repartitionists (Sokolov, Venden'ev and S. Bronshtein) reached an agreement to join forces. They organized a small underground library and collected for the treasury a 3 percent monthly contribution from each member of their circle.

In the late fall of 1887 Dmitrii Bekariukov joined the circle, and over the next several months read to its members "various compositions" of a socialist character.[13] In addition, under Bekariukov's leadership the circle raised money to help political prisoners and their families. In a series of propagandistic letters written by Bekariukov and distributed among the Kharkov workers in hectographed form, the doctor pointed to examples of economic exploitation among Russian peasants and workers and instances of judicial malfeasance. The letters also explained the nature of capitalism and exploitation of labor, while painting a general portrait of the future socialist society based on the works of Chernyshevskii and Mikhailovskii. Using the British Isles as an example, Bekariukov argued that the Russian people must learn to resist oppression. When Irish or Scottish peasants raised their pitchforks against the tax collectors, positive gains were won. "If all our peasants and workers had acted with such determination," he wrote, "they would have lived better long ago."[14]

Bekariukov's radical career represents a fascinating and little known variant of the revolutionary underworld of the 1880s. He was the son of a rich landowner in Volchansk district (Kharkov province) and attended Kharkov University. There, in 1883–84, he joined the highly secretive student group of the Conspirators. As much a Masonic-style fraternity as a radical circle, the Conspirators, led by the medical student (later doctor) M. D. Fokin, established an elaborate set of regulations to protect the group from police infiltration. At the core were strict rules governing the behavior of the "professional center." Only intelligentsia "Conspirators-revolutionaries" were admitted; no one could leave; and they were forbidden on pain of physical harm to reveal the names of their fellow members. In theory, the remaining members of the organization, those not admitted to the central circle of Conspirators, would never know the membership of the next level, of which there were four.[15]

Fokin demanded "iron discipline" from the group, not just in conspiratorial matters, but in attention to the members' studies and social behavior. Those who wavered were upbraided and sometimes purged. On the other hand, fictitious marriages and thievery were condoned as means to raise money for the organization. Like so many Jacobin groups before and since, the Conspirators demanded strength not only of the spirit, but of the body. The members of the group engaged in a variety of sports and in general physical culture in order "to be strong physically" and to present "an image of vitality."[16]

The ideology of the Conspirators was certainly secondary to their fraternal ties. Memoirists consider Fokin a narodovolets, devoted to peasant revolution and seizure of power, though opposed to terrorism as "a waste of strength in the fight against tsarism." Bekariukov, on the other hand, had extensive contacts with Black Repartition circles and was known for his advocacy of propaganda among urban workers, who would eventually play "an enormous role" in the revolution.[17] In both cases, the young Conspirators were convinced that political revolution lay far in the future and that what was necessary at the moment was patient and meticulous "preparatory work," which would produce the eventual upheaval. Their minimum program called simply for improved factory laws, more land to the peasants, and democratic reform in government.

When Fokin received his medical degree in 1885 and left for Kiev to assume a position, Bekariukov took his place at the Kazan center. At this point, there were some twenty circles tied to the Conspirators, including Fokin's new group in Kiev. Indeed, wherever the Conspirators went, to Riga, to St. Petersburg, to Kiev, and in Bekariukov's case, to Kharkov, they were obligated as members of the group to engage in "systematic, long-term conspiratorial work."[18] Between 1883, when Fokin started the circle, and 1893, when by mutual consent the Conspirators dispersed and joined the increasingly public liberation movement, some seventy-five to eighty young professionals experienced this Jacobin and Masonic-style organization.[19]

Bekariukov was not so much a leader as a tolerant *starosta* (elder) of the Kharkov workers' circle. In another circle the student Khaim Gel'rud read from Marx's *Dal Kapital* and Bakh's *Tsar-Hunger* and finally presented his listeners with a program for "an independent workers' organization."[20] The students Ivan Meisner and Vasilii Denisenko also visited the workers' circles. Meisner, who was well known to the police for having sent "letter bombs" to a number of Kharkov officials, encouraged the workers to adopt a terrorist program;[21] Denisenko conducted a separate circle devoted to the study of mathematics and geometry. Denisenko, Gel'rud, and Meisner were apprehended by the police, so the workers found another student,

Isaak Rodshtein, to take their place. But Rodshtein was disliked by the workers — "he was too much the pessimist" — and his place was taken by Semen Chaichenko and Ivan Radchenko.[22] Altogether, the relations between the workers and intelligentsia propagandists, Bekariukov included, can be described as cordial. But Veden'ev recalled that in the most important daily questions, "which apartment to use for studies, books, and money, we [the workers] were not dependent on anyone."[23]

Early in the spring of 1887 the Kharkov workers decided to write a program that would contain "a clearer formation of the goals and activities of the circle."[24] The testimony of the typesetter Iakov Alekseev described the origins of the program: "I am dissatisfied with the contemporary government structure, but I do not belong to any party. I searched for a means, a way in which it might be possible to improve the contemporary order, but I still have not found that means." With purely terrorist views, Alekseev added, "I am not fully in agreement."[25] In search of a program, Alekseev and his fellow Kharkov workers sent two of their members, Vasilii Sokolov and Ivan Veden'ev, to Belgorod to consult with Stepan Tkachenko, who was under police surveillance for Workers' Section activities, and with Sergei Veletskii, also under surveillance for his organization of Poltava railway workers in 1883–84. Despite police awareness of his antigovernment leanings, Veletskii led circles in the teachers' institute and seminary in Belgorod, while Tkachenko established a workers' circle among local wool-washers.[26] In consultation with the Kharkov delegates, Veletskii wrote a program which Tkachenko presented to a meeting of the Kharkov circle in May 1887. But, because of its length and complexity, the workers rejected Veletskii's proposal, adopting instead a draft program of their own, entitled "The Russian Social-Revolutionary Group of Workers."[27] "Every part of the program," Veden'ev recalled, "was formulated by the workers themselves, and then edited by . . . Bekariukov."[28]

The Kharkov workers' program began: "We are socialists, because we think that the best structure of a society is one in which the means of production belong to the producers," and "we are revolutionaries because we consider ourselves in the right to overthrow forcefully the contemporary structure to change it for the better." Except for this elevated *profession de foi*, the program is very careful in limiting the tasks of the Kharkov group. Socialism will come, but only after a long series of upheavals, and the closer Russia comes to socialism the better will be the conditions of life for the working class. Kharkov workers cannot lead a revolutionary struggle; instead, they should lend their support to a larger nationwide party. The propaganda of socialist ideas among peasants, workers, and intelligentsia is the key to creating the bases of socialism. The program did accept political terrorism as well as factory and agrarian terrorism, but "only in those cases when it carries a propagandistic character," and if it conforms with "our own demands." But terror "in the sense of self-defense from spies and enemies" they saw as useful "at all times, in any circumstances."[29] As Veletskii wrote to an exiled friend in Tomsk, the Kharkov workers' circle looked at terrorism "not in the narodovol'tsy sense as a way to bring about revolution, but as a provisional means of self-defense and struggle . . . along with other kinds of activities."[30]

Despite the Kharkov group's ability to unify around a program, serious internal squabbling at the end of 1887 succeeded in breaking it up. Some of the workers, led by Mikhail Konotopov and Solomon Bronshtein, resented Bekariukov and his tendency to conceal his activities. Others were unhappy that Bronshtein, Veden'ev, and Kondratenko seemed to act as an exclusive central committee of the group. Bronshtein agreed in the end with the criticism and demanded that the organization change "in such a way that more members of the group are informed about its activities."[31] The actual split was precipitated by a dispute over the entrance of Galina Krylova, a young, charming worker, into the circle's activities. Veden'ev and Kondratenko objected to her allegedly flirtatious behavior, claimed that she disturbed the work of the circle, and demanded that she be expelled. Bronshtein and Sokolov came to her defense and broke away to form their own separate organization, the New Southern Brotherhood, taking with them part of the library and two intelligentsia activists, Nikolai Kozhevnikov and Rabinovich. However, early in the spring of 1888, Bekariukov tried to patch up the quarrel, or at least presided at the meetings where the workers aired their differences and agreed on a new, more "democratic" form of organization.[32] Thereafter, there were seven members of a central group (Veden'ev, Sokolov, Bronshtein, Riabokon, Kondratenko, Chaichenko, and Sergei Kureliuk); each was to direct the activities of his own circle and report to the central group. Policy would be decided by a simple majority vote with at least five members present.

By the summer of 1888 the Kharkov workers' group had doubled in size to about fifty active members. A. Makarevskii, who had just returned from abroad, was astounded by the growth of the workers' organization, and he took on the job of establishing contacts with similar organizations in the North.[33] New members joined (among them Ruvim Ereivman, Grigorii Luk'ianov, and Iuvenalii Mel'nikov), and the original members of the central circle organized their own circles. Similarly, the Kharkov workers contacted a circle of local students (primarily from the Veterinary Institute), who provided important financial help, as well as a substantial number of illegal publications.

When Bekariukov was forced to leave Kharkov in December 1888 because the police were close on his heels, he suggested Sofia Siniavina as his replacement. But because of her earlier associations with Petr Shevyrev of the Terrorist Fraction, she was so carefully watched by the police that the workers halted any contact with her. Instead, the Montenegrin student Vladimir Perazich took Bekariukov's place in the group.[34] According to the police, "Perazich obtained illegal publications for the group; he read to the workers at Kondratenko's apartment various books of a social-political character; he took an active part in the meetings; and talking to the workers, he attempted to support and develop in them dissatisfaction with the existing political and social order."[35]

If Perazich took over the teaching functions in the circle, the workers themselves assumed responsibility for what they saw as their most critical task — the organization of other workers and propagandizing of socialist ideas in their midst. Luk'ianov and Tkachenko were sent to Aleksandrovsk to set up a circle among the railway workshop laborers. Kondratenko, Veden'ev, and Chaichenko traveled to Rostov-on-Don with the idea of allying with the workers' circle at the Vladikavkaz railway workshop. An Aleksandrovsk circle among train workers was quickly established; Tkachenko already had extensive contacts there and Kondratenko supported his efforts by allocating funds and printed materials from the Kharkov group's store. But in Rostov-on-Don, Chaichenko and Kondratenko met with the intelligentsia leaders of the railway machinists' circle, Nikolai Motovilov and Sergei (Lazar) Bogoraz, and found them opposed to and suspicious of a purely workers' circle. Motovilov and Bogoraz had developed a careful "system of circles' work," using only legal material for propaganda and shunning all contact with non-Rostov groups, and they refused to enter into an alliance.[36] But the Kharkov workers would not give up; the group sent "one of its most active and most sophisticated members," Iuvenalii Mel'nikov, to Rostov-on-Don in order to organize a circle of workers independent of the Bogoraz-Motovilov circle.[37]

Mel'nikov was born in Chernigov province, the son of a Ukrainian nobleman. While he attended secondary school, both of his sisters got involved in radical activities; Lidiia was expelled from the Bestuzhev School, while Vera was exiled to Siberia. Mel'nikov himself left school and learned the metal-working trade in order to get closer to "the people." In and out of trouble with the police for narodovol'tsy worker activities, he came to Kharkov at the end of 1887 to find a job at the Southern Railway. Mel'nikov was an "able, experienced, agitator," wrote his friend Boris Eidel'man; he was "simple, direct, sensitive, sincere, clear-headed, and absolutely consistent."[38] Mel'nikov's work in Rostov-on-Don supports this description. On arriving in Rostov, Mel'nikov signed up as a machinist in the railway workshop and quickly formed a circle of workers. He also contacted Bogoraz and Motovilov and won their sympathy by assuring them that he would not engage in propaganda among the intelligentsia. Frustrated by the worker-intelligentsia disagreements in Kharkov, Mel'nikov's idea in Rostov was to form an organization comprised exclusively of workers. He read theoretical works to his circle (including parts of *Das Kapital*) and engaged in wide-ranging discussions with them. His letters to his exiled wife are filled with enthusiasm for and confidence in the workers' movement.[39] Mel'nikov also led those Kharkov and Rostov workers who found their program's support of terrorism "out of place," except in the rare instance when it was carried out by the masses.[40] Whereas Tkachenko in Belgorod defended the terrorism of the program, Mel'nikov time and again attacked it as inimical to the development of the workers' movement.

The police had already infiltrated the Kharkov group in late 1886 and had placed a spy in its organization (probably Kureliuk), but the authorities were very careful not to move against the group until they had sufficient evidence to ensure a successful prosecution. Finally, during the summer of 1889, the police destroyed both the Kharkov and the Rostov-on-Don groups, with information based on secret reports and backed by Veletskii's complete confession. Despite all the evidence to the contrary, the judiciary once again placed the burden of guilt on the intelligentsia. The workers (Mel'nikov included) were, wrote the Kharkov prosecutor, "not so much active participants as passive victims of propaganda of an antisocial character." People like Bekariukov and Perazich "could not help but have a bad influence" on naive workers.[41]

Especially in the case of the Kharkov organization, the Russian authorities missed the importance of the development of the social-democratic movement. Russian workers, even in the provinces, had developed the capability of organizing themselves, contacting similar organizations, and issuing programs. From the diverse printed material found on the group's participants, as well as from their letters and program, it is apparent that the Kharkov workers' circle was neither Marxist nor narodovol'tsy in its orientation. Especially after Mel'nikov joined it, the group expressed a fledgling social-democratic world view, one that demanded workers' organization, enlightenment, and political and economic freedom as necessary steps towards the establishment of socialism. The Kharkov circle explicitly rejected classical narodovol'tsy formulations, yet there is no evidence that either the workers or the intelligentsia ever read or heard of Plekhanov's works. Instead, the group seems a logical step from the earlier Kharkov Workers' Section circles, a further step away from the original program of Narodnaia Volia and another step toward the demand for a social-democratic party.

Kazan, Vladimir, and Fedoseev

The development of social democracy in Kazan was even more closely tied to narodovol'tsy activities than it was in Kharkov. In 1885–86 Kazan had been the center of Sergei Ivanov's attempts to revive Narodnaia Volia, and a number of the small student circles that had fallen under his influence continued to operate in 1887–88.[42] Until the spring of 1887, Kazan zemliachestvo organizations among the city's students had also been extremely powerful. With their suppression the radicals went underground, joined with the remaining narodovol'tsy activists, and in late 1888 formed two new circles that crossed institutional and zemliachestvo boundaries. The goal of these circles, consisting of about thirty students at the university, the School for Doctors' Assistants, and the Midwife Institute, was to read and discuss social questions raised in the illegal literature. According to the testimony of one of these circles' veterans, Andrei Vydrin, the circles also committed themselves to "mutual help, aid for exiles, self-education, familiarization with and the spread of social revolutionary ideas."[43]

The two circles, which soon operated as one, were led by the students Konstantin Iagodkin and Nikolai Fedoseev.[44] Iagodkin organized a number of evening parties—replete with food, liquor, discussions, and singing—charging a fifty kopeck entrance fee that was to be used for aiding political exiles. Iagodkin also collaborated with Vladimir Sychev and Pavel Voronin in hectographing a brochure called "Political Russia," which recorded instances of political arrests, successful escapes from Siberian exile, and traced the advances of the revolutionary cause. Iagodkin and Sychev also supervised the circles' two libraries, which were later joined with the zemliachestvo library and served as the central focus of Kazan's democratic circles in the 1890s.[45]

One of the most influential members of the Kazan circles was Nikolai Fedoseev, though he was not their leader and moving force as Soviet historians insist, nor a Marxist in this period, as they claim.[46] To be sure, in 1891–92 Fedoseev did become a Marxist and exerted an important influence on Lenin. But during his Kazan years, Fedoseev, like so many other young students in Russia, was interested in adapting the teachings of Marx to a broad revolutionary ideology that would attract all elements of radical Russia into the liberation movement.

Fedoseev was born in Nolinsk (Viatka province), the son of a nobleman and civil servant. As a student at the first gymnasium in Kazan, Fedoseev already demonstrated an interest in radical politics, coming into contact with student radicals associated with Sergei Ivanov and his underground press as early as 1885, when he was sixteen. A year later Fedoseev and his friend Volkhov formed their own student self-education circle. At the same time, he joined a circle tied to the liberal P. A. Golubev, many of whose members later became social democrats. In 1887 Fedoseev petitioned to leave the eighth grade of the gymnasium and took his final examinations with the intention, he wrote to Nikolai Motovilov in December, of engaging in the study of the "factory question." Fedoseev added that he meant to study Russian workers not because they were inherently more important to the revolutionary process than peasants, but quite simply because so little work had been done on their situation in comparison to what had been written about the peasants.[47]

When the Kazan circles unified their efforts at the end of 1888, Fedoseev occupied a prominent role in their activities. He actively participated in the group's attempts to help political prisoners. He organized materials for the preparation of false passports and made lists of the names of recently arrested radicals, including those who escaped and those who died or went insane in exile.[48] Fedoseev's apartment, like that of Feiga Berkovich, was used by the leaders of the Kazan group for their regular meetings. Fedoseev told the police that these meetings were devoted primarily to reading and discussing "the programs of various revolutionary parties."[49]

In March 1889 the Kazan group agreed "unanimously" to adopt a program of action that was intended to satisfy all of its members' ideological leanings. Called "Young Russia," the program was neither narodovol'tsy nor social-democratic in its orientation; Fedoseev was quite correct to describe it in his deposition as nonideological.[50] First of all, a significant minority of the group's members held strongly narodovol'tsy views. One, Petr Maslov, supported "an extreme terrorist" program. Fedoseev and Sanin, representing the majority, were more interested in pure theory than they were in practical politics. As a result, "Young Russia" simply listed the activities the group intended to support: propaganda among young intelligentsia members, the peasantry, workers, and the military; the organization of forces for propaganda and active political struggle; the printing of materials that elucidated the group's socialist views; providing material and moral assistance for their members as well as for political prisoners; and the maintenance of libraries, treasuries, and repositories for illegal documents.[51]

The adoption of this statement was enough to prompt the police to break up the Kazan group in the summer of 1889. All of the group's participants were sentenced to fifteen months in jail. There is no archival evidence to support the Soviet contention that the group contacted workers' circles in Kazan or in any other cities or took any other steps towards organizing workers' circles of its own.[52] The primary contribution of the Kazan group to the development of Russian social democracy resides instead in its translating, printing, and collecting operations. At Iagodkin's apartment, the group hectographed large quantities of its own "Political Russia," as well as "An Abstract from Marx," which summarized his economic views.[53] On the suggestion of Fedoseev, Sanin translated Karl Kautsky's "The General Tenets of the Economic Teachings of Karl Marx," and the group hectographed Engels' "Development of Scientific Socialism."[54] Thanks primarily to Fedoseev, the Kazan group assembled one of the most impressive underground libraries in Russia; it included works of Marx and Plekhanov, narodovol'tsy literature, and legal works on Russian economic and social development.[55]

While Fedoseev was already interested in Marxism in his Kazan days, he had definitely become a Marxist by the time he was released from prison in January 1892 and sent to Vladimir under police surveillance. Unquestionably, the great famine of 1891–92 played an important role in the affirmation of his social-democratic leanings, as did his thorough study of Russian economic life while in prison. Even more important were his discussions with the Marxist statistician P. N. Skvortsov, who lived and worked in Vladimir. Skvortsov, like many Russian Legal Marxists of the 1890s, was politically a liberal and eschewed any contact with underground circles in Vladimir, just as the underground circles rejected him because of his doctrinaire Marxism and legalism.[56] Fedoseev, on the other hand, immediately entered a Vladimir circle consisting of both narodovol'tsy and social-democratic radicals including his fiance M. G. Gopfengauz, S. P. Shesternin, N. L. Sergievskii, and M. L. Sergievskii. "Among us," Shesternin wrote, "he was the first Marxist."[57]

While he was in Vladimir, Fedoseev was also approached by a workers' circle at the Morozov factory in nearby Orekhovo-Zuevo. The Morozov circle was led by Iakov Popkov, an Old Believer and a foreman in the weaving section of the factory. He had some elementary education, and from the police reports and the materials seized at the time of his arrest (which included Marx's *Communist Manifesto*, Plekhanov's "The Yearly International Holiday of Workers," and Diksztajn's *Who Lives from What?*), it was apparent that he was a committed social-democratic worker.[58] Popkov's circle consisted of eight workers – all in their mid-twenties or older, and all literate, Orthodox, and from the peasant estate. Except for Grigorii Kapranov and Fedor Khor'kov, who had come to the Orekhovo-Zuevo circle from Moscow in order to distribute illegal, mostly social-democratic literature, all the workers were employed at the Morozov factory. Vasilii Krivosheia, a twenty-three-year-old gymnasium drop-out and minor town official, also aided Popkov in his work, spreading underground materials and discussing the gains of Western social-democratic parties among the Morozov workers. Popkov, Krivosheia, and the circles' workers frequently organized meetings and regularly discussed the issues of Russian labor – in the prosecutor's words, "at every opportunity."[59] Most meetings were held in the forest, much vodka was imbibed, and the discussions went on late into the night. At one such meeting, an older worker, Aleksei Alektorskii, read illegal publications aloud and concluded, "The sovereign is always drunk, signs things without reading them, and only gets interested when they bring him a fine woman."[60]

In the summer of 1892 Krivosheia was fired from his civil service post and subsequently moved to Vladimir, where he met Fedoseev and apparently persuaded him to write a program for Popkov's group. On August 29 Fedoseev and Krivosheia returned to Orekhovo-Zueva where they presented the program to a meeting of Popkov's circle in the forest on the outskirts of town. The situation of Russian workers was "awful," Fedoseev's program began, but it was not hopeless. Russian workers must learn to struggle against the factory owners; only then would they understand that their economic emancipation will have to be accomplished by violent means: "seizing both political [state] power as well as all means of production from the hands of the owner-capitalists." For these purposes, all efforts must be placed in the organization of the working class. Without such political rights as "the freedom to publish workers' newspapers, freedom of assembly, and the legal operation of workers' unions, it would be impossible to form such an organization." Only *after* political freedom was achieved would the workers be in the position to struggle against the factory owners for a shorter workday and an increase in wages. For the moment, then, the task of the propagandists was to infuse the workers with an understanding of their broad interests, emphasizing that "pillage and destruction is definitely harmful to their cause." Fedoseev concluded his presentation of the program with a discussion of Western social democracy and the precepts "of the teacher of the workers of all the world, the German Karl Marx."[61]

Fedoseev visited the Morozov factory circle for two days (according to his confession only to see how the workers lived). On his return to Vladimir, he was immediately arrested by the police, who used his program as the pretext to round up Popkov, his workers' circle, and Krivosheia.[62] Fedoseev vehemently denied that he had anything to do with the program; "it completely contradicted his views and aroused in him the feeling of deep moral repulsion." Unlike Krivosheia, Fedoseev took no part in organizing activities. He had simply drafted the program and was desperately and understandably afraid of returning to prison. (After a few months in the Vladimir jail, Fedoseev suffered from a number of diseases, including a "general breakdown of his nervous system," which worried the authorities so much that they sent him off to a healthier Vologda exile.)[63]

From Fedoseev's program it is apparent that he was a fully convinced Marxist in 1892, and he unquestionably exerted an influence on the development of Lenin. More interesting for our purposes is the Marxist slant of the propaganda material—handwritten, typewritten, as well as illegal publications—which the police collected during their round-up of Morozov workers.[64] All of these materials pounded home one basic theme: the tsar was not a friend to the workers but the intimate confederate of the capitalist factory owners who were determined to suppress the workers' every aspiration. Typical was the proclamation "From Worker Socialists" (20 July 1892), undoubtedly written and circulated by the Popkov circle. The proclamation blamed the cholera epidemic that was sweeping through the Morozov factory on the tsar and the "owner-capitalists" who had brought on the famine. "Plague and famine," concluded the proclamation, "will scourge the Russian land as long as power remains in the hands of the tsar." [65] To the small social-democratic circle of Morozov workers, the connections among economic privation, social catastrophe, and political repression were clearly drawn, even without the help of Fedoseev. Equally clear was their solution—to organize the workers to overthrow the government, rather than to advocate terrorism or the seizure of power by intelligentsia conspirators.

Jewish Social Democrats

The first year-and-a-half of Alexander III's reign marked a crucial turning point in the development of political thinking and revolutionary action among Russian Jews.[66] During the 1870s, the Jewish intelligentsia had devoted itself primarily to the spreading of the *haskalah* (enlightenment), a movement that fit the expanding educational opportunities and the general aura of optimism among Jews under Alexander II. The small number of Jewish populists (about 4 percent of those arrested) expressed little interest in the Jewish question as such, and more often than not concealed their Jewishness in order to work among the Russian peasantry. The most fundamental assumption of both populists and haskalah publicists — that Russification in one form or another would lead inevitably to better life for all — was shattered by the pogroms of 1881–82. From April of 1881, when the Elizavetgrad pogroms began, to the spring of 1882, when the violence had spread to over two hundred cities, towns, and villages in the Pale of Settlement and the Kingdom of Poland, traditional anti-Semitism turned into a bloody attack on Jewish lives and property. By May 1882 the pogroms had died down; the Temporary Regulations of May 3 placed more severe restrictions on Jewish movement and economic activities in the empire; and the appointment of Dmitrii Tolstoi as Minister of Internal Affairs at the end of May signaled a firmer government approach against civil disturbances of any kind, even those directed against the Jews.

Order was restored, but Jewish political consciousness would never be the same. Surges of nationalist feeling rocked the Russian Jewish intelligentsia, producing an organized Palestinophile movement and also encouraging the growing impulse among Jews to emigrate. Some Jewish populists searched for ways to combine socialism and nationalism; others threw themselves into the narodovol'tsy struggle to overthrow the autocracy.

Although Narodnaia Volia initially treated the pogroms as the first stage of the social revolution, in some ways even encouraging them, during the course of the 1880s Jews and converted Jews played an increasingly important role in the narodovol'tsy movement. Dembo, Bogoraz, Bakh, Orzhikh, Kogan-Bernshtein, Shternberg, and scores of other Jewish radicals involved themselves in the terrorist struggle and the organizational efforts of Narodnaia Volia. In fact, the end of the 1880s witnessed a sharp rise of Jewish involvement in radical circles, not just in the capitals, but in the Pale of Settlement as well. Sitting in exile in Siberia, one rather anti-Semitic activist, I. I. Mainov, complained that large numbers of Jews were pouring into the exile centers of Iakutsk province: "Perelman from Minsk, Edel'man from Pinsk, Gegelman from Dvinsk, and so on and so forth." Who could figure out where all these people came from, he wrote. "The vast majority of these *gomeltsy* and *mintsy* appeared to be from the youth — intelligentsia, half-intelligentsia, and sometimes not intelligentsia at all."[67] George Kennan, who completed a tour of Siberia at the time, noted more sympathetically that inexperienced teenage Jewish girls and boys, sometimes still not graduated from the gymnasium, could be found in the worst corners of the tsarist exile system.[68]

Most of these young people were narodovol'tsy of one stripe or another, and generally they expressed no more interest in the Jewish question than did their forerunners, the Jewish populists of the 1870s. However, among Jewish social democrats, especially those in the Pale of Settlement and in large Jewish population centers of Odessa and Kiev, concern for the fate of the Jewish people in part motivated their revolutionary activity. By the late 1880s, there was also an observable growth in the *Palestintsy* or proto-Zionist movement among Jewish radicals, which sometimes overlapped with social-democratic circles. Jewish social democrats also differed from their narodovol'tsy coreligionists in that they were heavily influenced by the already mature Polish social-democratic movement. Despite the influence of the Poles and the newly emerging Zionist movement, Jewish social democrats, at least in the 1880s, shared the goals of Russian social democracy as a whole: integrating social-democratic and narodovol'tsy ideas; organizing intelligentsia and workers' circles with firm ties between them; and avoiding police infiltration and arrests by all means, even going as far as using terrorism in self-defense.

A number of the Jewish social-democratic circles, like their Russian counterparts, were barely distinguishable from those of the narodovol'tsy. Especially in Vilna, which served the Russian Empire as a kind of clearinghouse of revolutionary ideas, the outlook of Polish social democracy mixed with that of Narodnaia Volia in Jewish circles that adopted what they considered the best elements of both. In the same circle, one activist could be a Marxist, the second a terrorist, the third a follower of Mikhailovskii. Arkadii Kremer and his wife P. Srednitskaia became involved in narodovol'tsy circles in 1886 while they were secondary school students. Lidiia Aksel'rod led a "salon" for Jewish radicals of the city, in which she defended Marxist ideas.[69] Lev Iogikhes (Jogiches-Tyszko) also attended Aksel'rod's salon and devoted himself to conspiratorial activities, forming an illegal library and contacting Russian officers' circles in Vilna.

With Tsemakh Kopel'zon, who organized Jewish workers and intelligentsia, and Waclaw Selicki, who propagandized among Polish workers, Iogikhes was a chief figure in the Vilna underground. According to Kopel'zon, Iogikhes was an advocate of terror and of workers' propaganda, hoping to transform the most conscious workers into active terrorists.[70] To complicate matters further, both Kopel'zon (who considered himself a social democrat) and Iogikhes were affiliated with Dembo's narodovol'tsy circle of Poles and Jews, making it difficult to put them in the same category as other Jewish social democrats. Yet their primary concern was to carry out propaganda among Jewish workers. They spoke to the workers in a mixed Russian and Yiddish language and taught them all kinds of subjects. Iogikhes was well known for his lectures to workers on anatomy, complete with a skeleton that he dragged from circle to circle. Both Iogikhes and Kopel'zon also attempted to counter the growing interest among intelligentsia (more than among workers) in emigration to Palestine.

There were many Jewish social democrats, like Iogikhes, who simply were not attracted to Judaism or to the specific national development of Jewish workers. One of the most important was Leiba-Iudes Levinson, who was caught by the police (7 August 1888) trying to smuggle several suitcases full of Emancipation of Labor brochures into Russia. Although the police report that Levinson had earlier worked mainly with a fund to help poor Jews, her activities, like those of her friends Stepan Raichin (who had been sent to Moscow), Iosif Slobodskii, Khaia-Gitel Vaintrob, the Tsetseliia Gurevich, were closely tied to the Zurich group of Plekhanov and Zasulich.[71] All had been abroad for schooling, and all returned to Russia to work for and spread social-democratic ideas. Zasulich urged Levinson "to find serious and enterprising people in Russia," especially those "committed to the cause of propaganda among workers." Zasulich's last bit of advice to Levinson was to start in Odessa rather than Vilna, for there Plekhanov had many friends, whereas his relations with the Vilna circle were marred by mutual distrust.[72] Like other Jewish intelligentsia followers of Emancipation of Labor, Levinson assumed that the social-democratic revolution would automatically solve the problems of the Jewish proletariat. As she later confessed to the police, "In Russia, sooner or later, there will be an economic revolution, which will lead to a new social and collective structure. This revolution will be produced by the working class, conscious of its rights and interests as well as of the contradiction between their rights and interests and those of other classes." The bourgeoisie would cease to support the government, and the autocracy would be destroyed. Those who wished this revolution to come, Levinson concluded, should continue to explain to the workers their crucial position now and in the future, and also to organize workers' circles and societies.[73]

Even without the benefit of Plekhanov's direct influence, other Jewish social democrats moved in the same direction. A St. Petersburg couple, Berk (Boris) Ginzburg and his wife Elizaveta Breitman, translated Marx's works from the German in 1887 and wrote a series of short articles intended to illustrate the inevitability of an economic revolution.[74] In Kharkov, a group of Jewish and non-Jewish students led by Fedor Zandberg of the Veterinary Institute collected money for the families of arrested workers (Kondratenko, Riabokon, Chiachenko, and others) and spread social-democratic ideas (mixed with a devotion to terrorism) in circles around the city. Dr. Minna Fainberg, who had studied medicine in Bern (a major center of Russian Jewish Marxists in the 1880s), brought social-democratic propaganda to local gymnasium students, including Leiba Fainberg, Ivan Vileishis, Moisei Ganfman, Lev Dembo, and Enta Fainberg. Several Jewish social democrats worked in the Kharkov Sunday school, while others, like Vulf Liapidus and Grigorii Lifshits wrote for the local newspapers.[75]

According to most sources, the Jewish social-democratic movement among workers can be traced to the years 1886–87, when young Jewish students attempted to apply the ideas of the Polish Proletariat and of Plekhanov's Emancipation of Labor to the increasingly desparate situation of poor Jewish workers in the towns and cities of the Pale of Settlement.[76] Perhaps the most talented of these students was Emil Abramovich, who should be considered one of the pioneers of Russian social democracy. Abramovich was born into a poor Jewish intelligentsia family in Grodno in 1864. His father was a dentist, his mother had been educated in Breslau, and his maternal grandfather was a scholar who translated old Hebrew texts into German. Abramovich finished the gymnasium in Grodno with a gold medal in 1882 and went to Paris to study medicine. When he returned to Russia in 1884 to finish his studies in Derpt, he was already a confirmed social democrat. He spent every summer working in Minsk, where his family had moved to, and contacted underground Jewish circles, which until then had been dominated by Efim Khurgin, the "General" of at least a dozen Jewish narodovol'tsy groups in the city.[77] But with the help of Isaak Gurvich, Abramovich quickly set up a series of Jewish social-democratic circles, which Gurvich led when Abramovich was in Riga. Gurvich, who described his own ideology at this point as a mix of social-democratic and narodovol'tsy precepts, relied on the talented organizer and typesetter Iosif Reznik to contact dozens of workers' circles in town. By the end of 1886 Gurvich, Abramovich, and Reznik supervised three levels of circles: one of literate workers who read only legal publications, a second of literate workers, mostly typesetters, who read Russian underground publications, and a third level where Russian was taught to Jewish workers. Gurvich noted that these circles were not driven by assimilationism;

there was simply no Yiddish-language radical literature, and Jewish workers wanted to learn Russian.[78] A fourth, more centralized group of circles continued to be led by Khurgin; though predominantly narodovol'tsy in approach, its members exchanged materials and often cooperated in joint ventures with the social-democratic groups. According to Gurvich, some two hundred and thirty workers were involved, about half in the social-democratic camp and half in Khurgin's. One of the joint ventures involved setting up a legal Saturday school, which for a short time taught some one hundred Jewish workers to read Russian and addressed general scientific subjects, but, according to Isaak Gurvich, the antagonistic "Jewish bourgeoisie" in the city convinced the authorities that socialism was being taught so they closed the school.[79]

The best developed of the Minsk circles was that of the typesetters, led by Shlemo (sometimes Lev) Berkovich. Berkovich was born in Minsk and, like his father, was trained to be a Hebrew teacher.[80] However, he broke with his family, studied Russian and science, and worked as a typesetter. It was into this circle that Abramovich introduced Plekhanov's works in mid-1887. According to the testimony of one of its members, Girsh Polak, the 1887 Minsk circles (including one in nearby Nezhin) adopted no specific program. Instead, they read illegal propaganda, exchanged publications with other circles, and spent a great deal of effort avoiding police investigations, which were plaguing the city's radicals. As was typical of this generation of Jewish activists inside Russia, the Minsk group's primary concern was the desperate plight of poor Jews in the Pale. Yet they understood that the liberation of Jews was dependent on the general liberation of the Russian proletariat, a goal that Abramovich repeatedly emphasized in his propaganda. Shlemo Berkovich wrote to his future wife, Dveira Son'kina (April 1887):

> You paint me a picture of the unhappy position that has fallen to our brother Jews in Kiev and you write how sadly this picture affects you . . . I sympathize with your misery, but . . . if in society people suffer, that serves as a sign that the society is unsuitable, and if it is unsuitable then it is necessary to destroy it . . . to destroy the order that forces people to live in such a way . . . Not a single people can be made free if you do not give the others freedom . . . [Russia] imagines that if she oppresses the Jews, then she will become better . . . But no, this is great folly. The moment will come when she will awake from her deep sleep, and will see herself that it is not the unfortunate Jews who are the cause of her evil, but rather her own leaders, her own ex-

ecutioners, from whom she will exact vengeance, and she will have a bad conscience for having shed innocent Jewish blood.[81]

Jewish social democrats of the period also understood that the increasing attraction of Zionism in the Pale in the late 1880s could be explained by the hard lives of the population. In 1890 the police seized from a small Slutsk circle of young, poor, barely literate Jewish social democrats a handwritten propaganda piece which explained that the "dream of Palestine" derived from the "isolation, political injustice, and economic helplessness" facing Russian Jews. The only way to free the Jewish people was to make sure the "contemporary state structure" was destroyed, and a "new and better one" took its place.[82]

Although their goals were radical, the Minsk social democrats devoted themselves exclusively to propaganda. Girsh Polak met with several local circles in Minsk and in Nezhin, but did not attempt to draw them into a central organization. He encouraged them to exchange publications and discuss illegal works, but stopped at that. "The city is terrorized by searches," Berkovich wrote, and we are being "very careful."[83] Despite these attempts to stay clear of the police, the Minsk authorities decided that the social-democratic circles "should in no way be distinguished in their organization from a conspiratorial society." Consequently, in the beginning of 1889, the authorities arrested and sentenced nineteen circle members, almost all printers, fourteen of them Jews, one a Catholic converted from Judaism, and the other four Orthodox.[84] A number of the Minsk social democrats escaped arrest by emigrating. Gurvich himself left for the United States in 1890, as did Reznik in 1892 after serving his sentence. "In fact," Gurvich wrote, "we prepared socialist workers for America."[85]

Abramovich also managed to escape immediate prosecution. He had finished his medical studies in Derpt and lived in Kiev from February to May 1889, when he was finally arrested. According to the prosecutor, Abramovich spent his Kiev months "exclusively in various revolutionary undertakings."[86] Dressed in workers' garb, he distributed social-democratic literature among Kiev railway workers, whom he was able to contact through his old Minsk comrade, Shlemo Berkovich. In less developed labor circles, Abramovich lectured Jewish and Russian workers on the necessity of maintaining libraries, reading secular works, and building their intellectual prowess. He himself organized an illegal library, collecting a monthly fee from the library's members (twenty-three altogether) of twenty-five kopecks to buy new materials.[87] Gurvich wrote about him, that "Abramovich exerted an extraordinary influence . . . not only as a talented tutor, but as a person of rare spiritual qualities. He was a democrat not only in words, but also by nature; in him there were no abstractions, he dealt with the workers straightforwardly, as comrades, without the least hint of a patronizing tone . . . and the workers loved him and treated him with deep respect."[88] Abramovich lived extremely simply, rooming with the Kiev typesetters Izrail Golomb and David Gal'pern, and he turned over all of his money, earned by giving private lessons, to the cause. He continued his medical practice, but refused to treat the rich or to take money from the poor for his services. Even the gendarme agent Sergei Zubatov later sarcastically noted that Dr. Abramovich was "considered a saint, and [the workers] bowed before him."[89] "He was the first genuine social democrat in our midst," wrote the Kiev social-democratic worker L. Fedorchenko (Charov), "and everyone respected him."[90]

Abramovich's most lasting contribution to the development of Russian social democracy was the program called "Social-Revolutionary," which he probably wrote and to which he undoubtedly adhered. The program surfaced in dozens of circles from Odessa and Kiev in the South to Minsk and Vilna in the North during the period 1887–1889, reflecting Abramovich's own travels in this period.[91] Although Polak testified that the Minsk and Nezhin circles did not adopt a common program, the prosecutor thought otherwise, and claimed that they subscribed to "Social-Revolutionary."[92] The program, it is important to stress, never mentions the specific plight of the Jews, but instead concentrates on the importance of the political struggle for the working class as a whole. From everything we know about Abramovich (and that is too little), the principles of the program conform to the message he spread among workers: "The path of our development is the same as in Western Europe"; the goal is "the destruction . . . of the capitalist structure by means of the transfer into common ownership of all the means and objects of production"; "social revolution" is the only way to accomplish this goal and the revolution "can be carried out only by the people and for the people, that is, by the organizedproletariat"; and the timing of the revolution "depends not only on objective conditions, but also on the level of consciousness of the working class."

The program goes on to state that the duty of social revolutionaries (the word social democrat is never used) was to engage in a struggle on two fronts—among the working class, to raise its consciousness, and among the intelligentsia, to force the granting of a constitution that would give the workers the opportunity to liberate themselves. Terrorism is a fully legitimate means of such a struggle because it "disorganizes" the central state structure, making both tasks easier. But terrorism alone could not destroy despotism; therefore social revolutionaries must work among the only group that cared, and that is the "urban proletariat – the industrial workers." Much like the later brochure by Arkadii Kremer, the influential "On Agitation" (1893), Abramovich's "Social-Revolutionary" advocated agitation among workers as the primary focus of political activity. "Standing on the foundation of the most basic economic interests of the working masses," the party should interest workers "in political struggle – this is the difficult and significant task that should occupy one of the most important places in our program . . . *Every strike, every uprising, every conflict with a factory owner also leads the workers to a conflict with the government. All of these events can be transformed, under the influence of socialist workers, into political manifestations and demands for political freedom.*"[93]

This powerful program of political agitation undoubtedly prepared the social-democratic circles of the Pale for the emergence in the mid-1890s of the Jewish revolutionary organization called the Bund, and in almost every detail, save for the future welding of Jewish cultural nationalism to social democracy, presaged that party's theoretical underpinnings. The emergence of Jewish nationalism among social democrats in the Pale, already evident in the letters of Berkovich, exercised a particularly strong influence on Jewish intelligentsia social democrats in Odessa at the end of the 1880s, where, according to the local authorities, "the socialist views of Karl Marx are receiving special attention."[94] The leaders of the Odessa social-democratic movement were two Jewish students at Novorossiiskii University, Mikhail Morozov, who had earlier studied at the St. Petersburg Forestry Institute, and Khaim Ginzburg, who with his friends Lev Roizman and Faivel Ioshkevich-Rotkus' worked among Jewish and non-Jewish intelligentsia circles in Odessa. Morozov and Ginzburg went from circle to circle, spreading social-democratic literature, including Abramovich's "Social-Revolutionary." The most politically active circle in the Morozov-Ginsburg network was that of Nakhman (sometimes Naum) Shteinraikh.[95] The Odessa prosecutor noted, however, that the Jews in the Shteinraikh group wavered between social-democratic ideas and those of emerging Zionism: "Many Jews participated in this circle, but then, at the same time, the Palestine question emerged, and they changed their views somewhat and became captivated by their national movement. For instance, in such a frame of mind, Roizman and Ioshkevich left for Paris; there, however, under the influence of the ideas of Lavrov and Plekhanov, they returned again to the idea of the necessity of working in the interests of the transformation of the contemporary system in all of Russia."[96]

Indeed, the particularly strong ties between Jewish students in

Odessa and their coreligionists in Paris constantly supplied new leaders for the Odessa social-democratic movement.[97] With the arrests of Morozov and Ginzburg in 1890, a circle of young Jewish private teachers, led by David Simkha Gol'dendakh (D. B. Riazanov, later a Bolshevik), took charge of the social-democratic movement in the city. Gol'dendakh had been in Paris in 1880–90 and returned to Odessa in April 1890 with a packet of social-democratic materials and a letter of recommendation from Iudka Rapoport, the leader of the Paris group called Terrorist.[98] Along with Gershon Gurevich and Veniamin Rubinshtein, both private teachers, Gol'dendakh searched out workers' circles in the city and began holding weekly meetings among them to discuss illegal publications. About twenty workers consistently attended the meetings, and several of them later described to the police their format and content:

> Gol'dendakh usually took notes out of his pocket and discussed . . . the position of the working class in Russia [and that of] the peasants of a particular province, and always pointed out their sad position and their oppression by capitalism and the landowners. He pointed out the incompleteness, the unfitness, and even the harmfulness of government institutions in relation to the working class . . . He said that events in the future would demonstrate how to change this situation of the workers for the better, but that now it was only necessary to gather in circles and prepare people for reading illegal literature.[99]

The rapidly expanding social-democratic movement in Odessa supplied propagandists for the cities and towns of the South and West, and the police practice of banishing young Jewish activists from large university towns further encouraged the spread of social-democratic circles. In Ekaterinoslav, for instance, the banned Odessa activist Efim Mundblit served as the catalyst for the town's social-democratic movement. He joined forces with Boris Teitelbaum, who had recently returned from Switzerland, and with Pavel and Matvei Tochiskii (banished from St. Petersburg), to form a small, predominantly Jewish social-democratic circle in 1890–91. By the following winter the circle had contacted workers at the Briansk metallurgical factory in Ekaterinoslav and tied its efforts to a circle of Jewish artisans in the town (Kats, Fain, Metlitskii, and others).[100]

The police broke up Gol'dendakh's Odessa organization in the summer of 1891. The documents of his case reflect yet another example of the changing motives of Jewish involvement in the Russian revolutionary movement. In Gol'dendakh's confession, there was no special

Jewish dimension of his general commitment to radical politics. Instead, he stressed that he was a "scientific socialist" and came to the conclusion that the only way to improve Russia was to change "economic relations, the bases of all other relations."[101] Emil Abramovich perhaps best expressed the dilemma of the Jewish radicals, caught between their pained awareness of the particularly difficult situation of the Jewish masses and their desire to participate in the Russian revolutionary movement as a whole. In a letter of March 1914 to his old friend from the movement in the 1880s, E. A. Gurvich, Abramovich described what he saw as the increasing misery and persecution of Russian Jews: "Where is the escape from this situation? Neither emigration nor Palestine changes the reality of the Jewish masses, who, whether they want to or not, remain in the desert. And generally Jews are not in a position to change their situation through their own power. Only with the democratization of the state structure will this be possible. But when will that happen? And until then what will happen to the Jews?"[102]

Abramovich's own career reflects the tragic dilemma of Jewish social democrats. He was sentenced to ten years of exile in Eastern Siberia for his activities in the 1880s, after which he lived in a Lena mining camp and served as a doctor. In 1912 he was arrested again for writing an exposé of the Lena Goldfields Massacre, for which he received another four years in Siberia. In 1914, he volunteered to serve in the Russian army as a doctor among Jews who were drafted; their generally poor health and unwillingness to fight caused him great sorrow. According to Gurvich's short biography in *Katorga i ssylka* (1928), Abramovich was arrested in Saratov in 1919 and was in prison for about a half year "for belonging to the social-democratic party [Mensheviks]" before he died. The journal's editor, Boris Eidel'man, added the note, "for acting against Soviet power."[103]

By the end of Alexander III's reign, the social-democratic movement influenced the Russian underground in all the major cities of the empire. Even small towns like Nezhin, Slutsk, or Belgorod were the sites of social-democratic activities, as were the traditional troublespots of Odessa, Kiev, Kazan, and Kharkov and the better known capitals of St. Petersburg and Moscow. The movement was characterized by diverse combinations of intelligentsia and worker activists. There were circles comprised exclusively of workers, as in Tiflis, the Morozov factory, or the Rostov-on-Don circle (led by Mel'nikov). There were also intelligentsia and workers' circles which sought out each other, sometimes merging easily with one another, as in Minsk or Tula, sometimes establishing a formal structure for relations as in St.

Petersburg, and sometimes at odds, as in Kharkov. In all cases, the foundations of the social-democratic movement were much more spontaneously laid, much less influenced by Plekhanov's Emancipation of Labor group, and much more widespread than is usually asserted.

Former narodovol'tsy contributed directly to the growth of social democracy, most notably in Moscow and in Vilna. But former Black Repartitionists like Bekariukov and Krivosheia, and former Palestintsy like Lev Roizman, also became social-democratic activists. The varieties of social-democratic platforms were legion, as diverse if not more so than the narodovol'tsy programs they only sometimes criticized, reflecting the multifarious social, ethnic, and geographical origins and concerns of the hundreds of social democrats who made up the movement. The diversity of their programs also reflected a central problem for Russian social democracy in this period (and later): how to adopt the already ambiguous example of the Western, parliamentary social-democratic movement to the backward political and economic conditions of the Russian Empire. For social democrats like Abramovich, Iogikhes, or Egupov, terrorism was a perfectly appropriate means of struggle; for others, like Brusnev, Fedoseev, or the Afanas'ev brothers, terrorism contradicted the fundamental interests of social democrats. Just how political should the movement be? Should it help fight for those parliamentary institutions that would guarantee the emergence of the social-democratic party, or should the movement confine itself to building the organizational and intellectual forces of the workers, awaiting the further development of capitalism and the eventual bourgeois revolution that would accompany it? Most social democrats of the period, workers and intelligentsia, did not offer firm answers to these questions. Some leaned towards one solution, some to the other, but most tried to find a compromise between them. Part of that compromise involved uniting with other groups in society to struggle for a new and more liberal Russia, a proposition that also gained wide acceptance in narodovol'tsy circles.

Narodovol'tsy — Old and New

9

The revolutionary movement at the end of the 1880s and beginning of the 1890s was stimulated by a renewal of political life within Russian educated society, obshchestvo, during the same period. Especially zemstvo liberals — progressive gentry and "third element" professionals — chafed under the government's attacks on even the modest freedom of action granted the zemstvos in their 1864 statute and became increasingly dissatisfied with the "small deeds" mentality of the 1880s. The counterreforms in local government, promoted by Minister of Internal Affairs Tolstoi as early as 1884–85, were designed to tie the villages and zemstvos directly to the central bureaucracy, changing the autonomous character of local administration. Although Tolstoi's intention to eliminate zemstvo independence altogether was thwarted by his opponents in St. Petersburg, the government did abolish the elected post of justice of the peace (12 July 1889) and replaced it with the appointed land captain (*zemskii nachal'nik*), directly responsible to the central government. Less than a year later, 12 June 1890, a new decree was announced, bolstering the landed gentry's control of the rural zemstvo while increasing the provincial governor's ability to veto undesirable candidates for its offices.

Ironically, the government passed the restrictive decrees just as the zemstvos were about to exercise one of the most important functions in their history — that of famine relief. During the summer of 1891 the most serious crop failures in over half a century struck the Volga region and the central agricultural provinces; some 12.5 million people desperately required government help.[1] In 1892 cholera and typhus swept through the hungry villages, driving the death toll to

400,000. From the beginning of the famine the government took charge of relief efforts, providing the zemstvos with financial means and sufficient independence to administer many of the relief programs. At the same time the authorities encouraged private charitable efforts through a Special Committee on Famine Relief, founded in November 1891.

Despite distrust of the government's motives and abilities, famine relief was carried out by all parties with a minimum of rancor and with remarkable competence. By the time the crisis abated, however, the antagonisms between obshchestvo and government, which had been generally quite muted during the 1880s, reemerged in the aggravated form they had taken in the two decades following the 1861 emancipation. The zemstvos assumed that they had proven their worth during the famine and as a result would receive an expanded role in the countryside; the authorities on the other hand continued their program of the bureaucratization of the local governmemnt, which conceived of zemstvo autonomy as dangerous for the maintenance of the autocracy. After the famine, the simmering anger of zemstvo specialists and liberal gentry turned increasingly to political discussions about the need for a constitution and, by the turn of the century, to serious confrontations with the autocracy.

The famine of 1891–92 produced equally strident political reactions on the part of the cultural intelligentsia, the acknowledged leaders of obshchestvo. The government was uniformly and quite unfairly condemned for having badly mismanaged the famine relief. Even more important, the famine itself was interpreted as a sign of a deep-seated crisis in the economic and social policies of Alexander III's government. Much like the explosion of Russian self-criticism and questioning following the Crimean War and the Russo-Turkish War of 1877–78, the famine set off a new period of excited public debate over Russia's past and future.[2] Mikhailovskii, Vorontsov, and Danielson entered the fray in 1892 as new members of the editorial board of the journal *Russian Wealth* (*Russkoe bogatstvo*), railing against capitalism for having caused the famine, while accusing the Marxists of passivity, even compliance, in face of the destruction of the Russian village. The Marxist counterattack was led by Petr Struve, who analyzed the famine as a clear indication that class differentiation had triumphed in the countryside, beginning the welcome era of full-blown capitalism in Russia. Between 1892 and 1894, when Plekhanov and even the young Lenin entered the debate, the questions about the fate of capitalism in Russia and the role of the individual in history sparked a renewed interest in politics on the part of Russian obshchestvo. During the famine, it had seemed that the common efforts of government, zemstvos, and liberals to relieve peasant misery might introduce an era of cooperation between autocracy and educated society. Instead, in the wake of famine, the gap between them increased, while that between obshchestvo and the revolutionary movement, which often seemed unbridgeable in the mid-1880s, significantly narrowed, producing hopes in both camps for a united liberation movement.

Narodovol'tsy-Social Democrats

At the end of the 1880s more and more Russian radicals looked for an alternative to the traditional program of Narodnaia Volia. However, the growth of social democracy did not impede the development of narodovol'tsy circles; nor did it completely discredit narodovol'tsy thinking. To be sure, the spread of social-democratic circles influenced the ideology and tactics of narodovol'tsy groups, just as the narodovol'tsy workers' groups of an earlier period contributed to the development of Russian social democracy. Some social democrats and narodovol'tsy adopted elements of the other group's program, mixed both ideologies, worked together, and shifted from one camp to the other. Even within single radical groups like the Terrorist Fraction or the Moscow social democrats, some members could be classified as social democrats while others were narodovol'tsy.

Common in the late 1880s were the narodovol'tsy-social democrats, men and women who advocated terrorism, though of an allegedly new, "systematic" sort and who identified the working class as the central locus of the coming revolution. In the narodovol'tsy tradition, they also allotted to the peasantry a role in the revolution and assigned to the intelligentsia the function of directing propaganda and carrying out selective terrorism. They were voluntarists, convinced that revolution would come only if committed people worked consciously for it. Still, these radicals were not completely unjustified in identifying with social democrats. They rejected the "seizure of power" concept, so central to classical narodovol'tsy thinking. They hoped to organize workers into a fighting class that would lead the struggle for a constitution, then for socialism. The quicker the transition the better; yet the same radicals adhered to the principle that revolution was a scientific inevitability. In other words, they placed their voluntarism against the background of the scientific objectivity of the newer revolutionary world view.

These hyphenated radicals — the narodovol'tsy-social democrats — were for the most part astute underground politicians in search of an ideology that could provide a basis for broadening the revolutionary struggle. Narodovol'tsy programs continued to attract them because the autocracy persisted in its repressive course, denying any form of popular representation in government, hounding democratic elements in society, and confining the peasant masses to their poverty and ignorance. Terrorism was still relevant to persecuted radicals in an autocratic society, as were conspiracy, political struggle, and the hope for a peasant revolution. At the same time, the programs of the social democrats were attractive because they explained how the new forces in society had been unleashed by the quickening pace of industrialization. They also provided a framework for exploiting and identifying with the growing activism of the workers. In an era of the triumph of the Russian industrial revolution and of the concomitant victories of technology and science, Russian radicals found comfort in the scientific language of social democracy, in its assurance of victories in the future, in its promise that the isolation and backwardness of Russia would be eliminated.

Still, most of these narodovol'tsy-social democrats were not theoreticians and spent very little time working on ideological problems. Generally, there were either propagandists among workers, in which case they were primarily in the social-democratic camp, or they were terrorists and thus in the narodovol'tsy camp. After 1 March 1887, the second group was especially hounded by the government, which pursued a policy of indiscriminate arrest and of sentencing radicals to terms of exile that lost all reasonable relationship to the actual severity of the crime. The response to this pressure was predictable: hundreds of Russian radicals fled abroad, among them survivors of the Terrorist Fraction and significant numbers of Jewish students who had been expelled from Russian universities — having committed, in the words of a Ministry of Education circular, "the smallest infraction of student rules,"[3] not to mention having engaged in the slightest antigovernment activities. These émigré activists thereafter launched their plots from the relatively safe havens of Zurich and Paris. But even Western Europe was becoming dangerous for Russian radicals. The Foreign Okhrana, centered in Paris and active all over the continent, planned entrapments, worked for extraditions, planted spies, and even vandalized precious printing operations.

Most of the narodovol'tsy who remained in Russia carried on the traditions fo the Terrorist Fraction, fully accepting the precepts of workers' socialism and insisting on the need to strike at the government through terrorist activities. But a growing minority of narodovol'tsy activists, equally devoted to the cause of the urban proletariat, rejected the ideological justification and practical prospects for terrorism. They introduced a new concept of narodovol'tsy activities, which emphasized cooperation with the liberals in a drive for democratic rights. These "new narodovol'tsy," as they called themselves, responded to changes in Russian society, especially the

growth of the labor movement and the emergence of zemstvo and professional liberalism. Frustrated by the years of isolation wrought by
terrorist plots, the new narodovol'tsy searched for a democratic coalition that would finally end the nightmare of autocracy.

The Circle of Narodovol'tsy and Sofia Ginsburg

As the police began to investigate the Terrorist Fraction, a number
of its members and associates—including Isaak Dembo, Anton
Gnatovskii, Nikolai Rudevich, and Orest Govorukhin—escaped to
Zurich and regrouped as the Circle of Narodovol'tsy. With financial
support from the Russian community in Switzerland, the group
rededicated itself to the assassination of Alexander III or a high
government official. The preparations for the assassination, they
believed, would have to be carried out abroad, for the police were too
effective inside Russia itself. The circle set early fall of 1887 as an ap-
proximate target date for the attempt; in the meantime they planned
to prepare the explosives, organize support in the emigration, and
establish firm lines of communication with groups in St. Petersburg.[4]
Old friends in Jewish social-democratic circles facilitated communications: Rafail Soloveichik in Grodno, Lev Iogikhes in Vilna, and Isaak
Gurvich in Minsk put the smuggling and transportations operations of
their groups at Dembo's disposal.[5] The circle also sent a number of
messengers directly to Russia, keeping the home movement informed
about the progress of the plot in Zurich.

Searching for support in the emigration, Dembo paid the obligatory
visit to Lavrov in Paris, receiving the patriarch's blessing for his
circle's intentions. Sofia Ginsburg, a member of the circle and a special
favorite of Lavrov, later testified that the veteran radical hoped, as did
Dembo, that the Circle of Narodovol'tsy would serve as the new rallying point for Russian revolutionary activities in Europe.[6]
Tikhomirov's apostasy was final, irreparably discrediting the Executive Committee. Emancipation of Labor remained so financially
weak and politically isolated that its few supporters, again with
Aksel'rod in the lead, sought to unite with the narodovol'tsy in
emigration. However, like most Russian radicals, Dembo showed little interest in associating himself with Plekhanov's group. Instead, he
solicited support among German social democrats (he worked in their
Zurich press) and among Polish Marxists of the Proletariat, with
whom the circle maintained an especially close working relationship—so close that the police accused the group of "establishing relations between the 'Proletariat' and narodovol'tsy inside Russia."[7]
Several Proletariat members (Aleksander Debski among them) even
joined Dembo's group, as had former adherents of Emancipation of

Labor. He also maintained close contacts with Russian social-democratic students (mostly Jews) in Berlin, and with prominent émigré social democrats such as the Bulgarian Dimitr Blagoev and the Pole Stanislaw Mendelsohn. As a result of his organizational work, Dembo could claim with some justification that his circle was the genuine heir to the Executive Committee.

Unlike Tikhomirov, Dembo had no taste for ideological arguments or publicistic activities. Some émigrés considered him a social democrat; others called him a narodovolets; he made no attempt to distinguish between the two. Dembo and Gnatovskii had participated in predominantly Jewish self-education circles in Vilna in 1885–86, organizing various social events to raise money for political exiles and to buy illegal publications. Along with the Gordon sisters (Esfira and Elizaveta), Fanni Shtein, and Shifra Shavel', Dembo and Gnatovskii formed a small organization to conduct underground teaching and propaganda.[8] Even as a participant in the Terrorist Fraction's activities, Dembo only supplied chemicals for explosives and money. But when he was forced to emigrate, Dembo's ideology became maniacally simple; since it was impossible to propagandize peacefully for the betterment of the people, the only legitimate task was "to eliminate the tsar and systematically destroy every representative of the tsar's power until such time when it would be possible to work for the people."[9] Semen Stoianovskii, the circle's theorist, spelled out his organizational ideas in a similarly terse formula contained in a draft program. Under the conditions of political life in Alexander III's Russia, he wrote, no underground organization of the breadth of Zemlia i Volia (Land and Liberty) or Narodnaia Volia could possibly survive. Therefore, every individual revolutionary "must direct his strength to the accomplishment of terror" by joining small, isolated groups of like-minded assassins whose only goal would be "the carrying out of a terrorist act."[10]

Within the Circle of Narodovol'tsy, the political strategy of terrorism as developed by Narodnaia Volia had become an obsession. Dembo, Gnatovskii, and Debski worked incessantly in their laboratory, experimenting with explosives in the hope of developing a lighter, smaller, yet more powerful bomb. On 22 February 1889 (n.s.), Dembo and Debski climbed a mountain near Zurich to test their latest creation. Close to the top, the bomb accidentally exploded at Dembo's feet, fatally injuring him and badly mangling his companion. Before his death, "and in full possession of his faculties," Dembo told the Swiss police that he was a revolutionary and that his experiments with different kinds of bombs soon would have "paid off." Debski admitted to the police that a few days before the accident Dembo had excitedly informed him that his experiments had produced a new mixture of explosives with devastating power, and "that the study of this material would soon produce the desired results."[11]

From the mass of evidence accumulated by the St. Petersburg prosecutor and from Lavrov's reminiscences of Sofia Ginsburg (written in 1892), one can reasonably conclude, as did the tsarist authorities, that the Circle of Narodovol'tsy planned to assassinate Alexander III on 1 March 1889 and were held up only by the need to develop an easily transportable and effective bomb. Already in October 1888 Dembo had sent Ginsburg (traveling with false documents as a Swiss citizen Wilhelmina Braun) to St. Petersburg, to organize a select group of assassins. According to Lavrov, between her November 1888 arrival in St. Petersburg and the Zurich explosion in February 1889, she had almost completed the preparations for the assassination.[12] She had contacted a list of liberals provided by Lavrov in order to raise funds and had reentered the Kronstadt militaristy circle that she had originally helped to organize in 1885. But with the explosion in Zurich and the exposure of the plot, "Wilhelmina Braun" became the most wanted person in Russia. Ginsburg hid in Taganrog and then in a convent in the Crimea (under the new pseudonym of Lenina!) until the police finally caught up with her in May.

Ginsburg's career is particularly interesting, because she is considered the last of the narodovol'tsy. She also represents an entire generation of Russian-Jewish narodovol'tsy at the end of the 1880s, who demonstrated no particular concern for the plight of the Jewish masses but rather threw themselves wholeheartedly into the world of Russian intelligentsia radicalism. Ginsburg was born in Kerch in 1865, the daughter of Jewish intelligentsia parents steeped in the radical traditions of the 1860s. At the age of seventeen she moved to St. Petersburg in the hope of studying medicine, but as the military medical schools were now closed to women (the academies of medicine were already closed), she entered the Bestuzhev Higher Course for Women and enrolled in the school for midwives. In 1885 she also received a diploma as a private tutor in order to support herself by part-time teaching. Through contacts among the Bestuzhev radicals, Ginsburg participated in the militaristy movement in 1884–85, meeting with young Kronstadt officers and artillery school cadets. Although her role in these circles was a minor one, she feared arrest and left Petersburg for Switzerland early in the spring of 1885. Between March 1885 and October 1886, Ginsburg attended lectures at the medical faculty of Bern University, where she became involved with a group of twenty-five Russian-Jewish students who formed a social-democratic club. During that period she met Lavrov, who, entranced by her openness and self-assurance, became her intellectual and emotional mentor. They shared the same idea: a new and vital social-revolutionary party should be formed, one that would attempt neither to pick up the remains of the narodovol'tsy organization nor to revive the traditions of Narodnaia Volia, but would attract "the still lively and energetic elements" from the old party.[13]

With Lavrov's backing, Ginsburg returned to Russia in November 1886 for an "agitational trip" to test the possibilities for the formation of the new party.[14] She was shocked by what she found. In Odessa and Kharkov, she wrote to Lavrov, there was an appalling dearth of narodovol'tsy literature. At the same time, Plekhanov's writings "had their influence, and a strong influence at that." "Rejection of the political struggle" plus Plekhanov's tone, "self-assured, as if possessed of the truth," seemed to have a strong appeal for the intelligentsia. Passivity was the watchword of the day, whether it was that of Plekhanov or of the increasingly popular Lev Tolstoy. In Ginsburg's view, the individual was robbed of all social responsibility by the social democrats; the important role of the intelligentsia was obliterated. "I, of course, do not deny the efficacy of propaganda among the workers," she wrote; "on the contrary. But surely the military and the intelligentsia would be equally crucial participants in the making of a revolution."[15]

Ginsburg worked for a short time as a governess, converting to Russian Orthodoxy in January 1888 in order to get the job. But her lack of success in organizing a new party, coupled with the brutal experience of being assaulted by several men, prompted Ginsburg to leave Russia. After a brief stay in Bern, she made her way to Lavrov in Paris.[16] Hearing from him about the new Circle of Narodovol'tsy in Zurich, she returned to Switzerland, met Brinshtein (Dembo), and accepted his program. At the same time, she joined the German social-democratic party because, as she wrote Lavrov, "here, all of the Russians are always meeting with the Germans." Her German friends tried to convince her to stay in Europe and devote herself "to the struggle for the emancipation of women in Europe." (Ginsburg was a well-read feminist, and the Germans considered Russian women particularly advanced in comparison to their own educated women.) But Ginsburg insisted on working for the *rodina* — the motherland — though she admitted to Lavrov that there was some hypocrisy in her position because she was indifferent to the cause of the Jews, "which, first of all, I don't even understand." Ginsburg also soon grew weary of the many petty arguments that demoralized the émigré movement. None of the programs was sufficently thought through, she complained to Lavrov, and there were too many irritating personalities (not just Plekhanov!) associated with the movement.[17]

Ginsburg was therefore relieved when Dembo sent her back to Russia as the circle's agent in October 1888. She contacted the Petersburg narodovol'tsy and shared their bitterness that Tikhomirov had returned to Russia without being stopped by the narodovol'tsy emigration. "It is said," she wrote, "that he will remain here until his case is concluded. The question is now asked, what he did he pay to be able to walk freely around the streets of Petersburg? The Parisians, although they babbled a great deal, were, however, unable to prevent his exit from France."[18] She also met with the militaristy leaders Ivan Chizhevskii and Petr Dushevskii and was introduced by them to the growing social-democratic groups in the capital. She propagandized among workers' circles and attempted to convince the social-democratic intelligentsia that the political struggle in general and terrorism in particular should not be abandoned. "My listeners," Ginsburg wrote, "recoiled in horror from my words. First of all, in the opinion of the revolutionaries [Brusnev was among them], this was all totally unpoetical, and second of all, it was dangerous."[19] When the tsar's train accidentally crashed on 17 October 1888, Ginsburg was so elated — surely, she thought, this was the work of the narodovol'tsy — that she wrote a proclamation to "explain to Russian society the meaning of the accomplished deed." In fact, the proclamation differed little from dozens of other narodovol'tsy justifications for regicide. "We are convinced that peaceful means to work for the people do not exist." Therefore, the only way "to improve the lot of people of all social classes is unflinchingly to eliminate the tsar."[20]

The police discovery of this proclamation and the investigation of the Zurich explosion soon afterwards forced Ginsburg into hiding. Still, she continued to maintain that a broad party of social revolutionaries should be constituted; according to her plan, it would cooperate with liberals, workers, and the military, using terrorism as the fire to weld the new liberation coalition into being. She contacted Perazich and the Kharkov workers' group and recruited Semen Stoianovskii and Lev Freifel'd (from Odessa) into her new organization.[21] Finally arrested in May 1889 in Taganrog and sentenced to hard labor for life by the Supreme Judicial Court of the Senate on account of her regicidal writings, Ginsburg was locked up in the Shlisselburg fortress in an isolation ward. There she endured the constant screaming of her only ward-mate, V. P. Konashevich (one of Sudeikin's assassins), who had become insane. She wrote in her diary: "I brought to the attention of the prison authorities the situation of the insane prisoner. In order to pass the time, the gendarmes stand at his door and begin to taunt him in every kind of way, including the most unbelievable animal vileness. I stopped the gendarmes twice, but it was not enough to appeal to their moral feelings, and only the threat of complaining to the authorities succeeded in stopping this primitive behavior."[22] At the same time, the authorities refused her pleas of innocence and petitions for retrial. According to prison doctors, she suffered constant headaches and insomnia. On 7 January 1891, after only forty-eight days of Shlisselburg life, Ginsburg committed suicide.[23]

Sofia Ginsburg was typical of the Russian revolutionary emigration in the late 1880s both in her ideology, an uncomplicated mixture of social-democratic tenets and the terrorist imperative, and in her Jewish background. Of the one hundred fifty-four Russian émigrés linked by the Department of Police to antigovernment activities in 1888, eighty-six (56 percent) were Jews. Thirty-one were Orthodox, primarily Russians, and fifteen were Catholics, mostly Poles. Of the thirty-one radicals indicted in the Circle of Narodovol'tsy itself, twenty-four (77 percent) were Jews. Almost all of these were students in Swiss schools: twelve attended Zurich University, while nine were either preparing to enroll in or already attended the Zurich Polytechnical University.[24] The Russian government's practice of limiting educational opportunities for Russian Jewish youths and of expelling those Jewish students who had made it to the universities provided an explosive supply of revolutionary activists abroad. The general expulsion of Jews from Moscow in 1890 only fueled the resentment of Jewish youth. However, the Jewish radicals did not lose their Russian identity, nor did they express much interest in their new European lands or in Zionism. Rather, in Zurich and Bern, in Berlin and Dresden, they joined and sometimes led disaffected youth of Russian, Polish, and Ukrainian backgrounds in a series of planned assaults on the autocracy.

"Terrorist" and the "Petersburg Revolutionary Group," 1888–1891

Despite the capture of Ginsburg, the Russian police complained bitterly about the Swiss authorities' slow reaction to the Zurich explosion. As a result of the Swiss government's "complete ignorance" of the character and composition of the Russian revolutionary emigration, the Department of Police reported, "the main participants in the conspiracy escaped from Zurich and destroyed or hid the most important evidence."[25] Only second-level conspirators were brought before the Swiss authorities, whereas the principals, including Iudka Rapoport,

Boris Reinshtein, Nikolai Rudevich (Polozov), Rakhil Abramovich, and Beila Gurvich, escaped to Paris. The Russian police should have recalled their own inadequacies — during the previous two years Vladimir Burtsev, Ivan Kashintsev, E. A. Serebriakov, Aleksandr Bychkov, and Mikhail Sabunaev had escaped from exile in Eastern Siberia. Only Bychkov was caught and he committed suicide in prison. Burtsev, Kashintsev, and Serebriakov made their way to Paris where they formed a new center of narodovol'tsy activity. Sabunaev went underground in Kostroma, organizing yet another terrorist conspiracy.

With the addition of the fresh recruits from Switzerland after the Zurich explosion, the Paris emigration became the most dangerous foreign center of narodovol'tsy activity since Tikhomirov's 1882–1884 Executive Committee. The Parisian narodovol'tsy were quite poor, lived among students in the Latin Quarter, and spent most of their time learning the art of bomb-making. Also, they inherited two dozen bombs stored in Ginsburg's Paris apartment and began making arrangements to transport them into Russia for a fresh terrorist attack.[26] Sometimes called the Russian Social-Revolutionary Party Terrorist, or simply Terrorist, the Paris group sent a series of representatives into Russia to try to link the domestic and émigré movements in a major terrorist conspiracy.

Supported by Burtsev and Lavrov, and led by the enterprising Rapoport, Terrorist also attempted to launch a new publication called *Sotsialist* (*The Socialist*). The Okhrana agent A. A. Landeizen-Gekkel'man had provided information that led to the ransacking of the narodovol'tsy press in Geneva.[27] Rapoport now turned to the emigration to support a new publication that would replace *Vestnik "Narodnoi voli"*. He wrote the group's program with the idea of getting the support of Plekhanov and Aksel'rod and entered into negotiations with them.[28] Initially Plekhanov was quite pleased with Rapoport; he seemed to be supporting a Marxist position despite his terrorist inclinations. In the program of these "young narodovol'tsy," he wrote, there is "some naiveté, some blunders, but its general spirit, undoubtedly, is ours."[29] However, the first (and only) issue of *Sotsialist* (1889) contained articles by Lavrov, Kashintsev, and Serebriakov, and Plekhanov felt that Lavrov and Burtsev exercised too much influence over the young Rapoport. Disappointed and hurt that Rapoport had "betrayed" him and turned to his ideological opponents, Plekhanov wrote to Aksel'rod that the young terrorist "came to us in such a Machiavellian manner that I absolutely do not want to cooperate with him in the least."[30]

Rapoport himself was more interested in joining the Petersburg narodovol'tsy than in reaching an agreement with Plekhanov. In fact, by late 1887 narodovol'tsy circles inside Russia had recovered sufficiently from the arrests following the Terrorist Fraction investigation to become an outlet for the Paris bombs. In November 1887 a number of activists who had been associated with Petersburg self-development circles since 1885 joined in a group called the Revolutionary Cadres that was dedicated to spreading socialist ideas, as well as providing help for political prisoners.[31] Led by Nionila Istomina, Nikolai Beliaev, and Karl Kocharovskii, the group gradually became radicalized, in part by Ginsburg. Soon called the Petersburg Terrorist Circle and then the Petersburg Revolutionary Group, the Istomina-Beliaev-Kocharovskii organization drafted a program that combined some of Ginsburg's ideas with those of the growing St. Petersburg labor movement. We are all "social revolutionaries," the program stated, which means doing away with "the present capitalist social structure." In its place there would be a socialist system, in which "the means of production would belong to those who work." To accomplish the revolution that would make this socialist structure a reality, it would be necessary to form a great "workers' socialist party in Russia." But no party could be formed without the basic freedoms of press and assembly and without civil rights guaranteed by a constitution. Therefore the goal of the social revolutionaries was on the one hand to join educated society in its efforts to establish a constitution and on the other to engage in the political struggle against the autocracy. At that time political struggle was possible only by means of terrorism — "any number of attacks on the government." Through terrorism and agitation, the group would also "occupy an influential position among various classes of the population." The revolutionary party would have a twofold organization: "a propaganda section" to push for a constitution and a "fighting section" to carry out terrorist deeds.[32]

Like so many narodovol'tsy circles before it, the St. Petersburg Revolutionary Group set out to build an underground party that would direct the operations of revolutionaries in all corners of the empire. Istomina supervised the construction of an underground press in St. Petersburg; Kocharovskii saw to the building of a laboratory for the preparation of explosives. Beliaev and Izrail'son set up a section of the group in Penza, which soon demanded the assassination of the Chief Procurator of the Synod Pobedonostsev and Minister of Internal Affairs I. N. Durnovo.[33] Istomina and Beliaev objected — no terrorist attack should be carried out until a solid organizational base had been established. Disagreeing, Kocharovskii went his own way, attempting to convince Petr Kulakov and his circle of militaristy to organize a terrorist attempt on Alexander III. Indeed, the Revolutionary Group was plagued from its inception by internal conflicts and disorganization, making it impossible to unify efforts even in the capital alone. Vera Gurari, like Ginsburg a social democrat, terrorist, and narodovol'ka, refused to share resources with the central group. Moisei Garmidor, who returned from emigration in early 1888 to join the new group of activists, found the movement impossibly diffuse and working at cross-purposes with itself.[34]

The debate about how terrorism should be used, whether as a weapon of agitation in the context of a long-term struggle or as an immediate demonstration of the will of revolutionary Russia, divided the Petersburg movement and eventually subverted the Revolutionary Group's organizing attempts. This was especially evident after September 1889, when Beliaev attempted to join forces with Mikhail Sabunaev and his growing Volga narodovol'tsy organization.

Sabunaev was one of the most aggressive and least liked terrorist activists of the 1880s. Initially associated with Young Narodnaia Volia, Sabunaev immediately came over to the side of the "old" and was very useful in keeping his fellow Medical Surgery Academy students in the camp of Lopatin. But he had contracted a serious form of typhus and never recovered properly, sometimes leaving the impression, Sukhomlin wrote, that "he was not completely balanced psychologically."[35] Even the normally generous Lopatin called Sabunaev a "psychopath," and though Salova was somewhat more sympathetic, she nevertheless recognized that he was "sick" and offered to send him to Paris for treatment.[36] Thus Sabunaev was already a troubled young man, to say the least, when he was exiled for five years to Verkholensk. But he escaped in late October 1888 and made his way to the Volga region. That was when S. I. Mitskevich met him and was very impressed: "He was a great conspirator, went around in a wig, with his face made up, [and] had the appearance of some kind of revolutionary dictator-conspirator."[37] The ex-Okhrana agent Men'shchikov described Sabunaev as the most successful underground conspirator of the period. The Moscow Okhrana searched for him for two full years, Men'shchikov wrote, but never found him.[38]

During these two years, Sabunaev spent most of his time organizing young gymnasium and seminary students in Kostroma. By the spring of 1889 the circle was sufficiently well organized to hold a May first meeting on the banks of the Volga that included about twenty youngsters. At this first Russian *Maevka* (May Day celebration), the circle members discussed revolutionary questions and gave speeches "about the meaning of the May holiday and about the general condi-

tions of the country."[39] After this meeting Sabunaev started to push
the Kostroma youth (including N. A. Sanin, V. N. Tikhorskii, S. A.
Ostrovskii, and V. S. Turkovskii) to adopt increasingly radical
postures until the circle could become a fighting organization capable
of carrying out terrorist acts.

Sabunaev concentrated his efforts on the small towns of the Volga
region because of his fear of the capital and the university cities where
the secret police had concentrated its forces. He also directed his propaganda exclusively at school youths, believing that old radical and
liberal circles were so thoroughly penetrated by police agents that a
revolutionary organization had to be built from scratch. Like
Nechaev, Sabunaev wanted to train youngsters of fifteen to seventeen
years of age for the terrorist struggle. It was crucial, he insisted, "not
to confuse radicalism with fancy talk." Any vacillation or refusal to
obey roused his ire. A genuine revolutionary should be fully prepared
to accept the inevitable—"to be arrested, to languish in prison, to be
exiled to Siberia."[40] Sabunaev's fanatic devotion to the perfect revolutionary type, willing to endure any privations for the cause, alienated
several of his followers (G. A. Iablochkov, A. P. Preobrazhenskii,
and I. A. Povarennykh among them) and precipitated a number of
splits and internal crises in the Volga movement.

More important for the narodovol'tsy movement as a whole were
Sabunaev's attempts to subject all narodovol'tsy circles to his
methods. At a meeting of ten narodovol'tsy leaders in Kazan (15
September 1889), Beliaev from Petersburg willingly turned over considerable power to Sabunaev in a new nationwide organization.[41] The
assembled narodovol'tsy divided Russia into various "main centers"
and "local councils," giving the latter the right to carry out terrorist
acts on their own initiative. A number of possible terrorist projects
were discussed, but no definite agreement was reached except to meet
again in the spring of 1890. Sabunaev, along with two fellow Siberian
escapees, Vasilii Gusev and Beila Gurvich, left the meeting with a
mandate to organize the Moscow and Volga regions.[42] His subsequent
propaganda efforts in Simbirsk and Samara met with indifference
from local students. Kostroma remained loyal, and in Moscow,
Vologda, and Iaroslavl, a number of student circles pledged their
loyalty to the new organization.[43] Although Sabunaev never
succeeded in bullying any of his subgroups into terrorist actions, he
did manage to raise significant funds for the narodovol'tsy cause.

Within two months of the Kazan meeting, there was trouble between the Volga and Petersburg organizations. The problem was
partly Sabunaev's visceral mistrust of the Petersburg radicals, with
their supposed ties to the inherently untrustworthy emigration and

also to the capital's ever-dangerous secret police agents. On the other side, the Petersburg organization, especially Beliaev, Istomina, Beila Gurvich, and Vasilii Gusev, gradually succumbed to the spell of the successful social-democratic movement. In December 1889 Gusev sent Sabunaev a letter proclaiming that the Petersburg Revolutionary Group had adopted the new orientation of "workers' socialism" and inviting the leader and his Volga groups to accept the new program. Sabunaev's reaction was predictable: he demanded that his followers choose between him and the "renegade" Petersburg Group, and when they chose him, he forbade any further contact with the Petersburg activists, especially Beliaev and Gusev.[44] Sabunaev's harsh reaction prompted an all-out struggle with the Petersburg group for control of narodovol'tsy strongholds. Gurvich and Istomina went to Penza in May 1890, where they hoped "to direct the Volga cities and little by little to dispel the influence of Sabunaev."[45] Beliaev and Izrail'son attempted to wrest the Riazan group from Sabunaev's control. Now alone at the head of his own organization, Sabunaev concentrated his efforts in "old" narodovol'tsy towns — Iaroslavl, Vladimir, Kostroma, and Voronezh. He set up his own press, reprinted a number of narodovol'tsy classics, and planned a new terrorist journal.[46] In the end, Sabunaev's paranoid fears of the connection with Petersburg proved justified. Gusev, Beliaev, and Istomina were arrested in the fall of 1890 and with the information from the Revolutionary Group's depositions, the police moved on Sabunaev and the Kostroma circle in December.[47] With Sergei Zubatov of the Moscow Okhrana in the lead, the authorities systematically swept through the Volga region and broke up the last Sabunaev circle in Vladimir in April 1891.

The Petersburg Revolutionary Group was indicted primarily for its ties to the emigration, especially to Terrorist. One of the Paris group's members was Beirish Grosman, arrested by the police as he was trying to cross the border with terrorist publications financed by Burtsev; another was Beila Gurvich, who had returned to Petersburg and worked initially with Sabunaev and then with the Petersburg group. The program of the Paris circle called for a series of attacks on high government officials organized by émigrés and domestic narodovol'tsy.[48] In the beginning of 1889, when Ginsburg was forced into hiding, the Paris group sent Iudka Rapoport to the capital to contact the Petersburg Group and to Minsk to arrange transportation of the bombs with Kivel Shmulevich.

Ia. L. Iudelevskii, an advocate of "systematic" terror (and later a social-revolutionary "Maximalist"), conducted the actual negotiations with Rapoport in the name of the Petersburg Revolutionary Group. According to the prosecutor's reports on these meetings, Rapoport and Iudelevskii concentrated on editorial policy for the new Paris journal, *Sotsialist*, and also discussed ways to organize dispersed narodovol'tsy circles and raise funds from domestic sources for the emigration. Istomina, herself wavering on the question of terrorism, wanted to find out Lavrov's attitude toward the Sabunaev-Petersburg Group split but Rapoport refused to speak in the name of Lavrov. As a result, in May 1889, Iudelevskii and Mariia Sheffer went to Paris themselves and called on Lavrov. Of course Lavrov gave his official blessings to the Petersburg Group, agreed to serve as its official representative at international socialist congresses, and even to edit a party journal if the group decided to issue one.[49] However, his attitude toward the growing dispute within the internal movement on the terrorist struggle (and the differences between Istomina and Rapoport on the same question) was the same as that expressed in a "Dear Comrades" letter he sent to St. Petersburg with the terrorist Moisei Garmidor in early 1888. He would support any serious radical group inside Russia as long as its program was "social-revolutionary," but he refused to become involved in disputes between or within these groups.[50]

Burtsev, on the other hand, was less hesitant to support an immediate terrorist conspiracy (though he, unlike Lavrov, favored more active cooperation with Russian liberals). On behalf of the Paris group Terrorist, he sent a certain "Dr. Miller" to Russia in November 1889 to continue the negotiations begun by Rapoport. Miller met with Foinitskii of the St. Petersburg Group in the capital in November and again in Kiev in December. Both times the two agreed to work out a common program and to have a delegate from the group sent to Paris to work out the details. But when Miller returned to Petersburg in the middle of January (1890), he could not convince Istomina to join the efforts of the emigration. She objected to his insistence on the "immediate carrying out of terrorist acts," without first establishing a network of personal ties and material stores that would insure their success.[51] Also, Miller was too inquisitive for Istomina's tastes; he wanted to know the group's program, the names of its members, and the sources of its finances.

Only because she needed the emigration's contacts with other radical groups inside the empire did Istomina agree, in the end, both to provide Miller with an outline program and to dispatch Foinitskii to Paris in May in order to continue negotiations. Before Foinitskii could leave, he and the rest of Istomina's group were arrested in a March-April series of police raids that totally destroyed the St. Petersburg Revolutionary Group. (These arrests also led to the discovery and destruction of Sabunaev's Volga organization.) At the same time, the

French police, using information provided by Landeizen-Gekkel'man, moved in on the Paris group Terrorist. Five émigrés were indicted for experimenting with explosives in a forest outside Paris.[52] Each was sentenced to three years in jail and fined two hundred French francs. A number of other émigrés were seized by the French, questioned, and released with the warning not to engage in any further violent activities. Iudelevskii and Rapoport were both arrested by the Russian police as they attempted to reenter the country in the spring of 1890. Like most Jewish radicals during this period, they received an extremely harsh sentence—five years in solitary confinement and ten years exile in Eastern Siberia.

Narodovol'tsy of a New Type

Before its destruction, Istomina's revolutionary circle had inched towards a fresh concept of narodovol'tsy activity, one which subordinated the terrorist struggle to the broad interests of the liberation movement. They had rebuffed Sabunaev's attempts to recreate Narodnaia Volia and rejected the Paris group's insistence on an immediate assassination attempt. Impressed by the growth of the workers' movement, Istomina, Gusev, Beliaev, and Gurvich, among others, adopted a program more in concert with the social democrats of the capital than with the Narodnaia Volia. To be sure, not all Petersburg narodovol'tsy approved of this transformation. Kocharovskii, for instance, responded to Burtsev's call for the formation of a Union of Russian Social-Revolutionary Groups, which would focus its attention on the broad needs of the liberation struggle, by writing a counterproposal that defended the primacy of terrorism: "Of all the systems of struggle with the government for the achievement of political freedom, the only one accessible at this time [and] . . . having any chance of success, is the system of political terror."[53] Kocharovskii echoed here the sentiments of a decade of narodovol'tsy terrorists, who advocated unrelenting violent attacks on government personnel. However, as the 1880s wore on, these terrorists grew ever more isolated from society as a whole. A major assassination might have saved their cause; but repeated defeats in the form of foiled plots and police arrests reinforced the inclination of a majority of narodovol'tsy to turn away from the terrorist underground and to join a broader struggle for democratic rights in Russia.

Even in the first half of the 1880s, narodovol'tsy had been unhappy with the terrorist program and tried to alter it by making it more "scientific," that is, "systematic," or at least more closely tied to the interests of the people in the form of "factory and agrarian terror." But neither terrorism as agitation nor systematic terror bore fruit, and the isolation of narodovol'tsy from society only increased. Some of the narodovol'tsy turned to social-democratic ideas, while others, like Abram Bakh, the author of *Tsar-Hunger* and an earlier terrorist associate of Sergei Ivanov, attacked terrorism as inconsistent with the principles of narodovol'tsy activity. In an open letter to his comrades (late 1886), meant specifically as a rejection of Lavrov's hopes for terrorism, Bakh wrote that "terror exerts exactly no political influence and is only a fruitless waste of strength." Worse still, "terrorism . . . lies in basic contradiction at present with the fundamental goals of the party — to take an active role in the social movement, to become a political force." As a result of terrorism and conspiracy, Bakh asserted, society has forgotten about its liberators, and the liberators have forgotten about society. Therefore "we must reject at this time the organization of revolutionary force with the goal of an overthrow and reject terror as a weapon of political activity."[54] Bakh's sentiments were shared by several well-known leaders of the emigration, including Stepniak-Kravchinskii and Debagorii-Mokrievich. Under their leadership, the emigration published four numbers of the journal *Self-Government* (*Samoupravlenie*) (Geneva, 1887–1889), which also called for unification among Russian radicals and the formation of a powerful democratic party by radical activists from both narodovol'tsy and social-democratic camps.[55]

Inside Russia there was a spontaneous growth of what might be called liberal-narodovol'tsy circles at the end of 1887 and 1888. These circles were made up of self-designated "narodovol'tsy of a new type," "new narodovol'tsy," or "young narodovol'tsy," whose immediate goals included minimal economic reforms (factory and agrarian legislation) as well as steps in the direction of complete political freedom. The means of struggle, an 1888 programmatic letter stated, would be "the organization of revolutionary elements around propaganda among workers and intelligentsia." Terror would continue to be used "episodically" but would play "a secondary role." There was no justification, the letter continued, for all organizational and propaganda work to be subordinated to the terrorist cause. In addition, the liberal narodovol'tsy rejected the traditional and, in their view, "chimerical" concept of the seizure of power. The new groups also accepted without question the notion "that at this moment capitalism is growing [and] the *obshchina* [village commune] is being destroyed." As a result, they would tie their interests "to those of the factory and agricultural proletariat," thus promoting the "creation of a future workers' socialist party" that would be formed after the revolution. The task at present was to recruit factory labor to the liberation movement in the name of a nationwide social-revolutionary movement.[56] A young narodovolets from Vologda, Aleksandr Brodskii, preferred to call himself a "social-revolutionary," meaning, he wrote, that he rejected terrorism as an outmoded means of struggle, but that he "recognized the need to struggle against the Russian government for the good of the people" by attempting to arouse a liberation movement.[57] Other new narodovol'tsy, like the Moscow Socialist Federalists (1887), a group of students from the Petrovskii Academy and the Technical School, advocated terrorism as "one of the means of struggle with absolutism," but insisted that it be combined with "legal agitation" among the zemstvos and within obshchestvo as a whole. The Socialist Federalists, like many liberal narodovol'tsy of the period, expressed hesitancy about organizing a revolution, which "might lead to undesirable results. We do not want to exchange one despotism for another."[58]

The young narodovol'tsy circles spread rapidly from Kazan and Moscow in late 1887 to Tobolsk, Orel, Tver, Suwalki, and the Novo-Aleksandriisk Institute of Agronomy near Lublin. Even the Kharkov workers' group, which we earlier placed in the social-democratic camp, called itself at one time "new narodovol'tsy."[59] In Moscow, three university students, Aleksandr Gukovskii, Sofia Kondorskaia, and Pavel Kraft organized a young narodovol'tsy group to update the old program with "scientific data." The new group would represent the interests of "the working class, joined with the representatives of science and art."[60] In Kursk, the once fiery leader of Young Russia (1861), Petr Zaichnevskii, at the age of forty-seven still charming radical youth (especially women) with his fervor, organized an illegal circle of some thirty-five young narodovol'tsy. In his several trips to Moscow, one veteran wrote, Zaichnevskii "made an enormous impression" on several student circles "with his revolutionary enthusiasm, his passionate eloquence."[61] Although part of the new movement because they rejected terrorism, Zaichnevskii's followers aped his Jacobinism—the intelligentsia should lead the revolution, seize power, run the revolutionary dictatorship, and hand over its power to the "people" by means of a representative assembly only at "that time when it had reached the level of the intelligentsia."[62] There was much in Zaichnevskii that resembled Bolshevism, Mitskevich recalled, and many of his followers, A. I. Orlov, V. P. Artsybushev, and M. P. Iasneva-Golubeva among them, became social democrats and Bolsheviks.[63] Literally hundreds of other new narodovol'tsy circles sprang up all over the empire in 1888–1890, each advocating a slightly different revision to the traditional program of Narodnaia Volia, yet insisting—like the circle in Tver—"that a plan of struggle . . . be worked out that would unite all forces hostile to the government."[64]

Operating out of London, Vladimir Butrsev was one of the few to recognize the strength of this movement, and he attempted to unite it around a broadly based program of political freedom. Already in early 1887 he had supported the distribution of *Self-Government*, which demanded that Russian liberal and revolutionary forces unite in the name of a struggle for political rights.[65] By February 1889 he began publishing his own newspaper, *Free Russia* (*Svobodnaia Rossiia*), which chronicled the developments in all branches of the revolutionary movement, pleading all the while for unity. In the spring of 1890 Burtsev attempted to cross the Rumanian border into Russia, but gave up the notion of personally organizing the movement when his traveling companion, Iudka Rapoport, was seized by the police. Returning to London, Burtsev left the leadership of the narodovol'tsy effort to a St. Petersburg "central bureau" which, in the course of 1890–91, issued a dozen pamphlets and proclamations supporting Burtsev's call for a united revolutionary-liberal movement. An announcement of a new journal, *Revolutionary Union* (*Revoliutsionnyi soiuz*), summarized the bureau's platform: no single movement was strong enough to overthrow the autocracy, and the country was too "underdeveloped" for the success of a "narrow" party. At the same time, tsarism was too strong and indeed was thriving on the "disunity of its enemies." Therefore the only means of struggle was "unified action in the name of a minimal program of political freedom."[66]

Burtsev's attempts to spearhead a new alliance between the liberal and social-revolutionary liberation movements foundered on the growing efficiency of police countermeasures. The arrests of the spring and summer 1890 wiped out Istomina's organization, Ginsburg's Sevastopol group, Sabunaev's Volga narodovol'tsy, and several dozen liberal narodovol'tsy circles. The year 1891, the police reported with great satisfaction, "passed peaceably in comparison to the previous years, and among the number of political cases, there was not one that could be considered a serious assault on the contemporary order."[67] In the face of the terrible famine of 1891–92, which left hundreds of thousands of Russian peasants hungry or dead from starvation and sickness, the obtuseness of this statement is striking, demonstrating again the police obsession with terrorism and terrorist conspiracy as the only "serious" threats to the autocracy. In fact, the famine of 1891–92 had political reverberations throughout the Russian Empire; no underground organization could have aroused the political consciousness of the Russian intelligentsia the way the famine did.

The first political reaction to the famine came from the St. Petersburg narodovol'tsy who had avoided the terrorist-oriented circles and propagandized among the capital's workers. Like their 1882–83 counterparts, they had escaped police arrest by avoiding ties to any of the prominent conspiracies of the period. Since the destruction of the St. Petersburg Craftsmen in early 1888, the labor movement had prospered as an informally linked series of workers' circles. Some of their leaders leaned toward the old program of the Workers' Section; others considered themselves social democrats. But in both cases they worked easily with one another and invited intelligentsia activists of all parties to talk to their members. In contrast to the beginning of the 1880s, when intelligentsia propagandists outnumbered the workers' circles, the situation was now reversed: workers' circles were desperately searching for propagandists and narodovol'tsy filled the need.

Some bickering between narodovol'tsy and social-democratic propagandists arose as a result of the May 1 demonstration in 1891, when the narodovol'tsy managed to publish the speeches in hectograph form before the social democrats could act. In January 1892, the narodovol'tsy worker-propagandists also reacted more quickly to the devastating results of the famine, forming themselves into a political circle, the Group of Narodovol'tsy. There were no theoretical discussions involved, the group's leader, Mikhail Aleksandrov (Ol'minskii) recalled; the narodovol'tsy had the printing facilities, they maintained ties to workers, so they launched an underground publishing campaign, the goal of which was to reinvigorate the liberation movement.[68] Inside the Petersburg workers' circles the narodovol'tsy continued to operate harmoniously with the social democrats, but formal rivalry between the intelligentsia groups of the two parties grew more intense.

The first proclamation of the Group of Narodovol'tsy ("Free Word"—January 1892) was written by Mikhailovskii, who, the narodovol'tsy hoped, would serve as their ideological leader. But the renowned populist social thinker remained true to his nonrevolutionary stance. He called only for an open discussion of Russia's situation and suggested that elections be held for an assembly of the land.[69] (By 1894 Mikhailovskii had broken completely with the group; they were simply too radical for him.)[70] The second proclamation, "From the Group of Narodovol'tsy" (January 1892), was written by A. A. Fedulov and approved by the five-man central committee of the group. This programmatic document advocated, as did Burtsev, the unification of old and new narodovol'tsy into a single decentralized revolutionary party which would use "the favorable moment" to engage in an "open struggle" with the autocracy.[71] There was no mention of terrorism in either proclamation. Clearly, the group was trying to convince Russian society that narodovol'tsy were revolutionaries devoted to the people, rather than obsessed terrorists. In this spirit, the group republished in February 1892 Narodnaia Volia's anti-Jacobin "Preparatory Work of the Party" (1880), which minimized the role of terror and emphasized propaganda among the workers, military, students, and professionals as a means to develop a broadly based revolutionary force. Also in February, Nikolai Astyrev, a radical statistician who led a circle of Moscow activists, proposed that the group publish a series of letters to the peasantry on the causes and dimensions of the famine. Written in the peasant vernacular, the first letter enjoyed wide popularity (it was printed in eighteen hundred copies) and became one of the most important pieces of agitational literature in the 1890s.[72] Astyrev's first letter was also the last; he was arrested in April and died after four years in prison.

By the summer of 1892 the group was prepared to issue the first number of its underground newspaper, the *Express Leaflet* (*Letuchii listok*). Lack of funds and materials delayed publication of the second number until April 1893. The articles in both issues reiterated the group's determination "to raise the Russian people" to the historical stage by "unifying society and the working masses."[73] The immediate task, therefore, was to organize a broad coalition for the political struggle, one that would include liberals, social democrats, and populists. An article on the famine even suggested presenting a popular petition to the government, requesting that more intensive help be given to the peasantry.[74] Nevertheless, the group would exclude liberals from the party itself, "for two reasons—socialism and revolution."[75]

In the *Express Leaflet*, the narodovol'tsy also distinguished themselves from other underground movements by their position as political realists. The social democrats had an "uncritical," "myopic" attachment to the catechism of scientific socialism. The populists had their own "fetish" of the village commune and the artel, not to mention "a strange pretension to [Russian] uniqueness." The arguments between the two groups, though interesting and mutually correcting each other, did not meet the "sharp character" of the contemporary crisis. There were, of course, some unique aspects of Russian peasant life, the group noted; anyone who did not understand that did not know Russia. Yet the development of capitalism in the countryside could not simply be ignored, and one did not have to be a social democrat to analyze capitalism's effects. It was common sense that the peasants were not going to turn into workers overnight, so why deny them a socialist future. In their own eyes, then, the narodovol'tsy had an unassailable case for exclusive leadership of the liberation movement. They supported the growth of socialism among workers in the cities and among peasants in the countryside. They were willing to ally themselves with the liberals in the struggle for political freedom and ready to use terror "as a surrogate for agitation" in the name of the revolutionary intelligentsia. They also considered themselves the heirs to fourteen years of revolutionary heroism and commitment to the still applicable slogan of revolutionary work: "the seizure of power, won by the people."[76]

The efficiency of the Russian police in striking down any revolutionary circle in Russia subverted the seemingly impeccable logic of the group. In April 1894 the narodovol'tsy's press was seized and their ranks decimated. Moreover, the premises of the group's program were highly unrealistic. The possibilities of a "seizure of power" or even of a terrorist struggle were never so remote as in 1892 and 1893. Narodovol'tsy were not even in the position to experiment with bombs or plan assassinations, much less mobilize students or young officers for an assault on the government. The revolutionary intelligentsia with whom the group hoped to spearhead the liberation movement was dispersed by exile in Siberia, emigration, and banishment from university centers. Within the cultural intelligentsia, the famine had sparked sharp intellectual debates on the broad questions of Russian economic development, instead of serving as an impulse for revolutionary action. The new zemstvo and urban professional intelligentsia groups expressed little interest in the narodovol'tsy underground and turned rather to liberal (constitutional) solutions to Russia's political problems. Populists and social democrats, to whom the narodovol'tsy condescendingly granted a role in the "future" democratic society, now proved strong antipodal magnets for revolutionary and nonrevolutionary (legal) elements in the Russian intelligentsia. Even the leadership of the political struggle, rejected in principle by populists and social democrats, fell to the liberals, whose social base in the professional classes expanded with the industrialization and modernization of Russia in the late 1880s and early 1890s.

The Party of People's Rights

The most effective group of new narodovol'tsy emerged out of liberal and radical circles in Saratov, the so-called Athens of the Volga. In early 1890 Mark Natanson, the leader of the Chaikovskii Circle (1870–1873), returned from exile and joined Saratov liberals as a member of the Society of Fine Arts. Natanson began immediately to propagandize among its younger members and to absorb the new spirit among radicals for a broad liberation movement. Joining with other former populists, O. V. Aptekman (at this point a zemstvo doctor) and N. S. Tiutchev, who had settled in Novgorod after his exile, Natanson gradually wove a network of contacts incorporating circles of populists who had returned from exile, Volga narodovol'tsy who had survived the Sabunaev arrests, and the now more assertive zemstvo liberals. As a manager of the Riazan-Urals Railway, the enterprising Natanson also went to St. Petersburg, met with Mikhailovskii, and secured the writer's agreement to edit a new journal. Other old friends and intelligentsia leaders, like V. G. Korolenko and N. F. Annenskii in Nizhnii Novgorod, also agreed to participate in the journal, though they refused, like Mikhailovskii, to join an illegal party.

Although the new *Kolokol* that was to come from these discussions never got off the ground, Natanson found enthusiastic support for his ideas about forming a new party.[77] During the spring and summer of 1892, he moved to Orel to work for the railway; there he was joined by A. V. Gedeonovskii, a returned exile earlier associated with the narodovol'tsy Bogoraz and Orzhikh.[78] The two pooled their contacts with pockets of former populist and narodovol'tsy exiles, mostly in Saratov and Orel but some as far as Baku and Tiflis. (In the latter city, the ex-Workers' Section propagandists N. M. Flerov and V. A. Bodaev led a small circle that agreed to join the new party.) With these contacts firmly in place, Natanson held a founding meeting in Saratov in September 1893. Attended by some twenty activists, primarily narodovol'tsy, a program of the Social-Revolutionary Party of People's Rights was drafted and unanimously accepted.

"One question" takes precedence over all others at this time of crisis, the program began, "the question of political freedom." It was in every person's interest that "the autocracy be replaced by representative institutions." But in taking the name of People's Rights, the party understood not just the rights of the people to political freedom, but also "its right to the satisfaction of its material needs." With this program of constitutional and civil rights, the party itself would then "unify all oppositional elements in the country and organize an active force, which, with the aid of all moral and material means that it can muster, would secure the destruction of the autocracy and guarantee everyone the rights of a citizen and a human being."[79] Terrorism was not mentioned in the program, though it certainly could fall under the rubric, often used, of mustering all "material means." There was also no direct mention of socialism, though one could read that into the guarantee of "material needs." Perhaps most striking, given the populist background of its authors, is that the program omitted any mention of Russian uniqueness, save for the political backwardness of the autocracy, and neglected altogether any consideration of the peasant commune or an imminent peasant revolution. No doubt, part of the explanation for these omissions derived from the extreme disappointment of populist intellectuals with the peasants' politically passive reaction to the famine. All the same, the members of People's Rights were socialists, Aptekman later wrote, but "we are not going to take the second step without taking the first."[80] As A. I. Bogdanovich emphasized in the only other publication of the party, "The Vital Question" (spring 1894), socialism needs political freedom; it is "not only the first step" to it, "but it is a necessary condition for its existence." One or two bombs cannot destroy the autocracy, Bogdanovich concluded, nor can a circle of conspirators; only a "political party in the real sense of this word can do the job."[81]

With their program in hand, Natanson, Tiutchev, Gedeonovskii, and others traveled the length and breadth of the country searching for allies. In Petersburg Natanson hoped to absorb the Group of Narodovol'tsy, but they were too attached to the narodovol'tsy tradition to give up their name. Few liberals joined, for even if the party was constitutionalist, it was, as Martov noted, "revolutionary constitutionalist."[82] Despite these setbacks, Natanson continued working. With the help of Gedeonovskii and the cooperation of the Poles (Pilsudski and the Polish Socialist Party PPS), he set up one small press in Smolensk and made arrangements to construct a bigger one in St. Petersburg that could print his long-planned journal. But the police picked up his trail from his contacts with the Group of Narodovol'tsy. On the night of 21 April 1894, the authorities moved in concert all over the country, arresting members of both the Group of Narodovol'tsy and the Party of People's Rights, not distinguishing between the two until the investigations were completed. Some fifty members of People's Rights and sixty narodovol'tsy were indicted.[83]

The history of the Party of People's Rights after the April 1894 arrests is a fascinating study in itself, crucial for the development of the liberation movement and also closely linked to the beginnings of the Socialist-Revolutionary party and the Kadets. But for our purposes, a glimpse at the early years of the Party of People's Rights (1892–1894) provides a fitting conclusion to the period of the new narodovol'tsy, 1888–1894. The new narodovol'tsy wanted to strip their party of what they saw as its main encumbrance, terrorism, and focus on its main strength, its members' devotion to political change. Allied with other liberation movements in society, indeed at their forefront, the narodovol'tsy hoped to forge ahead with a struggle for political freedom; socialism would follow in due time. Natanson and the Party of People's Rights followed this logic to its final step, eliminating the narodovol'tsy name in the process. Natanson was only in part a neopopulist, for he did not deny the advances of capitalism nor the destruction of the village commune, nor, most important, the significance of the political struggle. On the other hand, unlike the vast majority of activists in the 1880s, he felt no particular attachment to the narodovol'tsy tradition. He was in essence a new narodovolets, without any devotion to terrorism or conspiracy. He ran his new party much as he had the Chaikovskii circle twenty years earlier, with an openness to liberals and the legal world of the intelligentsia that would have been impossible, practically and psychologically, to the vast majority of his narodovol'tsy predecessors. In 1886 Bakh had advocated stripping Narodnaia Volia of terrorism, conspiracy, and the isolation they begot; when this was accomplished at the beginning of the 1890s, Narodnaia Volia lost its *raison d'être* and ceased to exist. The political struggle alone was not enough to keep the party together.

Many narodovol'tsy joined the Party of People's Rights, comprising at least forty of its one hundred and twelve known members; and many of these went on to play important roles in the liberation movement.[84] Even the Group of Narodovol'tsy, Aleksandrov (Ol'minskii) noted, ceased to be narodovol'tsy before its members understood that fact.[85] Most joined the social democrats.

In 1878 the terrorist struggle gave birth to Narodnaia Volia; beginning in 1888, with terrorism under attack from narodovol'tsy themselves, the name of Narodnaia Volia began to lose its magic appeal. In 1893–94, with the demise of the Group of Narodovol'tsy and the emergence of the Party of People's Rights, the name and the party Narodnaia Volia finally expired. But the cumulative ideas of its many programs lived on, altered by the new circumstances of Nicholas II's Russia, in the Socialist-Revolutionary and Social-Democratic parties.

Conclusion

Between the assassination of Alexander II in 1881 and the end of Alexander III's reign in 1894, the Russian revolutionary movement underwent profound changes. The most important of these was to drop once and for all the utopian peasant orientation of the early populist phase and to replace it with the political struggle as interpreted by the narodovol'tsy, though one must be careful not to exaggerate either the idealism of the populists or the realism of the narodovol'tsy. There were urban, worker-oriented populists just as there were narodovol'tsy who continued to count on a peasant uprising. However, by the end of the 1880s most radicals—social democrats, narodovol'tsy, and neopopulists alike—shared the belief that the autocratic government had to be overthrown and a constituent assembly established before a social revolution could take place. In attempting to find the right combination of forces to overthrow the autocracy, Russian radicals moved from program to program, picking and choosing from the ideologies available to them, and integrating those ideologies into their own day-to-day views of the tasks at hand. Among underground activists, in contrast to intellectuals in the emigration, practical, antigovernment politics dominated revolutionary thinking to the point where ideology itself became secondary. Ideology justified the actions of revolutionary practitioners; it seldom determined them. As a result, ideological distinctions between narodovol'tsy, social democrats, and new narodovol'tsy (or neopopulists) carried only minor implications for the development of the revolutionary movement. There was no struggle between new ideas and old, new classes and old ones, as so often portrayed in

Soviet historical literature. Rather, mutual cooperation in practical matters and mutual borrowing in ideological questions characterized the period. Groups and individuals that can be identified as prototypes of one persuasion or another were the exception, whereas those that combined elements of relevant theories of revolution were the rule.

By the end of the 1880s, practical politics led radical activists to conclude that the likelihood of either a genuine social revolution or a violent overthrow of the government by a conspiratorial party was minimal; consequently they must find strength in numbers and cooperation, joining in a unified front of revolutionary groups of all types to force the government to grant a constitution and civil rights. Socialists of all ideological persuasions could only be served by government reform; this was the conclusion of the early 1890s, a departure from both the populist wisdom of the 1870s and the Jacobinism of the early history of Narodnoia Volia.

Another important change in the revolutionary movement was that it paid more attention to the Russian urban work force. The emergence of the working class as a major social and even political factor during the 1880s helped push the narodovol'tsy toward a new kind of politics. In the face of depression, unemployment, and declining real wages, the Russian workers of the 1880s organized and engaged in strikes, which to some extent induced the government to undertake reforms in factory law. First the narodovol'tsy, then the social democrats, and even the new narodovol'tsy, saw in the urban working class the crucial popular support for the revolutionary process. The social democrats and many narodovol'tsy also fully accepted Marx's dictum that the working class was historically determined to bring about the socialist revolution. Not that the peasants should be ignored (as Plekhanov advised), for they would necessarily be an ally of the revolution. But the urban workers were strategically located, easily accessible to propagandists, and most important, they themselves searched for answers to the question "What Is to be Done?" As such, the workers were natural allies of politically minded radicals. The more advanced workers formed their own circles, sought out the help of radical organizations, and in some cases joined narodovol'tsy and social-democratic groups. But even the "simple" workers had a straightforward desire to learn and to understand, which contributed to the growing momentum of socialism in their ranks.

The relationship between intelligentsia propagandists and worker activists was usually a good one, though exceptions were numerous and general statements difficult to substantiate. There was trust and there were instances of enmity; sometimes workers insisted on more

radical activities, sometimes less. But for the revolutionary movement, social-democratic and narodovol'tsy alike, contacting existing
workers' circles and forming new ones became a firm principle of
theory and practice. There is little evidence in the period 1881–1894 to
suggest that workers were somehow inherently drawn to social
democracy. The Workers' Section, for instance, was much more successful among workers than was the contemporaneous Petersburg
Party of Social Democrats. At the same time, the Petersburg
Technologists, people like Rodziewicz, Brusnev, Sviatlovskii, and
Cywinski, gradually won worker converts to social democracy
because of their patience and consistency, their devotion, and their
ability to listen as well as teach, not because their ideology suited
workers more than that of the contemporaneous and successful Group
of Narodovol'tsy. The general lack of tolerance in workers' circles for
ideological disputes between propagandists forced those few
narodovol'tsy and social democrats who were inclined to exclude the
other from "their" circles to curb rivalries and to cooperate.

It is worth reiterating that social democracy emerged in Russia in
the 1880s independent of the direct influence of Plekhanov and his
Emancipation of Labor group. "Direct" is the significant word, for it is
clear that the publications of Plekhanov, Aksel'rod, and other émigré
Marxists did contribute to the growth of the internal movement. Yet
even in the realm of radical literature, Diksztajn's *Who Lives from
What?* and Bakh's *Tsar-Hunger* played a more vital role for domestic
social democrats than *Socialism and the Political Struggle* or *Our Differences*. There was no father of Russian social democracy, but there
were dozens of big brothers and sisters—workers like Afanas'ev-
Klimanov, Mefodiev, or Karelina; Polish students like Cywinski and
Lelewel; narodovol'tsy activists like Popov, Istomina, and Ol'minskii;
and many others, Russians, Jews, and Ukrainians, army officers, technologists, and university students. Plekhanov may have been the first
Russian Marxist, but more significant for the development of Marxism
in the 1880s were activists like Abramovich, Brusnev, and Fedoseev,
the men and women in the movement itself who recognized and
directly aided the political character of the long-term struggle for the
emancipation of Russian labor.

The emergence of Russian social democracy in the 1880s occurred in
part because of another major change in the period, the shifting social
composition of revolutionary activists. In percentage terms, the
number of revolutionaries from the noble estate declined between
1881 and 1894, as did the number of students. More workers became
involved, and more children of townspeople (*meshchane*) and merchants. The social portrait of the revolutionary movement became as

complex as the social structure of Imperial Russia itself; there were students of peasant background, gymnasium-trained workers, Jewish agronomists, and Cossack university students, to name only a few of the varieties, which became the rule rather than the exceptions. The emergence of a technical intelligentsia to service the needs of Russian industrialization also altered the traditional social patterns of revolutionary groups. Those technologists who opted for illegal activities proved to be an instrumental force behind the proliferation of social-democratic circles.

Ethnic and geographic diversity of the revolutionary movement increased greatly under Alexander III. By the early 1880s, provincial towns like Kharkov, Ekaterinoslav, Rostov-on-Don, and Saratov housed radical circles as important as those in Petersburg, Moscow, or Kiev. Odessa, Minsk, and Vilna grew in importance as revolutionary centers with the emergence of Jewish political consciousness in the late 1880s. Jews and Poles now made up a significant percentage of radicals in the *Russian* movement, not to speak of the powerful Polish, and somewhat later, Jewish movements. Increasingly, too, Ukrainians, Armenians, Georgians, as well as other minority nationalities, joined the revolutionary cause. By the early 1890s, the revolutionary movement was even less ethnically Russian than the Empire itself.

In registering these shifts in the revolutionary movement under Alexander III, we must think about the elements that did not change. Most important, Narodnaia Volia did not expire with the emergence of Russian social democracy, nor did it even change its most important characteristics. The narodovol'tsy remained, above all, political, which meant that they searched for ways to begin the political revolution while maintaining faith in the ultimate social upheaval. Terrorism was rejected by some, altered by others to fit the "scientific" ethos of the day, and embraced as a panacea by a minority. Updated and put into perspective, terrorism was accepted by the vast majority of radicals, both social democrats and narodovol'tsy, in the 1880s. When it was raised, the argument against terrorism was usually tactical: it could not succeed and only brought havoc from the government authorities. For the activists of the 1880s and early 1890s, then, there was no inherent contradiction in being a social-democratic terrorist or, for that matter, in being an antiterrorist narodovolets.

Jacobinism and Blanquism—the seizure of power by a revolutionary elite—continued to be relevant to narodovol'tsy activists, though even this concept evolved along the lines of the idea of terrorism. As was often the case in revolutionary Russia, the psychologically unstable activists of the 1880s gravitated to both the terrorist and Jacobin solutions. But more quickly than terrorism, Jacobinism faded when confronted with political realism. Certainly, Jacobins like Sabunaev, some of the militaristy, and Zaichnevskii are examples to the contrary. But for the most part, as the improbability of a violent overthrow of the autocracy by an elite group of revolutionaries became more evident, Jacobin solutions appeared more outdated, both for narodovol'tsy and for the social democrats. For the same reason, the social democrats rejected the "seizure of power" — on grounds of ineffectiveness rather than out of theoretical purity.

A Bolshevik, wrote Lenin, "is a Jacobin, unalterably tied to the organization of the proletariat, conscious of its class interest." Both elements were present in the 1880s, and in some ways Lenin's mature thinking resembled that of the narodovol'tsy-social democrats of the period. Like them, he saw no reason either to await the further development of capitalism to strike at the autocracy or to let the bourgeois revolution run its course before beginning the socialist one. Like the narodovol'tsy of the 1879–1881 period, Lenin believed that the "seizure of power" could advance the timetable of the socialist revolution. For Lenin, as for the narodovol'tsy, capitalism was an absolute evil with none of the progressive characteristics attributed to it by Plekhanov or the Legal Marxists. Also, Lenin adapted the narodovol'tsy's general views of the primacy of politics and of the ultimate importance of the peasantry in the revolution to his own essentially social-democratic ideology.

Mature Leninism was also a departure from the traditions of the narodovol'tsy of the 1880s. Unlike his older brother Aleksandr, Vladimir Il'ich used theory to divide rather than unite his organization. He also flatly rejected the efficacy of terrorism and renounced any possible advantage that might accrue from an alliance with Russian liberals. In this sense, the Socialist-Revolutionary party, a broadly based movement anchored in the desire for democratization of government institutions as the first step to the revolution, was the much more likely heir to the narodovol'tsy of the period 1881–1894. The Battle Organization of the party reflected the consistent attraction and relevance of terrorism to Russian radicals. Even the splits in the movement itself were presaged by the tensions between various narodovol'tsy factions in the 1880s. While the socialist revolutionaries were a logical extension of the new narodovol'tsy movement, the Mensheviks and the Jewish Bund had their precursors in the social-democratic groups of the period. In short, Bolshevism alone was hardly the sole heir of the Russian revolutionary movement under Alexander III.

The closer all of these parties came to their goal of revolution, the more they sought to distinguish themselves from each other. The opportunity to participate in parliamentary institutions after 1905 only increased the antagonism among them. Just as they had done in the 1880s, the émigré party centers seemed determined to exacerbate ideological distinctions. Their competition for power soon erupted into bloody fighting. The heritage of the revolutionary movement of the 1880s — unity among radicals, ideological flexibility, and mutual help and tolerance — disappeared as Russian revolutionaries marched towards October 1917 and the construction of a new order.

Abbreviations
Notes
Selected Bibliography
Index

Abbreviations

DP	Departament politsii
GM	*Golos minuvshego*
GOT	*Gruppa "Osvobozhdenie truda": Iz arkhivov G. V. Plekhanova, V. I. Zasulich i L. G. Deicha*
HI	Hoover Institution Archives
IISH	International Institute of Social History Archives
IRS	*Istoriko-revoliutsionnyi sbornik*
IZ	*Istoricheskie zapiski*
KA	*Krasnyi arkhiv*
KL	*Krasnaia letopis'*
KS	*Katorga i ssylka*
LNV	*Literatura sotsial'no-revoliutsionnoi partii "Narodnoi voli"*
LR	*Letopis' revoliutsii*
MG	*Minuvshie gody*
OVD	*Obzor vazhneishikh doznanii po delam o gosudarstvennykh prestupleniiakh*
PR	*Proletarskaia revoliutsiia*
RB	*Russkoe bogatstvo*
TSGAOR	Tsentral'nyi gosudarstvennyi arkhiv oktiabr'skoi revoliutsii i sotsialisticheskogo stroitel'stva
TSGIA SSSR	Tsentral'nyi gosudarstvennyi istoricheskii arkhiv SSSR
VI	*Voprosy istorii*

Notes

1. Background to Radicalism

1. *Skorb' naroda: Podrobnosti uzhasnogo prestupleniia protiv sviashchen-noi osoby Gosudaria Imperatora Aleksandra II 1-go marta 1881 goda* (St. Petersburg, 1881), pp. 1–6.

2. *LNV*, p. 904. I use here F. Haskell's translation in; Franco Venturi, *Roots of Revolution*, tr. F. Haskell (New York, 1970), p. 716.

3. I have relied on the standard sources for this section: Venturi, *Roots of Revolution*; V. Bogucharskii, *Aktivnoe narodnichestvo semidesiatykh godov* (Moscow, 1912); and B. S. Itenberg, *Dvizhenie revoliutsionnogo narod-nichestva* (Moscow, 1965). See also D. Field, "Movement to the People Reap-praised" (unpublished), which attributes more political acumen to the populists of 1874 than traditionally assumed.

4. "Iz stat'i 'Pis'mo k byvshim tovarishcham' (*Chern. pered.* no. 1)," in *Za sto let*, ed. V. Burtsev (London, 1897), p. 202.

5. "Iz stat'i (Plekhanova), *Chernyi peredel* (*Chern. pered.*, no. 1)," in ibid., p. 198.

6. "Programma ispolnitel'nogo komiteta," *Narodnaia Volia*, 3 (1880), in *LNV*, pp. 162–165.

7. S. Iu. Witte, *Vospominaniia*, 3 vols. (Moscow, 1960), I, 433.

8. *K. P. Pobedonostsev i ego korrespondenty: Pis'ma i zapiski*, 2 parts (Moscow-Petrograd, 1923), pt. 1, 327. See P. A. Valuev, *Dnevnik, 1877–1884* (Petrograd, 1919), p. 157.

9. Pobedonostsev was not as hostile to the idea of a separate ministry of the police as he was to the "incapable and inexperienced people" of the brotherhood (*Pobedonostsev i ego korrespondenty*, pt. 1, 92).

10. See Ignat'ev's 22 December 1881 *doklad* on the necessity for police reorganization in the appendix of P. A. Zaionchkovskii, *Krizis*

samoderzhaviia na rubezhe 1870–1880-kh godov (Moscow, 1964), pp. 485–490.

11. This was published on 4 September 1881 as the "Ukase on state security," in TsGIA SSSR, f. 1405, op. 435, d. 84 (1881). Archival citations use the following abbreviations: *fond* – f.; *opis'* – op.; *deloproizvodstvo* – d-vo; *tom* – t.; *chast'* – ch.; and *delo* – d. References to archival *listy* use the abbreviations p. and pp. instead of l. and ll. throughout to avoid confusion between letters and numbers.

12. V. A. Tvardovskaia, *Ideologiia poreformennogo samoderzhaviia* (Moscow, 1978), p. 222.

13. *Dnevnik gosudarstvennogo sekretaria A. A. Polovtsova*, 2 vols. (Moscow, 1966), I, 106. See also Tvardovskaia, *Ideologiia*, p. 223.

14. *Vospominaniia E. M. Feoktistova* (Leningrad, 1929), pp. 228–229; Valuev, *Dnevnik*, p. 257.

15. *Vospominaniia Feoktistova*, p. 228.

16. Valuev, *Dnevnik*, p. 226.

17. *Dnevnik Polovtsova*, I, 106.

18. P. A. Zaionchkovskii, *Rossiiskoe samoderzhavie v kontse XIX stoletiia* (Moscow, 1970), pp. 162–163.

19. Valuev, *Dnevnik*, p. 205.

20. *Vospominaniia Feoktistova*, pp. 228–230. He notes as well that the "despicable" Orzhevskii exploited Tolstoi's paranoia in order to advance his position vis-à-vis his natural rival in the police hierarchy, V. K. Plehve.

21. *Pobedonostsev i ego korrespondenty*, pt. 1, 668–672.

22. Ibid., p. 327. Fursov was removed from his position and tried for negligence for not discovering the 1 March 1881 plot.

23. As inspector, Sudeikin was given control over the St. Petersburg and Moscow secret police as well as over the investigative sections of the gendarme administrations in Kiev, Odessa, Kharkov, and Kherson provinces. N. A. Troitskii, "Degaevshchina," *VI*, 3 (1976): 128.

24. Valuev, *Dnevnik*, p. 246.

25. *Dnevnik Polovtsova*, I, 244. Plehve calmed down when he was appointed Deputy Minister in 1884. Apparently Plehve told Sudeikin that the assassination of Tolstoi would be a personal tragedy, but would not be a bad thing for Russia. See L. Tikhomirov, "V mire merzosti i zapusteniia," *Vestnik "Narodnoi voli"*, 5 (1884), in "Degaevshchina (materialy i dokumenty)," *Byloe*, 4 (1906): 30.

26. These are Tolstoi's notes in the margins of Vasilii Karaulov's deposition; see TsGAOR, f. 102–DP, op. 168, d. 7 (1884), p. 91.

27. *Dnevnik Polovtsova*, I, 157. To be sure, Tolstoi was not alone. Valuev noted in his diary (19 December 1883): "Strong impact. Great alarm . . . with him [Sudeikin] dead all clues are gone" (Valuev, *Dnevnik*, p. 246).

28. *Pobedonostsev i ego korrespondenty*, pt. 1, 321–326.

29. *Dnevnik Polovtsova*, II, 189–191.

30. *Pobedonostsev i ego korrespondenty*, pt. 2, 252; Valuev, *Dnevnik*, p. 86; S. Ivanov, "K kharakteristike obshchestvennykh nastroenii v Rossii v nachale 80-kh godov," *Byloe*, 9 (1907): 201; "K biografii Aleksandra III,"

Byloe, 9–10 (1909): 70.

31. The government attributed a May 1884 train wreck to an attempt by the nihilists to kill Grand Prince Sergei Aleksandrovich. The 17 October 1888 accidental crash of the tsar's train, in which the tsar and his family were "miraculously saved," sent the government into even greater paroxysms of antinihilist rhetoric; see TsGAOR, f. 102–DP, d–vo III, d. 43 (1889), ch. 33, p. 3. As a result of the scare, the train administration was purged, railway police were reinforced, and there was a ministerial order to observe strictly the 1886 censorship law that forbade any discussions of the movements of the tsar or his family. See TsGIA SSSR, f. 776, d. 52 (1881), ch. I, p. 191. For an example of a simple murder turned into a "nihilist" attack, see ibid., f. 1405, op. 85, d. 10942, pp. 111–113. For the wild overreaction by Pobedonostsev to a supposed nihilist holdup of a monastery, see *Pobedonostsev i ego korrespondenty,* pt. 1, 309.

32. *Pobedonostsev i ego korrespondenty,* pt. 1, 309, 319; pt. 2, 920. Pobedonostsev demanded that the trial of the railway officials remain closed. After all, he wrote to the tsar, "the people saw in it [the tsar's survival] a miracle of God," and that attitude should not be changed. See *Pis'ma Pobedonostseva k Aleksandru III,* 2 vols. (Moscow, 1925), II, 216.

33. *Pis'ma Pobedonostseva,* I, 381; M. N. Katkov, *Sobranie peredovykh statei "Moskovskikh vedomostei," 1882* (Moscow, 1898), p. 234.

34. *Pobedonostsev i ego korrespondenty,* pt. 2, 69, 506; TsGIA SSSR, f. 1093, op. 1, d. 365, p. 6.

35. *Pobedonostsev i ego korrespondenty,* pt. 2, 468; *Dnevnik Polovtsova,* II, 38, 141–142.

36. "Iz dnevnika senatora V. P. Bezobrazova," *Byloe,* 9 (1907): 17.

37. *Dnevnik Polovtsova,* II, 403.

38. Katkov, *Sobranie peredovykh statei, 1882,* p. 142.

39. *Dnevnik Polovtsova,* II, 197.

40. See H. W. Whelan, *Alexander III and the State Council: Bureaucracy and Counter-Reform in Late Imperial Russia* (New Brunswick, N.J., 1982), pp. 73–74.

41. Quoted in T. Taranovski, "The Politics of Counter-Reform: Autocracy and Bureaucracy in the Reign of Alexander III, 1881–1894" (Ph.D. diss., Harvard University, 1976), p. 344.

42. Zaionchkovskii, *Rossiiskoe samoderzhavie,* p. 9.

43. *Dnevnik D. A. Miliutina 1878–1880,* 4 vols. (Moscow, 1947–1950), III, 140.

44. *Pis'ma Pobedonostseva,* II, 29.

45. Quoted in Zaionchkovskii, *Krizis samoderzhaviia,* p. 380.

46. J. F. Baddeley, *Russia in the "Eighties"—Sport and Politics* (London, 1921), p. 186.

47. See Hans Rogger, "Russian Ministers and the Jewish Question," *California Slavic Studies,* 8 (1975): 70–71.

48. G. Kennan, *Siberia and the Exile System,* 2 vols. in one (New York, 1970, first printed in 1891), II, 25. See also "Krovavaia istoriia v Iakutske" (Mimeograph, n.d.), in TsGIA SSSR, f. 1410, op. 1, d. 542, p. 2.

49. *Pobedonostsev i ego korrespondenty*, pt. 2, 479.

50. See A. Gerschenkron, "The Rate of Industrial Growth in Russia since 1885," *Journal of Economic History*, suppl. 7 (1947): 144–174, and R. W. Goldsmith, "The Economic Growth of Tsarist Russia 1860–1913," *Economic Development and Cultural Change*, 9 (1961): 441–475. Both Gerschenkron and Goldsmith warn the reader that their figures (somewhat lower in the former and higher in the latter case) must be seen, in Gerschenkron's words, "as very uncertain indeed."

51. See P. A. Khromov, *Ekonomicheskoe razvitie Rossii v XIX–XX vekakh, 1800 – 1917* (Moscow, 1950), pp. 88–89, 211; A. G. Rashin, *Formirovanie rabochego klassa Rossii: Istoriko-ekonomicheskie ocherki* (Moscow, 1958), p. 119; P. I. Liashchenko, *History of the National Economy of Russia to the 1917 Revolution* (New York, 1949), pp. 423–424; I. Gindin, *Gosudarstvennyi bank i ekonomicheskaia politika tsarskogo pravitel'stva* (Moscow, 1960), p. 65; and A. V. Pogozhev, *Uchet chislennosti i sostava rabochikh v Rossii: Materialy po statistike truda* (St. Petersburg, 1906), pp. 75–76.

52. M. I. Tugan-Baranovskii, *Statisticheskie itogi promyshlennogo razvitiia Rossii* (St. Petersburg, 1898), p. 18; Liashchenko, *History*, pp. 528–530; Rashin, *Formirovanie*, p. 13; V. I. Lenin, *The Development of Capitalism in Russia*, tr. from *Sochineniia*, vol. III, 4th ed. (Moscow, 1956), pp. 556–557; Ginden, *Gosudarstvennyi bank*, p. 53; and Ministerstvo Finansov, Departament Torgovli i Manufaktur, *Fabrichnozavodskaia promyshlennost' i torgovlia Rossii*, 2nd ed. (St. Petersburg, 1898), pp. 370–371.

53. T. S. Fedor, *Patterns of Urban Growth in the Russian Empire During the Nineteenth Century* (Chicago, 1975), pp. 192, 198. For declining death rates, see J. H. Bater, *St. Petersburg: Industrialization and Change* (Montreal, 1976), p. 311.

54. Tugan-Baranovskii, *Statisticheskie itogi*, p. 32.

55. A. G. Rashin, *Naselenie Rossii za 100 let (1811–1913 gg.)* (Moscow, 1956), pp. 93, 113–114; *Formirovanie*, pp. 12–13.

56. Much of the following discussion of peasant agriculture and the role of the commune is from L. Volin, *A Century of Russian Agriculture* (Cambridge, Mass., 1970), pp. 62–86, and Liashchenko, *History*, pp. 368–375. See also T. H. Von Laue, *Sergei Witte and the Industrialization of Russia* (New York, 1963), pp. 23–32.

57. See T. Shanin, *The Awkward Class: Political Sociology of Peasantry in a Developing Society* (Oxford, 1972).

58. See the "Programma ispolnitel'nogo komiteta," *Narodnaia Volia*, 3 (1880), in *LNV*, p. 162, and "Polozhenie partii v dannyi moment," *Narodnaia Volia*, 8–9 (1882), in ibid., p. 494.

59. See "Vnutrennee obozrenie," *Narodnaia Volia*, 6 (1881), in *LNV*, pp. 425–437, and "Peredovaia stat'ia," *Narodnaia Volia*, 10 (1884), in ibid., p. 674.

60. "Peredovaia stat'ia," *Narodnaia Volia*, 10 (1884), in *LNV*, pp. 669–670.

61. R. Wortman, *The Crisis of Russian Populism* (Cambridge, Eng., 1967), p. 78.

62. V. R. Leikina-Svirskaia, *Intelligentsiia v Rossii vo vtoroi polovine XIX*

veka (Moscow, 1971), pp. 317–318. Her numbers cover only the period 1884–1890. The only comprehensive list of statistics for the revolutionary movement under Alexander III are in *OVD* for the period 1890–1894: *Vedomost' doznanii* (1890) pp. 54–55; (1891) pp. 54–59, 114; (1892–93) pp. 90–102, 145–147; (1894) pp. 81–88, 125. The *OVD* figures generally corroborate those of Leikina-Svirskaia. The percentage of women is taken from the *OVD* figures; the percentage of nobles is taken from Leikina-Svirskaia's tables.

63. The percentage of workers in the revolutionary movement for 1884–1890 and 1901–1903 is taken from Leikina-Svirskaia, *Intelligentsiia*, p. 318; for 1890–1894, from *OVD*.

64. Ia. T. Mikhailovskii, "O zarabotnoi plate i prodolzhitel'nosti rabochego vremeni v russkikh fabrikakh," in *Fabrichno-zavodskaia promyshlennost'*, pp. 465, 581–592; M. Tugan-Baranovskii, *Geschichte der russischen Fabrik* (Berlin, 1900), p. 185.

65. For seasonal labor, see Mikhailovskii, "O zarabotnoi plate," pp. 468–469; Lenin, *The Development of Capitalism*, p. 574; Bater, *St. Petersburg*, p. 313; R. E. Johnson, *Peasant and Proletarian: The Working Class of Moscow in the Late Nineteenth Century* (New Brunswick, N.J., 1979), pp. 28–50; and R. Zelnik "The Peasant and the Factory," in *The Peasant In Nineteenth Century Russia*, ed. W. S. Vucinich (Stanford, 1968), pp. 158–190.

66. TsGAOR, f. 102-DP, d. 88 (1884), ch. 35, p. 48.

67. TsGIA SSSR, f. 20, op. 2, d. 1802, p. 25 ("Ob"iasnitel'naia zapiska k proektu pravil o nadzore za zavedeniiami fabrichnoi promyshlennosti.i ob otnosheniiakh khoziaev onykh k rabotaiushchim u nikh liudiam," p. 2).

68. TsGAOR, f. 102-DP, d. 88 (1884), ch. 35, p. 53.

69. Mikhailovskii, "O zarabotnoi plate," p. 479.

70. TsGIA SSSR, f. 20, op. 2. d. 1794a, pp. 54–58 (Ministerstvo Finansov — Deprt. Torgovli i Manufaktur, "O vospreshchenii nochnoi raboty nesovershennoletnim i zhenshchinam na fabrikakh, zavodakh i manufakturakh," pp. 5–13).

71. TsGAOR, f. 102-DP, d-vo III, d. 9 (1887), ch. 46, pp. 91–92; op. 168, d. 9 (1885), pp. 39–40, 150. Some strikes in 1885–1886 were caused in part by the new laws against female night work and child labor.

72. TsGIA SSSR, f. 20, op. 2, d. 1794a, pp. 35–36.

73. Mikhailovskii, "O zarabotnoi plate," p. 471.

74. *Vospominaniia I. I. Ianzhula o perezhitom i vidennom v 1864–1909 gg.* (St. Petersburg, 1910), p. 116; S. S. Sviatlovskii, *Fabrichnyi rabochii* (Warsaw, 1889), pp. 115, 120; TsGAOR, f. 102-DP, d-vo III, d. 59 (1885), ch. 45, p. 5.

75. See Bater, *St. Petersburg*, pp. 347–348.

76. *Rabochee dvizhenie semidesiatykh godov: sbornik arkhivnykh dokumentov*, ed. E. A. Korol'chuk (Moscow, 1934), p. 9.

77. Quoted in R. Luxemburg, *Die industrielle Entwicklung Polens* (Leipzig, 1898), p. 47. See also I. Janżuł [Ianzhul], *Przemysl fabryczny w Królestwie Polskiem, studium ekonomiczne* (St. Petersburg, 1887).

78. Rashin, *Formirovanie*, pp. 20–21.

79. TsGAOR, f. 102-DP, d. 88 (1884), ch. 41, pp. 46–47.

80. *Istoriia rabochego klassa Rossii, 1861–1900 gg.*, ed. L. M. Ivanov (Moscow, 1972), pp. 132–133.

81. TsGAOR, f. 102-DP, op. 168, d. 8 (1885), p. 14.

82. Ibid., d-vo III, d. 9 (1887), ch. 46, pp. 122–123.

83. Ibid., d. 88 (1884), ch. 41, pp. 3–4.

84. TsGIA SSSR, f. 20, op. 2, d. 1802, pp. 3–4.

85. Ibid., pp. 29–39 ("Ob"iasnitel'naia zapiska," pp. 10–29).

86. Ibid., pp. 67–163 ("Postanovleniia ob otvetstvennosti za narusheniia zakonov o naime na fabriki i zavody," pp. 18–19; "Ob uvelichenii chisla chinov fabrichnoi inspektsii," pp. 1–15; "Vypiska iz zhurnala Obshchego 5obraniia Gosudarstvennogo Soveta, 19 Maia 1886 g.").

87. A. M. Pankratova, "Vstupitel'naia stat'ia," in *Rabochee dvizhenie v Rossii v XIX veke* (Moscow, 1952), III, (1), 72, 79.

88. See *Istoriia rabochego klassa*, pp. 190–191. For government assessements and statistics, see the report of the Moscow Factory Inspector (Ianzhul) on strikes from 28 November 1885 to 1 January 1888, in TsGIA SSSR, f. 20, op. 13, d. 3, pp. 238–248.

89. TsGIA SSSR, f.20, op. 13, d. 3, pp. 228–243; f. 1286, op. 41, d. 485, p. 2; and TsGAOR, f. 102-DP, d-vo III, d. 59 (1885), ch. 45, p. 12.

90. TsGIA SSSR, f. 1405, op. 535, d. 182, p. 5; TsGAOR, f. 102-DP, op. 168, d. 8 (1885), p. 248.

91. "Delo o stachke," in *Morozovskaia stachka, 7–13 (19–25) Ianvaria 85 goda*, ed. D. B. Riazanov (Gol'dendakh) (Moscow, 1923), pp. 41–42.

92. The description of the events of the Morozov strike is taken from the report of the Vladimir prosecutor (TsGIA SSSR, f. 1405, op. 530, d. 974, pp. 1–12). See also ibid. op. 86, d. 10836, pp. 6–48. A number of documents on the Morozov strike were published in *Morozovskaia stachka* and in *Rabochee dvizhenie*, III (1), 123–302.

93. "Delo o stachke," in *Morozovskaia stachka*, p. 24.

94. R. Zelnik, *Labor and Society in Tsarist Russia* (Stanford, 1971), pp. 331–369.

95. "Peredovaia stat'ia Katkova (29 May 1886)," in *Morozovskaia stachka*, pp. 71–72.

96. G. Plekhanov, "Morozovskaia stachka," in ibid., p. 2.

97. V. Zasulich, "Znachenie Morozovskoi stachki," in ibid., p. 4.

2. Narodnaia Volia after the First of March

1. N. A. Troitskii, *"Narodnaia volia" pered tsarskim sudom* (Saratov, 1971), pp. 18, 106, 162; M. G. Sedov, *Geroicheskii period revoliutsionnogo narodnichestva* (Moscow, 1966), p. 361.

2. "Podgotovitel'naia rabota partii," *LNV*, p. 874.

3. M. N. Pokrovskii, *Ocherki po istorii revoliutsionnogo dvizheniia v Rossii XIX i XX vv.* (Moscow, 1924), p. 79. My description of the organization is summarized from N. I. Rysakov's deposition (TsGIA SSSR, f. 1405, op. 521, d. 409, ch. II, pp. 43–44).

4. The *Worker's Newspaper* (*Rabochaia gazeta*) appeared in two numbers (1880–1881). The arrests of the spring of 1881 interrupted the preparations for the third number.

5. TsGIA SSSR, f. 1045, op. 521, d. 409, ch. II, pp. 43–44.

6. Ibid., p. 45.

7. I. I. Popov, "Revoliutsionnye organizatsii v Peterburge v 1882–1885 godakh," in *Narodovol'tsy posle 1-go marta*, p. 53. See also P. A. Tellalov's observations quoted in V. Levitskii, "'Narodnaia volia' i rabochii klass," *KS*, 1 (62) (1930): 55.

8. TsGIA SSSR, f. 1405, op. 521, d. 409, ch. II, pp. 46–47, 98.

9. Ibid., d. 410, p. 248. For the history of the Nagornyi and Bulanov groups, see ibid., pp. 239–261; V. Ia. Bogucharskii, *Iz istorii politicheskoi bor'by v 70-kh i 80-kh gg.* (Moscow, 1912), p. 141.

10. "Proekt vozzvaniia ot imeni iuzhno-russkoi boevoi druzhiny," in TsGAOR, f. 102-DP, op. 168, d. 7 (1884), p. 163.

11. "Ot iuzhnogo rabochego soiuza: Ko vsem rabochim," in TsGIA SSSR, f. 1410, op. 1, d. 382, p. 112. Typical of the ideological mixing of the period was that the group advocated terrorism in the name of Black Repartition. For a history of this group, see I. I. Popov, "Leonid Samoilovich Zalkind," *KS*, 11 (60) (1929): 172–176, and V. Manilov, "Ocherki iz istorii sots.-dem. dvizheniia v Kieve," *LR*, 3 (1923): 123.

12. Tellalov later became the leader of the Petersburg Workers' Section. See L. A. Kuznetsov, "Iz dalekogo proshlogo," in *Narodovol'tsy posle 1-go marta*, pp. 26–29, and N. Volkov, "Narodovol'cheskaia propaganda sredi moskovskikh rabochikh v 1881 godu," *Byloe*, 2 (1906): 179. Some 100–120 workers were involved in Tellalov's group.

13. TsGIA SSSR, f. 1405, op. 83, d. 11020, p. 309.

14. Popov, "Revoliutsionnye organizatsii," p. 53.

15. TsGAOR, f. 102-DP, op. 168, d. 7 (1884), pp. 199–200.

16. Popov, "Revoliutsionnye organizatsii," p. 54.

17. Troitskii, "*Narodnaia volia*", p. 155.

18. Venturi, *Roots of Revolution*, p. 657.

19. Between 1881 and 1883, there were dozens of attempts to unify the disparate émigré factions, primarily on the initiative of Petr Lavrov. See his letters from this period in *Lavrov: Gody Emigratsii*, ed. B. Sapir, 2 vols. (Dordrecht, Holland, 1974).

20. TsGIA SSSR, f. 1405, op. 83–84, d. 11053, pp. 10–11. A further cause for unification, the prosecutor noted, was that each party needed the other to restore depleted funds and arrested personnel. See also *Sredi rabochikh v 1880–1884 gg.* (n.p., 1905), p. 8.

21. TsGIA SSSR, f. 1405, op. 530, d. 974, p. 26; op. 85, d. 11000, pp. 9–13.

22. TsGAOR, f. 102-DP, op. 168, d. 9 (1885), pp. 155–156.

23. See ibid., pp. 176–87, and TsGIA SSSR, f. 1405, op. 521, d. 415, pp. 1–10.

24. P. L. Lavrov, *German Aleksandrovich Lopatin* (Petrograd, 1919), pp. xv–xvi.

25. TsGIA SSSR, f. 1405, op. 521, d. 415, pp. 13–37, 145.

26. Ibid., pp. 192–194

27. Ibid., d. 410, pp. 382, 390–392. The discovery of the bombs among the pianos led to the arrest of the Shreder group.

28. Ibid., d. 413, pp. 176, 204.

29. Ibid., op. 85, d. 11000, p. 36.

30. TsGAOR, f. 102-DP, op. 168, d. 10b (1886), p. 228.

31. V. Figner, *Polnoe sobranie sochinenii* (hereafter *PSS*), 6 vols. (Moscow 1928), I, 270–273.

32. *OVD 1882*, IV, 52.

33. Ibid., p. 94, n. 1.

34. The letter is quoted in full in M. Balabanov, *K istorii rabochego dvizheniia na Ukraine: "Iuzhno-russkii rabochii soiuz"* (Kiev, 1925), pp. 139–140. See also *OVD 1881*, II, 29.

35. Balabanov, *K istorii*, p. 141.

36. Troitskii, "Narodnaia volia", pp. 33–34.

37. S. N. Valk, "Neizdannyi nekrolog N. A. Zhelvakova," *KS*, 12 (61) (1929): 173–179.

38. A. Rubach, "Ubiistvo gen. Strel'nikova i kazn' Khalturina i Zhelvakova," *LR*, 2 (1924): 188–191.

39. Quoted in ibid., p. 186.

40. Figner, *PSS*, I, 340.

41. Ibid., p. 332.

42. For a somewhat different view of the Degaevshchina, see A. B. Ulam, *In the Name of the People* (New York, 1977), pp. 380–392. See also "Degaevshchina (materialy i dokumenty)," *Byloe*, 4 (1906): 18–33; A. Pribyleva-Korba, "Sergei Petrovich Degaev," *Byloe*, 4 (1906): 1–3; and especially the article by N. A. Troitskii, "Degaevshchina," *VI*, 3 (1976): 125–133.

43. Tikhomirov, "V mire merzosti," p. 33.

44. N. I. Sidorov, "Statisticheskie svedeniia o propagandistakh 70-kh godov v obrabotke III otdeleniia," *KS*, 1 (38) (1928): 32–33; *Khronika sotsialisticheskogo dvizheniia v Rossii, 1878–1887* (Moscow, 1906), p. 332.

45. The following account of Sudeikin's method is taken from K. Ia. Zagorskii, "V 1881–1882 gg. (Vospominaniia)," *KS*, 3 (76) (1931): 167–177, and Figner, *PPS*, I, 330–340.

46. Pribyleva-Korba, "Sergei Petrovich," pp. 5–9, 12–14; Tikhomirov, "V mire merzosti," p. 36. On Vladimir Degaev, see TsGIA SSSR, f. 1405, op. 83, d. 11132, p. 174.

47. [S. N. Valk], "Pobeg Sergeia Degaeva," *KA*, 6 (1928): 220–222.

48. In ibid., pp. 221–222, Valk notes that to reinforce Degaev's story the police spread the word that a dangerous political prisoner had escaped. Durnovo and Plehve were also wired this message. By January 20 a circular on the escaped narodovolets was sent out to all police and gendarme authorities in the empire.

49. Degaev also played a role in the assassination of police spy F. Shkrioba, whom Sudeikin apparently considered expendable; TsGAOR, f. 102-DP, op. 168, d. 8 (1885), p. 166; TsGIA SSSR, f. 1405, op. 539, d. 208, p. 12.

50. Sudeikin was already feeding selected information to his superiors in

order to bolster his position. It is likely that he passed on Degaev's information that the terrorists would take no part in the Turgenev burial proceedings, which delighted Tolstoi; see *Dnevnik Polovtsova*, I, 115, 117.

51. According to Karaulov's deposition, Degaev and Sudeikin had already chosen the place and the procedures to carry out the plan: TsGAOR, f. 102-DP, op. 168, d. 7 (1884), p. 93.

52. In his deposition Stepan Rossi insisted that Degaev was intent on killing Tolstoi, Plehve, and Sudeikin: TsGIA SSSR, f. 1405, op. 530, d. 974, p. 30. Karaulov stated that a primary target would be the Grand Prince Vladimir Aleksandrovich: TsGAOR, f. 102-DP, op. 168, d. 7 (1884), p. 92. The plot to kill Tolstoi was near completion at the time of Sudeikin's death. Sudeikin had given Degaev instructions on how to follow the minister (Tikhomirov, "V mire merzosti," p. 37), while at approximately the same time Tolstoi was informed, by whom he did not say, "that the nihilists had decided to kill him." This person, who may well have been Sudeikin himself, told Tolstoi that "it was necessary to change the directions of his walks, and not go the same way as he had the day before" (*Dnevnik Polovtsova*, I, 116). In an interview with Baddeley Tolstoi said that Sudeikin had warned him a number of times of an assassination attempt (*Russia in the "Eighties"*, pp. 19–91) and advised him to be especially careful of "petitioners with muffs" (*Dnevnik Polovtsova*, I, 106). In all these cases Sudeikin may have warned Tolstoi of the plots in order to become more informed about his routine or to throw the minister even more off balance. It is also conceivable, as Ulam argues, that the entire story of joint plots between Sudeikin and Degaev was just a fabrication and should not be taken seriously (*In the Name of the People*, p. 387).

53. The two trips abroad are the most obscure parts of the Degaev story, and the explanation given by Tikhomirov strikes me as questionable. I would speculate that in the first meeting Tikhomirov actually told Degaev to continue with his activities as before in the hope of assassinating high government officials. A noted advocate of political terrorism, Tikhomirov must have felt that a continuing Degaev-Sudeikin partnership could be a positive factor in bringing political change to Russia, despite the inevitable losses in the domestic narodovol'tsy movement. Indeed, the summer of 1883 following Degaev's return from Geneva was the period of intense assassination plans involving other government officials. Then, when confronted with the entire Executive Committee in August, Tikhomirov was forced to drop his ambitious hopes for Degaev. As soon as Degaev returned to Russia from the August meeting, he told Rossi that the Paris committee had "demanded that he put off all the other assassination projects and kill Sudeikin as soon as possible" (TsGIA SSSR, f. 1405, op. 530, d. 594, p. 93). Whatever his role in promoting the Degaev-Sudeikin partnership, we can be sure that Tikhomirov's account of his meetings with Degaev omits some important details. Degaev himself, after reading these accounts, wrote to Tikhomirov that such a version of events might well be necessary for internal consumption in Russia, but, added Degaev, "you, you *know*, that the matter was considerably more complicated" (*Lavrov*, II, 154). In fact, Degaev eventually threatened that if Tikhomirov did not tell the full story he would "defend himself," "reporting on revolutionaries

'knowing but not saying anything' about his case." See *Vospominaniia L'va Tikhomirova* (Moscow-Leningrad, 1927), p. 187.

54. Tikhomirov vehemently denied this and wrote that the moment when Degaev made his bargain with the Executive Committee (June or August?), "all such activities were unconditionally brought to an end" (Tikhomirov, "V mire merzosti," p. 37).

55. TsGAOR, f. 102-DP, op. 168, d. 19a, p. 146 (Deposition of Sergei Ivanov); A. V. Pribylev, *Ot Peterburga do kary: Vospominaniia* (Moscow, 1923) p. 7.

56. Lopatin learned of Degaev's double role only when he arrived in St. Petersburg and Degaev told him about it in a restaurant. See I. I. Popov, *German Aleksandrovich Lopatin* (Moscow, 1926), p. 48; V. Ia. Iakovlev-Bogucharskii, "K biografii P. F. Iakubovicha," *RB*, 5 (1911): 132–133.

57. TsGAOR, f. 102-DP, op. 168, d. 8 (1885), pp. 164–165. Actually, Lopatin took an active, perhaps even dominant role in the discussions that led to Sudeikin's murder. According to his deposition, he "explained to those who were chosen to kill Sudeikin exactly where they were to conceal themselves in the apartment, how to carry out the attack, and how to 'finish off' Sudeikin." He also "gave these instructions to them [Starodvorskii and Konashevich] in the presence of Degaev and based on the layout of the apartment brought by the latter [Degaev]." See also TsGIA SSSR, f. 1405, op. 86, d. 10937–10938, p. 27.

58. TsGIA SSSR, f. 1405, op. 86, d. 10937–10938, p. 27; "Ubiistvo podp. Sudeikina (iz arkhiva V. L. Burtseva)," *Na chuzoi storone*, 9 (1925): 205–219; "Degaevshchina (materialy)," pp. 25–27.

59. Sudovskii was badly beaten by Konashevich but lived. He remained conscious enough after the attack to name Degaev as leader of the assassins.

60. On the considerable involvement of the Polish party Proletariat in the Degaev affair, see F. Kon, *Narodziny wieku: Wspomnienia* (Warsaw, 1969), p. 52.

61. Starodvorskii and Konashevich were sentenced to death, but the sentences were commuted to life with hard labor. Konashevich suffered repeated mental breakdowns, and in 1905, when Starodvorskii was released, Konashevich remained in a Kazan mental hospital; see "Degaevshchina (materialy)," p. 27, n. 1; *Dnevnik Polovtsova*, I, 159.

62. The proclamation was printed by Starodvorskii at R. Krantsfel'd's apartment and was later reprinted in number 10, *Narodnaia Volia* (TsGIA SSSR, f. 1405, op. 530, d. 974, p. 31).

63. *Pobedonostsev i ego Korrespondenty*, pt. 1, 326.

64. In a January 1884 letter to M. N. Oshanina, Sergei complained about the hostility and "loathing" that greeted him as a result of the article in *Today* (*Lavrov*, II, 149–150).

65. "V. Degaev to Tikhomirov, 20 November 1884," in ibid., p. 150. Vladimir also complained in this letter that the narodovol'tsy harrassed him, as well as his sister, who was still living in Saratov.

66. HI, Nicolaevsky Collection, no. 184, folder 9; I. Genkin, "Predatel' S. P. Degaev v Amerike," *KS*, 9 (106) (1933): 132–135 .

67. L. Kulczycki, *Rewolucja rosyjska*, 2 vols. (Lwów, 1911) I, 497.

68. Bogucharskii, *Iz istorii*, p. 93. See also, V. Kistiakovskii, *Stranitsy proshlogo* (Moscow, 1912), p. 9.

69. *Khronika*, p. 245; Volk, *Narodnaia volia*, p. 149.

70. M. G. Shebalin, "Peterburgskaia narodovol'cheskaia organizatsiia v 1882–1883 godakh," in *Narodovol'tsy posle l-go marta*, p. 42. For an English-language portrait of Iakubovich, see Wortman, *Crisis of Populism*, pp. 182–187.

71. TsGAOR, f. 102-DP, op. 168, d. 8 (1885), pp. 253–258. Serious negotiations began with the Workers' Section in the fall of 1883. Shebalin and Iakubovich set up a printing press in the summer of 1884. The project for *The Revolutionary* was finally given up in the spring of 1884.

72. TsGIA SSSR, f. 1405, op. 87, d. 10128, p. 29.

73. These talks were arranged for the purpose of defining the relationship between the Polish Proletariat and Narodnaia Volia. Undoubtedly, both the Proletariat's demand for autonomy and its lack of interest in political terror encouraged Iakubovich as well as the Workers' Section (Popov, "Revoliutsionnye organizatsii," p. 61; Shebalin, "Peterburgskaia organizatsiia," pp. 46–47).

74. While rumors circulated about the role of Degaev, no one in Young Narodnaia Volia knew for sure in the winter of 1883–84. In response to the government's announcement of a ten-thousand-ruble price on the head of Degaev, the group printed a "counter-announcement" (26 February 1884) defending the assassination and praising Degaev (TsGAOR, f. 102-DP, op. 168, d. 8 (1885), p. 306).

75. Ibid., p. 259. Iakubovich also claimed that he was prompted to revolt by several other concrete manifestations of anticentralist, antiterrorist feeling among the Petersburg radical intelligentsia. First, a brochure appeared in April 1883 indicating that the "old" Narodnaia Volia was under attack from within (ibid., p. 320). This text of the brochure, "Ot revoliutsionerov k russkomu obshchestvu," indeed claimed that there was "a crisis in the party," and that a "transformation of the organization on new principles, determined by changing conditions and by the broad goals of the future," was in order (TsGIA SSSR, f. 1410, op. 1, d. 441, pp. 22–27). Iakubovich was also encouraged by the favorable reception the intelligentsia gave to Plekhanov's *Socialism and the Political Struggle* in the fall of 1883. See TsGAOR, f. 102-DP, op. 168, d. 8 (1885), pp. 319–320.

76. TsGIA SSSR, f. 1405, op. 530, d. 973, pp. 46–47.

77. TsGAOR, f. 102-DP, op. 168, d. 7 (1884), p. 202.

78. TsGIA SSSR, f. 1405, op. 530, d. 973, p. 47.

79. TsGAOR, f. 102-DP, op. 168, d. 7 (1884), pp. 104–106.

80. Shebalin, "Peterburgskaia organizatsiia," pp. 70–71.

81. TsGAOR, f. 102-DP, op. 168, d. 7 (1884), pp. 384–385; Zhuikov, *Peterburgskie marksisty*, pp. 165–72; Sedov, *Geroicheskii period*, p. 335.

82. TsGAOR, f. 102-DP, op. 168, d. 7 (1884), p. 332; d. 8 (1885), p. 319.

83. M. V. Bramson, "Otryvki iz vospominanii, 1883–1886 gg.," in *Narodovol'tsy posle l-go marta*, p. 82.

84. TsGIA SSSR, f. 1405, op. 86, d. 10939, p. 59.

85. Ibid., op. 539, d. 224, p. 3. Lopatin was Tikhomirov's personal choice (and was strongly recommended by Lavrov), although he was not formally a member of Narodnaia Volia. Besides, there were no other logical candidates: Oshanina was ill, Nionila Salova was too young, and Tikhomirov saw himself as a publicist rather than an organizer. An underlying reason behind the commission was the Executive Committee's desperate need for funds from domestic Russian sources. At this point, a Paris police agent reported, the Executive Committee could not even pay for stamps (TsGIA SSSR, f. 1405, op. 530, d. 1079, p. 130).

86. Valk, "K istorii protsessa 21," pp. 138–141. See also "Sotsial'naia revoliutsiia i zadachi nravstvennosti (otkrytoe pis'mo k molodym tovarishcham)," Vestnik "Narodnoi voli", 3 (1884): 1–6. The letter was signed by "the members of various organizations" but was probably the work of German Lopatin.

87. Despair and disillusionment over the lack of popular or liberal reaction to the March 1 assassination and the Strel'nikov killing caused an intensification of the "takeover" mentality expressed in the editorial article of no. 8–9 Listok "Narodnoi voli". There is no sense in waiting for a constitution or a popular uprising: "now our immediate task is to organize a conspiracy, with the goal of overthrowing the state structure." Any alternative to "smashing the despotic state" was seen as foolhardy and useless (LNV, pp. 489–494.) For an evaluation of this important article, see especially Kuz'min [Kolosov], Narodovol'cheskaia zhurnalistika, pp. 118–119.

88. Gots, "Moskovskaia gruppa," p. 107.

89. TsGIA SSSR, f. 1405, op. 86, d. 10838, pp. 77–79. Iakubovich was purposely excluded from these meetings (ibid., op. 87, d. 10128, p. 30). Other Workers' Section propagandists more readily joined with the Youth. For instance, Iakov Samoilovich and Fedor Olesnikov (both students at the St. Petersburg Technological Institute) became members of its "central circle"; ibid., op. 85, d. 10948, pp. 1–27; TsGAOR, f. 102-DP, d-vo III, d. 31 (1887), ch. 11, pp. 17–26.

90. TsGAOR, f. 102-DP, op. 168, d. 8 (1885), pp. 317–318. Ovchinnikov, because of his age and senior status in the party, often took the position of negotiator for the Youth. Still, it was Iakubovich who provided him with precise, written instructions of the positions that he should defend in the negotiations (TsGIA SSSR, f. 1405, op. 87, d. 10939, p. 229).

91. TsGAOR, f. 102-DP, op. 168, d. 8 (1885), p. 323.

92. Ibid., d. 7 (1884), p. 386.

93. Ibid., d. 8 (1885), pp. 324–25; TsGIA SSSR, f. 1405, op. 530, d. 973, pp. 86–88. See also "German Lopatin," HI, Okhrana Archives, spravka no. 33, 1908, index no. XVIb (I), "Narodovol'tsy."

94. Kuz'min [Kolosov], Narodovol'cheskaia zhurnalistika, p. 120; Kulczycki, Rewolucja rosyjska, II, 512.

95. TsGAOR, f. 102-DP, op. 168, d. 7 (1884), pp. 272–72. See also ibid., d. 8 (1885), p. 323.

96. TsGIA SSSR, f. 1405, op. 530, d. 1079, p. 131; "German Lopatin," HI, Okhrana Archives, spravka no. 33, 1908, index no. XVIb (I), "Narodovol'tsy."

97. TsGAOR, f. 102-DP, op. 168, d. 7 (1884), p. 333.

98. TsGIA SSSR, f. 1405, op. 85, d. 10939, p. 38.

99. Ibid., op. 530, d. 973, p. 83.

100. Ibid., op. 86, d. 10838, pp. 40–41.

101. TsGAOR, f. 102-DP, op. 168, d. 7 (1884), pp. 348–352. Iakubovich's letter claimed also that contacts with Paris had been reestablished and that the pace of arrests was slowing down.

102. TsGIA SSSR, f. 1405, op. 86, d. 10838, p. 66.

103. TsGAOR, f. 102-DP, op. 168, d. 8 (1885), p. 322.

104. Ibid., d. 7 (1884), pp. 328–38. See V. I. Sukhomlin, "Iz epokhi upadka partii 'Narodnaia volia'," *KS*, 7–8 (28–29) (1926): 61.

105. TsGAOR, f. 102-DP, op. 168, d. 7 (1884), p. 336; d. 8 (1885), pp. 18–19; and Popov, "Revoliutsionnye organizatsii," p. 78.

106. A. Shekhter-Minor, "Iuzhno-russkaia narodovol'cheskaia organizatsiia," in *Narodovol'tsy posle l-go marta*, p. 131.

107. "Zasulich to Engels, 1880–1890s" HI, Nicolaevsky Archives, folder 3, no. 16.

108. "Zasulich to Engels, undated," in ibid.

3. Social Democrats in St. Petersburg, 1884–1888

1. *K. Marks, F. Engels i revoliutsionnaia Rossiia* (Moscow, 1967), p. 427.

2. *Iz arkhiva P. B. Aksel'roda* (Berlin, 1924), p. 16.

3. Quoted in Geierhos, *Vera Zasulič*, p. 201.

4. G. V. Plekhanov, *Sochineniia*, 2nd ed. (Moscow, 1927), XXIV, 178–179. See Baron, *Plekhanov*, p. 75.

5. See Baron, *Plekhanov*, pp. 81–88, and Geierhos, *Vera Zasulič*, pp. 198–216.

6. TsGIA SSSR, f. 777, op. 3, d. 97 (1885), p. 3. Volume II of *Das Kapital*, edited by A. A. Bubnov, was printed in three thousand copies; ibid., pp. 1–4.

7. "Katalog sistematicheskogo chteniia (Odessa, 1882)," in TsGIA SSSR, f. 1410, op. 1, d. 463. See S. S. Volk, *Karl Marks i russkie obshchestvennye deiateli* (Leningrad, 1969), pp. 183–187.

8. TsGIA SSSR, f. 1405, op. 87, d. 10145, p. 43.

9. Ibid., op. 521, d. 414, p. 149.

10. See N. Naimark, *The History of the "Proletariat"* (New York, 1979), pp. 155–159.

11. The best Soviet works on Blagoev and the Party of Social Democrats include: N. L. Sergievskii, *Partiia russkikh sotsial-demokratov: Gruppa Blagoeva* (Moscow, Leningrad 1929); Polevoi, *Zarozhdenie marksizma*, pp. 283–323; Zhuikov, *Peterburgskie marksisty*, pp. 151–224; and B. N-skii [Nicolaevsky], "K istorii 'Partii russkikh sotsial-demokratov' v 1884–86 gg.," *KS*, 5 (54) (1929): 44–68.

12. D. Blagoev, *Kratki belezhki iz moia zhivot* (Sofia, 1954), p. 34. See also Blagoev's memoirs in Russian, *Moi vospominaniia* (Moscow, 1928).

13. "Dmitrii Blagoev in Russia: An Autobiographical Letter (Blagoev to D. Kol'tsov, Sofia, 1903)," ed. D. Labelle, *International Review of Social History*, 9 (1964): 294. A reprint of this article, as well as other material on Blagoev,

was collected by Nicolaevsky and is held in his archives at the Hoover Institution: see B. Nicolaevsky, "K istorii s.d. dvizheniia v 1880-kh godakh," (manuscript), no. 168, folder 7; B. Nicolaevsky, "Zametki i bibliografiia po voprosy o s.d. dvizhenii v 1880-kh gg.," (letters to Nicolaevsky about Blagoev), no. 168, folder 3.

14. Vladimir Barybin, a member of the Perm zemliachestvo, organized a group of approximately twenty-eight workers called Vzaimnost', whose primary task, according to the prosecutor, was to obtain cheap goods for its members. This cooperative group maintained a small press and may have played a role in the political education of Blagoev and the social democrats (TsGIA SSSR, f. 1405, op. 88, d. 10094, p. 102, and Zhuikov, *Peterburgskie marksisty*, pp. 187–191).

15. TsGAOR, f. 102-DP, d-vo III, d. 545 (1885), p. 41; op. 168, d. 8 (1885), p. 88.

16. "Dmitrii Blagoev in Russia," p. 294. In addition to Blagoev, Latyshev, and Kharitonov, other important members of the group were: Ivan Gil'genburg, David Gofman (who had ties to the *militaristy*), Petr Budkov (who killed himself in prison on 5 September 1886), Ivan Moshkovtsev, Orest Govorukhin (later involved in Terrorist Fraction activities), and the Serb Mark Nikolich. Also directly involved in the group were the brothers Andreev (Petr and Nikolai), the Technological Institute student Pavel Shat'ko, the Cossack Nikolai Borodin, the worker Apollinarii Gerasimov, and Prince V. A. Kugushev. Soviet historians usually date the founding of the party in 1884, even sometimes in late 1883. See Ia. K. Dukhin, "Blagoevets Vasilii Kharitonov," *VI*, 1 (1982): 173.

17. M. S. Ol'minskii, "Davnie sviazi," *Ot gruppy Blagoeva k "Soiuzu bor'by"* (Rostov-on-Don, 1921), p. 69.

18. O. M. Govorukhin, "Vospominaniia o terroristicheskoi gruppe Aleksandra Il'icha Ul'ianova," *Oktiabr'*, 3 (1927): 129–130.

19. "Dmitrii Blagoev in Russia," p. 293.

20. [B. Nicolaevsky], "Programma pervogo v Rossii sotsial-demokraticheskogo kruzhka," *Byloe*, 13 (1918): 40; Ovsiannikova, *Gruppa Blagoeva*, pp. 40–41. The only evidence that the Party of Social Democrats actually organized circles comes from Kugushev, who wrote that he put together four such circles in the Vyborg district and knew all the workers in them. See "Kugushev to Kharitonov [February 1924]," in V. Kharitonov, "Iz vospominanii uchastnika gruppy Blagoeva," *PR*, 72 (1928): 165. Blagoev, Kharitonov, and I. I. Popov (of the Workers' Section) refer to some fifteen social-democratic circles all over Petersburg, but do not claim, as does Nicolaevsky, that they were originally organized by the group. See I. I. Popov, *Minuvshee i perezhitoe: iz vospominanii* (Moscow, 1933), p. 126.

21. TsGAOR, f. 102-DP, d-vo III, d. 100 (1886), p. 164.

22. Ibid., op. 168, d. 9 (1885), p. 171; d. 10b (1886), p. 170.

23. The main contact man for the Party of Social Democrats was Isaak Magat, who often was counted as a member of the group. Magat and his fellow Vilna Jewish radicals imported literature for Narodnaia Volia, as well as for the social democrats. Periodic meetings were held by the Petersburg social democrats to raise money for the importation of literature. Among the works

smuggled in for the social democrats by the Vilna group were the *Communist Manifesto*, Engels' *The Development of Scientific Socialism*, Plekhanov's *Socialism and the Political Struggle* and *Our Differences*, and Diksztajn's *Who Lives from What?* See TsGIA SSSR, f. 1405, op. 87 d. 10268, p. 108; TsGAOR, f. 102-DP, d-vo III, d. 100 (1886), pp. 28–29.

24. TsGAOR, f. 102-DP, d-vo III, d. 100 (1886), pp. 134, 144, 147.

25. G. N. Lavrov was N. N. Lavrov's brother and may have been in contact with his brother's circle at the Shreder factory. It is likely that the notes found on Lavrov were copied from Latyshev, who was an experienced propagandist among workers. Lavrov's deposition is uncommonly honest and there is every reason to believe him when he wrote that though he intended to organize workers, he had not yet been in touch with them, and that although he considered himself a social democrat, he was not actually a member of the group because he could not locate them (TsGIA SSSR, f. 1405, op. 87, d. 10268, pp. 87, 98). For a different reading of Lavrov's papers, see Zhuikov, *Peterburgskie marksisty*, pp. 184–186.

26. TsGIA SSSR, f. 1405, op. 87, d. 10268, p. 71, 95–96.

27. [Nicolaevsky], "Programma pervogo," p. 50.

28. "Kugushev to Kharitonov (February 1924)," p. 165. According to the police, Debora Pozner and Ekaterina Ivanova worked both for Lopatin and for the social democrats (*OVD 1884*, IX, 31; *OVD 1885*, X, 40–41).

29. TsGIA SSSR, f. 1405, op. 87, d. 10268, p. 87.

30. Ol'minskii, "Davnie sviazi," p. 69.

31. Popov, "Revoliutsionnye organizatsii," pp. 79–80. See Bramson, "Otryvki iz vospominanii," p. 82.

32. Blagoev, *Kratki belezhki*, p. 56.

33. Polevoi, *Zarozhdenie marksizma*, p. 517.

34. Baron, *Plekhanov*, p. 117. Emphasis added.

35. N. L. Sergievskii: "Gruppa Osvobozhdenie truda i marksistkie kruzhki," *IRS*, II: 86–260; "Dmitrii Blagoev v Peterburge 1880–1885 gg.," *KL*, 2 (11) 1924): 45–48; *Rabochii: Gazeta partii russkikh sotsial-demokratov (blagoevtsev), 1885 g.* (Leningrad, 1928), p. 17; "Kogda i po kakomu povodu byl napisan Plekhanovym 'Proekt programmy russkikh sotsial-demokratov'," *PR*, 72 (1928): 88–89. See the hostile introduction, "Ot Istparta," to Sergievskii's work, *Partiia russkikh sotsial-demokratov*, pp. 3–5. M. Liadov [Akimov] argues somewhat differently. He claims that the domestic social democrats forced Plekhanov to abandon aspects of his Marxism and adopt elements of their "populist" program; M. Liadov [Akimov], *Istoriia rossiiskoi sotsial-demokraticheskoi rabochei partii* (St. Petersburg, 1906), pt. 1, pp. 46–49.

36. "Pis'mo Peterburgskoi gruppy russkikh sotsial-demokratov (Blagoevtsy), 20 Marta 1885 g. So prilozheniem kritiki broshiura Plekhanova 'Nashi raznoglasiia'" (handwritten), HI, Nicolaevsky Archives, no. 168, folder 1. The letter is also in *GOT*, VI, 130.

37. TsGIA SSSR, f. 1405, op. 87, d. 10268, p. 2.

38. TSGAOR, f. 102-DP, op. 168, d. 8 (1885), pp. 269–274.

39. *Perepiska G. V. Plekhanova i P. B. Aksel'roda*, 2 vols. (Moscow, 1925), I, 21.

40. "Grinfest to Aksel'rod (9 February 1885)," IISH, Axelrod Archives, A (15), 62-I, p. 26.

41. TsGAOR, f. 102-DP, d-vo III, d. 91 (1893), pp. 6–7; TsGIA SSSR, f. 1405, op. 87, d. 10143, pp. 59–60. Govorukhin mentioned that surprisingly few copies of *Our Differences* were received by the Party of Social Democrats in his "Vospominaniia," p. 130.

42. See the letters from the "Blagoevtsy" (Latyshev) to Emancipation of Labor in [Nicolaevsky], "Programma pervogo," pp. 48–52. See also "Prilozheniia," *IRS*, II, 187–191; V. I. Nevskii, "K istorii 'Partii russkikh sotsial-demokratov," *PR*, 5 (1922): 298; TsGIA SSSR, f. 1405, op. 87, d. 10143, p. 1. The letters were initially directed to the Executive Committee in Paris and were finally given over to Emancipation of Labor; see "Grinfest to Aksel'rod," IISH, Axelrod Archives, A-(15), 62-I, p. 26. The police recommended the deportation of Blagoev primarily on evidence that through these letters he was in contact with Tikhomirov and Lavrov; see TsGAOR, f. 102-DP, d-vo III, d. 545 (1885), p. 4.

43. This was apparently the second progam of Emancipation of Labor. See V. Iu. Samedov, "K voprosu o pervonachal'nom proekte programmy gruppy 'Osvobozhdenie Truda'," *Voprosy istorii KPSS*, 2 (1965): 97–101.

44. The first number of *Rabochii* appeared in January 1885 under the editorship of Blagoev, the second in July 1885 under Latyshev. A third number was in preparation under Kharitonov when he was arrested. Kharitonov was in charge of the printing operations of all three numbers (TsGIA SSSR, f. 1405, op. 87, d. 10268, p. 84). Between two and three hundred copies of each issue were printed and distributed by the social democrats, usually among workers for propaganda purposes.

45. "Chego ne dostaet rabochemu narodu?" and "Chego dobivat'sia rabochemu narodu," *Rabochii*, 1 (1885), reprinted in Sergievskii, *Rabochii*, pp. 24–25, 33–36.

46. Blagoev and Kharitonov both claim the authorship of the draft program; most likely, since the two lived together, it was a joint product (Ovsiannikova, *Gruppa Blagoeva*, p. 30). The program, called "Proekt programmy russkikh sotsial-demokratov," was first published by Nicolaevsky in *Byloe* ("Programma pervogo"). A more detailed but less reliable prosecutor's copy of the program is located in TsGIA SSSR, f. 1405, op. 87, d. 10143, pp. 90–93.

47. "Proekt programmy," in [Nicolaevsky], "Programma pervogo," pp. 43–44.

48. "Dmitrii Blagoev in Russia," p. 293.

49. "Proekt programmy," in [Nicolaevsky], "Programma pervogo," p. 46.

50. Ibid., p. 47. Kharitonov, in recalling the terrorist aspect of the program, noted that terrorism was too deeply embedded in the Russian radical tradition to be rejected outright ("Iz vospominanii," p. 156).

51. TsGAOR, f. 102-DP, d-vo III, d. 100 (1886), p. 52.

52. "Programma sotsial-demokraticheskoi gruppy 'Osvobozhdenie truda'" (Geneva, 1884), in TsGIA SSSR, f. 1410, op. 3, d. 618, p. 9.

53. Quoted in N. L. Sergievskii, "Plekhanov i gruppa Blagoeva," *PR*, 8 (1928): 146. See N-skii [Nicolaevsky], "K istorii," pp. 62–63.

54. G. Plekhanov, "Sovremennye zadachi russkikh rabochikh (Pis'mo k peterburgskim rabochim kruzhkam)," *Rabochii*, 2 (1885), repr. in Sergievskii, *Rabochii*, p. 56. With this article, Deich wrote, Plekhanov "hoped to facilitate the transformation of the Blagoev group from Lassallean-Lavrist-narod-ovol'tsy social democrats into genuine Marxists" (L. Deich, "Vmesto biblio-grafii," *GOT*, III, 351).

55. "Blagoevtsy to Emancipation of Labor," in [Nicolaevsky], "Programma pervogo," p. 49.

56. "Blagoev to Plekhanov (28 May 1885)," in "Pis'ma," *GOT*, VI, 129. This letter is particularly interesting in that Blagoev supports his arguments with references to both Marx and Lassalle. Plekhanov's letters to Blagoev were un-fortunately destroyed in the fire of the latter's library in Plovdiv (1898).

57. For a short description of workers' circles in the late 1880s and early 1890s, see R. Pipes, *Social Democracy and the St. Petersburg Labor Movement* (Cambridge, Mass. 1963), pp. 1–14.

58. I use Tochiskii's own spelling of his name (about which there is some dispute) in a signed petition to the authorities (TsGAOR, f. 102-DP, d-vo III, d. 1112 [1892], ch. II, p. 5). There is also some question about identifying him as a Pole since Tochiskii, unlike many Polish activists in the empire, was fully Russianized. In 1888 he formally converted from Catholicism to Orthodoxy and took the Russian name Pavel (ibid., p. 1). On Tochiskii's Polish identity see Z. Łukawski, *Polacy w rosyjskim ruchu socjaldemokratycznym* (Cracow, 1970), pp. 24–25. Further biographical information on Tochiskii is available in A. Breitfus, "Tochiskii i ego kruzhok," *KL*, 7 (1923): 325–327, and in "Doklad Departamenta Politsii Ministru Vnutrennikh Del'," *KL*, 7 (1923): 375. This lat-ter report, containing materials from the Department of Police, Ministry of Justice, and Ministry of Internal Affairs, is reprinted from TsGAOR, f. 102-DP, d-vo III, d. 1112 (1892), ch. 1. I use the *KL* printed version, hereafter referred to as "Doklad Politsii." Other first-hand information on Tochiskii is available in his sister's memoirs: M. Lebedeva [Tochiskaia], "K biografii P. V. Tochisskogo (Vospominaniia sestry)," *IRS*, III, 296–297.

59. Sergievskii provides the most independent assessment of Tochiskii in "Gruppa Osvobozhdenie Truda," *IRS*, II, 158–161, and in "O kruzhke Tochisskogo," *KL*, 7 (1923): 340–343. Zhuikov employs a very elaborate argu-ment to demonstrate that Plekhanov exerted an influence on the Tochiskii group through the Perm zemliachestvo (*Peterburgskie marksisty*, pp. 187–195). For the traditional approaches, see Kazakevich, *Sotsial-demokraticheskii organizatsii*, pp. 31–77; Polevoi, *Zarozhdenie marksizma*, pp. 323–337; and N. K. Lisovskii, *P. V. Tochiskii* (Moscow, 1963). G. V. Khlopin was the only actual member of the Party of Social Democrats to have contact with the society. Breitfus clearly states in his memoirs that the group had no idea there even were such people as Russian "social democrats" (Breit-fus, "Tochiskii i ego kruzhok," p. 335).

60. An associate of Tochiskii's, Ivan Shelaevskii, also found himself in this predicament. He had intended to enter the Institute of Communications, but was refused. He then entered the work force and enrolled in the Artisan School.

61. TsGAOR, f. 102-DP, d-vo III, d. 1112 (1892), ch. 2, p. 2.

62. *OVD 1888*, XIII, 19.

63. Lebedeva, "K biografii Tochisskogo," p. 298.

64. TsGAOR, f. 102-DP, d-vo III, d. 1112 (1892), ch. 2, p. 2.

65. "Doklad Politsii," pp. 350–351. Even Lazarev admitted to the police that he was fully in sympathy with Narodnaia Volia. Ibid., p. 352.

66. Breitfus, "Tochiskii i ego kruzhok," p. 326.

67. Ibid., pp. 326–327, 367. Still, in Tochiskii's propaganda among workers, Breitfus wrote, there "was not a word about revolution."

68. "Doklad Politsii," p. 352.

69. Five hundred and forty books were seized by the police, including science textbooks, language grammars, and literature. There were also seventy-five articles from various journals. Many books were rebound; some were copied and bound. The police never uncovered the illegal library. It is likely, as A. Breitfus reports, that the illegal library was turned over to the workers' circle leader and member of the society, I. I. Timofeev, who passed it on to the 1890–91 social democrats (Breitfus, "Tochiskii i ego kruzhok," p. 337, and "Doklad Politsii," pp. 353, 361).

70. Breitfus lists the titles in the illegal library in "Tochiskii i ego kruzhok," p. 329. There were only twenty-one titles in the illegal library (as compared to six hundred in the legal). Of these, only four can be considered social-democratic literature: Diksztajn's *Who Lives from What?*, Marx's *Communist Manifesto*, Plekhanov's *Our Differences*, and one number of *Rabochii*.

71. Ibid., p. 339.

72. *OVD 1888*, XIII, 19.

73. The other leaders of the workers' circles were V. A. Shelgunov, a certain "Semenich," "Fomich" — probably V. Fomin, "Fimka" — most likely Aleksandr Filimonov, and Nil Vasil'ev. Probably Gavril Mefodiev and Vasilii Buianov were also members of the society, though there is no direct evidence for this. With the exception of Vasil'ev, all these workers played an important role in the 1889–1893 social-democratic movement in St. Petersburg. However, in 1886–1887 Buianov and Vasil'ev were clearly associated with populist ideas, while Shelgunov and Fomin could be considered narodovol'tsy ("Doklad Politsii," p. 354; Breitfus, "Tochiskii i ego kruzhok," p. 337; Kazakevich, *Sotsial-demokraticheskie organizatsii*, pp. 37–38). See also E. A. Korol'chuk's introduction to *V nachale puti: Vospominaniia peterburgskikh rabochikh 1872–1897 gg.* (Leningrad, 1975), pp. 64–70.

74. Breitfus, "Tochiskii i ego kruzhok," p. 336.

75. "Doklad Politsii," p. 367.

76. Ibid., p. 354.

77. Ibid., p. 349.

78. Ibid., pp. 354–355. See *OVD 1888*, XIII, 20.

79. "Doklad Politsii," pp. 384, 386.

80. TsGIA SSSR, f. 1405, op. 87, d. 10268, p. 9.

81. "Deich to Aksel'rod (27 November 1883)," IISH, Axelrod Archives, A (3), II, III, pp. 17–18.

82. Tochiskii spent six months in prison in 1890, after which he was sent to Ekaterinoslav under police surveillance (TsGAOR, f. 102-DP, d-vo III, d.

1112 (1892), ch. 2, pp. 1-2). There, according to Liudmila Stal', he and his brother Matvei joined her circle and "educated the youth in the spirit of Marxist ideas"; see L. Stal' [Zaslavskaia], "Ot narodnichestva k marksizmu," *Istoriia ekaterinoslavskoi sotsial-demokraticheskoi organizatsii, 1889-1903*, ed. M. A. Rubach (Ekaterinoslav, 1932), p. 3. But Tochiskii also maintained contacts with narodovol'tsy worker activists. Kazakevich's claim that Tochiskii was always a revolutionary Marxist and died as a Bolshevik fighting the counter-revolutionaries in 1919 is unconvincing. For instance, Stal' says that he committed suicide in 1919 and stresses his pre-1917 union activities. See Kazakevich, *Sotsial-demokraticheskii organizatsii*, p. 40, and Lisovskii, *Tochiskii*, p. 24.

4. Narodnaia Volia in the South, 1884-1887

1. TsGIA SSSR, f. 1405, op. 87, d. 10317, p. 24. A similar statement appears in TsGAOR, f. 102-DP, op. 168, d. 10b (1886), pp. 273-274.

2. *OVD 1886*, XI, 7.

3. It is apparent from available data that the national and social composition of the movement changed radically in comparison to the decade 1873-1883. The earlier movement was about 50 percent noble, 30 percent *meshchane* (town dwellers, sometimes including workers), and only 4.3 percent Jewish, corresponding to the number of Jews in European Russia, about 4 percent; see "K statistike gosudarstvennykh prestuplenii v Rossii" (pt. II), *Narodnaia Volia*, 2 (1881), in *LNV*, p. 356; Sidorov, "Statisticheskie svedeniia," pp. 27-58. Troitskii's list of all those tried for political crimes between 1885 and 1890 (almost all of whom were narodovol'tsy), shows a jump of Jewish participation to 33 percent, a fall of nobles to 33 percent, and a rise of children of *meshchane* and merchants to 48 percent. My own collection of Ministry of Justice statistics on various revolutionary groups (mostly narodovol'tsy) indicted for political crimes during the same period also shows a marked rise in Jewish participation to 21 percent (Orthodox at 50 percent), while nobles (grouped with offspring of *chinovniki*) made up 30 percent and *meshchane* and merchants 39 percent. (The Ministry of Justice, less blatantly anti-Semitic than the Department of Police, listed converted Jews as Orthodox, while the police tended to identify Jews by nationality rather than religion.) The statistics are derived from TsGIA SSSR, op. 85, d. 10897, pp. 76-79; op. 85, d. 10858, pp. 145-146; op. 87, d. 10212, p. 314; op. 87, d. 10294, p. 245; op. 87, d. 10240, pp. 30a-30b; op. 87, d. 10165; op. 87, d. 10317; op. 87, d. 10147; op. 88, d. 10008, pp. 55-56; op. 89, d. 11043, pp. 168-170; op. 89, d. 11130, pp. 191-192; op. 90, d. 10832, pp. 172-173; op. 91, d. 10742, pp. 135-135; op. 91, d. 107438, pp. 182-183. Other relevant statistical studies of the revolutionary movement generally corroborate these data. See A. Kappeler, "Zur Charakteristik russischer Terroristen (1878-1887)," *Jahrbücher für Geschichte Osteuropa*, 27 (1979): 522-547; L. Ia. Lur'e, "Nekotorye osobennosti vozrastnogo sostava uchastnikov osvoboditel'nogo dvizheniia v Rossii," in *Osvoboditel'noe dvizhenie v Rossii* (Saratov, 1976), VIII, 64-84; Leikina-Svirskaia, *Intelligentsiia*, pp. 314-317; and R. J. Brym, *The Jewish Intelligentsia and Russian Marxism* (New York, 1978), pp. 104.

4. *OVD 1884*, IX, p. 32.

5. TsGAOR, f. 102-DP, op. 168, d. 7 (1884), p. 242.

6. "Iz perepiski gruppy 'Osvobozhdenie truda'," *KL*, 2 (1924): 194–195.

7. I. I. Popov, "S. A. Ivanov," *KS*, 2 (39) (1928): 166–169; TsGIA SSSR, f. 1405, op. 530, d. 1079, pp. 14, 21, 53.

8. A. Bakh, *Zapiski narodovol'tsa*, 2nd. ed. (Leningrad, 1931), p. 124. Kalegaev was arrested in 1884. The police found out that he had once given Bakh as much as 1500 rubles (*OVD 1885*, X, 4).

9. Antonov was the son of a worker, finished a Nikolaev Craft School in 1876, and went to work at the Nikolaev Admiralty. At first, he devoted himself exclusively to the study of the workers' questions, then gradually became involved in the revolutionary movement, apparently through the encouragement of Iakov Berdichevskii whom he met in Poltava. After March 1, Antonov led a Workers' Section group in Libiatin and in April 1883 went underground. In the fall of 1884 Antonov played a leading role in the reorganization of the southern narodovol'tsy, first in Rostov-on-Don, then in Voronezh, where he worked closely with Ivanov in his robbery attempts. See *OVD 1885*, X, 15–17; TsGIA SSSR, f. 1405, op. 86, d. 10760, p. 82; see also A. N. Makarevskii, "Rabochii-narodovolets P. L. Antonov," *KS*, 5 (12) (1924); 272–281.

10. TsGIA SSSR, f. 1405, op. 530, d. 1079, pp. 28, 73. Ivanov later testified that he planned these postal raids as much for the "morale" of the party as for its coffers. TsGAOR, f. 102-DP, op. 168, d. 10b (1886), p. 297; *OVD 1883*, VII, 13.

11. TsGIA SSSR, f. 1405, op. 86, d. 10765, pp. 47–48.

12. Ibid., d. 10760, p. 80. TsGAOR, f. 102-DP, op. 168, d. 10a (1886), pp. 347–348. Pribylev claims that Ulanovskaia was completely innocent. A. V. Pribylev, "V gody nevoli (Perepiska E. L. Ulanovskoi-Kranikhfel'd s mater'iu)," *KS*, 3 (24) (1926): 223.

13. In Lisianskii's apartment, the police found a fully operating secret press, bombs, guns, and false documents. Because of the "strong outcry of public opinion" the Minister of Justice recommended an "urgent passing of sentence." On 20 June 1885, on the orders of the Kharkov Military Tribunal, Lisianskii was hanged. TsGIA SSSR, f. 1405, op. 86, d. 10760, pp. 82, 172.

14. TsGAOR, f. 102-DP, op. 168, d. 8 (1885), p. 296.

15. TsGIA SSSR, f. 1405, op. 530, d. 1079, p. 28.

16. TsGAOR, f. 102-DP, op. 168, d. 9 (1885), p. 310.

17. M. A. Krol', "Vospominaniia o L. Ia. Shternberge," *KS*, 8–9 (57–58) (1929): 214–224.

18. L. Ia. Shternberg, "Politicheskii terror v Rossii, 1884" (Prilozh. 1), in *Lavrov*, II, 579.

19. Krol', "Vospominaniia o Shternberge," p. 226.

20. TsGIA SSSR, f. 1405, op. 87, d. 10145, pp. 196, 227–235; B. Orzhikh, "V riadakh 'Narodnoi voli' (Vospominaniia)," in *Narodovol'tsy: sb. III*, p. 85.

21. TsGIA SSSR, f. 1405, op. 85, d. 10925, pp. 3–6; *OVD 1884*, XI, 12. Kaliuzhnaia had been suspected of being a police agent before Degaev's treachery was uncovered. She was therefore eager to carry out an assassination to clear her name.

22. Feofan Krylov, for instance, objected to the seizures because private individuals, not the government, would suffer; see TsGAOR, f. 102-DP, op. 168, d. 10b (1886), pp. 277–278.

23. G. N. Dobruskina-Mikhailova, "Lopatinskii protsess (Protsess 21)," in *Narodovol'tsy: sb. III*, p. 206.

24. *OVD 1885*, X, 18.

25. Benevol'skii himself became a police informant. TsGIA SSSR, f. 1405, op. 530, d. 975 (1886), pp. 20–22; TsGAOR, f. 102-DP, op. 168, d. 10b (1886), pp. 237-238.

26. There is little doubt that El'ko was a provocateur, that is, working for the police *before* his arrest; see L. P. Men'shchikov, *Okhrana i revoliutsiia*, 3 vols. (Moscow, 1925), I, 17; TsGIA, SSSR, f. 1405, op. 88, d. 9988, p. 9. It has been estimated that some one hundred and fifty activists were arrested because of El'ko's information. A. A. Kulakov, "Avtobiografiia," *KS*, 3 (64) (1930): 178.

27. TsGAOR, f. 102-DP, op. 168, d. 10a (1886), p. 172.

28. Bakh, *Zapiski narodovol'tsa*, pp. xix, 167. See also L. Kuznetsov, "K istorii 'Narodnoi voli' (Zapiska A. N. Bakha 1886 g.)," *KS*, 6 (67) (1930): 54–59.

29. TsGIA SSSR, f. 1405, op. 87, d. 10145, p. 221; op. 88, d. 10064, p. 187; TsGAOR, f. 102-DP, op. 168, d. 10b (1886), pp. 279–285. Bogoraz was arrested at the end of 1883 in Rostov-on-Don and spent three months in prison. See also N. F. Kuleshova, *V. G. Tan-Bogoraz: Zhizn' i tvorchestvo* (Minsk, 1975), pp. 5–15.

30. Orzhikh, "V riadakh," pp. 75–76; TsGIA SSSR, f. 1405, op. 88, d. 10064, p. 169.

31. Jacewicz was an attractive, experienced twenty-eight-year-old revolutionary, who was successful in recruiting both workers and gymnasium students to the cause. Tan [Vladimir (Natan) Bogoraz], "Povesti proshloi zhizni," *RB*, 9 (1907): 107.

32. TsGIA SSSR, f. 1405, op. 88, d. 10064, p. 189; op. 88, d. 10075, pp. 30–63.

33. Tan [Bogoraz], "Povesti," *RB*, 9 (1907): 108; 10 (1907): 151.

34. TsGIA SSSR, f. 1405, op. 88, d. 10075, pp. 34–35, 56; op. 87, d. 10251, p. 34; op. 88, d. 10064, p. 131.

35. TsGIA SSSR, f. 1405, op. 88, d. 10064, p. 189. Tan [Bogoraz], "Povesti," *RB*, 9 (1907): 107–115.

36. TsGAOR, f. 102-DP, op. 168, d. 10a (1886), p. 293; Tan [Bogoraz], "Povesti," *RB*, 9 (1907): 111.

37. TsGIA SSSR, f. 1405, op. 88, d. 10064, pp. 187–189.

38. Ibid., p. 117.

39. Ibid. See also Orzhikh, "V riadakh," p. 125.

40. A. Makarevskii, "Iz istorii revoliutsionnogo dvizheniia 1885–1887 godov," *LR*, 2 (1924): 66.

41. TsGAOR, f. 102-DP, op. 168, d. 10a (1886), p. 175.

42. TsGIA SSSR, f. 1405, op. 88, d. 10064, pp. 130–131.

43. "Bor'ba obshchestvennykh sil v Rossii" (Tip. Narodnoi voli, 1886), in TsGIA SSSR, f. 1410, op. 3, d. 531, pp. 84–85.

44. *Narodnaia Volia*, 11–12 (1885), in *LNV*, p. 729.

45. Bogoraz did recall that several members of the organization had read the first volume of Marx's *Das Kapital*; See "Povesti," *RB*, 9 (1907): 120.

46. TsGAOR, f. 102-DP, op. 168, d. 10a (1886), pp. 267–269.

47. *OVD 1887*, XII, 6.

48. TsGIA SSSR, f. 1405, op. 88, d. 10064, p. 129.

49. *Narodnaia Volia*, 11–12 (1885), in *LNV*, pp. 729–730.

50. Orzhikh, "V riadakh," p. 151. See TsGIA SSSR, f. 1405, op. 88, d. 10064, pp. 169–170.

51. Orzhikh, "V riadakh," p. 144.

52. Ibid., p. 125. See Tan [Bogoraz], "Povesti," *RB*, 9 (1907): 111.

53. See Tikhomirov's letters to Plehve in K. Malakhov and Kamartin, "Lev Tikhomirov i Plehve," *KL*, 7 (1923), pp. 203–207, and A. Gleason, "The Emigration and Apostasy of Leo Tikhomirov," *Slavic Review*, 26 (1968), 414–429.

54. TsGAOR, f. 102-DP, op. 168, d. 9 (1885), p. 74.

55. Ibid., d. 10a (1886), pp. 125, 204–205. Also in *OVD 1886*, XI, 22–27, n. 2.

56. TsGIA SSSR, f. 1405, op. 88, d. 10064, pp. 127–28. Parts are also in *OVD 1887*, XII, 33.

57. Orzhikh, "V riadakh," p. 134.

58. TsGIA SSSR, f. 1410, op. 1, 1886, d. 523, pp. 82a–93.

59. TsGAOR, f. 102-DP, op. 168, d. 10a (1886), pp. 208–209. Also in *OVD 1886*, XI, 28–29.

60. Makarevskii, "Iz istorii," p. 71.

61. "Dorogie tovarischi na dalekoi rodine, 18 July 1885," in TsGAOR, f. 102-DP, op. 168, d. 9 (1885), pp. 143–144. (Police copy.)

62. TsGIA SSSR, f. 1405, op. 530, d. 1079, p. 76.

63. *OVD 1884*, IX, 32.

64. The proclamation was signed "From the circles and groups of the southern Russian organization of the party 'Narodnaia Volia'." TsGIA SSSR, f. 1410, op. 1, d. 525 (1886), p. 5.

65. "Dorogie tovarishchi," in TsGIA SSSR, f. 1410, op. 1, d. 520, pp. 29–30.

66. For other works seized by the police at the Taganrog press, see TsGIA SSSR, f. 1410, op. 1, d. 525 (1886); d. 526; d. 527; and Z. V. Kogan, "O rabote taganrogskoi i novocherkasskoi tipografii partii 'Narodnoi voli'," in *Narodovol'tsy, sb. III*, pp. 183–85.

67. TsGAOR, f. 102-DP, op. 168, d. 10a (1886), pp. 405–406.

68. TsGIA SSSR, f. 1410, op. 1, d. 504, pp. 10, 163–253. This *delo* contains what can only be described as an amazing collection of the most diverse forged stamps, designs, documents, and passports.

69. TsGIA SSSR, f. 1405, op. 87, d. 10134, pp. 29–30; op. 87, d. 10165, pp. 77–78; op. 87, d. 10147, pp. 100–2; op. 530, d. 975 (1886), pp. 2–3. The Iaroslavl Demidov Juridical School was the only institution of higher education that accepted seminarians as a matter of course; it became an especially important center for revolutionary activity in the last half of the 1880s.

70. Orzhikh, "V riadakh," p. 100. TsGAOR, f. 102-DP, op. 168, d. 10a

(1886), pp. 246–250.

71. *OVD 1885*, X, 5. Among the archives of evidence collected by the police and judiciary are almost one hundred lithographed and hectographed lists of collections for political exiles and prisoners. Contributions generally ranged from a single ruble to fifty rubles. The contributors were almost always anonymous ("from a Melitopol chinovnik . . . 10 rubles"). The Moscow Red Cross collected 1,119 rubles and 32 kopecks between May and November of 1885 alone. TsGIA SSSR, f. 1410, op. 1, d. 504, pp. 130–162.

72. Ivanov's list consisted of sixty different addresses (Popov, "S. A. Ivanov," p. 168). Bakh concluded that this was approximately the number of active narodovol'tsy in the organization. Kuznetsov, "K istorii," p. 54.

73. TsGIA SSSR, f. 1405, op. 88, d. 10025, p. 52; op. 87, d. 10160, pp. 81–96; M. P. Gots, "S. V. Zubatov," *Byloe*, 9 (1906): 63–69; Men'shchikov, *Okhrana*, I, 51. Zubatov began his career as an agent by tailing the Gots group in Moscow. Before their arrests, Kogan and Bogoraz managed to print the last number of *Listok "Narodnoi voli"* in a hastily constructed press in Tula. Orzhikh, "V riadakh," p. 170.

74. See *Iakutskaia tragediia 22 marta 1889 goda; Sb. vospominanii i materialov* (Moscow, 1925).

75. TsGAOR, f. 102-DP, op. 168, d. 10b (1886), pp. 41–45; *OVD 1888*, XIII (*Vedomost'*), 40. Apparently Orzhikh survived his traumatic imprisonment. Bogoraz describes a visit with him in Vladivostok, where he had withdrawn completely from politics and was the proprietor of a prosperous florist business. Later, he allegedly emigrated to Chile. Tan [Bogoraz], "Povesti," *RB*, 9 (1907): 118.

76. TsGIA SSSR, f. 1405, op. 88, d. 10075, pp. 44–45, 161–165.

77. Ibid., op. 87, d. 10317, p. 14.

78. For short biographies of the leading socialist revolutionaries, see Hildermeier, *Die Sozialrevolutionäre Partei*, pp. 404–412.

5. Russian Radicals and the Military

1. R. Kantor, "K istorii voennoi organizatsii 'Narodnoi voli' (Pokazaniia F. I. Zavalishina)," *KS*, 5 (18) (1925): 236. These remarks by the tsar are noted in the margins of Zavalishin's deposition sent to him by Tolstoi.

2. TsGAOR, f. 102-DP, d. 88 (1884), ch. 41, pp. 6–7.

3. TsGIA SSSR, f. 1405, op. 85, d. 10999, p. 67; *Dnevnik Polovtsova*, I, 212.

4. See P. A. Zaionchkovskii, *Samoderzhavie i russkaia armiia na rubezhe XIX–XX stoletii* (Moscow, 1973), p. 64; Shchetinina, *Universitety*, p. 131.

5. Zaionchkovskii, *Samoderzhavie i armiia*, p. 234.

6. Apparently, Zaionchkovskii's sources do not include the officers arrested during 1883, those arrested and released for lack of evidence, and those who were not arrested at all (ibid., p. 234, n. 230). See L. N. Godunova, "Voennaia organizatsiia partii 'Narodnaia volia' " (Kand. diss., avtoref., Moscow, 1971), pp. 17–19; L. T. Senchakova, *Revoliutsionnoe dvizhenie v russkoi armii i flote v kontse XIX nachale XX vv.* (Moscow, 1972), pp. 46–47. Godunova firmly establishes the existence of thirty-four military narodovol'tsy circles with 192

full-fledged members. For ninety-seven other officers, there is evidence of association, though not membership. Of the thirty-four circles, seventeen were infantry. Both Godunova and Senchakova estimate that a total of four hundred officers were involved, though clearly half of these were associates and sympathizers, and therefore did not "belong" to the Military Organization.

7. For the numbers in the Central Military Circle, see *OVD 1886*, XI, p. 52, and Troitskii, "*Narodnaia volia*", p. 191.

8. P. A. Argunov, "Moskovskii kruzhok militaristov," in *Narodovol'tsy posle I-go marta*, p. 87.

9. "Programma Ispolnitel'nogo Komiteta," *Narodnaia Volia*, no. 3 (1880), in *LNV*, p. 165.

10. "Podgotovitel'naia rabota partii," in ibid., p. 875.

11. *OVD 1883*, VII, 32–33. See also Figner, *PPS*, I, 227, and "Iz istorii narodovol'cheskogo dvizheniia sredi voennykh v nachale 80-kh godov," *Byloe*, 8 (1906): 158–193.

12. E. A. Serebriakov,*Revoliutsionery vo flote* (Petrograd, 1920), p. 60; Kulczycki, *Rewolucja rosyjska*, II, 459; TsGIA SSSR, f. 1405, op. 85, d. 10898, p. 40.

13. Figner, *PPS*, I, 213.

14. TsGIA SSSR, f. 1405, op. 83, d. 11020, p. 313.

15. Ibid. Nearly 400 different, mostly narodovol'tsy, journals, proclamations, and programs were found on Butsevich at the time of his arrest. See Senchakova, *Revoliutsionnoe dvizhenie*, pp. 46–47.

16. M. Frolenko, *M. Iu. Ashenbrenner* (Moscow, 1930), pp. 21–22; TsGIA SSSR, f. 1405, op. 85, d. 10898, p. 40.

17. TsGIA SSSR, f. 1405, op. 85, d. 10898, pp. 41–42.

18. Ibid., d. 10999, p. 173.

19. Ibid., pp. 174–175, 213. Here, ten Petersburg circles are listed along with the leaders of each.

20. Ibid., d. 10897, p. 149; d. 10898, p. 44.

21. TsGIA SSSR, f. 1405, op. 85, d. 10898, p. 44.

22. For the Tiflis narodovol'tsy organizations in the military and among Georgians (led by Prince Shervashadze), see TsGIA SSSR, f. 1405, op. 83, d. 11312, pp. 42–44; op. 521, d. 414, pp. 183–189. For Armenian narodovol'tsy in Tiflis, see R. G. Suny, "Populism, Nationalism and Marxism: The Origins of Revolutionary Parties Among the Armenians of the Caucasus," *The Armenian Review*, 32 (1979): 139.

23. *OVD 1883*, VII, 8.

24. B. Kubalov, "Veteran Narodnoi voli (M. P. Ovchinnikov)," *KS*, 5 (12) (1924): 95–96.

25. "Ispolnitel'nyi komitet ofitseram russkoi armii (26 August 1881)," in TsGIA SSSR, f. 1410, op. 1, d. 359, p. 1. Also in *LNV*, 908–912.

26. Ivanov, "K kharakteristike," p. 197.

27. Only Captain Arkadii Kunaev of the Kronstadt Artillery Academy was described by the judiciary as a "dangerous terrorist." He became a leader of the Petersburg Military Organization at the end of 1882; see TsGIA SSSR, f. 1405, op. 85, d. 10999, p. 14.

28. TsGAOR, f. 102-DP, d. 88 (1884), ch. 41, p. 7.

29. TsGIA SSSR, f. 1405, op. 85, d. 10898, pp. 43, 185. See Tolstoi's report to the tsar on the Military Organization in Kantor, "K istorii," p. 214. See also O. Bulanov, "A. P. Bulanov," *KS*, 5 (12) 1924), pp. 291–296. In some cases, sons of army and navy officers working as skilled laborers on railways or at the ports engaged in propaganda for the Military Organization among common soldiers (TsGIA SSSR, f. 1405, op. 83–84, d. 11133, pp. 8–18).

30. Valuev, *Dnevnik*, p. 242; see also pp. 219, 238, and *Dnevnik Polovtsova*, I, 119.

31. TsGAOR, f. 102-DP, d. 88 (1884), ch. 35, p. 3.

32. TsGIA SSSR, f. 1405. op. 85, d. 10858, p. 174; *OVD 1886*, XI, 58; *OVD 1884*, VIII, 35. Archival information is very scant on the union, its relationship to various radical circles, and the extent to which it overlapped with the military circles or the Society of Translators and Publishers. The report of the Moscow prosecutor (TsGIA SSSR, f. 1405, op. 85, d. 10858) is full of internal contradictions as well as differences with the gendarme reports in *OVD*.

33. "Ot redaktsii," *Sbornik obshche-studencheskoi organizatsii*, vyp. I (Moscow, 1884), p. 5, in TsGIA SSSR, f. 1410, op. 1, d. 527, p. 80.

34. *OVD 1886*, XI, 59–60.

35. Ibid., pp. 61–62. See also TsGIA SSSR, f. 1405, op. 85, d. 19858, p. 92.

36. For recent discussions of the Raspopin group, see Polevoi, *Zarozhdenie marksizma*, pp. 337–349, and Johnson, *Peasant and Proletarian* pp. 103–105. The best study of the group is P. Anatol'ev, "Obshchestvo perevodchikov i izdatelei," *KS*, 100 (1933): 82–141. See also Argunov, "Moskovskii kruzhok," pp. 87–96.

37. TsGIA SSSR, f. 1405, op. 85, d. 10858, p. 90.

38. Anatol'ev, "Obshchestvo perevodchikov," p. 95; TsGIA SSSR, f. 1405, op. 85, d. 10858, p. 95.

39. Quoted in TsGIA SSSR, f. 1405, op. 85, d. 10858, p. 95.

40. Quoted from an unpublished Argunov manuscript in Anatol'ev, "Obshchestvo perevodchikov," p. 82.

41. TsGIA SSSR, f. 1405, op. 85, d. 10858, p. 218.

42. The group included V. T. Raspopin, P. A. Argunov, I. I. Vorzheikin, Elena Maslova, A. G. Miasnikova, M. I. Sukhanov, N. P. Fomin, and R. Tsimmerman. The Poles Ludwik Janowicz and Boleslaw Malinowski were also close to the group.

43. Quoted in Anatol'ev, "Obshchestvo perevodchikov," p. 96.

44. Ibid., p. 97.

45. The Moscow prosecutor mentions Malinowski as another important contact with Warsaw (TsGIA SSSR, f. 1405, op. 85, d. 10858, p. 218). The police also established several ties between the Moscow Society and the St. Petersburg Student Corporation (TsGAOR, f. 102-DP, d-vo III, d. 776, pp. 103–4). The publications served as the basis of underground libraries for years to follow. See TsGIA SSSR, f. 1405, op. 88, d. 10076, pp. 335–338.

46. Anatol'ev, "Obshchestvo perevodchikov," pp. 96, 102–105.

47. Ibid., p. 124. Certainly Deich did not think much of Janowicz's reports on the Moscow movement when the Pole visited in Switzerland. "He speaks a great deal, but says nothing (very) comforting"; see "L. Deich to P. Aksel'rod (12 January 1884)" (copy), IISH, Axelrod Archives, A (3), II–III, p. 26.

Janowicz was arrested after a shootout in a Warsaw milk-bar (July 1884) involving him, the police, and two other Proletariat activists.

48. Figner, *PPS*, I, 299; M. A. Braginskii, "Iz vospominanii o voennorevoliutsionnoi organizatsii (1884–1886 gg.)," in *Narodovol'tsy 80-kh i 90-kh godov*, p. 118.

49. TsGIA SSSR, f. 1405, op. 87, d. 10319, p. 210.

50. Ibid. Several other narodovol'tsy activists also participated in the Junkers' meetings; Fedor Alekseev, Samuil Zalkind, Sofia Ginsburg, and Moisei Bramson. Petr Dushevskii of the Mikhailovskii Artillery School was a military leader of the Junkers. See Braginskii, "Iz vospominanii," p. 118.

51. Senchakova, *Revoliutsionnoe dvizhenie*, p. 1.

52. Ibid., p. 36.

53. TsGIA SSSR, f. 1405, op. 87, d. 10319, p. 211. Braginskii, "Iz vospominanii," pp. 123–124. There were radical circles among the Junkers at the Mikhailovskii Artillery School, the Nikolaevskii Engineering School, and at the Konstantinovskii and Pavlovskii Military Schools.

54. On Red'ko, see TsGIA SSSR, f. 1405, op. 87, d. 10319, p. 165; on Kuchin, see ibid., p. 217.

55. *OVD 1886*, XI, 53. The police indicate that Braginskii initially wavered between Shelgunov and Bruevich, but in the end sided with Shelgunov.

56. TsGIA SSSR, f. 1405, op. 87. d. 10319, p. 424; *OVD 1886*, XI, 53.

57. TsGIA SSSR, f. 1405, op. 87, d. 10319, pp. 8, 132, 294.

58. This copy of the program, reproduced in full in the report of Kiev prosecutor (19 December 1886), was sent to Kiev by Shelgunov and seized there from Mikhail Mauer (ibid., pp. 18–32). The program is summarized in *OVD 1886*, XI, 55.

59. Senchakova, *Revoliutsionnoe dvizhenie*, p. 66. See also TsGIA SSSR, f. 1405, op. 521, d. 429, p. 231.

60. The engineer technologists were P. Shat'ko, N. G. Grigor'ev, V. F. Danilov, M. Iu. Beliavskii, and F. M. Pol'skii. See TsGIA SSSR, f. 1405, op 87, d. 10319, pp. 218–219.

61. Zhuikov and Polevoi insist that the Party of Social Democrats influenced the Central Military Circle; Senchakova thinks influences flowed in the opposite direction. See Zhuikov, *Peterburgskie marksisty*, p. 202; Polevoi, *Zarozhdenie marksizma*, pp. 321–323; and Senchakova, *Revoliutsionnoe dvizhenie*, pp. 64–65.

62. TsGIA SSSR, f. 1405, op. 87, d. 10319, p. 218.

63. Ibid., pp. 8, 212, 440.

64. *OVD 1886*, XI, 56.

65. TsGIA SSSR, f. 1405, op. 87, d. 10219, pp. 212, 218; Senchakova, *Revoliutsionnoe dvizhenie*, p. 70. Fifty-two were finally sentenced (*OVD 1886*, XI, 52). Troitskii lists eighteen officers who faced trial in the St. Petersburg Military Court, 13–18 October 1887, including Shelgunov, Mauer, Chernevskii, and Aksentovich; see his "*Narodnaia volia*", p. 191.

66. TsGIA SSSR, f. 1405, op. 87, s. 10240, p. 13; op. 89, d. 11058, pp. 83, 109, 128. See Senchakova, *Revoliutsionnoe dvizhenie*, pp. 78–80, 82.

67. TsGIA SSSR, f. 1405, op. 521, d. 429. pp. 163–164.

68. Ibid., pp. 164-165.

69. Ibid., p. 165; Senchakova, *Revoliutsionnoe dvizhenie*, p. 89.

6. The St. Petersburg Student Movement and the Terrorist Fraction

1. "Pravitel'stvennoe soobshchenie o dele 1 marta 1887 g.," *Aleksandr Il'ich Ul'ianov i delo 1 marta 1887 g.*, ed. A. I. Ul'ianova-Elizarova (Moscow-Leningrad, 1927), pp. 411-413.

2. Among the most useful Soviet studies are the one just cited; A. S. Poliakov, *Vtoroe 1-e marta: Pokushenie na imperatora Aleksandra III* (Petrograd, 1919); B. S. Itenberg and A. Ia. Cherniak, *Zhizn' Aleksandra Ul'ianova* (Moscow, 1966); and I. D. Lukashevich, *1 marta 1887 g.: Vospominaniia* (Petrograd, 1920). See also N. Valentinov (N. V. Volski), *The Early Years of Lenin*, ed. and tr. R. H. W. Theen (Ann Arbor, 1969).

3. *Dnevnik Polovtsova*, I, 38; Shchetinina, *Universitety*, p. 220.

4. (John Darlington) Board of Education. Special Reports on Educational Subjects, *Education in Russia* (London, 1909), p. 147.

5. S. V. Rozhdestvenskii, *Istoricheskii obzor deiatel'nosti Ministerstva Narodnogo Prosveshcheniia, 1802-1902* (St. Petersburg, 1902), pp. 616-623; S. D. Kassow, "The Russian University in Crisis: 1899-1911," 2 vols. (Ph.D. diss., Princeton, 1976), I, 49, 79.

6. TsGIA SSSR, f. 1405, op. 86, d. 10877, pp. 32-33; op. 87, d. 10212, pp. 18-19. According to the police, the Corporation had representatives from twenty different provinces and, at its height, consisted of six circles. Most of the students were poor; fifteen of them lived on less than twenty rubles per month. TsGAOR, f. 102-DP, d-vo III, d. 776 (1884), p. 103.

7. TsGIA SSSR, f. 1405, op. 86, d. 10877, pp. 32-34.

8. Zhuikov, *Peterburgskie marksisty*, pp. 166-167.

9. *Studenchestvo*, 2 (1883): 2-5, in TsGIA SSSR, f. 1410, op. 1, d. 422, pp. 247-248; *Studenchestvo*, 1 (1883): 6, in ibid., p. 249.

10. *Studenchestvo*, 3-4 (1883): 6, in TsGIA SSSR, f. 1410, op. 2, d. 427, p. 7; *Svobodnoe slovo*, 1-2 (1884): 14, in ibid., d. 428, p. 8.

11. *Studenchestvo*, 7-8 (1883): 1, in TsGIA SSSR, f. 1410, op. 1, d. 494, p. 37.

12. *Svobodnoe slovo*, 1-2 (1884): 9, in ibid., op. 2, d. 428, p. 6.

13. *Studenchestvo*, 3-4 (1883): 9; 2 (1882): 5-13; 5-6 (1883): 59-71; *Svobodnoe slovo*, 3 (1883): 7-13, all in ibid., d. 427, pp. 55-58; d. 422, pp. 256-262; d. 185, pp. 59-70. The newspapers also carried announcements of newly hectographed editions of Marx's works, such as the 1883 publication of the Russian translations of *The Civil War in France*.

14. *Studenchestvo*, 2 (1882): 5, in TsGIA SSSR, f. 1410, op. 1, d. 422, p. 256.

15. *Svobodnoe slovo*, 1-2 (1884): 11, in ibid., op. 2, d. 428, p. 7.

16. *Svobodnoe slovo*, 3 (1884): 12-13, in ibid., pp. 57-58.

17. *Svobodnoe slovo*, 3 (1884): 7, in ibid., p. 55. An offshoot of the Corporation, the Union of Young Russian Intelligentsia published one number of its lithographed journal *Voice of the Youth*, which placed particularly heavy emphasis on the need to contact workers. In fact, the copy of the journal found

by the police was confiscated from a workers' circle. *Golos molodezhi*, 1 (1886): 1–81, in TsGIA SSSR, f. 1410, op. 1, d. 532, pp. 2–24.

18. *Studenchestvo*, 5–6 (1883): 2–3, in TsGIA SSSR, f. 1410, op. 3, d. 185, p. 2. For ties with the Moscow Society and with the provinces, see ibid., f. 1405, op. 86, d. 10877, p. 59.

19. V. P. Krikunov, *A. I. Ul'ianov i revoliutsionnye raznochintsy Dona i Severnogo Kavkaza* (Nal'chik, 1963), pp. 19–20; Łukawski, *Polacy w rosyjskim ruchu*, pp. 15–17.

20. TsGAOR, f. 102-DP, d-vo III, d. 776 (1884), ch. III, p. 99.

21. Ibid., ch. II, p. 3.

22. TsGIA SSSR, f. 1405, op. 87, d. 10212, p. 25.

23. TsGAOR, f. 102-DP, d-vo III, d. 776 (1884), ch. II, p. 119.

24. Ibid., 118.

25. Ibid., ch. III, p. 3. See also Rozhdestvenskii, *Obzor MNP*, p. 179.

26. Rozhdestvenskii, *Obzor MNP*, p. 148; Shchetinina, *Universitety*, p. 215.

27. TsGIA SSSR, f. 1405, op. 88, d. 10143, pp. 75–76.

28. Krikunov, *A. I. Ul'ianov*, pp. 61, 74–75. Zhuikov is less willing to label the circle "social-democratic," but he does emphasize the important influence of Marxism on its maturation (Zhuikov, *Peterburgskie marksisty*, pp. 210–211).

29. Police Chief Gresser called in the remaining leaders of the petition campaign and threatened them with expulsion (*Svobodnaia Rossiia*, 1 [1889]: 59). See also S. G. Sviatikov, "Uvol'nenie V. I. Semevskogo i peterburgskoe studenchestvo," *GM*, 12 (1916): 230–232.

30. On the Union of the Zemliachestvos and the Circle of the Don and Kuban, see S. A. Nikonov, "Vospominaniia revoliutsionera (1884–1920)" (manuscript of 1925), in TsGIA SSSR, f. 1093, op. 1, d. 145, pp. 112–115; *OVD 1887*, XII, 14–15; and Govorukhin, "Vospominaniia," p. 137.

31. For a history of the Scientific-Literary Society, see I. M. Grevs', "V gody iunosti," *Byloe*, 12 (1918): 42–88. See also TsGIA SSSR, f. 1405, op. 88, d. 9991, p. 10.

32. Itenberg and Cherniak, *Zhizn' Ul'ianova*, p. 70.

33. TsGAOR, f. 102-DP, d-vo III, d. 100 (1886), p. 88; TsGIA SSSR, f. 1405, op. 88, d. 9991, pp. 10, 46–47; *OVD 1887*, XII, 14–15. Ul'ianov resigned as secretary shortly before the plans were drawn for the March 1 attempt; he wanted to avoid compromising the society.

34. *Svobodnaia Rossiia*, 1 (1889): 59. S. A. Nikonov, "Zhizn' studenchestva i revoliutsionnaia rabota kontsa vos'midesiatykh godov," in *Aleksandr Il'ich*, p. 146.

35. The Dobroliubov demonstration is described in Nikonov, "Zhizn' studenchestva," pp. 146–147; *OVD 1887*, XII, 15–16; *Svobodnaia Rossiia*, 1 (1889): 59; "17 noiabria v Peterburge," in *A. I. Ul'ianov*, p. 355; and M. A. Braginskii, "Dobroliubovskaia demonstratsiia," *Byloe*, 5 (1907): 306–309.

36. *OVD 1887*, XII, 4. See E. I. Iakovenko, "K sorokaletiiu 1-go marta 1887 g.," *KS*, 3 (32) (1927): 19.

37. *OVD 1887*, XII, 22; Nikonov, "Zhizn' studenchestva," p. 154.

38. Nikonov, "Zhizn' studenchestva, " p. 154. See also the copy of Andreiushkin's letter to Ivan Nikitin (*OVD 1887*, XII, 13–14). Rudevich, who knew Andreiushkin well, described him as "amazingly cold-blooded," "able to look death in the eye and calmly ascend the scaffold." See "Rudevich to Lavrov (fall 1887)," *Lavrov*, II, 201.

39. Lukashevich, *1 marta 1887 g.*, p. 5. For a similar description of Shevyrev, see "Rudevich to Lavrov (fall 1887)," *Lavrov*, II, 203. Even Govorukhin, who exaggerates the role of Ul'ianov, admits that Shevyrev initiated the Fraction. "A. I. Ul'ianov i P. Ia. Shevyrev po vospominaniiam Govorukhina," *PR*, 7 (1925): 125.

40. *Aleksandr Il'ich*, p. 336. See also Lukashevich, *1 marta 1887 g.*, p. 13.

41. Lukashevich, *1 marta 1887 g.*, p. 45.

42. Typical was Govorukhin's report to the Paris narodovol'tsy (May 1887): Ul'ianov was a "very gifted personality . . . kind, a humane person of the highest sort, a loving nature," *Lavrov*, II, 175.

43. Lukashevich, *1 marta 1887 g.*, p. 45.

44. Govorukhin, "Vospominaniia," p. 133. Anna Elizarova (Ul'ianov's sister) began the long tradition in Soviet historiography of exaggerating Aleksandr's devotion to Marxism. See her memoirs, "Vospominaniia ob Aleksandre Il'iche Ul'ianove," in *Aleksandr Il'ich*, pp. 30–124.

45. Nikonov, "Zhizn' studenchestva," pp. 157–158; S. Khlebnikov, "Vospominaniia ob Aleksandre Il'iche Ul'ianove, 1886–1887," in *Aleksandr Il'ich*, p. 264. See also *OVD 1887*, XII, p. 17, and "Rudevich to Lavrov (fall 1887)," *Lavrov*, II, 202. The police constantly refer to Ul'ianov as a narodovolets while Rudevich noted only that Ul'ianov was an advocate of terrorism but opposed to the seizure of power.

46. Smirnov, "Otgoloski 'Narodnoi voli'," p. 243. See also Iakovenko, "K sorokaletiiu," p. 24.

47. "Soobshchenie iz Vil'no" (letter to the Paris narodovol'tsy from an unidentified Vilna conspirator, March-April, 1887), *Lavrov*, II, 168–169.

48. *OVD 1887*, XII, pp. 13–14. Andreiushkin had been in close contact with the narodovolets Natan Bogoraz and apparently shared his terrorist views. Similarly, Osipanov had been recruited to the movement by Boris Orzhikh in Tomsk in 1882–83. Lukashevich, *1 marta 1887 g.*, p. 38.

49. Nikonov, "Zhizn' studenchestva," pp. 156–157.

50. "Govorukhin to the Paris Narodovol'tsy (May 1887)," *Lavrov*, II, 176.

51. Govorukhin, "Vospominaniia," p. 130.

52. Lukashevich, *1 marta 1887 g.*, p. 26. Govorukhin praises Lukashevich as a "social democrat," a "superb chemist," and generally as a talented individual; see "Govorukhin to the Paris Narodovol'tsy (May 1887)," *Lavrov*, II, 176.

53. Lukashevich, *1 marta 1887 g.*, p. 28; TsGIA SSSR, f. 1405, op. 88, d. 9961, p. 79.

54. "Programma terroristicheskoi fraktsii partii 'Narodnaia volia'," in *Aleksandr Il'ich*, pp. 375–380 (emphases added); *OVD 1887*, XII, 5. The program was never printed; the one reproduced in the above collections was taken from a police version dictated by Ul'ianov to his captors while in prison. Contemporaneous accounts of the program are very close to Ul'ianov's

verbal version. See, for instance, "Soobshchenie iz Vil'no," *Lavrov*, II, 171–172, and "Govorukhin to Lavrov (June 1887)," ibid., pp. 184–185.

55. "Rudevich to Lavrov (fall 1887)," *Lavrov*, II, 198.

56. The police were convinced at the time that the Fraction consisted of a melding of two groups: the Circle of the Don and Kuban, led by Shevyrev, and the Vilna narodovol'tsy, led by Dembo (TsGIA SSSR, f. 1405, op. 88, d. 10047, p. 145). On the activities of the Vilna group, see ibid., d. 10080, pp. 1–65.

57. This version seems the most likely of a number of possible scenarios for the procurement of the explosives (TsGIA SSSR, f. 1405, op. 88, d. 9961, pp. 73–74, and *OVD 1887*, XII, 18–19).

58. Govorukhin was indeed followed by the police. He left Petersburg in February, went underground in Vilna, and with the help of Joseph Pilsudski, Gnatovskii, and Pashkovskii, emigrated to Switzerland. He left behind a suicide note, but the police did not fall for the ruse. Apparently, Rudevich never agreed with plans for regicide and for this reason asked Shevyrev to be sent out of the country (TsGIA SSSR, op. 88, d. 10047, pp. 54–92; *OVD 1887*, XII, 20–21).

59. Lukashevich, *1 marta 1887 g.*, p. 22; *OVD 1887*, XII, 22–23.

60. *OVD 1887*, XII, 13–14.

61. *Svobodnaia Rossiia*, 1 (1889): 60.

62. Lukashevich, *1 marta 1887 g.*, p. 37.

63. "Delo 1 marta 1887 goda: Sudoproizvodstvo," in *Aleksandr Il'ich*, p. 3.

64. Nikonov, "Zhizn' studenchestva," p. 172.

65. *Svobodnaia Rossiia*, 1 (1889): 60.

66. Poliakov, *Vtoroe 1-e marta*, p. 47.

67. "Obvinitel'nyi akt po delu 1 marta 1887 g.," in *Aleksandr Il'ich*, p. 407; "Delo 1 marta 1887," pp. 330, 332, 335. The case against the Terrorist Fraction ("Obvinitel'nyi akt") is also in TsGIA SSSR, f. 1405, op. 88, d. 9961, pp. 95–109. The sentencing is recorded in ibid., d. 9981, pp. 171–176.

68. See Poliakov, *Vtoroe 1-e marta*, p. 47.

69. TsGIA SSSR, f. 1405, op. 88, d. 9981. See also the petition of 28 March 1887 quoted in Poliakov, *Vtoroe 1-e marta*, p. 56.

70. "Delo 1 marta 1887," p. 346.

71. Ibid., p. 336. TsGIA SSSR, f. 1405, op. 88, d. 9981, p. 342.

72. Confronted by the hostility of his fellow exiles on Sakhalin, Kancher committed suicide. Gorkun soon died in exile; B. Pilsudski apparently died on Sakhalin during World War I, while Mariia Anan'ina, who became involved with Lev Deich in exile, died while serving hard labor.

73. "Delo 1 marta 1887," p. 351.

74. *OVD 1887*, XII, 65–66, 118–121. "Rudevich to Lavrov (fall 1887)," *Lavrov*, II, 197.

75. Poliakov, *Vtoroe 1-e marta*, p. 10.

76. Shchetinina notes that as a result of March 1, 261 students were expelled from the universities, 4.15 percent of all students at that time (*Universitety*, pp. 220–222).

77. *Pobedonostsev i ego korrespondenty*, pt. 1, 739.

78. Ibid., pt. 2, 661. Orzhevskii's gendarmes had nothing to do with the arrests; Gresser's city police gained in stature, reigniting the long-standing feud between the two. Apparently Tolstoi's nerves failed him again and he left the city on March 16. B. Kazanskii, "Novye dannye o dele 1 marta 1887," *KS*, 10 (71) (1930): 142.

79. *OVD 1887*, XII, 27.

80. "P. L. Lavrov to V. N. Smirnov (13 May 1887)," *Lavrov*, II, 434.

81. Quoted in full in Poliakov, *Vtoroe 1-e marta*, p. 62.

82. "Donesenie Direktora dep-ta Politisii," in *Aleksandr Il'ich*, p. 363.

83. "Proklamatsiia," in *Aleksandr Il'ich*, pp. 364–365; TsGAOR, f. 102-DV, d-vo III, d. 12 (1887), ch. 1, pp. 3–7.

84. Others involved in the group included the students V. P. Petrovy, I. I. Eisymont, P. I. Zakharov, the teacher N. P. Estifeev, and the worker P. A. Zysser (TsGIA SSSR, f. 1405, op. 88, d. 10094, p. 67, and *OVD 1887*, XII, 168–170). See also S. N. Valk, " 'Studencheskii soiuz' i kazn' 1 maia 1887 goda," *KA*, 21 (1927): 226–227.

85. TsGIA SSSR, f. 1405, op. 88, d. 10094, p. 60; Iakovenko, "K sorokaletiiu," p. 22. Iakovenko notes here that he and M. N. Sosnovskii composed the proclamation and Estifeev hectographed it.

86. *OVD 1887*, XII, 68–70; Poliakov, *Vtoroe 1-e marta*, p. 63; Valk, "Studencheskii soiuz," pp. 230–231.

87. TsGIA SSSR, f. 1405, op. 88, d. 10094, p. 74.

88. Ibid., p. 61.

7. Social Democracy in St. Petersburg and Moscow, 1889–1893

1. In his testimony Egupov implicated 138 radicals; the names are listed in TsGAOR, f. 102-DP, d-vo VII, d. 220 (1893), t. I, pp. 105–172. See also *OVD 1892*, XVII, 29–37.

2. For instance, the Moscow prosecutor writes that "there remains no doubt as to the truthfulness of his confession"; TsGIA SSSR, f. 1405, op. 93, d. 10547, p. 33.

3. See the standard Soviet studies of this period: Kazakevich, *Sotsialdemokraticheskie organizatsii*, and Polevoi, *Zarozhdenie marksizma*. For the importance of the period to Soviet conceptions of Bolshevik history, see Pipes, *Social Democracy*, and the clumsy rejoinder by R. A. Kazakevich and F. M. Suslov, *Mister Paips fal'sifitsiruet istoriiu* (Leningrad, 1966). For a thorough study of the role of Poles in the movement, see A. M. Orekhov, *Sotsialdemokraticheskoe dvizhenie v Rossii i pol'skie revoliutsionery* (Moscow, 1973). For collections of documents and workers' memoirs, see *V nachale puti*, and *Rabochee dvizhenie*, III (2).

4. See Pipes, *Social Democracy*, p. 18.

5. Naimark, *The History of the "Proletariat"*, pp. 55–80.

6. TsGIA SSSR, f. 1405, op. 91, d. 10748, ch. II, p. 151; d. 10749, ch. III, p. 247. See also Pipes, *Social Democracy*, pp. 24–26; Polevoi, *Zarozhdenie marksizma*, pp. 376–377; and B. Lelewel, "Przyczynek do dziejów udziału Polaków w rosyjskim ruchu rewolucyjnym (1886–1890)," *Niepodległość*, 1 (24) (1934): 138.

7. V. Golubev, "Stranichka iz istorii rabochego dvizheniia," *Byloe*, 12 (1906): 11.

8. TsGIA SSSR, f. 1405, op. 91, d. 10747, ch. I, p. 236.

9. V. V. Fomin, "Vospominaniia o podpol'noi rabote revoliutsionnykh kruzhkov na Baltiiskom zavode," in *V nachale puti*, p. 185.

10. Orekhov, *Sotsial-demokraticheskoe dvizhenie*, p. 146.

11. TsGIA SSSR, f. 1405, op. 91, d. 10749, ch. III, p. 230.

12. *OVD 1891–92*, XVII, 17.

13. Golubev, "Stranichka, " p. 113.

14. "Stenogram of the memoirs of M. I. Brusnev in the Museum of the Revolution (8 May 1929)," p. 6, quoted in *V nachale puti*, p. 75.

15. Golubev, "Stranichka," p. 113.

16. Brusnev, "Vozniknovenie," p. 23.

17. Fomin, "Vospominaniia," pp. 184–185, 190–191.

18. TsGIA SSSR, f. 1405, op. 92, d. 10979, pp. 43–44. The police never uncovered the first stage of the Central Circle's activities, 1889–90. Only Filimonov and Bogdanov were arrested for propagandizing among workers and their papers and depositions, contained in this *delo*, demonstrate a high level of "workers' consciousness."

19. Ibid., pp. 39–40.

20. Ibid., pp. 14–15.

21. Fomin, "Vospominaniia," pp. 200–201. On the workers' zemliachestvos in Moscow factories, see Johnson, *Peasant and Proletarian*, pp. 68–70.

22. Fomin, "Vospominaniia, " pp. 181–182, 202.

23. Ibid., p. 212.

24. I. I. Egorov, "Iz vospominanii o rabochikh kruzhkakh v Peterburge 1888–1892 godov," in *V nachale puti*, p. 238.

25. V, M. Karelina, "Vospominaniia o podpol'nykh rabochikh kruzhkakh Brusnevskoi organizatsii," in *V nachale puti*, p. 274; A. G. Boldyreva, "Minuvshie gody," in ibid., p. 403; Fomin, "Vospominaniia," pp. 192, 204.

26. A. P. Il'in, "V. I. Ul'ianov v rabochikh kruzhkakh Peterburga," in *V nachale puti*, p. 367.

27. Boldyreva, "Minuvshie gody," pp. 249–268.

28. Karelina, "Vospominaniia," p. 276.

29. The circle consisted of former Institute workers, weavers, and wives of prominent worker-activists: Anna Egorova (Boldyreva), Natalia Grigor'eva, Vera Nikolaeva, Masha Ivanova (Makhlakova), Pasha Zheliabina, Fenia Norinskaia, Natasha Keizera, and Elizaveta Aleksandrova. Some women of the intelligentsia also met with the circle, including L. Krasin's wife, Liubov' Milodova.

30. Golubev, "Stranichka," p. 115. For the circle at the Eccelesiastical Academy, led by Kanavin and Favorskii, see TsGIA SSSR, f. 1405, op. 92, d. 10928, pp. 87–88.

31. *OVD 1892–93*, XVII, 3.

32. The names "Workers' Union" and "Central Workers' Circle" were sometimes used interchangeably. However, the former generally referred to the combined worker and intelligentsia organizations and the latter to their ex-

ecutive committee.

33. Golubev, "Stranichka," p. 116.

34. Brusnev "Vozniknovenie," p. 24.

35. See the full address in Golubev "Stranichka," pp. 120-121, and in *Rabochee dvizhenie*, III (2), 129-130.

36. Golubev, "Stranichka," p. 119.

37. N. D. Bogdanov, "Na zare sotsial-demokratii," in *V nachale puti*, p. 231.

38. Brusnev, "Vozniknovenie," p. 20.

39. V. V. Sviatlovskii, "Na zare rossiiskoi sotsial-demokratii," *Byloe*, 19 (1922): 119-122. "V. B.", "Vospominaniia peterburzhtsa o vtoroi polovine 80-kh godov," *MG*, 2 (1908): 196-197. For a discussion of Brusnev's tactics, see Sergievskii, "Gruppa 'Osvobozhenie truda'," *IRS*, II, 119-122.

40. L. Krasin, "Dela davno minuvshikh dnei (1887-1892)," *PR*, 3 (1923): 10-11.

41. Sviatlovskii, "Na zare," p. 152.

42. OVD 1892-93, VII, 24-25. See also *Rabochee dvizhenie*, III (2) 131-132.

43. Bogdanov exaggerates when he writes that there were 150-200 worker demonstrators ("Na zare," p. 231). See Orekhov, *Sotsial-demokraticheskoe dvizhenie*, p. 166; Brusnev, "Vozniknovenie," p. 25.

44. The workers were banished from St. Petersburg for three years. TsGIA SSSR, f. 1405, op. 92, d. 10979, p. 78.

45. "Brusnev stenogram," p. 2, quoted in *V nachale puti*, p. 90. The speeches were printed and distributed in hectographed form by the Group of Narodovol'tsy. In 1892 they were printed by Plekhanov abroad; S. N. Valk, "Materialy k istorii prazdnovaniia 1 Maia v Rossii," *KL*, 4 (1922): 262-263.

46. See Korol'chuk, "Peredovye proletarii," *V nachale puti*, p. 90.

47. TsGIA SSSR, f. 1405, op. 93, d. 10573, pp. 95-133; R. Pipes, *Struve: Liberal on the Left 1870-1903* (Cambridge, Mass., 1970), I, 70.

48. TsGIA SSSR, f. 1405, op. 93, d. 10573, pp. 101-102. Stranden also collected and distributed hectographed copies of a dozen revolutionary poems.

49. Ibid., pp. 108-109.

50. Ibid., p. 111.

51. Ibid., pp. 112-113.

52. At least in his depositions, Sivokhin noted that the workers were not particularly interested in these studies. Some fell asleep during his lectures and others asked "irrelevant" questions, such as how to make liquor out of apples (ibid., p. 125; d. 10547, p. 19).

53. Ibid., d. 10573, p. 96. TsGAOR, f. 102-DP, d-vo III, d. 558 (1892), p. 8.

54. V. M. Karelina, "Na zare rabochego dvizheniia v S. Petersburg," *KL*, 4 (1922): 16.

55. TsGAOR, f. 102-DP, d-vo III, d. 558 (1892). p. 8.

56. TsGIA SSSR, f. 1405, op. 93, d. 10573, p. 96; TsGAOR, f. 102-DP, d-vo III, d. 558 (1892), p. 10.

57. TsGIA SSSR, f. 1405, op. 93, d. 10573, p. 96. See Sviatlovskii, "Na zare," p. 159, and Karelina, "Na zare," pp. 16-17.

58. TsGAOR, f. 102-DP, d-vo III, d. 558 (1892), p. 9.

59. "Otkrytoe pis'mo k pol'skim rabocham," (police copy) in ibid., pp. 21–22. See also *Rabochee dvizhenie*, III (2), 130–131.

60. TsGAOR, f. 102-DP, d-vo III, d. 558 (1892), p. 10.

61. The workers indicted in August 1892 for collecting funds were Petr Lopatin, Raskol'nikov, Pashin, Evgrafov, Fomin, and Konstantin Norinkov (ibid., p. 23).

62. TsGIA SSSR, f. 1405, op. 93, d. 10573, p. 89.

63. TsGAOR, f. 102-DP, d-vo III, d. 558 (1892), pp. 12–15; TsGIA SSSR, f. 1405, op. 521, d. 441, p. 248.

64. TsGIA SSSR, f. 1405, op. 93, d. 10573, p. 129.

65. Ibid., pp. 140–142; TsGAOR, f. 102-DP, d-vo III, d. 558 (1892), pp. 23–30. Of the twenty-five workers, all were between 19 and 30 years of age, about half were from the peasant estate, and four were women. Most were literate, at least eight were metal workers, and together they represented diverse factories from around the city. All but three or four were single.

66. TsGIA SSSR, f. 1405, op. 93, d. 10573, p. 142. The gendarmes were somewhat more impressed with the ability of workers to organize themselves (*OVD 1894*, XVIII, 32).

67. TsGIA SSSR, f. 1405, op. 93, d. 10573, p. 95.

68. Golubev, "Stranichka iz istorii," p. 111.

69. "Aksel'rod to Bernstein," *Perepiska Plekhanova i Aksel'roda*, I, 243.

70. See Pipes, *Social Democracy*, p. 42.

71. TsGIA SSSR, f. 1405, op. 521, d. 441, pp. 228–236; op. 530, d. 1050, p. 9.

72. For Radchenko and his importance in the development of Bolshevism, see Pipes, *Social Democracy*, pp. 42–56, and J. H. Billington, *Fire in the Minds of Men* (New York, 1980), pp. 455–461.

73. Forty members of the reconstituted organizations were indicted. TsGIA SSSR, f. 1405, op. 521, d. 441, pp. 229–249.

74. The meetings are described in Norinskii, "Kratkaia avtobiografiia," in *V nachale puti*, p. 296, and V. A. Shelgunov, "Moi vospominaniia o voskresnykh shkolakh," in ibid., p. 337.

75. Norinskii, "Kratkaia avtobiografiia," pp. 295–296; Iakovlev, "Vospominaniia o V. I. Lenine," in *V nachale puti*, p. 358.

76. For the group's history, see Iu. Martov, *Zapiski sotsial-demokrata* (Berlin, 1922), pp. 129–161.

77. TsGAOR, f. 102-DP, d-vo III, d. 741 (1891), pp. 68–69; d-vo VII, d. 220 (1893). t. IV, p. 14. For a brief English-language discussion of the group, see Johnson, *Peasant and Proletarian*, pp. 106–109; for a Soviet point of view, see Polevoi, *Zarozhdenie marksizma*, pp. 399–400.

78. TsGAOR, f. 102-DP, d-vo III, d. 741 (1891), p. 69.

79. Ibid., d-vo VII, d. 220 (1893), t. I, pp. 30–31.

80. Krasin, "Dela davno," p. 21; TsGAOR, f. 102-DP, d-vo VII, d. 220 (1893), t. I, pp. 30–31; Brusnev, "Vozniknovenie," pp. 28–29.

81. Orekhov, *Sotsial-demokraticheskoe dvizhenie*, p. 248; Krasin, "Dela davno," p. 21.

82. TsGAOR, f. 102-DP, d-vo VII, d. 220 (1893), t. I, pp. 29–30. Egupov

says here that they both participated in the Shelgunov demonstration, for which Nemtsov was deported from St. Petersburg.

83. Ibid., pp. 30–35.

84. Ibid., d-vo III, d. 741 (1891), p. 56; d-vo VII, d. 220 (1893), t. I, p. 31.

85. TsGAOR, f. 102-DP, d-vo VII, d. 220 (1893), t. I. p. 35.

86. Ibid., p. 38–39.

87. Ibid., p. 40. Ivanitskii was a Russian from Ekaterinoslav province, who finished his education in Warsaw. His activities are described by Orekhov, *Sotsial-demokraticheskoe dvizhenie*, pp. 268–303. Egupov also held discussions with the most important radicals in the Polish socialist camp: the "national-socialist" M. Potocki and the social democrat L. Krzywicki.

88. TsGAOR, f. 102-DP, d-vo VII, d. 220 (1893), t. I, p. 46.

89. Brusnev, "Vozniknovenie," p. 31.

90. TsGIA SSSR, f. 1405, op. 93, d. 10547, p. 320.

91. TsGAOR, f. 102-DP, d-vo VII, d. 220 (1893), t. I, p. 50.

92. TsGIA SSSR, f. 1405, op. 93, d. 10543, p. 19. (Copy of "Brusnev to Sivokhin, 22 January 1892").

93. TsGAOR, f. 102-DP, d-vo VII, d. 220 (1893), t. I. p. 52.

94. Ibid., pp. 55–56.

95. Ibid., pp. 52, 57, 94. Kashinskii, according to a secret police agent, was an "ardent opponent" of Plekhanov's style of social democracy, and refused to distribute Plekhanov's works among his acquaintances; see ibid., d-vo III, d. 741 (1891), p. 98. Egupov noted that Kashinskii and Leonid Krasin, "an experienced circles' activist and by conviction a 'Marxist'," fought over the issue of terror. Kashinskii accused Krasin of being an "egotist" for opposing terrorism. Krasin responded that "he who wants to carry on terror, let him do so, but for an organization to which Krasin belonged, he completely rejected terrorist activity"; ibid, d-vo VII, d. 220 (1893), t. I, p. 94.

96. Boris Groman, Ivan Punev, and Vasilii Plekhanov, the *tekhniki* as the police called them, were the most effective propagandists among the Russian Caucasian circle. They were assigned to public works projects as engineers and carried out propaganda on the job; see TsGAOR, f. 102-DP, d-vo III, d. 741 (1891), p. 1. In Moscow, Egupov maintained especially good relations with the Bureau, a central zemliachestvo organization, and with Elena Strel'nikova's women's circle. Ibid., pp. 3–4; d-vo VII, d. 220 (1893), t. IV, p. 60.

97. TsGAOR, f. 102-DP, d-vo VII, d. 220 (1893), t. I, p. 60.

98. Ibid., p. 61.

99. TsGIA SSSR, f. 1405, op. 93, d. 10547, pp. 5–7.

100. TsGAOR, f. 102-DP, d-vo VII, d. 220 (1893), t. I, p. 80; TsGIA SSSR, f. 1405, op. 93, d. 10547, pp. 212, 257. Raichin, a metal worker, traveled under the name of the Austrian citizen Franz Liakhovich. He had worked with Emancipation of Labor's press in Switzerland, had little formal education, but was considered an able advocate of the social-democratic program.

101. TsGAOR, f. 102-DP, d-vo VII, d. 220 (1893), t. I, pp. 77–78.

102. Raichin was arrested in Warsaw (11 April 1892). His deposition prompted the police to destroy the Kashinskii-Egupov-Brusnev group.

103. The meeting was also attended by Epifanov, Afanas'ev, Teren'tev, Kwiatkowski, Vanovskii, Avaliani, Groman, Petrov, A. M. Pervushin, and A. P. Ryzhkina.

104. TsGAOR, f. 102-DP, d-vo VII, d. 220 (1893), t. I, p. 79.

105. Brusnev, "Vozniknovenie," p. 33.

106. TsGAOR, f. 102-DP, d-vo VII, d. 220 (1893), t. I, p. 80.

107. Ibid., pp. 79, 81. TsGIA SSSR, f. 1405, op. 93, d. 10547, p. 257.

108. TsGAOR, f. 102-DP, d-vo VII, d. 220 (1893), t. I, pp. 81–82.

109. The program, found on Brusnev at the time of his arrest, was (according to the police) "doubtlessly written in Kashinskii's hand." Kashinskii's deposition said that he copied the program "from somewhere" and gave Brusnev the copy, but that the program was never discussed at a meeting (TsGIA SSSR, f. 1405, op. 93, d. 10547, p. 276). "Programma vremennogo organizatsionnogo Ispolnitel'nogo Komiteta," in OVD 1892–93, XVII, 22–24. The program was reprinted in Ot gruppy Blagoeva, pp. 87–88.

110. Polevoi, Zarozhdenie marksizma, pp. 397–398, and Kazakevich, Sotsial-demokraticheskie organizatsii, pp. 116–117, 175–176.

111. The police seized from Egupov and Brusnev an extraordinary collection of social-democratic literature, including most of the works of Marx, Aksel'rod, and Plekhanov. TsGIA SSSR, f. 1405, op. 93, d. 10547, pp. 8–9, 320.

112. It was also typical of the Russian judicial system that Brusnev did not find out about this allegation until 1895. At this point, he appealed to the Ministry of Justice for his release, claiming, probably correctly, that he had nothing to do with the Fraction's activities. In 1896 his term was shortened by three years. In 1901, Brusnev took part in a Russian polar expedition as a technical expert, for which he received a special commendation. TsGIA SSSR, f. 1405, op. 93, d. 10548, pp. 86, 243.

113. Johnson, Peasant and Proletarian, p. 115.

114. See especially Zelnik's "Russian Bebels: An Introduction to the Memoirs of Semen Kanatchikov and Matvei Fisher, II," The Russian Review, 35 (1976): 432–439.

115. See ibid., pp. 425–426; no. 37 (1976), pp. 432, 437. Here Zelnik comments on Wildman's discussion of worker and intelligentsia relations in the mid-1890s. See A. K. Wildman, The Making of a Workers' Revolution (Chicago, 1967), pp. 89–97.

8. Social Democrats in the Provinces, 1887–1892

1. L. Haimson, The Russian Marxists and the Origins of Bolshevism (Cambridge, Mass., 1955), p. 60.

2. "Ot Ivanovo-Voznesenskoi rabochei druzhiny," (4 June 1890), in TsGIA SSSR, f. 1405, op. 91, d. 10759, p. 2.

3. Ibid., op. 89, d. 11128, pp. 1–3.

4. Ibid., op. 521, d. 429, pp. 152–154.

5. OVD 1888, XIII, 20.

6. Ibid. TsGIA SSSR, f. 1405, op. 521, d. 429, pp. 106–107.

7. OVD 1888, XIII, 22.

8. TsGAOR, f. 102-DP, d-vo VII, d. 220, t. II (1893), pp. 5, 34.

9. Ibid., p. 4; t. I (1893), pp. 50–51.

10. TsGAOR, f. 102-DP, d-vo VII, d. 220, t. II (1983), pp. 16–18; d-vo III, d. 741 (1891), p. 143.

11. TsGIA SSSR, f. 1405, op. 90, d. 10847, p. 99.

12. *OVD 1890*, XV, 74. See V. Nevskii, "Khar'kovskoe delo Iuvenaliia Mel'nikova," *Ot gruppy Blagoeva*, pp. 98–99, and I. Veden'ev, "V khar'kov-skikh revoliutsionnykh kruzhkakh," *LR*, 5 (1923): 98–101.

13. TsGIA SSSR, f. 1405, op. 90, d. 10847, p. 100.

14. [Bekariukov], "Gol' na vydumki khitra," (Prilozheniia k st. V. Nevskogo), *Ot gruppy Blagoeva*, p. 120. See also V. Perazich, *Iu. D. Mel'nikov (na zare sotsial-demokraticheskogo dvizheniia)* (Khar'kov, 1930), pp. 65–66.

15. I. N. Moshinskii (Iuz. Konarskii), "Devianostye gody v kievskom pod-pol'e," *KS*, 5 (34) (1927): 12; "Istoricheskaia zapiska o tainom obshchestve 'zagovorshchikov'," *KS*, 12 (49) (1928): 49–52. This last article was signed by the main participants of the group: M. D. Fokin, L. D. Sinitskii, and D. D. Bekariukov, and was cosigned by V. I. Skliarevich and S. Rodzevich. As far as I know, the organization was never discovered by the authorities.

16. Moshinskii, "Devianostye gody," pp. 11–14; V. Skliarevich, "O Kievskoi 'gruppe zagovorshchikov'," *KS*, 5 (42) (1928): 68–69.

17. Moshinskii, "Devianostye gody," p. 15; "Istoricheskaia zapiska," p. 49. Perazich, *Iu. D. Mel'nikov*, p. 48.

18. "Istoricheskaia zapiska," p. 51. Indirect references to the organization are evident in V. V. Agapov's letters in TsGAOR, f. 102-DP, d-vo III, d. 776 (1884), p. 303. See also M. E. Berezin *et. al.*, "Vospominaniia o zhizni narod-nicheskikh kruzhkov v Kazani," *KS*, 10 (71) (1930): 121.

19. For the names of members, many of whom became distinguished profes-sionals, see Skliarevich, "O 'gruppe zagovorshchikov'," p. 70.

20. Veden'ev, "V khar'kovskikh kruzhkakh," p. 102; V. Perazich, "O predatel'stve S. M. Ratina," *KS*, 4 (53) (1929): 106.

21. For Meisner and the Kharkov terrorist circles, see Spiridovich, *Revoliu-tsionnoe dvizhenie*, p. 6.

22. Perazich, *Iu. D. Mel'nikov*, pp. 39–42; Veden'ev, "V khar'kovskikh kruzhkakh, pp. 104–105.

23. Veden'ev, "V khar'kovskikh kruzhkakh," p. 108.

24. TsGIA SSSR, f. 1405, op. 90, d. 10847, p. 100.

25. Quoted in Nevskii, "Khar'kovskoe delo," p. 104.

26. TsGIA SSSR, f. 1405, op. 90, d. 10847, pp. 35–36. See also Veden'ev, "V khar'kovskikh kruzhkakh," p. 103.

27. "Opyt Programmy russkoi sotsial'no-revoliutsionnoi gruppy rabo-chikh," in TsGIA SSSR, f. 1405, op. 90, d. 10847, pp. 22–23. Reprinted in "Prilozheniia k st. V. Nevskogo," *Ot gruppy Blagoeva*, pp. 117–118.

28. Veden'ev, "V khar'kovskikh revoliutsionnykh kruzhkakh," p. 110. The authorship of the program has never been established.

29. TsGIA SSSR, f. 1405, op. 90, d. 10847, pp. 22–23.

30. See Veletskii's letters to Vera Denish (1886–1888), in ibid., pp. 35–39. In

this correspondence Veletskii's positions resemble those of the later "Economists."

31. Perazich, *Iu. D. Mel'nikov*, pp. 49–50; Veden'ev, "V khar'kovskikh kruzhkakh," pp. 106–107.

32. TsGIA SSSR, f. 1405, op. 90, d. 10847, p. 100; Nevskii, "Khar'kovskoe delo," p. 99. The Kharkov prosecutor and Nevskii state that Bekariukov led the reunification; Veden'ev and Perazich indicate that the workers themselves ceased their quarreling, seeing the benefits of unity (Veden'ev, "V khar'kov-skikh kruzhkakh," p. 107; Perazich, *Iu. D. Mel'nikov*, p. 51).

33. A. Makarevskii, "Iz istorii revoliutsionnogo dvizheniia 1885–1887 godov," *LR*, 2 (1924): 88.

34. Perazich studied at the medical faculty of the university and later played an important role in the Southern Russian Union of Struggle. See Nevskii, "Khar'kovskoe delo," p. 103; *OVD 1890*, XV, 75.

35. TsGIA SSSR, f. 1405, op. 90, d. 10847, p. 102.

36. Ibid., p. 101. Perazich, *Iu. D. Mel'nikov*, pp. 93, 102.

37. TsGIA SSSR f. 1405, op. 90, d. 10847, p. 101.

38. Quoted in Nevskii, "Khar'kovskoe delo," p. 109. See also Veden'ev, "V khar'kovskikh kruzhkakh," p. 104.

39. TsGIA SSSR, f. 1405, op. 90, d. 10847, pp. 76–77.

40. Ibid., p. 102.

41. Ibid., p. 103.

42. Ibid., op. 521, d. 433 (1890), p. 236; TsGAOR, f. 102-DP, d-vo III, d. 776 (1884), ch. III, p. 307.

43. TsGIA SSSR, f. 1405, op. 90, d. 10832, pp. 3, 14.

44. Other leaders of the group included Vladimir Sychev, Aleksei Sanin, Pavel Voronin, Pavel Lavrovskii, and the female students Feiga Berkovich, Pelageia Zakharova, and Anna Sementovskaia. Twenty-four activists were eventually arrested in the Kazan case of Iagodkin and Fedoseev (ibid., pp. 172–173). All were either students or graduates. Nineteen were Orthodox, two, Old Believers, and three, Jews. Twenty out of twenty-four were between the ages of 17 and 24. Only three were nobles while six were children of clergy-men.

45. Ibid., pp. 15, 136. Maxim Gorky supposedly received his political education in this library; see N. Fedoseev, *Stat'i i pis'ma* (Moscow, 1958), p. 7.

46. See Polevoi, *Zarozhdenie marksizma*, p. 353; Fedoseev, *Stat'i i pis'ma*, and the collection of memoirs about him, *Fedoseev, Nikolai Evgrafovich; sbornik vospominanii* (Moscow, 1923). Soviet literature is particularly em-phatic on the point of Fedoseev's Marxism because Lenin wrote that he belonged to one of these Kazan circles from the fall of 1888 to May 1889 (Fedoseev, *Stat'i i pis'ma*, p. 7). There is no mention of the young Ul'ianov in the detailed archive materials on the Kazan group.

47. "Fedoseev to N. A. Motovilov, December 1887," in Fedoseev, *Stat'i i pis'ma*, pp. 31–32.

48. TsGIA SSSR, f. 1405, op. 90, d. 10832, p. 72.

49. Ibid., p. 139. *OVD 1890*, XV, 64–65.

50. TsGIA SSSR, f. 1405, op. 90, d. 10832, p. 137; op. 521, d. 433 (1890), p. 228.

51. TsGIA SSSR, f. 1405, op. 90, d. 10832, pp. 74–75; op. 521, d. 433 (1890), pp. 224–225. The program was written in Sychev's hand, though most likely its authors were Iagodkin and Fedoseev. The latter, perhaps correctly, told the police that he was the "initiator" of the programmatic effort.

52. See *Fedoseev, Nikolai Evgrafovich*, p. 7; Fedoseev, *Stat'i i pis'ma*, pp. 7–8.

53. TsGIA SSSR, f. 1405, op. 521, d. 433 (1890), p. 222; op. 90, d. 10832, p. 74.

54. I. L. Reshin, "Ot narodnichestva k marksizmu: Iz istorii revoliutsionnykh kruzhkov Rossii vtoroi poloviny 80-kh — nachale 90-kh godov XIX v.," (Kand. diss., avtoref., Moscow, 1967), p. 40.

55. *OVD 1890*, XV, 66. TsGIA SSSR, f. 1405, op. 90, d. 10832, pp. 177–84.

56. S. Shesterin, "Vladimirskii kruzhok molodezhi i N. E. Fedoseev," in *Fedoseev, Nikolai Evgrafovich*, p. 108. Skvortsov later moved to Nizhnii Novgorod where he exerted an important influence on the Marxist circle led by the Krasin brothers.

57. Ibid. See also P. F. Savinova, "N. E. Fedoseev vo Vladimirskoi gubernii (1892–1893 gody)," *Sovetskie arkhivy*, 2 (1972): 69–75.

58. TsGIA SSSR, f. 1405, op. 93, s. 10592, pp. 2, 13, 76–77. The police also found on Popkov his own notes on the economic and political exploitation of workers and on a wide variety of underground revolutionary publications.

59. Ibid. p. 76.

60. Ibid., p. 50.

61. Ibid., pp. 51–52; op. 521, d. 438 (1893), pp. 216–217.

62. The police uncovered the Popkov circle and later Fedoseev's fleeting participation with characteristic thoroughness. One of the Morozov workers, Kliuev, reported to the management of the factory that he had been given an illegal brochure. The Morozov management then contacted the local police, who sent a secret agent going by the name of Naumov to work at the factory. Naumov contacted Kliuev, who brought him into the Popkov circle. Naumov's reports are a part of the prosecutor's case, and he disappeared when the arrests were made. Kliuev actually organized the forest meetings between Fedoseev, Krivosheia, and the workers.

63. TsGIA SSSR, f. 1405, op. 93, d. 10592, pp. 56, 65, 101–102. Krivosheia, who admitted that Fedoseev had nothing to do with spreading revolutionary materials, also suffered a complete nervous breakdown in prison and was likewise sent to Vologda.

64. Ibid., pp. 2–3, 53.

65. Ibid., p. 3.

66. J. Frankel, *Prophecy and Politics: Socialism, Nationalism, and the Russian Jews, 1862–1917* (Cambridge, Eng., 1981), pp. 49–132.

67. Saratovets (I. I. Mainov), "Na zakate narodovol'tchestva," *Byloe*, 5–6 (27–28) (1917): 73–74.

68. See especially vol. II of Kennan, *Siberia and the Exile System*.

69. T. M. Kopel'zon, "Evreiskoe rabochee dvizhenie kontsa 80-kh i nachala 90-kh godov," *Revoliutsionnoe dvizhenie sredi Evreev; sbornik pervyi*, ed. Sh. Dimanshtein (Moscow, 1930), pp. 66–67; L. Aksel'rod-Ortodoks, "Iz moikh vospominanii," *KS*, 2 (63) (1930): 23.

70. Kopel'zon, "Evreiskoe dvizhenie," pp. 67–69.

71. TsGIA SSSR, f. 1405, op. 89, d. 11114, pp. 1–2, 42; op. 521, d. 429, pp. 274–275.

72. TsGIA SSSR, f. 1405, op 89, d. 11114, pp. 11–17.

73. Ibid., op. 521, d. 429, pp. 279–280.

74. TsGAOR, f. 102-DP, d-vo V, d. 6563 (1885), pp. 25–27.

75. M. Rubach, "Ot narodnichestva i narodovol'chestva k marksizmu," LR, 1 (1924): 229–237.

76. "Doklad o Russkom sotsialdemokratich. dvizhenii mezhdunarodnomu sotsialistich. kongressu v Parizhe 1900 g.: Istoriia Evreiskogo rabochego dvizheniia v Rossii i Pol'she" (Geneva, 1901), p. 7; in TsGIA SSSR, f. 1410, op. 3, d. 212, p. 5. Especially for the Vilna circles, see H. J. Tobias, The Jewish Bund in Russia from Its Origins to 1905 (Stanford, 1972), pp. 11–13, and E. Mendelson, Class Struggle in the Pale (Cambridge, Eng., 1970) pp. 27–44.

77. I. Gurvich, "Pervye evreiskie rabochie kruzhki," Byloe, 6 (1907): 65; "Vospominaniia M. A. Makarevicha" in "Pamiati Emiliia Aleksandrovicha Abramovicha," KS, 3 (40) (1928): 131; N. A. Bukhbinder, Istoriia evreiskogo rabochego dvizheniia v Rossii (Leningrad, 1925), pp. 44–45.

78. Gurvich, "Pervye kruzhki," pp. 66–68.

79. Ibid. p. 69. Evgeniia Gurvich claimed that the Saturday school was closed because of objections from the Palestintsy (E. A. Gurvich, "Evreiskoe rabochee dvizhenie v Minske v 80-kh g. g.," Revoliutsionnoe dvizhenie sredi Evreev, pp. 36–37.)

80. V. Eidel'man, "Vospominaniia o L've Efimoviche Berkoviche i Emilii Aleksandroviche Abramoviche," KS, 3 (40) (1928): 136.

81. TsGIA SSSR, f. 1405, op. 90, d. 10807, pp. 101–102.

82. Ibid., op. 91, d. 10779, p. 21.

83. Ibid., op. 90, d. 10807, pp. 34, 103.

84. Ibid., p. 83. An impressive library of both social-democratic and narodovol'tsy propaganda materials was seized from the circle.

85. Gurvich, "Pervye kruzhki," p. 75.

86. TsGIA SSSR, f. 1405, op. 90, d. 10807, p. 128.

87. N. A. Bukhbinder, "K istorii sotsial-demokraticheskogo dvizheniia v Kievskoi gubernii," KL, 7–9 (1923): 264.

88. Gurvich, "Pervye kruzhki," p. 75.

89. Quoted in Bukhbinder, "K istorii," p. 264.

90. L. Fedorchenko (N. Charov), "Pervye shagi sotsial-demokratii v Kieve," KS, 6 (27) (1926): 21.

91. It is impossible to establish Abramovich's authorship of the program. In his very circumspect depositions, he says only that he had printed copies of the program and passed it on to those who wished to see it. See "Pokazaniia E. A. Abramovicha (Pril. 1, 2)," in Bukhbinder, "K istorii," pp. 265–274.

92. TsGIA SSSR, f. 1405, op. 90, d. 10807, p. 41. Here the prosecutor calls it the "Hand-written program for activists among workers."

93. Ibid., pp. 1–6. (Emphases added.)

94. Ibid., op. 521, d. 439, p. 101.

95. Ibid., op. 93, d. 10552, pp. 76–79, 119–120. About one-half of the forty-

one activists implicated were Jewish. In the summer of 1891, Shteinraikh and Leviash hectographed hundreds of copies of various social-democratic pamphlets.

96. Ibid., p. 131.

97. The circles at Novorossiiskii University continued to function under the leadership of Vladimir Gernet until 1892, when they were completely destroyed by the police. TsGIA SSSR, f. 1405, op. 521, d. 439, p. 100; op. 93, d. 10552, pp. 85–86.

98. TsGIA SSSR, f. 1405, op. 92, d. 10963, p. 107; *OVD 1891*, XVI, p. 7.

99. TsGIA SSSR, f. 1405, op. 92. d. 10963, pp. 62–63.

100. *Istoriia ekaterinoslavskoi sotsial-demokraticheskoi organizatsii, 1889–1903*, ed. M. A. Rubach (Ekaterinoslav, 1932), pp. xvi–xvii.

101. TsGIA SSSR, f. 1405, op. 92, d. 10963, p. 69.

102. "Pis'ma E. A. Abramovich k E. A. Gurvich," *KS*, 3 (40) (1928): 143.

103. "Vospominaniia E. A. Gurvich," in "Pamiati Emiliia Aleksandrovicha Abramovicha," *KS*, 3 (40) (1928): 136.

9. Narodovol'tsy — Old and New

1. The information and data on the famine and famine relief are from R. G. Robbins Jr., *Famine in Russia 1891–1892* (New York, 1975).

2. See, for instance, Pipes, *Struve*, pp. 60, 86; Billington, *Mikhailovsky*, pp. 164–165; and A. P. Mendel, *Dilemmas of Progress in Tsarist Russia* (Cambridge, Mass., 1961), pp. 119–127.

3. A. I. Georgievskii, *Kratkii istoricheskii ocherk pravitel'stvennykh mer i prednachertanii protiv studencheskikh besporiadkov* (St. Petersburg, 1890), p. 160.

4. TsGIA SSSR, f. 1405, op. 90, d. 10782, pp. 97–98.

5. Especially Soloveichik was useful in this context. He traveled back and forth between Switzerland and Grodno and was a member of the Polish Proletariat, a social democrat, and a firm supporter of the Dembo conspiracy (ibid., pp. 60–65). For the role of Iogikhes and Gurvich, see ibid., op. 91, d. 10747, pp. 5–8; d. 10749, ch. III, pp. 173, 244.

6. Ginsburg's deposition in TsGIA SSSR, f. 1405, op. 90, d. 10782, p. 169; P. L. Lavrov, "Vospominaniia o Sof'e Mikhailovne Ginsburg," *GM*, 7–8 (1917): 225–227.

7. TsGIA SSSR, f. 1405, op. 90, d. 10782, pp. 98–99; op. 91, d. 10747, pp. 23–45.

8. For Dembo's early radical activities (1884–86), see TsGIA SSSR, f. 1405, op. 88, d. 10080, p. 208.

9. Ibid., op. 90, d. 10783 (1889), ch. II, p. 100.

10. Ibid., p. 119.

11. Ibid. See also *OVD 1889*, XIV, 23–24. and Spiridovich, *Revoliutsionnoe dvizhenie*, p. 15.

12. Lavrov, "Vospominaniia o Ginsburg," p. 250.

13. Ibid., p. 230. See also TsGIA SSSR, f. 1405, op. 90, d. 10783, ch. II, pp. 225–230; L. Freifel'd, "Svetloi pamiati Sofii Mikhailovny Ginsburg," *KS*, 5 (12) (1924): 259–271; and "K biografii S. M. Ginsburg," *KS*, 3 (24) (1926): 211–222.

14. In her deposition, Ginsburg claimed she returned to Russia in order to check out a rumor that women educated abroad would no longer be able to take examinations to become doctors. TsGIA SSSR, f. 1405, op. 90, d. 10783, ch. II, pp. 225-226; Lavrov, "Vospominaniia o Ginsburg," p. 203.

15. Lavrov, "Vospominaniia o Ginsburg," pp. 231-232.

16. Ibid., p. 236. See also TsGIA SSSR, f. 1405, op. 90, d. 10783, ch. II, p. 133; d. 10782, pp. 22-24.

17. Lavrov, "Vospominaniia o Ginsburg," p. 241.

18. TsGIA SSSR, f. 1405, op. 90, d. 10783, ch. II, p.142.

19. Lavrov, "Vospominaniia o Ginsburg," p. 249; *OVD 1889*, XIV, 16.

20. The proclamation exists in several hand-written copies. The original is in TsGIA SSSR, f. 1410, op. 1, d. 538, p. 181.

21. "K delu S. M. Ginsburg," *Byloe*, 7 (1908): 87-89; Perazich, "Iuvenalii Mel'nikov," p. 109.

22. B. S. Nikolaevskii, "S. M. Ginsburg v Shlissel'burge," *Byloe*, 15 (1919): 98; E. E. Kolosov, *Gosudareva tiur'ma — Shlissel'burg* (Petrograd, 1924), p. 88.

23. Nikolaevskii, "S. M. Ginsburg," pp. 93-95.

24. TsGIA SSSR, f. 1405, op. 90, d. 10783, ch. II, pp. 135-136, 142.

25. *OVD 1890*, XV, 3.

26. E. Stepanov, "Iz zagranichnykh vospominanii starogo narodovol'tsa," *KS*, 3 (24) (1926): 124; *OVD 1890*, XV, 3.

27. For the role of the Okhrana and especially of Landeizen-Gekkel'man in counterrevolutionary provocation, see Stepanov, "Iz vospominanii," pp. 123-144; Cherniavskaia-Bokhanovskaia, "Iz istorii bor'by russkogo samoderzhaviia s 'Narodnoi volei' zagranitsei," *KS*, 4 (65) (1930): 97; and F. S. Zuckerman, "The Russian Political Police at Home and Abroad (1880-1917)," 2 vols. (Ph. D. diss., New York University, 1973), I, 213-258.

28. *Iz arkhiva Aksel'roda*, pp. 109-110. In 1886 Rapoport had engaged in propaganda among Odessa students and in 1888 he organized an Odessa-centered Southern Russian Central Workers' Circle. As a student at Zurich University in 1888-89, Rapoport worked with Dembo and then left for Paris after the explosion. He was the cofounder of Terrorist along with Boris Reinshtein (TsGIA SSSR, f. 1405, op. 91, d. 10748, ch. II, p. 143).

29. "Plekhanov to Aksel'rod (March 1889)," *Perepiska Plekhanova i Aksel'roda*, I: 58-59.

30. *Iz arkhiva Aksel'roda*, p. 110.

31. The core of the Cadres was organized by the underground circle of Istomina, Ginsburg, Sleptsova, and Rodzevicha at the Bestuzhev Higher School for Women.

32. *OVD 1890*, XV, 14-17. TsGIA SSSR, f. 1405, op. 91, d. 10748, ch. II, p. 72.

33. TsGIA SSSR, f. 1405, op. 91, d. 10749, ch. III, p. 195; d. 10748, ch. II, p. 73. The large and important Penza section was broken up by the police in May 1890.

34. *OVD 1890*, XV, p. 9. TsGIA SSSR, f. 1405, op. 91, d. 10749, ch. III, p. 187.

35. V. I. Sukhomlin, "Iz epokhi upadka partii 'Narodnaia volia'," *KS*, 7-8

(28–29) (1926): 78–79.

36. Ibid., p. 82.

37. Mitskevich, "Na grani," p. 47.

38. Men'shchikov, *Okhrana,* I, 97–98. Here Men'shchikov writes that Sabunaev was a "giant" in the field of conspiracy. In his many precautions, "Sabunaev was right, a thousand times right."

39. "Iz avtobiografii S. A. Ostrovskogo," in *Narodovol'tsy, sb. III,* p. 248.

40. "Vospominaniia Vasiliia Serapionovicha Turkovskogo," in ibid., p. 258. See also Men'shchikov, *Okhrana,* I, 97, and TsGIA SSSR, f. 1405, op. 92, d. 10904, pp. 80–81.

41. Also in attendance were Trofimov from Kazan, A. V. Sazonov from Saratov, Lev Osinskii from Iaroslavl, Petr Manuilov from Voronezh, Vasilii Gusev, Beila Gurvich, Poviazina, and Chetvergova. See M. S. Aleksandrov (Ol'minskii), " 'Gruppa narodovol'tsev' (1891–1894)," *Byloe,* 11 (1906): 5; Spiridovich, *Revoliutsionnoe dvizhenie,* p. 21.

42. TsGIA SSSR, f. 1405, op. 91, d. 10749, ch. III, pp. 188–189.

43. In Iaroslavl Sabunaev set up a circle of eight under Vladimir Neklepaev, and in Kostroma a circle of fourteen under Semen Aleksandrov (ibid., op. 92, d. 10904, pp. 161–163).

44. "Iz avtobiografii Ostrovskogo," p. 252; "Vospominaniia Turkovskogo," p. 262.

45. *OVD 1890,* XV, 43.

46. "Vospominaniia Turkovskogo," p. 259.

47. "Iz avtobiografii Ostrovskogo," p. 253.

48. TsGIA SSSR, f. 1405, op. 912, d. 10749, ch. III, pp. 170–171.

49. Ibid., p. 224.

50. *OVD 1890,* XV, 93–94.

51. TsGIA SSSR, f. 1405, op. 91, d. 10749, ch. III, p. 191; d. 10748, ch. II, p. 74.

52. Boris Reinshtein, Aleksei Teplov, and Evgenii Stepanov (like Dembo before them) attempted to develop a new and better bomb. Teplov was wounded in one experiment, prompting the investigation by the French police. *OVD 1890,* XV, 5–6; TsGIA SSSR, f. 1405, op. 521, d. 438 (1893), pp. 286–298a.

53. Men'shchikov, *Okhrana,* I, 84, 86.

54. Kuznetsov, "K istorii," pp. 56–59.

55. TsGIA SSSR, f. 1405, op. 89, d. 11130, p. 308. See Shirokova, *Partiia "Narodnogo prava",* pp. 20–21.

56. *OVD 1888,* XIII, 44–46.

57. TsGIA SSSR, f. 1405, op. 89, d. 11121, pp. 87–88.

58. The program of the Moscow Socialist Federalists was published in no. 1 *Self-Government* (December 1887); see Spiridovich, *Revoliutsionnoe dvizhenie,* pp. 9–12.

59. Perazich, "Iuvenalii Mel'nikov," p. 108.

60. TsGIA SSSR, f. 1405, op. 90, d. 10789, p. 21.

61. Mitskevich, "Na grani, " p. 46.

62. TsGIA SSSR, f. 1405, op. 90, d. 10788, pp. 1–97, 125.

63. Mitskevich, "Na grani," p. 46.

64. Spiridovich, *Revoliutsionnoe dvizhenie*, p. 29. At the turn of the century, Minister of Justice Murav'ev estimated that in 1890 there were 106 such social-revolutionary groups; in 1891, 138; in 1892, 134; and in 1893, 149. No such data was gathered for 1888 and 1889; I would estimate in those years about 150 groups per year. See Murav'ev's "O sotsial'no-revoliutsionnom dvizhenii Rossii za poslednie gody po svedeniem ministerstva iustitsii" (1900), in TsGIA SSSR, f. 1405, op. 530, d. 1022, p. 2.

65. See TsGIA SSSR, op. 89, d. 11130, p. 308, on the distribution of *Self-Government*.

66. "Ob"iavlenie ob izdanii zhurnala 'Revoliutsionnyi soiuz'," in TsGIA SSSR, f. 1410, op 1, d. 552, p. 30.

67. *OVD 1891*, XVI, 3.

68. Aleksandrov, "Gruppa narodovol'tsev," pp. 12–15.

69. "Svobodnoe Slovo," reprinted in ibid., p. 17.

70. For Mikhailovskii's attitudes in this period, see Billington, *Mikhailovsky*, pp. 153–160, and V. A. Tvardovskaia, "N. K. Mikhailovskii i 'Narodnaia volia'," *IZ*, 82 (1968): 202.

71. "Ot gruppy narodovol'tsev," reprinted in Aleksandrov, "Gruppa narodovol'tsev," p. 17.

72. For Astyrev's Moscow circle see TsGIA SSSR, f. 1405, op. 93, d. 10522, pp. 161–213; Aleksandrov, "Gruppa narodovol'tsev," p. 20.

73. *Letuchii listok "Gruppy narodovol'tsev"*, 1 (1892), in appendix to P. Kudelli, *Narodovol'tsy na pereput'i: delo lakhtinskoi tipografii* (Leningrad, 1925), p. 49.

74. "K raschetu" in ibid., p. 69.

75. "Nakanune," in ibid., p. 75.

76. Ibid., pp. 73–75.

77. The history of the party is ably recounted in Shirokova, *Partiia "Narodnogo prava"*. See also Hildermeier, *Die Sozialrevolutionäre Partei*, pp. 36–38; O. V. Aptekman, "Partii 'Narodnogo prava'," *Byloe*, 7 (1907): 177–204; and S. Galai, *The Liberation Movement in Russia, 1900–1905* (Cambridge, Eng., 1973), pp. 58–65.

78. I. I. Popov, "Aleksandr Vasil'evich Gedeonovskii," *KS*, 8–9 (45–46) (1928): 243; Gedeonovskii, "Iaroslavskii kruzhok," p. 108.

79. The program is quoted in full in Aptekman, "Partiia 'Narodnogo prava'," pp. 197–198. It was written by an editorial commission of A. I. Bogdanovich from Petersburg, P. F. Nikolaev from Moscow, and M. A. Plotnikov from Nizhnii Novgorod. Mikhailovskii neither wrote the program nor participated in the founding meeting of the party, contrary to what is so often maintained. Shirokova, *Partiia "Narodnogo prava"*, p. 63.

80. Aptekman, "Partiia 'Narodnogo prava'," p. 190.

81. Quoted in ibid., p. 201.

82. A Egorov [Martov], "Zarozhdenie politicheskikh partii i ikh deiatel'nost'," *Obshchestvennoe dvizhenie v Rossii*, 4 vols. (St. Petersburg, 1909–1911), I, 374.

83. Shirokova, *Partiia "Narodnogo prava"*, pp. 107, 129, 134.

84. See the list of members in ibid., pp. 182–95. See also Galai, *Liberation Movement*, p. 59.

85. Aleksandrov, "Gruppa narodovol'tsev," p. 13.

Selected Bibliography

For the history of the narodovol'tsy, the best guide to early Soviet sources is M. A. Drei, *Opyt ukazatelia literatury po istorii partii "Narodnoi voli"* (Moscow, 1929). The journal *Katorga i ssylka* is an especially rich source of narodovol'tsy memoir literature and published documents, which have been catalogued by R. M. Kantor, "Katorga i ssylka za desiat' let (1921-1930): Sistematicheskii-predmetnyi ukazatel'," *KS*, 11-12 (84-85) (1931). The illegal literature published by the narodovol'tsy and social democrats is listed in *Svodnyi katalog nelegal'noi i zapreshchennoi pechati XIX veka*, pts. 1-3 (Moscow, 1977). The voluminous secondary literature published by the Soviets after 1953 on the history of the populist movement was indexed by N. Ia. Kraineva and P. V. Pronina, "Narodnichestvo v rabotakh sovetskikh issledovatelei za 1952-1970 gg., " *Obshchestvennoe dvizhenie v poreformennoi Rossiia* (Moscow, 1965), pp. 370-381. For the social democrats in the period 1881-1894, the best bibliographical source is *Gruppa "Osvobozhdenie truda" (Bibliografiia za 50 let)*, ed. V. I. Nevskii (Moscow, 1934). For more recent works, see the complete bibliography in Iu. Z. Polevoi, *Zarozhdenie marksizma v Rossii* (Moscow, 1959), pp. 523-556. Further important bibliographical (and biographical) information on both the social democrats and the narodovol'tsy is contained in the unfortunately incomplete *Deiateli revoliutsionnogo dvizheniia v Rossii: Biobibliograficheskii slovar'*. Two parts were printed on the 1880s (the narodovol'tsy), "Vos'midesiatye gody," vol. III, vyp. I and II (Moscow, 1933-34); and two parts on the social democrats, "Sotsial-demokraty, 1880-1904," vol. V. vyp. 1 and 2 (Moscow, 1931-1933).

Archival Sources

Hoover Institution Archives (Stanford, California)
  Collection   Boris Nicolaevsky Archives
  Collection   Okhrana Archives
International Institute for Social History (Amsterdam)
  Collection   Axelrod Archives
Tsentral'nyi arkhiv oktiabr'skoi revoliutsii i sotsialisticheskogo stroitel'stva (Moscow)
  fond 102-DP   Departament Politsii
Tsentral'nyi gosudarstvennyi istoricheskii arkhiv SSSR (Leningrad)
  fond 20   Departament torgovli i manufaktur
  fond 776   Glavnoe upravlenie po delam pechati
  fond 777   SPb. komitet po delam pechati
  fond 1282   Kantseliariia ministra vnutrennikh del
  fond 1286   Departament politsii ispolnitel'noi MVD
  fond 1354   Pravitel'stvuiushchii senat: Soedinennoe prisutstvie l-go i kassatsionnykh departamentov
  fond 1405   Ministerstvo iustitsii
        op. 82-95   Dela departamenta ministerstva iustitsii vtorogo ugolovnogo otdeleniia
        op. 521   Vsepoddanneishie doklady ministra iustitsii
        op. 530   Doneseniia prokurorskogo nadzora sudebnykh palat i okruzhnykh sudov
        op. 535   Dela III-go reestra vtorogo ugolovnogo otdeleniia
        op. 539   "Bumagi" ministra iustitsii
  fond 1410   Veshchestvennye dokazatel'stva k delam ministerstva iustitsii

Published Documents

Aleksandr Il'ich Ul'ianov i delo 1 marta 1887 g. Ed. A. I. Ul'ianova-Elizarova. Moscow-Leningrad, 1927.

Arkhiv "Zemli i voli" i "Narodnoi voli". Ed. S. N. Valk. Moscow, 1932.

Burtsev, Vl. *Za sto let (1800–1896).* 2 vols. in 1. London, 1897.

"Degaevshchina (materialy i dokumenty)." *Byloe,* 4 (1906): 18–33.

"Dmitrii Blagoev in Russia: An Autobiographical Letter." Ed. D. Labelle. *International Review of Social History,* vol. IX, pt. 2 (1964): 286–297.

Dnevnik gosudarstvennogo sekretaria A. A. Polovtsova. 2 vols. Moscow, 1966.

"Doklad departamenta politsii ministru vnutrennikh del (po delu Tochiskogo)." *KL*, 7 (1923): 344–388.

Fedoseev, N. E. *Stat'i i pis'ma*. Moscow, 1958.

Gruppa "Osvobozhdenie truda" (*Iz arkhivov G. V. Plekhanova, V. I. Zasulich, i L. G. Deicha*). Ed. L. G. Deich. 6 vols. Moscow-Leningrad, 1924–1928.

Istoriko-revoliutsionnyi sbornik. Ed. V. I. Nevskii. 3 vols. Moscow-Leningrad, 1924–1926.

Iz arkhiva P. B. Aksel'roda. Berlin, 1924.

K. B. Pobedonostsev i ego korrespondenty: Pis'ma i zapiski. 2 pts. Moscow- Petrograd, 1923.

Kantor, R. "K istorii voennoi organizatsii 'Narodnoi voli' (Pokazaniia F. I. Zavalishina)." *KS*, 5 (18) (1925): 210–240.

Khronika sotsialisticheskogo dvizheniia v Rossii, 1878–1887 gg. Moscow, 1906.

Kuznetsov, L. "K istorii 'Narodnoi voli' (Zapiska A. N. Bakha 1886 g.)." *KS*, 6 (67) (1930): 51–61.

Lavrov: Gody emigratsii. Ed. Boris Sapir. 2 vols. Dordrecht, Holland, 1974.

Literatura sotsial'no-revoliutsionnoi partii "Narodnoi voli". Ed. V. Ia. Iakovlev-Bogucharskii. Paris, 1905.

Ministerstvo Finansov. Departament torgovli i manufaktur. *Fabrichno- zavodskaia promyshlennost' i torgovlia Rossii*. 2nd ed. St. Petersburg, 1896.

Morozovskaia stachka 7–13 (19–25) Ianvaria 85 goda. Ed. D. B. Riazanov (Goldendakh). Moscow, 1923.

[Nicolaevsky, B.], "Programma pervogo v Rossii s.-d. kruzhka." *Byloe*, 13 (1918): 38–52.

Obzor vazhneishikh doznanii po delam o gosudarstvennykh prestupleniiakh; Vedomost' doznaniiam, proizvodivshimsia v Zhandarmskikh Upravleniiakh Imperii. 1 June 1881–1 Jan. 1895. 18 vols.

Ot gruppy Blagoeva k "Soiuza bor'by" (1886–1889 gg.). Rostov-on-Don, 1921.

Perepiska G. V. Plekhanova i P. B. Aksel'roda. 2 vols. Moscow, 1925.

Pis'ma Pobedonostseva k Aleksandru III. 2 vols. Moscow, 1925.

Rabochee dvizhenie v Rossii v XIX veke: Sbornik dokumentov i materialov. Ed. A. M. Pankratova (vol. IV, ed. L. M. Ivanov). 4 vols. Moscow- Leningrad, 1950–1963.

"*Rabochii*": *Gazeta partii russkikh sotsial-demokratov (blagoevtsev) 1885*. Ed. N. L. Sergievskii. Leningrad, 1928.

" 'Studencheskii soiuz' i kazn' 8 maia 1887g." Ed. S. N. Valk. *KA*, 2 (1927): 226–231.

Valk, S. N. "K istorii protsessa 21 (Pis'ma i pokazanii P. F. Iakubovich)." *KA*, 5 (1929): 122–179; 6 (1929): 102–137; 1 (1930): 70–108.

Valuev, P. A. *Dnevnik, 1877–1884*. Petrograd, 1919.

Memoirs and Memoir Collections

Aleksandrov (Ol'minskii), M. S. " 'Gruppa narodovol'tsev' 1891–1894." *Byloe*, 11 (1906): 1–29.

Aptekman, O. V. "Partiia 'Narodnogo prava'," *Byloe*, 7 (1907): 177–204.

Argunov, P. A. "Moskovskii kruzhok militaristov," pp. 87–96 in *Narodovol'tsy posle 1-go marta*. Moscow, 1928.

Ashenbrenner, M. Iu. *Voennaia organizatsiia "Narodnoi voli"*. Moscow, 1924.

Bakh, A. N. *Zapiski narodovol'tsa*. 2nd ed. Leningrad, 1931.

Blagoev, Dimitr. *Kratki belezhki iz moia zhivot*. Sofia, 1954.

Braginskii, M. " 'Dobroliubovskaia' demonstratsiia (17 XI 1886g.)." *Byloe*, 5 (1907): 306–309.

Breitfus, A. "Tochisskii i ego kruzhok." *KL*, 7 (1923): 324–339.

Brusnev, M. I. "Vozniknovenie pervykh sotsial-demokraticheskikh organizatsii (Vospominaniia)." *PR*, 2 (1923): 17–33.

Fedoseev Nikolai Evgrafovich: Odin iz pionerov revoliutsionnogo marksizma v Rossii (sb. vospominanii). Moscow-Petrograd, 1923.

Figner, V. N. *Polnoe sobranie sochineniia*. 6 vols. Moscow, 1929.

Gedeonovskii, A. V. "Iaroslavskii revoliutsionnyi kruzhok 1881–1886 gg." *KS*, 3 (24) (1926): 95–109.

Golubev, V. "Stranichka iz istorii rabochego dvizheniia (Pamiati N. V. Shelgunova)." *Byloe*, 12 (1906): 104–120.

Gots, M. R. "Moskovskaia tsentral'naia gruppa part. 'Narodnoi voli'," pp. 96–108 in *Narodovol'tsy posle 1-go marta 1881 g*. Moscow, 1928.

Govorukhin, O. M. "Vospominaniia o terroristicheskoi gruppe Aleksandra Il'icha Ul'ianova." *Oktiabr'*, 3 (1927): 127–141; 4 (1927): 146–162.

Gurvich, I. "Pervye evreiskie rabochie kruzhki." *Byloe*, 6 (1907): 65–66.

Iakovenko, E. I. "O vtorom 1-m marte." *KS*, 3 (32) (1927): 7–42.

Ivanov, S. "K kharakteristike obshchestvennykh nastroenii v Rossi v nachale 80-kh gg." *Byloe*, 9 (1907): 193–207.

"K istorii Sabunaevskoi revoliutsionnoi organizatsii 1889–1890 gg. (Iz vospominanii S. A. Ostrovskogo i V. S. Turkovskogo)," pp. 248–267 in *Narodovol'tsy, sb. III*. Moscow, 1931.

Karelina, V. M. "Na zare rabochego dvizheniia v S.-Peterburge." *KL*,

4 (1922): 12-20.

Krasin, L. B. "Dela davno minuvshikh dnei (1887-1892 gg.)." *PR*, 3 (1923): 3-28.

Krol', M. A. "Vospominaniia o L. Ia. Shternberge." *KS*, 8-9 (57-58) (1929): 214-236.

Lavrov, P. L. *German Aleksandrovich Lopatin*. Petrograd, 1919.

———— "Vospominaniia o Sof'e Mikhailovne Ginsburg." *GM*, 7-8 (1917): 225-256.

Lukashevich, I. *1 marta 1887 g. Vospominaniia*. Petrograd, 1920.

Makarevskii, A. "Iz istorii revoliutsionnogo dvizheniia 1885-87 gg. (Vospominaniia narodovol'tsa)." *LR*, 2 (1924): 63-93.

Men'shchikov, L. P. *Okhrana i revoliutsiia*. Pt. 1: "gody reaktsii, 1885-1898." Moscow, 1925.

Mitskevich, S. I. "Na grani dvukh epokh." *PR*, 2 (1923): 34-54.

Moshinskii, I. N. "Devianostye gody v kievskom podpol'e." *KS*, 5 (34) (1927): 1-27.

Narodovol'tsy, sb. III. Ed. A. V. Iakimova-Dikovskaia et al. Moscow, 1931

Narodovol'tsy 80-kh godov. Ed. A. V. Iakimova-Dikovskaia et al. Moscow, 1928.

Narodovol'tsy posle 1-go marta 1881 g. Ed. A. V. Iakimova-Dikovskaia et al. Moscow, 1928.

Nikonov, S. "Iz vospominanii ob A. I. Ul'ianove." *PR*, 2-3 (1929): 172-190.

Ol'minskii, M. S. "Davnie sviazi," pp. 60-79 in *Ot gruppy Blagoeva k "Soiuza bor'by"*. Rostov-on-Don, 1921.

Orzhikh, B. D. "V riadakh 'Narodnoi voli' (Vospominanii)," pp. 75-177 in *Narodovol'tsy, sb. III*. Moscow, 1931.

"Pamiati Emiliia Aleksandrovicha Abramovicha." *KS*, 3 (40) (1928): 131-136.

Perazich, V. *Iu. D. Mel'nikov (na zare sotsial-demokraticheskogo dvizheniia Ukrainy)*. Khar'kov, 1930.

———— "Iuvenalii Mel'nikov i khar'kovskii rabochii kruzhok." *LR*, 3 (1923): 108-115.

Popov, I. I. "Revoliutsionnye organizatsii v Peterburge v 1882-1885 gg." pp. 49-81 in *Narodovol'tsy posle 1-go marta 1881 goda*. Moscow, 1928.

Revoliutsionnoe dvizhenie sredi Evreev; sbornik pervyi. Ed. Sh. Dimanshtein. Moscow, 1930.

Serebriakov, E. *Revoliutsionery vo flote*. Petrograd, 1920.

Shebalin, M. P. "Peterburgskaia narodovol'cheskaia organizatsiia v 1882-1883 gg.," pp. 40-48 in *Narodovol'tsy posle 1-go marta 1881 goda*. Moscow, 1928.

Skliarevich, V. "O Kievskoi 'gruppe zagovorshchikov'." *KS*, 5 (42)

(1928): 68–72.

Stepanov, E. "Iz zagranichnykh vospominanii starogo narodovol'tsa." *KS*, 3 (24) (1926): 123–144.

Sukhomlin, V. I. "Iz epokhi upadka partii 'Narodnaia volia'." *KS*, 3 (24) (1926): 75–89; 4 (25) (1926): 29–45; 6 (27) (1926): 65–88; 7–8 (28– 29) (1926): 61–103.

Sviatlovskii, V. V. "Na zare Rossiiskoi sotsial-demokratii." *Byloe*, 19 (1922): 139–160.

Tan [Bogoraz, Natan (Vladimir)]. "Povesti proshloi zhizni." *RB*, 9 (1907): 107–31; 10 (1907): 150–64.

Tikhomirov, L. "V mire merzosti i zapusteniia," *Vestnik "Narodnoi voli"*, 5 (1884), in "Degaevshchina (materialy i dokumenty)." *Byloe*, 4 (1906): 30–36.

Vospominaniia L'va Tikhomirova. Moscow-Leningrad, 1927.

Secondary Works

Anatol'ev, P. "Obshchestvo perevodchikov i izdatelei." *KS*, 3 (100) (1933): 82–141.

Antonov, V. S. "K voprosu o sotsial'nom sostave i chislennosti revoliutsionerov 70-kh godov." *Obshchestvennoe dvizhenie v poreformennoi Rossi*. Moscow, 1965: 336–343.

Balabanov, M. *K istorii rabochego dvizhenie na Ukraine: "Iuzhnorusskii rabochii soiuz"*. Kiev, 1925.

Baron, Samuel H. *Plekhanov: The Father of Russian Marxism*. Stanford, 1963.

Baynac, Jacques. *Les Socialistes-Révolutionnaires*. Paris, 1979.

Billington, James H. *Mikhailovsky and Russian Populism*. Oxford, 1958.

Bogucharskii, V. Ia. *Iz istorii politicheskoi bor'by v 70-kh i 80-kh gg. XIX v.: Partiia "Narodnoi voli." Ee proiskhozhdenie, sud'by i gibel'*. Moscow, 1912.

Bukhbinder, N. A. "K istorii sotsial-demokraticheskogo dvizheniia v Kievskoi gubernii." *KL*, 7–9 (1923): 263–285.

Galai, Shmuel. *The Liberation Movement in Russia, 1902–1905*. Cambridge, Eng., 1973.

Geierhos, Wolfgang. *Vera Zasulic und die russische revolutionäre Bewegung*. Munich-Vienna, 1977.

Geyer, Dietrich. *Lenin in der russischen Sozialdemokratie*. Cologne-Graz, 1962.

Gleason, Abbott. "The Emigration and Apostasy of Leo Tikhomirov." *Slavic Review*, 26 (1968): 414–429.

Godunova, L. N. "Voennaia organizatsiia partii 'Narodnaia volia' 1880–1884." Kandidatskaia dissertatsiia, avtoreferat.Moscow, 1971.

Haimson, Leopold. *The Russian Marxists and the Origins of Bolshevism. Cambridge, Mass., 1955.

Hildermeier, Manfred. *Die Sozialrevolutionäre Partei Russlands: Agrarsozialismus und Modernisierung im Zarenreich (1900–1914).* Cologne-Vienna, 1978.

"Istoricheskaia zapiska o tainom obshchestve 'zagovorshchikov'." *KS,* 12 (49) (1928): 49–58.

Itenberg, B. S., Cherniak, A. Ia. *Zhizn' Aleksandra Ul'ianova.* Moscow, 1966.

Ivanov, L. M., ed. *Rabochii klass i rabochee dvizhenie (1861–1917).* Moscow, 1966.

Johnson, Robert Eugene. *Peasant and Proletarian: The Working Class of Moscow in the Late Nineteenth Century.* New Brunswick, N. J., 1979.

Kazakevich, R. A. *Sotsial-demokraticheskie organizatsii Peterburga kontsa 80-kh–nachala 90-kh godov.* Leningrad, 1960.

Kassow, Samuel D. "The Russian University in Crisis, 1899–1911." Ph.D. diss. Princeton, 1976.

Kennan, George. *Siberia and the Exile System.* 2 vols. in one. New York, 1970 [first printed in 1891].

Krikunov, V. P. *A. I. Ul'ianov i revoliutsionnye raznochintsy Dona i Severnogo Kavkaza.* Nal'chik, 1963.

Kudeli, P. "Narodovol'tsy na pereput'i (delo lakhtinskoi tipografii)." *KL,* 2 (11) (1924): 53–90.

Kulczycki, Ludwik. *Rewolucja rosyjska.* 2 vols. Lwów, 1911.

Kuz'min, D. (Kolosov, E. E.) *Narodovol'cheskaia zhurnalistika.* Moscow, 1930.

Leikina-Svirskaia, V. R. *Intelligentsiia v Rossii vo vtoroi polovine XIX veka.* Moscow, 1971.

Lukawski, Zygmunt. *Polacy w rosyjskim ruchu socjaldemokratycznym w latach 1883–1893.* Cracow, 1970.

Mendel, A. P. *Dilemmas of Progress in Tsarist Russia: Legal Marxism and Legal Populism.* Cambridge, Mass., 1967.

Naimark, Norman M. *The History of the "Proletariat": The Emergence of Marxism in the Kingdom of Poland, 1870–1887.* New York, 1979.

Nevskii, V. *Ot "Zemli i voli" k gruppe "Osvobozhdenie truda".* Moscow, 1930.

N-skii [Nicolaevsky, B.] "K istorii Partii russkikh sotsial-demokratov." *KS,* 5 (54) (1925): 44–68.

Orekhov, A. M. *Sotsial-demokraticheskoe dvizhenie v Rossii i pol'skie revoliutsionery.* Moscow, 1973.

Ovsiannikova, S. *Gruppa Blagoeva.* Moscow, 1959.

Pipes, Richard. *Social Democracy and the St. Petersburg Labor Movement 1885–1897.* Cambridge, Mass., 1963.

_____ *Struve: Liberal on the Left 1870–1903*. Cambridge, Mass., 1970.

Polevoi, Iu. Z. *Zarozhdenie marksizma v Rossii*. Moscow, 1959.

Pomper, Phillip. *Peter Lavrov and the Russian Revolutionary Movement*. Chicago, 1972.

Rashin, A. G. *Formirovanie rabochego klassa Rossii*. Moscow, 1959.

Robbins, Richard G. Jr. *Famine in Russia, 1891–1892*. New York, 1975.

Rozhdestvenskii, S. V. *Istoricheskii obzor deiatel'nosti Ministerstva narodnogo prosveshcheniia*. St. Petersburg, 1902.

Sedov, M. G. *Geroicheskii period revoliutsionnogo narodnichestva*. Moscow, 1966.

Senchakova, L. T. *Revoliutsionnoe dvizhenie v russkoi armii i flote v kontse XIX nachale XX v.* Moscow, 1972.

Sergievskii, N. "Dmitrii Blagoev v Peterburge (1880–1885 gg.)." *KL*, 11 (1924): 42–52.

_____ "Gruppa 'Osvobozhdenie truda' i marksistskie kruzhki." *IRS*, II, 86–260.

_____ *Partiia russkikh sotsial-demokratov: Gruppa Blagoeva*. Moscow-Leningrad, 1929.

Shchetinina, G. I. *University v Rossii i ustav 1884 goda*. Moscow, 1976.

Shirokova, V. V. *Partiia "Narodnogo prava."* Saratov, 1972.

Spiridovich, A. I. *Revoliutsionnoe dvizhenie v Rossii: Partiia Sotsialistov- Revoliutsionerov i eia predshestvenniki*. Petrograd, 1916.

Taranovski, Theodore. "The Politics of Counter-Reform: Autocracy and Bureaucracy in the Reign of Alexander III, 1881–1894." Ph.D. diss. Harvard, 1976.

Troitskii, N. A. *"Narodnaia volia" pered tsarskim sudom*. Saratov, 1971.

_____ "Degaevshchina." *VI*, 3 (1976): 125–133.

Tvardovskaia, V. A. *Ideologiia poreformennogo samoderzhaviia (M. N. Katkov i ego izdaniia)*. Moscow, 1978.

_____ *Sotsialisticheskaia mysl' Rossii na rubezhe 1870–1880-kh godov*. Moscow, 1969.

Ulam, Adam B. *In the Name of the People: Prophets and Conspirators in Prerevolutionary Russia*. New York, 1977.

Utechin, S. V. "The 'Preparatory' Trend in the Russian Revolutionary Movement in the 1880s." *Soviet Affairs*, 3 (1962): 7–22.

Valk, S. N. "Rasporiaditel'naia komissiia i 'Molodaia partiia Narodnoi voli'." *KS*, 2 (75) (1931): 98–131.

Venturi, Franco. *Roots of Revolution: A History of the Populist and Socialist Movement in Nineteenth Century Russia*. Trans. F. Haskell. New York, 1970.

Volk, S. S. *Narodnaia volia, 1879–1882.* Moscow-Leningrad, 1966.

von Borcke, Astrid. *Die Ursprünge des Bolschewismus.* Munich, 1977.

Walicki, Andrzej. *The Controversy over Capitalism.* Oxford, 1969.

Whelan, Heide W. *Alexander III and the State Council: Bureaucracy and Counterreform in Late Imperial Russia.* New Brunswick, N. J. 1982.

Wortman, Richard. *The Crisis of Russian Populism.* Cambridge, Eng., 1967.

Yarmolinsky, Avrahm. *Road to Revolution: A Century of Russian Radicalism.* London, 1957.

Zaionchkovskii, P. A. *Krizis samoderzhaviia na rubezhe 1870–1880-kh godov.* Moscow, 1964.

———— *Rossiiskoe samoderzhavie v kontse XIX stoletiia: Politicheskaia reaktsiia 80-kh–nachala 90-kh godov.* Moscow, 1970.

———— *Samoderzhavie i russkaia armiia na rubezhe XIX–XX stoletii.* Moscow, 1973.

Zelnik, Reginald. "Russian Bebels: An Introduction to the Memoirs of Semen Kanatchikov and Matvei Fisher." *Russian Review*, 35 (1976): 249– 289, 417–447.

Zhuikov, G. S. *Peterburgskie marksisty i gruppa "Osvobozhdenie truda".* Leningrad, 1975.

Index

Russian Research Center Studies

29. *Doctor and Patient in Soviet Russia*, by Mark G. Field.
30. *Russian Liberalism: From Gentry to Intelligentsia*, by George Fischer.
31. *Stalin's Failure in China, 1924–1927*, by Conrad Brandt.
32. *The Communist Party of Poland: An Outline of History*, by M. K. Dziewanowski. Second edition.
33. *Karamzin's Memoir on Ancient and Modern Russia: A Translation and Analysis*, by Richard Pipes.
34. *A Memoir on Ancient and Modern Russia*, by N. M. Karamzin, the Russian text edited by Richard Pipes.
35. *The Soviet Citizen: Daily Life in a Totalitarian Society*, by Alex Inkeles and Raymond A. Bauer.
36. *Pan-Turkism and Islam in Russia*, by Serge A. Zenkovsky.
37. *The Soviet Bloc: Unity and Conflict*, by Zbigniew Brzezinski. (Sponsored jointly with the Center for International Affairs, Harvard University.) Revised and enlarged edition. Also in Harvard Paperbacks.
38. *National Consciousness in Eighteenth-Century Russia*, by Hans Rogger.
39. *Alexander Herzen and the Birth of Russian Socialism, 1812–1855*, by Martin Malia.
40. *The Conscience of the Revolution: Communist Opposition in Soviet Russia*, by Robert Vincent Daniels.
41. *The Soviet Industrialization Debate, 1924–1928*, by Alexander Erlich.
42. *The Third Section: Police and Society in Russia under Nicholas I*, by Sidney Monas.
43. *Dilemmas of Progress in Tsarist Russia: Legal Marxism and Legal Populism*, by Arthur P. Mendel.
44. *Political Control of Literature in the USSR, 1946–1959*, by Harold Swayze.
45. *Accounting in Soviet Planning and Management*, by Robert W. Campbell.
46. *Social Democracy and the St. Petersburg Labor Movement, 1885–1897*, by Richard Pipes.
47. *The New Face of Soviet Totalitarianism*, by Adam B. Ulam.
48. *Stalin's Foreign Policy Reappraised*, by Marshall D. Shulman.
49. *The Soviet Youth Program: Regimentation and Rebellion*, by Allen Kassof.
50. *Soviet Criminal Law and Procedure: The RSFSR Codes*, translated by Harold J. Berman and James W. Spindler; introduction and analysis by Harold J. Berman. Second edition.
51. *Poland's Politics: Idealism vs. Realism*, by Adam Bromke.
52. *Managerial Power and Soviet Politics*, by Jeremy R. Azrael.
53. *Danilevsky: A Russian Totalitarian Philosopher*, by Robert E. MacMaster.
54. *Russia's Protectorates in Central Asia: Bukhara and Khiva, 1865–1924*, by Seymour Becker.
55. *Revolutionary Russia*, edited by Richard Pipes.
56. *The Family in Soviet Russia*, by H. Kent Geiger.
57. *Social Change in Soviet Russia*, by Alex Inkeles.

58. *The Soviet Prefects: The Local Party Organs in Industrial Decision-Making*, by Jerry F. Hough.

59. *Soviet-Polish Relations, 1917–1921*, by Piotr S. Wandycz.

60. *One Hundred Thousand Tractors: The MTS and the Development of Controls in Soviet Agriculture*, by Robert F. Miller.

61. *The Lysenko Affair*, by David Joravsky.

62. *Icon and Swastika: The Russian Orthodox Church under Nazi and Soviet Control*, by Harvey Fireside.

63. *A Century of Russian Agriculture: From Alexander II to Krushchev*, by Lazar Volin.

64. *Struve: Liberal on the Left, 1870–1905*, by Richard Pipes.

65. *Nikolai Strakhov*, by Linda Gerstein.

66. *The Kurbskii-Groznyi Apocrypha: The Seventeenth-Century Genesis of the "Correspondence" Attributed to Prince A. M. Kurbskii and Tsar Ivan IV*, by Edward L. Keenan.

67. *Chernyshevskii: The Man and the Journalist*, by William F. Woehrlin.

68. *European and Muscovite: Ivan Kireevsky and the Origins of Slavophilism*, by Abbott Gleason.

69. *Newton and Russia: The Early Influence, 1698–1796*, by Valentin Boss.

70. *Pavel Axelrod and the Development of Menshevism*, by Abraham Ascher.

71. *The Service Sector in Soviet Economic Growth: A Comparative Study*, by Gur Ofer (also Harvard Economic Studies).

72. *The Classroom and the Chancellery: State Educational Reform in Russia under Count Dmitry Tolstoi*, by Allen Sinel.

73. *Foreign Trade under Central Planning*, by Franklyn D. Holzman.

74. *Soviet Policy toward India: Ideology and Strategy*, by Robert H. Donaldson.

75. *The End of Serfdom: Nobility and Bureaucracy in Russia, 1855–1861*, by Daniel Field.

76. *The Dynamics of Soviet Politics*, edited by Paul Cocks, Robert V. Daniels, and Nancy Whittier Heer.

77. *The Soviet Union and Social Science Theory*, by Jerry F. Hough.

78. *The Russian Levites: Parish Clergy in the Eighteenth Century*, by Gregory L. Freeze.

79. *Commissars, Commanders, and Civilian Authority: The Structure of Soviet Military Politics*, by Timothy J. Colton.

80. *Struve: Liberal on the Right, 1905–1944*, by Richard Pipes.

81. *The Limits of Reform: The Ministry of Internal Affairs in Imperial Russia, 1802–1881*, by Daniel T. Orlovsky.

82. *Terrorists and Social Democrats: The Russian Revolutionary Movement under Alexander III*, by Norman M. Naimark.

(Some of these titles may be out of print in a given year. Write to Harvard University Press for information and ordering.)